AHMANSON · MURPHY
FINE ARTS IMPRINT

THE AHMANSON FOUNDATION
has endowed this imprint
to honor the memory of
FRANKLIN D. MURPHY
who for half a century
served arts and letters,
beauty and learning, in
equal measure by shaping
with a brilliant devotion
those institutions upon
which they rely.

THE PUBLISHER AND THE UNIVERSITY OF CALIFORNIA PRESS FOUNDATION GRATEFULLY ACKNOWLEDGE THE GENEROUS SUPPORT OF THE AHMANSON • MURPHY IMPRINT IN FINE ARTS.

THE PUBLISHER AND THE UNIVERSITY OF CALIFORNIA PRESS FOUNDATION ALSO GRATEFULLY ACKNOWLEDGE THE GENEROUS SUPPORT OF THE KORET FOUNDATION IN MAKING THIS BOOK POSSIBLE.

MODELS OF INTEGRITY

Art and Law in Post-Sixties America

Joan Kee

UNIVERSITY OF CALIFORNIA PRESS

University of California Press, one of the most distinguished university presses in the United States, enriches lives around the world by advancing scholarship in the humanities, social sciences, and natural sciences. Its activities are supported by the UC Press Foundation and by philanthropic contributions from individuals and institutions. For more information, visit www.ucpress.edu.

University of California Press
Oakland, California

Library of Congress Cataloging-in-Publication Data

Names: Kee, Joan, author.
Title: Models of integrity : art and law in post-sixties America / Joan Kee.
Description: Oakland, California : University of California Press, [2019] | Includes bibliographical references and index. |
Identifiers: LCCN 2018034894 (print) | ISBN 9780520299382 (cloth : alk. paper) |
Subjects: LCSH: Law and art—United States—History—20th century. | Law and art—United States—History—20th century—Case studies. | Artists—United States—History—20th century.
Classification: LCC KF4288 (ebook) | LCC KF4288 .K44 2019 (print) | DDC 344.73/097—dc23
LC record available at https://lccn.loc.gov/2018034894

Printed in Thailand

26 25 24 23 22 21 20 19
10 9 8 7 6 5 4 3 2 1

For Ross

CONTENTS

ACKNOWLEDGMENTS

The debts I have accumulated in writing this book are many. I thank James Boyd White for his unflagging encouragement and the example he has set for me and for countless others in the name of expanding humanistic legal scholarship. No less is due to Sonia Katyal and Miwon Kwon, whose respective areas of expertise in property law and contemporary art brought much-needed light to bear on an unruly early version of the manuscript. Joshua Chambers-Letson and Suzanne Hudson must be acknowledged for providing typically incisive and generous feedback on a revised draft as well as for their friendship. In Nadine Little and her colleagues at the University of California Press, I have found dedicated advocates. My home department, the History of Art at the University of Michigan, has been a wellspring of continued support. To both the department and the university I owe profuse thanks for their support in defraying the costs of image acquisition and reproduction.

Insightful conversations with Marlyse Baptista, Danny Herwitz, and David Porter at the Institute for the Humanities at the University of Michigan motivated my early thinking. Pat Simons commented on an early draft of Chapter 2 that set me on a more fruitful path. The Clark Art Institute opened its doors to a colloquium on art and law whose participants, including Amy Adler, Ariella Azoulay, Robin Kelsey, Frederic Schwartz, Cristina Vatulescu, and Bess Williamson, offered a bracing environment for navigating new paths and reassessing past lines of inquiry. The *Brooklyn Rail* likewise offered a much-needed platform for thinking through and around the thorny intersection of art and law; many thanks to Phong Bui. I have benefited greatly from rewarding discussions with Katherine Biber, Matt Biro, Jennifer DeVere Brody, Martha Buskirk, Kris Cohen, Scott Hodes, Kibum Kim, Michelle Kuo, Maud Lavin, Judge Pierre Leval, Eng-Beng Lim, Jill Magid, Daniel McClean, Jonas Mekas, Les Moran, Jeremy Pilcher, Alex Potts, Sergio Muñoz Sargimento, and Carey Young. For their generosity and assistance, I am indebted to Jonathan Henery, Tehching Hsieh, Jay Jaroslav, Les Krims, Sally Mann, Ann Messner, Joan Rothfuss, Carolee Schneemann, John and Thomas Solomon, and the Felix Gonzalez-Torres Foundation, particularly Emilie Keldie, as well as the staffs of the Fales Library and Special Collections at New York University, the Museum of Modern Art Archives, the Canadian Centre for Architecture, the Archives of American Art, the CCS Bard Library and Archives, and the Getty Research Institute Special Collections. Audiences at Cambridge University, York University, Cornell Law School, Ohio State University, the School of the Art Institute at Chicago, and the Tate patiently listened to early versions of various sections, and their probing questions sparked new ways of thinking. A special tip of the hat to my students for their probing comments and questions as well as to John Alan Farmer. My appreciation to H. Jean Rim and Woo Sik Kee for being witnesses, jurors, and judges at various opportune moments.

Portions of Chapter 4 previously appeared in *American Art* 30(1) (March 2016) as "Orders of Law in the One Year Performances of Tehching Hsieh."

INTRODUCTION

ON AN EARLY FALL DAY IN 1971, Vito Acconci sat blindfolded for three hours at the bottom of the stairs to the basement of 93 Grand Street, New York City. The basement was home to the offices of the legendary art magazine *Avalanche*. Holding metal pipes and a crowbar, he swung them while repeatedly muttering phrases like "I want to be alone" and "I will not let anyone down here."[1] Titled *Claim*, his action became a representative example of performance art, a category of artistic production based on live human action. Although performance art had long-standing ties with theater, concerts, and other forms of live public presentation, it became prominent in many parts of the world during the 1960s, particularly as a means of compelling audiences to reflect on the nature of everyday life. In *Claim*, Acconci's threats of unmitigated violence reflected a city now notorious for violent crime; brute violence in the name of defending one's property and space was vigilante fantasy writ large.

Far less notorious is the document Acconci signed with *Avalanche* publishers Willoughby Sharp and Liza Béar, who invited the artist to perform his work in 93 Grand Street (fig. 1). In it, he assumed "total responsibility" for any damage occasioned by the performance of *Claim.* Too formal to be merely a well-meaning personal gesture to pacify nervous friends, the document amounts to a liability release, executed to release *Avalanche* and its publishers from legal responsibility for Acconci's actions. According to common law principles, or regulations derived from historically accepted customs endorsed by courts, occupants of a property are responsible for injuries occurring on that property, regardless of its actual owner. At the time Acconci signed the release, courts and legislatures were pushing to impose absolute responsibility for any harm caused by a given party, irrespective of fault.[2] Known in legal parlance as "strict liability," this standard became increasingly conspicuous in cases involving physical harm to people, as opposed to those concerning property damage. That the release was signed by Sharp in his capacity as the occupant of 93 Grand Street—which he and Béar used not only as office space for *Avalanche* but also to show artworks whose content, intentions, or presentation made them unlikely candidates for display in museums and galleries—resonated with how risk management became a primary concern for U.S. institutions, including legislatures, corporations, and museums.

The liability release undercut not only the artist's threats of assault, projected through video monitors installed in the ground-floor gallery, but the popular myth of the renegade artist unfettered by concern over what the law or the public might say and do. Moreover, the release anticipated a third potential audience for *Claim* in addition to Acconci's immediate artistic contemporaries and passersby on the street. Hypothetically, Sharp and Béar could have used the liability release to exonerate themselves from any charges brought by audience members injured by Acconci. Doing so would involve lawyers, police, and judges as part of the work's extended audience. Equally important was that Acconci willingly assumed the risk of an adverse legal encounter. He chose to assume personal responsibility that recognized how his actions affected others. By voluntarily subjecting himself to legal standards, he modeled a kind of integrity that merged personal accountability into his overall project.[3]

For art made in the United States between the early 1970s and the mid-1990s, law conditioned, in expanded ways, the complex relationships between artists, artworks, and audiences. Significant legal changes, from the growth of consumer rights legislation to the heightened visibility of women's rights, affected everyday life at an unprecedented pace, converging unavoidably with how an increasing number of artists made works that deliberately blurred the boundary allegedly separating art from everyday life as well as those participating directly in political and legislative processes. Likewise, the law became visually present in daily life in ways and to a magnitude virtually unmatched in any other nation. From warnings on cigarette packs required by Congress in 1966 to labels on products containing hazardous substances mandated in 1973, legislative management of risk became part of the everyday physical landscape. After the U.S. Supreme Court overturned a general prohibition against lawyers publicizing

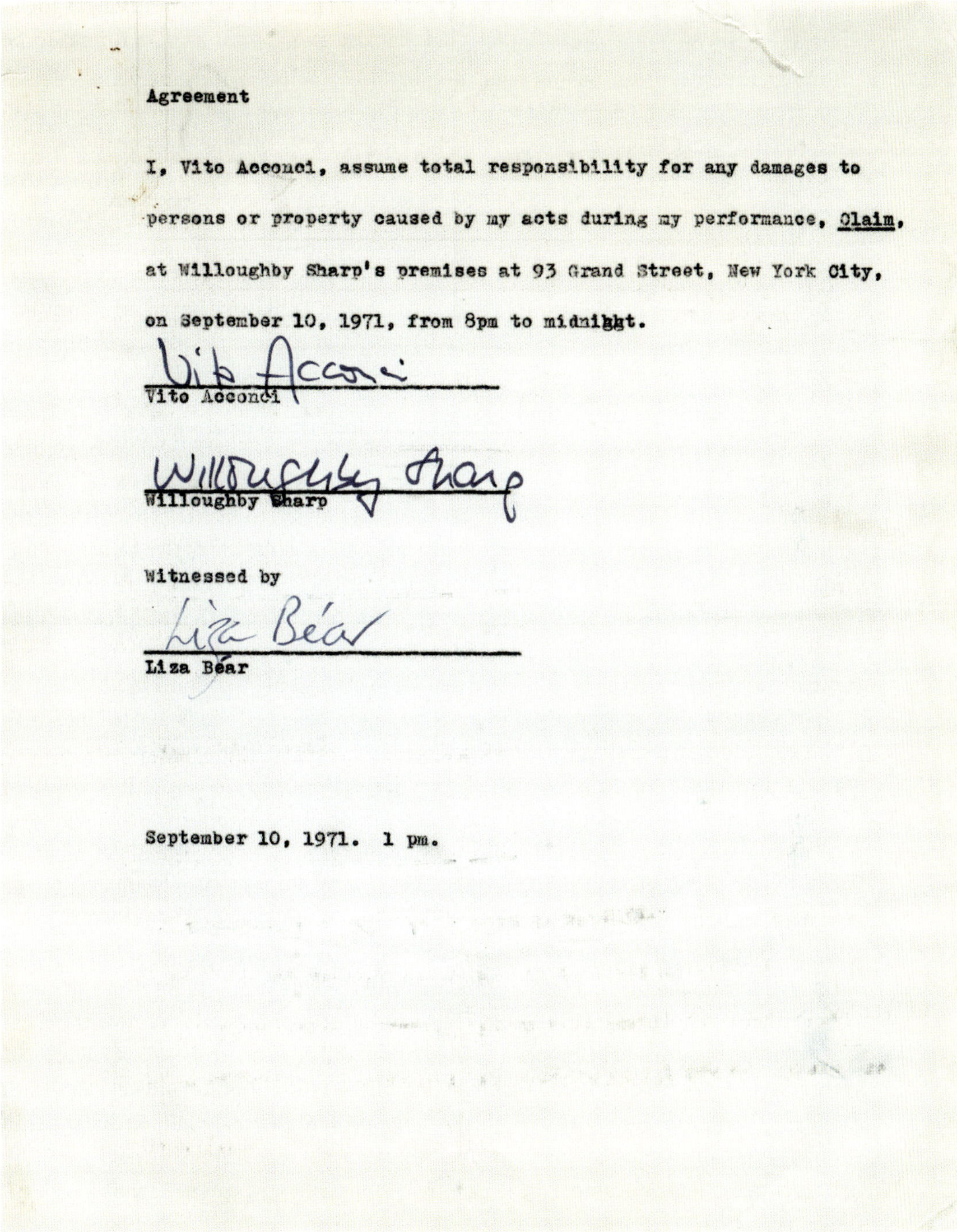

Agreement

I, Vito Acconci, assume total responsibility for any damages to persons or property caused by my acts during my performance, Claim, at Willoughby Sharp's premises at 93 Grand Street, New York City, on September 10, 1971, from 8pm to midnight.

Vito Acconci

Willoughby Sharp

Witnessed by

Liza Bear

September 10, 1971. 1 pm.

FIGURE 1

Vito Acconci, claim (signed agreement), September 10, 1971. Typed text and signatures in ink on paper, 11 × 8½ inches. Avalanche Magazine Archives, I.A.118. Museum of Modern Art Archives, New York. © 2018 Vito Acconci/Artists Rights Society (ARS), New York, and Museum of Modern Art/Licensed by SCALA/Art Resource, New York.

their services in 1977, advertisements for legal services appeared in newspapers, in subway cars, on radio, and on billboards.[4] Legal authority was further expressed through the categorization and regulation of space, including the emergence of environmental law in the early 1970s and rising concerns over vandalism and homelessness in the 1980s. Whether through the "best interests" doctrine that became a watchword of family law in the 1970s or Title IX, the federal law created in 1972 that prohibits gender discrimination at universities receiving federal funds, the workplace, the home, and the university campus were progressively defined by regulation intended to safeguard public interests. At the same time, legal constants such as abiding beliefs in originality and authorship clashed with strategies of visual artistic production like appropriation (the use of existing forms with little or no modification), which gained special traction in the 1980s.

Working with the law through its agents, or invoking and even challenging its bedrock doctrines, was thus a crucial opportunity for artists to whom integrity represented a necessary expansion of artistic identity in a tin age of political malfeasance. Against examples such as the notorious Watergate scandal that led to Richard Nixon's resignation in 1974, the abuses of power by the FBI and CIA, and the long-term bribery of foreign government officials by aircraft manufacturer Lockheed, several artists produced work that made calls for accountability a systemic part of their creative process. They modeled values different from those of corporations, institutions, governments, and other traditional sources of authority that were attempting to minimize, disclaim, or abort their own social responsibilities. What might be called the "hunt for integrity" was embedded in a crisis of citizenship forged in the crucible of deeply polarizing attitudes toward the Vietnam War, civil rights legislation, and the social improvement efforts of the "Great Society" that Lyndon B. Johnson urged Americans to build in 1964.

But integrity also concerned self-determination expressed through direct relationships to property, whether in the form of land, goods, or ideas. Deeply affected by the scarcity of housing and studio space, along with the prominence of the art market, artists engaged with property as a subject and means of production, often to make themselves intelligible to a legal regime that held private property interests as sacrosanct. Legal scholar Margaret Radin wrote an influential reminder of how the most powerful indications of selfhood consisted of the ability to control one's environment through the possession of goods and land.[5] Published soon after Ronald Reagan's landslide victory over Jimmy Carter in the 1980 presidential election, Radin's article implied that the defense of property underpinned state regulation. Since his 1966 California gubernatorial campaign, Reagan had staunchly advocated "law and order."[6] Characterized by a zero-tolerance policy toward crime and demands for harsher punishment, the call for so-called law and order was intended to address widespread discontent toward government failure to protect private property in the wake of civil dissent and riots taking place in numerous U.S. cities.[7] Although a political tactic aimed at wresting control from liberal hands, the law and order campaign resonated with a plurality of Americans, including minoritarian bodies and those subject to exceptions due to age, race, gender, sexual orientation, and citizenship status, for whom the status of property owner has often been a shield against a variety of economic, political, and social forces conspiring to erase or suppress their existence. Property law gained new significance by the end of the 1970s, when the crisis of citizenship often played itself out through dynamics of inclusion and exclusion. Scattershot policies marking the end of the Carter administration paved the way for Reagan, who rehabilitated the concept of U.S. exceptionalism, successfully wooing voters with promises of restored military glory and economic recovery.[8] The mirage of unity and the moralistic tone of rhetoric encouraged ideologues to discount from the polity those who either failed to share their beliefs or appeared to flout them. Not surprisingly, law became visible in the art world through the optics of critique or dissent.[9]

Integrity as a form of self-expression through property coincided with mounting interest in the "right of integrity," or the legal right of creators to prevent others from destroying or changing their work without authorization.[10] An idea central to moral rights, a legal concept referring to rights given to creators of copyrighted works, the right of integrity was eventually written into law in 1990. Another legal notion of integrity worth considering is legal philosopher Ronald Dworkin's influential description of "law as integrity." Widely circulated in the 1980s, the argument held that the primary responsibility of law is not to uphold consensus norms or maximize efficiency but to consistently administer moral principles that are equally applicable to all citizens. The constraints that law imposes "benefit society not just by providing predictability or procedural fairness, or in some other instrumental way, but by securing a kind of equality among citizens that makes their community more genuine and improves its moral justification for exercising the political power it does."[11] The definition is intimately linked to the "rule of law," a legal concept holding that the necessity of law is rooted in its capacity to prevent the arbitrary and unwarranted exercise of political and military power. Yet the rule of law is authoritative because it works for and through a community, something artists tried to remind viewers by realizing works through acts of transparency, reciprocation, trust, and conviction. In some works, integrity took shape through specific commitments to an abstract ideal, whether it was the utopian creation of a commons in the United States, one of the most privatized places on earth, or creating a space for moral disagreement without moral character attacks.

In this book, using multiple conceptions of integrity, I discuss how law and art can serve as integrated sources of creative thinking through close analysis of how specific works were conceived, executed, and received. I ask readers who may be accustomed to characterizations of law as an extension of ill-conceived politics to understand law not as a set of paternalistic and forbiddingly esoteric rules imposed by a self-serving autocracy, but as a plastic, and even liquid, condition collectively shaped by turns of language, aesthetic decisions, and individual behavior. The experience generated by many contemporary artworks made possible conversations that were different from those pitting art against the law, and different from those familiar to jurists for whom artworks were yet another subset of property readily converted into forms of capital. As with the liability release in *Claim,* such dialogue was often channeled through actions that were not directly part of a specific work but were nevertheless integral to their creation or circulation. By the end of this book, I hope readers might be persuaded of how artworks and artists frame the authority of law as a question of sympathy and vulnerability. Lawyers have to contend with an ever-expanding array of objects and forms of visual expression, and I argue that for law to do justice it must address some of the questions raised by art history, especially the challenge of description.[12] This book, then, seeks to realize a coalition of imaginations pooled from artists, critics, and historians committed to thinking about the structural and social conditions of art and from lawyers and law scholars interested in looking outside legal discourse to improve law's ability to deliver justice both accessible and relevant to daily life. What kinds of futures become possible if we pair the communities of thinking represented by the categories of art and law?

CONTEMPORARY ART AND LAW IN HISTORICAL RELATION

If contemporary art is an epistemological rather than temporal category, its distinguishing characteristics include how representative examples provoke and unsettle the structuring capacity of law. Precisely for this reason, the nexus of art and law offers intriguing possibilities for modeling communities of thought beyond compliance and consensus. The legal history of visual art in the twentieth century etched into relief the fundamental question of what art is *for* via competing definitions of visual art among lawmakers, police, jurists, and witnesses. This was made clear in *Brancusi v. United States,* the first case that compelled U.S. courts to verbalize their assumptions regarding art.[13] Decided in 1928, it began when the U.S. Customs Service treated a bronze cast of Constantin Brancusi's sculpture *Bird in Space* as a manufactured metal, taxable as "Kitchen Utensils and Hospital Supplies"[14] (fig. 2). Although the Customs Court ruled that Brancusi's sculpture was in fact art, and thus entitled to a less onerous taxation rate, the law has been reluctant to expand the definition of art, so as to minimize the risk of tax evaders who might invoke "art" as a loophole to shirk their civic duties.[15]

The impasse between contemporary art and law registers most clearly through attitudes toward medium. The idea of artistic medium has been absorbed into larger questions of mixed media, of media inflected by context. Today, the Code of Laws of the United States of America (the U.S.C.), the official compilation of permanent federal statutes passed by Congress, defines a "work of art" in terms of artistic medium and authorship. It applies to paintings, drawings, prints, sculptures, and photographs, but not to posters, charts, films, or books. To an artist, art critic, or art historian, the definition reads as a sign of excessive prudence at best and simpleminded philistinism at worst. To a lawyer or judge compelled to decide a course of action, sometimes within very short timeframes, however, the definition provides clarity and guidance in

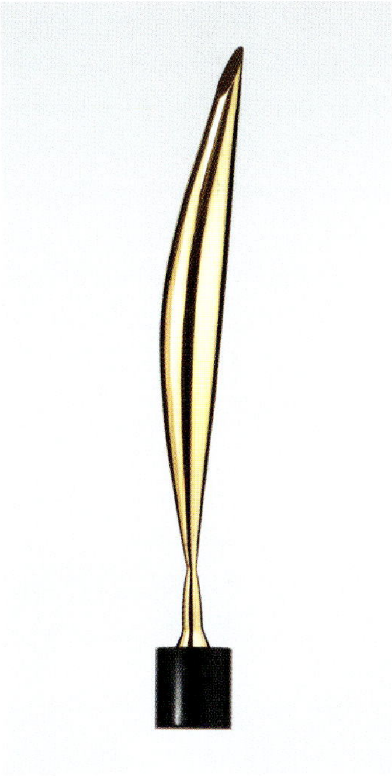

FIGURE 2
Constantin Brancusi, *Bird in Space,* 1924. Polished bronze; black marble base. Height: 50 5⁄16 inches. Circumference: 17 11⁄16 inches. Base: 6 5⁄16 inches. Philadelphia Museum of Art, Louise and Walter Arensberg Collection, 1950-134-14, 15.

the absence of any real instruction about how best to consider objects and visual images. Clear definitions persist in legal attitudes toward art because of how legality is a function of exclusion embodied in the unit of the category.

From the 1960s on, the art-law impasse became even more pronounced as new forms of artistic production made obsolete the very questions underpinning so many legal cases involving visual art, namely what art is or should be. Conceptual art, for example, identified the idea as the artwork, rather than the completed physical object, even if the object resulted from the idea. As Sol LeWitt, one of conceptual art's best-known and most eloquent representatives, declared, "the idea becomes a machine that makes the art."[16] Ranging from drawings produced from verbal instructions to artists' declarations regarding the status of objects, conceptual art was popularly construed in critical and art historical circles through *dematerialization,* a term coined in 1968 by the critic Lucy Lippard to emphasize how "the thinking process" takes precedence over all other considerations and "may result in the object becoming wholly obsolete."[17] These definitions ran counter to entrenched ideas of copyright, a branch of law granting exclusive rights to the creator of original works. One of the most commonly encountered areas of law for artists, U.S. copyright law revolves around a strict separation between the idea responsible for a work's creation and its subsequent expression in a "tangible medium."[18]

Contemporary art in the 1960s and '70s was characterized by the emergence of artworks whose conception and appearance not only differed radically from painting and sculpture—media legally recognized as "fine art"—but were intended to overlap, encroach on, or even usurp structures and functions necessary in everyday life and ordinarily undertaken by nonart entities. For some artists, particularly those of a conceptual bent, the law served as art's executive arm. Lawyer Ira Lowe of Washington, D.C., whose clients included the artists Frank Stella, Louise Bourgeois, and Larry Rivers, enabled Ed McGowin to legally change his name twelve times between 1970 and 1971.[19] Intended to challenge an art world that required artists to establish a consistent brand identity, particularly through affiliation with a distinct "school or group," these multiple name changes formed the basis of McGowin's work *Name Change*.[20] But the open-ended nature of conceptual art could frustrate lawyers charged with preparing clients for all eventualities. Los Angeles attorney Clifford Schaffer, who represented conceptual artist Michael Asher in the early 1970s, found it difficult to protect his client's desires for creative control when Asher himself could confirm neither the parameters of his work nor its final manifestation.[21] The difficulty Schaffer encountered because of Asher—whose early work consisted of altering gallery spaces, including removing partition walls and adjusting sound levels—instructively points to a root incompatibility between art and law: where law takes as its baseline the idea that humans are sovereign agents primed to act intentionally, art often depends on how materials and material properties act upon, and even thwart, human intention.

Law, particularly from the realms of property and contract, continued to seep into artistic production, especially with the rise of artworks made directly in the natural environment during the 1960s and '70s. Categorized as "land art," "earthworks," or "environmental art," such works highlighted competing property interests arising from works built on land not owned by their creators. Public artworks relied on contracts to realize their projects, and artists frequently grappled with increased regulation of land use through new laws concerning zoning, environmental protection, and landlord-tenant relations. Particularly tricky were works, such as examples of land-based art, in which land owned by someone other than the artist was used to create intellectual property owned by the artist.

Some artists worked with land in order to engage directly with social, political, and legal frameworks. Especially popular was the idea that artworks could double as land reclamation projects, as evident in works like Robert Morris's *Johnson Pit #30* (1979), one of the first publicly funded earthworks in the United States (fig. 3). Located in a sand-and-gravel pit outside Seattle, it was completed shortly after the enactment of the Federal Surface Mining Control and Reclamation Act of 1977 gave states a financial incentive to restore lands damaged by mining.[22] Like many artworks occupying large tracts of land, it came to fruition only after the land in question was seen as having no economic value. Abandoned in the 1940s, the pit was used as a dumping ground for household goods and automobiles and became a hotbed of illegal activity—even to the point that traffic signs near it were being vandalized. Although the land was offered for sale, no buyers appeared and the local government finally offered the pit to artists in the name of reclamation. Morris cleared the pit, terraced it, and planted it with rye grass for public use.

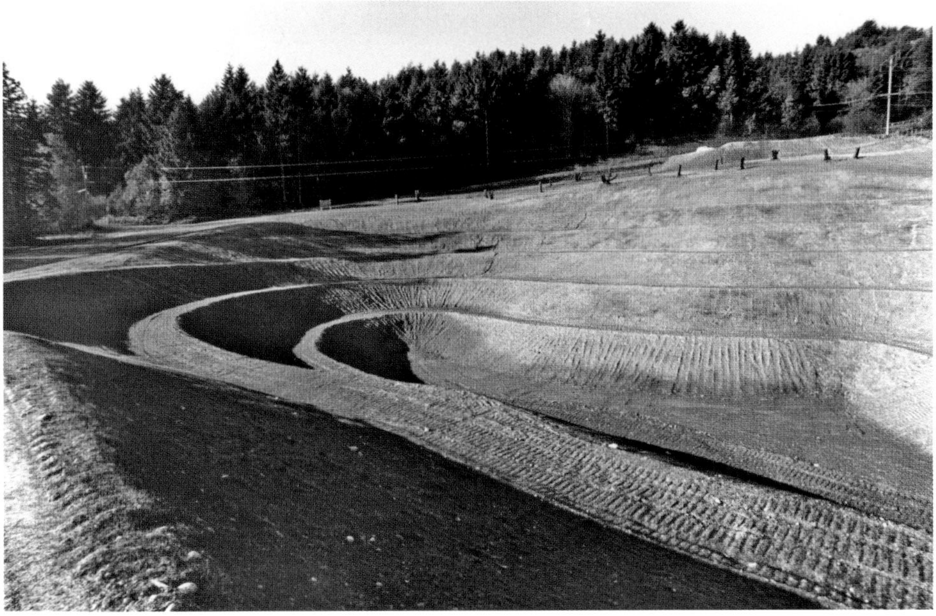

FIGURE 3
Robert Morris, *Johnson Pit #30*, 1979. Earthwork. Photo: Colleen Chartier. © 2018 Robert Morris/Artists Rights Society (ARS), New York. Courtesy of King County Archives, Maryland.

Helping propel the creation of works outside institutional settings that could engage directly with audiences outside galleries, museums, and other common display venues was a renewed sense of artistic production as a form of commons building. Artists professed interest in using publicly accessible works to fulfill a sense of social responsibility. *Johnson Pit #30* exemplifies how many artists tried to prove the social worth of their activities by finding a practical, or at least a socially beneficial, use for something that was seemingly beyond recuperation. The work recalled a longer discussion about the place of art in society, particularly regarding its significance. Efforts to repurpose artworks for social use were also symptoms of a fundamental anxiety over art's social purpose. As Morris insinuated in his essay on art as land reclamation, it was not enough to be useless. Yet he was deeply ambivalent toward the drive for art to impart some practical function, lest it make resource extraction socially acceptable and art merely its "public-relations" arm, "incapable of signaling any protest."[23]

The unprecedented scale of resources needed to produce a single work further brought up another property claim, one based on John Locke's theory of just desserts: those who work to improve the land should, as a matter of principle, acquire the rights to that land. A case in point was *The Wall*, an installation by Forrest Myers consisting of forty-two painted aluminum braces bolted to an eight-story-high wall located at the entrance of the SoHo district in New York City (fig. 4). Completed in 1973, it required permits from city engineers, local governments, and the owner of the building to which the sculpture was

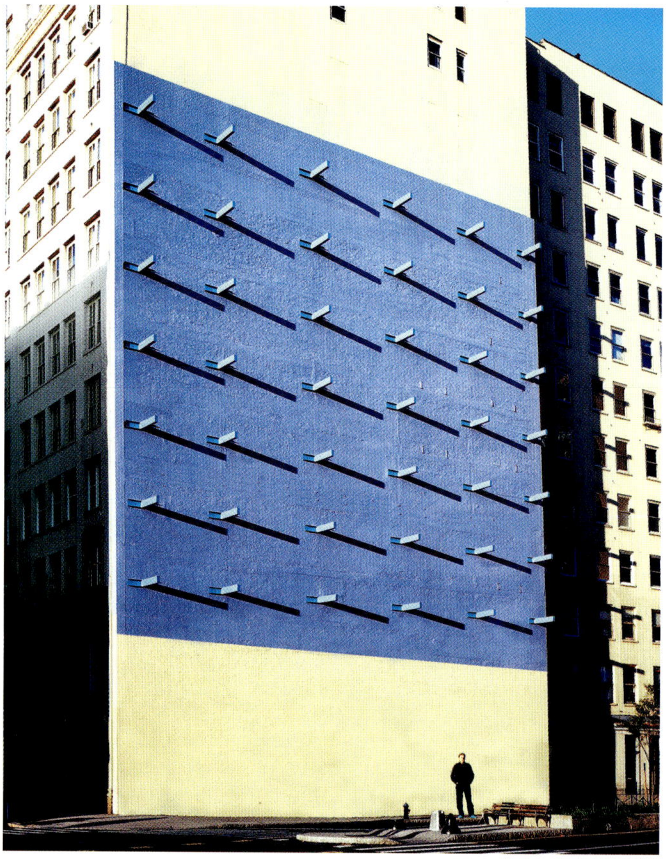

FIGURE 4
Forrest Myers, *The Wall*, 1973/2009.
Located at 599 Broadway, New York City.
Courtesy of the artist. © Forrest Myers.

attached.[24] Yet subsequent litigation surrounding the restoration of *The Wall* to its original SoHo location (now a condominium building) also showed how courts were loath to conflate ownership of the underlying property with that of the artwork.[25]

"All of us are looped together in a new and unsettling connectivity," critic Lawrence Alloway memorably wrote in his influential assessment of the "art world" in 1972.[26] Both confirming and challenging this heightened interconnectedness was institutional critique, or the artistic strategy of examining how institutions operate. Several of the most representative examples of institutional critique in the early 1970s made information disclosure the medium, often in hopes that such transparency might lead to policy change. At the very least, institutional critique became a system of accountability directed toward both the art world and civil society at large. A foundational example was Hans Haacke's *Shapolsky et al. Manhattan Real Estate Holdings, a Real-Time Social System, as of May 1, 1971* (fig. 5). For this multipart work, Haacke photographed 142 properties owned by a New York developer and his family, including tenements in Harlem, the East Village, and the Lower East Side of Manhattan, which he then

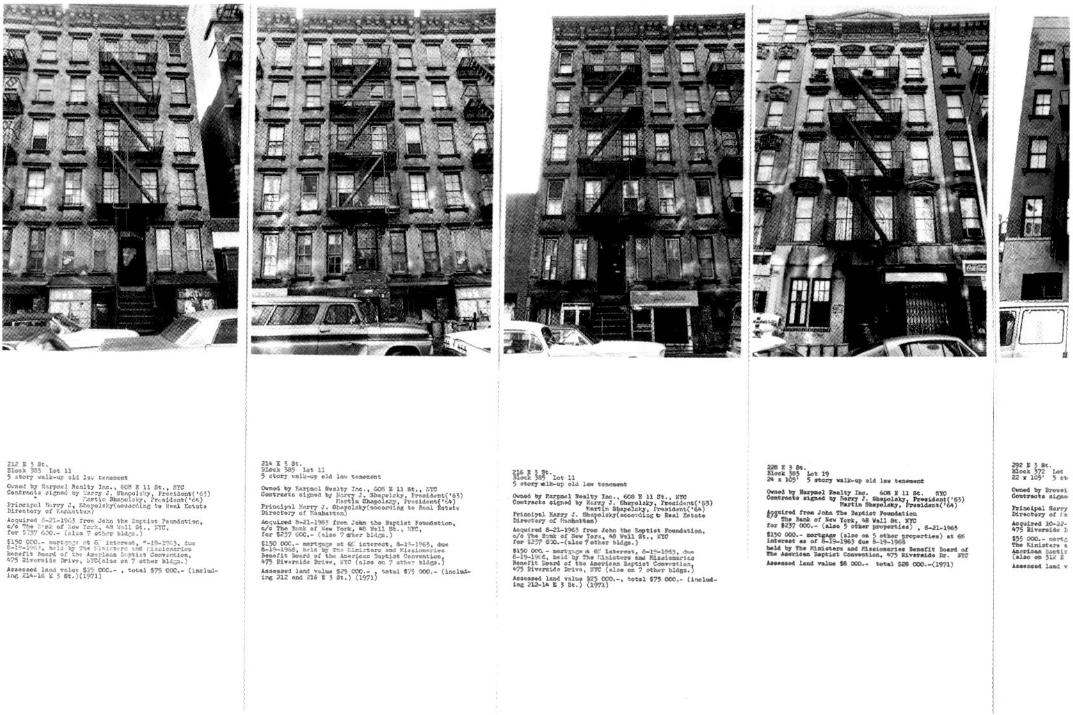

FIGURE 5

Detail of Hans Haacke, *Shapolsky et al. Manhattan Real Estate Holdings, a Real-Time Social System, as of May 1, 1971*, 1971. Nine photostats, 142 gelatin silver prints, and 142 photocopies, dimensions variable. © Hans Haacke/Artists Rights Society (ARS), New York/VG Bild-Kunst, Bonn.

displayed with information about each building, including its address, type, land value, date of acquisition, and the names of those involved in the property's acquisition. Foreshadowing Alloway's comparison of the "art world" to economist James March's classic description of all organizations as shifting, multiple-goal political coalitions in which bargaining for certain interests preceded rational decision making, Guggenheim Museum director Thomas Messer demanded that Haacke withdraw his work, for fear of possible retribution from museum trustees potentially connected with the Shapolsky family.[27] Although Haacke gleaned his information from New York City's Department of Records, the Guggenheim claimed that showing the work might expose the museum to a lawsuit—a bluff the artist called after speaking with lawyer Jerry Ordover, who stated that the work was not libelous, as it displayed information without commentary.[28] The Guggenheim ultimately canceled the exhibition, reflecting its fear of liability but also anxiety over how even the presentation of abundant data, even within the contained environment of a museum, posed a threat to calcified systems of power. At the same time, Haacke's diligence and the dispassionate manner

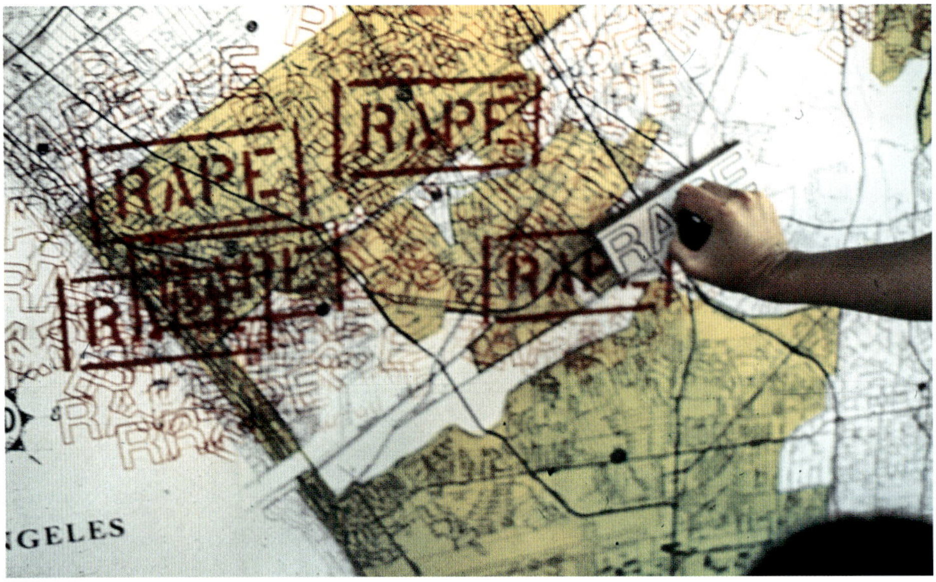

FIGURE 6
Suzanne Lacy, Detail of *Three Weeks in May,* 1977. Courtesy of the artist. © Suzanne Lacy.

of information display made him a credible authority in the eyes of the press and the police, who later used his work to investigate some of the properties exhibited.[29]

Paralleling the rise of institutional critique was what Acconci described as a "reaction against the isolationism of the museum, a bursting of art out of the museum and into the street."[30] Widely recognized for what she dubbed "new genre public art," or artworks brought directly to audiences outside institutional structures for activist purposes, Suzanne Lacy has noted how, from around 1972, artists tried to bring art and its aesthetic concerns into "real life" by producing works that have legitimate political impact.[31] In a revealing demonstration of how different periods within the general category of contemporary art might be parsed according to what was legally possibly at a given time, Lacy secured city and police cooperation for her complex, multipart work *Three Weeks in May* on a level unlikely to happen in a post-2001 world of heightened surveillance.[32] Created in 1977 and supported by Los Angeles City Attorney Burt Pines, *Three Weeks in May* addressed the inadequacy of law to bring rapists to justice. Among its most visually striking components was the public display of a twenty-five-foot-long map of Los Angeles showing occurrences of rape in the city (fig. 6). Installed in an underground shopping arcade near Los Angeles City Hall, an area deserted after working hours and likely a prime zone for criminal activity, the map used information provided by the Los Angeles city police. In dark red ink highly evocative of blood, the hypervisible "RAPE" stamp served as a visual counter to the gross underreporting of rape, a tendency aggravated by prevailing rape laws that put the credibility of victims on trial as much as the actions of the suspect.[33] The stamped words exude a particular literalism that reads as a will to transparency, a far cry from systems of authority engrossed in concealing or minimizing their accountability to others.

Together with new genre public art, performance art, or live enactments taking place over a specific period and often in front of an audience, became prominent. Addressing the prominence of performance art as a means of thinking about law, the artist and writer Lewis MacAdams claimed that if "law was power," performance was especially relevant as it enabled artists to use "the only power that any of us ever really has—the power to take our own lives in our hands."[34] Certainly a disproportionate number of performance artists tended to attract more than their share of negative legal scrutiny, because performance may have been too successful in showing just how far outside the bounds of legal regulation visual art could in fact be. As performance artist Linda Montano declared:

> The reason there is so much censorship in America now is because it's very difficult to be "authentically" bodied in America . . . when real artists use real bodies in real time to make a real statement, they are censored and seen as perverse. Actually the populace is projecting their own guilt on real-time based performance artists. The first amendment is being crushed.[35]

Montano was referring to the infamous "NEA Four" case of the early 1990s involving her friend, the performance artist Karen Finley. Along with John Fleck, Holly Hughes, and Tim Miller, Finley saw her proposal for government funding vetoed by the chairman of the National Endowment for the Arts (NEA) on the basis of her work's supposed content. The rejection triggered a highly publicized set of trials leading all the way up to the Supreme Court, which upheld the government's decision to deny funding.[36] Montano's comment suggests how performance deliberately tampered with the perceived distinction between politics and aesthetics, especially in the United States during the 1980s and '90s. Yet the goal was not to destroy the law by championing illegality for its own sake. Rather, it was to be outside the law, or to establish ways of existing outside the structures reified by the perceptions embedded in law's rule.

The rise of performance triggered other legal quandaries, especially when mapped against the multiple histories of photography. From its commercial popularization in the mid-nineteenth century, photography has been defined as much by the artistic and legal debates concerning its nature and use as by the techniques and materials needed for its creation. The law was especially divided, with police regarding photography as a useful means of cataloging criminal types that might enable them to predict future wrongdoing and judges initially suspicious of photography's reliance on technology. About a century later, photography enjoyed almost inviolable status as a key source of legitimate evidence. This status contrasted sharply with the uneven rise of photography as a mainstream artistic practice. The cataclysmic wars of the twentieth century, particularly the Vietnam War and World War II, contributed dramatically to the rise of photography as a key form of rhetoric production, a point that was given an artistic gloss with exhibitions like "The Family of Man," the mammoth traveling show of photographs that made its debut at the Museum of Modern Art in New York in 1955 and that celebrated humanism in the face of a constant nuclear threat.

Despite its institutional and general visibility, photography struggled to gain the same recognition as paintings and sculptures. Complicating the artistic status of photography was that the sale of conceptual art often depended on photographic documentation of a work's existence.[37] Since at least the mid-2000s, many performance artists have treated documentation of their performances as theirs, even when created by a third party.[38] Under U.S. copyright law, such documentation would belong to the photographer, barring any prior agreement.[39] But although museums and galleries credit individual photographers, they recognize the performer as the sole author. In the legal context, the expanded availability of cameras and development facilities exposed photographers to heightened public scrutiny, which in turn collided with police and court tendencies to regard photographs as documentation. This was borne out by the inordinate number of obscenity cases involving photographs, as opposed to paintings or sculptures, including situations where the photograph was explicitly presented as an artwork and not as a journalistic image or as evidence.

Acconci later wrote that the expansion of art was intended to break "the boundaries of convention and law."[40] Certainly, artists and art proved to be among the most enduring and potent challenges to law, namely in how agents of the law have failed to dismiss completely the grounds for artists claiming exceptions to lawful standards or special privileges based on the intrinsic value of artistic creation being incommensurate to economic barometers of value or systems of exchange. A key example was Congress partially adopting moral rights legislation through the Visual Artists Rights Act (VARA). Signed into law in 1990 by then president George H.W. Bush, VARA acknowledged, at the federal level, visual art as a unique legal subject.[41] Arguably the most important law to directly affect visual artists as a specific occupational class, VARA granted artists an unprecedented number of noneconomic rights, including the right to claim or disclaim authorship, the right to prevent the work from being changed or destroyed in a way that would harm the artist's reputation, and the right to disclaim authorship if such change or destruction occurs. But although the law granted unprecedented concessions to visual artists demanding what amounted to special treatment from legislatures, its language is deeply circumspect, a measure of lawmaker skepticism. Only paintings, sculptures, and prints "existing in a single copy, in a limited edition of 200 copies or fewer" and still photographs "produced for exhibition purposes only" and existing in a single copy "signed by the author" qualified for VARA protection.[42] Above all, the works had to be those of an artist with "recognized stature." Judicial interpretation has expanded the scope of VARA. In 2018, New York federal judge Frederic Block affirmed a jury's finding that a property developer's effacement of graffiti works on buildings he owned constituted a violation of the artists' rights under VARA. Called the "5Pointz case" after the building complex, the decision not only paved the way for other site-specific, ephemeral works to claim VARA protection, but also emphasized the importance of self-presentation. Telling was Block's approbation: the artists testifying were "respectful, articulate and credible," the latter affirmed not only by traditional benchmarks of professional achievement such as exhibition record and media attention but also by their "social media presence."[43]

Yet for every judge who accepted expert testimony regarding the artistic status of a particular object or action, there were many more who refused to accept new artistic media or strategies.[44] As legal scholar Amy Adler has noted, lawyers often regard contemporary art as "an insider's game" whose conventions are just as opaque to them as the law is for artists.[45] The classic instance was the 1994 case *Rogers v. Koons*, one of the most important decisions in copyright law, in which the U.S. Court of Appeals for the Second Circuit—arguably the most influential U.S. court ruling on matters of visual art, by virtue of its location in New York City—found the artist Jeff Koons to have unlawfully copied an image depicted in a black-and-white photograph taken by a professional photographer, Art Rogers.[46] The photograph showing a smiling elderly couple displaying a litter of puppies served as the basis of a large, colored wooden sculpture (fig. 7). Despite significant physical and affective differences, including the facial

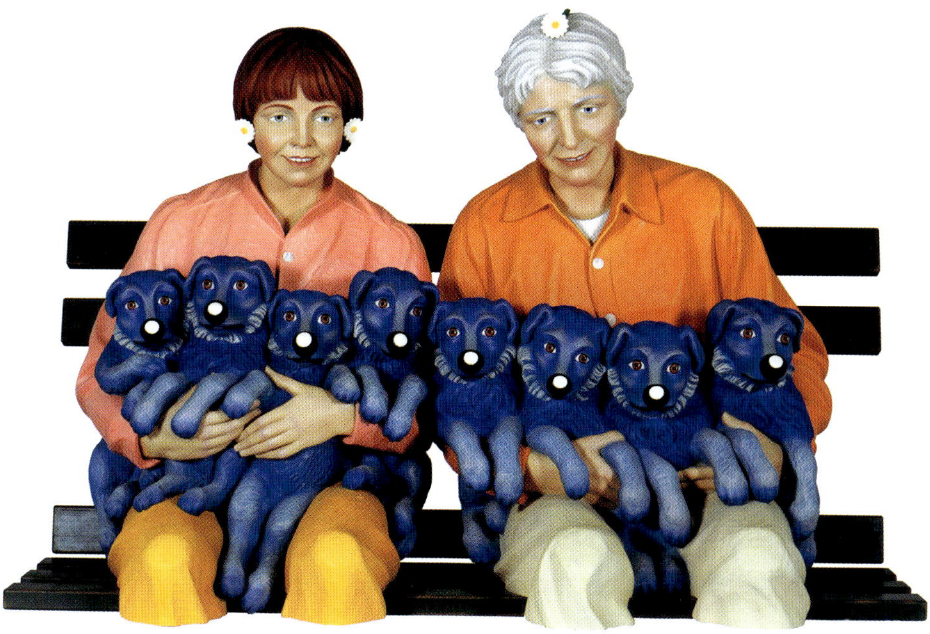

FIGURE 7
Jeff Koons, *String of Puppies*, 1988. Polychromed wood, 42 × 62 × 37 inches. © Jeff Koons.

expressions of the couple—which, under Koons's instruction, turned into catatonic stares—the court found in Rogers's favor, claiming that the "average lay person" would recognize Koons's work as a copy. In their influential treatise on copyright, frequently used by judges to support court decisions, Melville and David Nimmer likewise contended that the copy of an image from one medium to another would constitute infringement.[47]

The *Rogers* case was decided on principles articulated by Pierre Leval, then a district court judge in New York. In what has now become the governing standard for deciding permissible copying known as "fair use," a 1990 law journal article by Leval proposed the standard of "transformative use," which tasked judges presiding over infringement cases to consider how much quoted matter is "transformed in the creation of new information, new aesthetics, new insights and understandings."[48] But unlike the *Rogers* court, which deployed "transformative use" as a bar that new approaches to creation had to meet, Leval proposed it to emphasize copyright as a stimulant to knowledge production. Tacitly gesturing toward the creative commons paradigm that would gain traction in the 2000s, Leval's article was consequently cited in *Blanch v. Koons,* where the Second Circuit ruled in favor of the artist who used for his painting an image that had originally appeared in a photographed advertisement.[49]

The continued muddling of art and everyday life, where artworks resemble or are in fact nonartistic objects or where artists perform activities typical in other professions, rests on the conviction that such intentional confusion enhances the social and political relevance of artistic production. Such muddling assumes particular significance when it triggers legal intervention, in turn revealing law's inconsistencies, limits, and inchoate parts—that is, law as another kind of form. Since the early 1980s, the artist Richard Prince has used other photographers' images in his work, often with very little modification. The subject of numerous copyright infringement lawsuits that doubled as a rare opportunity for dialogue between different sectors of the contemporary art world, Prince turned in 2014 to using photographs culled from Instagram accounts without the consent of the image creators or account holders. Drawn to these images because they did not look "like art," Prince reproduced them wholesale, though at a greatly magnified size (one work measures five by four feet, for example) that mimicked how dramatic enlargement helped cement the fine-art status of photography from the late 1970s.[50] While contemporary art is crucially defined by the expansion of media, categories of medium persist in legal attitudes toward art, precisely because of how legality is produced through bounded categories that not only provide clarity but hopefully reduce the likelihood of additional lawsuits. Should Prince successfully defend his use of images, for instance, he could potentially file future claims against anyone else using the same images now legally recognized as his intellectual property. Yet different attitudes toward medium also emphasize the incongruence between art and law, one of the best places for thinking about the motivations, assumptions, and functions of both realms.

LIFE IN THE RISK SOCIETY

In 1974, the Japanese American sculptor Isamu Noguchi was commissioned to create *Shinto*, a 1,600-pound stainless steel sculpture, for the lobby of the Bank of Tokyo, Japan's leading foreign exchange institution (fig. 8). Suspended from the ceiling of the lobby of the bank's New York headquarters, the rhomboid work was a cornerstone of the newly renovated 100 Broadway. Located a stone's throw from the New York Stock Exchange, the grand Beaux Arts exterior of the building (completed in 1896) had been home to the bank since 1952. The bank made the most of its prime location when it co-underwrote a massive renovation. Spearheaded by the firm of Nobutaka Ashihara, the renovation was hailed by the influential *New York Times* architecture critic Ada Louise Huxtable as a "vote of confidence" in a city popularly characterized as a cess-pool of decay.[51] Widely acclaimed for his large-scale works, Noguchi seemed an ideal choice to revitalize the building, with Huxtable describing *Shinto* as enabling a "dramatically successful counterpoint of new and old."[52] But in 1980, the bank removed

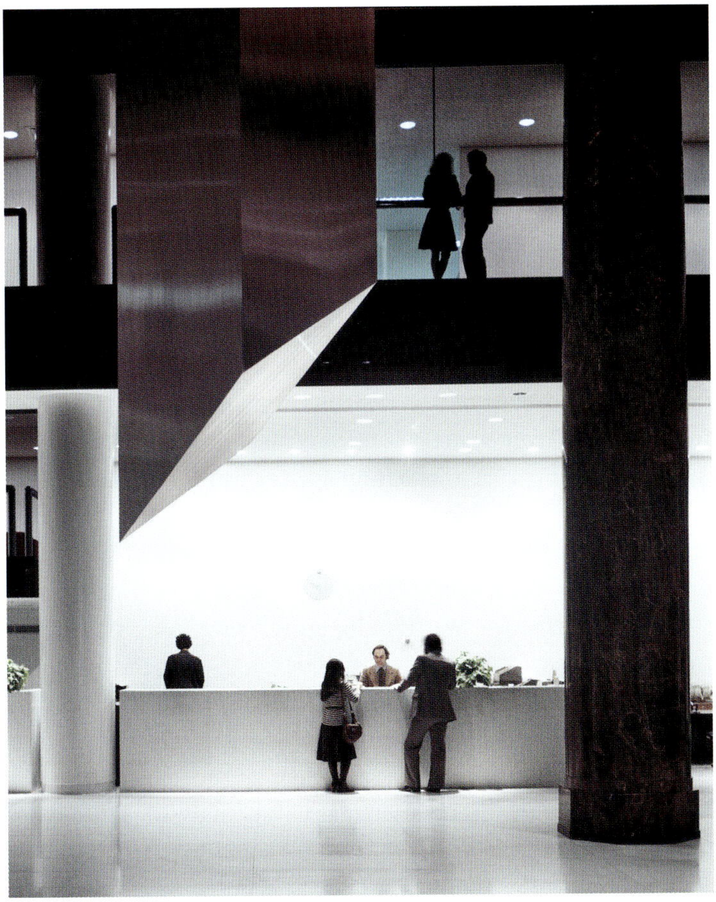

FIGURE 8
Ezra Stoller, interior view of Bank of Tokyo, New York headquarters, 1976. Foreground: Isamu Noguchi, *Shinto*, 1974–75. Stainless steel public sculpture. Photo: Ezra Stoller. © Ezra Stoller/Esto.

the sculpture on the grounds that a few unidentified customers and employees perceived the sculpture as looking "like a guillotine."[53] Despite Noguchi's protests, the removal was not illegal, a stark reminder of just how far the legal regime esteemed the interests of owners over creators. Bank officials defended their decision, citing how the work could seem "threatening or unsafe."[54] Their concern was likely affected by what had been, since the 1960s, a steady move toward strict liability in personal injury cases, where courts imposed absolute legal responsibility for any harm caused by a given party, irrespective of fault.[55]

The *Shinto* situation highlighted a broader culture of risk management, or what sociologist Ulrich Beck popularly described as the "risk society." Here the risk in question indicated what sociologist Anthony Giddens defined as manufactured uncertainties, or risks directly caused by human action, particularly technological and industrial development: "The idea of risk is bound up with the aspiration to control and particularly with the idea of controlling the future."[56] Defined by various branches of law as the probability of bodily or psychological harm, risk became as central to the definition of *artist* as conceptions of labor or intention had been previously.[57] As artworks became more complicated to produce, and as litigation increased exponentially—with the rate of civil lawsuits filed in state courts actually outpacing U.S. population growth in the late 1970s—addressing the issue of responsibility through risk management became an increasing part of artistic production.[58] Think, for example, of Experiments in Art and Technology founder Billy Klüver's anxious insistence on a safety consultant to guard against "lawsuits, [and] crackpots."[59] Museums found themselves adjusting the scope of their operation. Display venues, particularly museums and other public spaces, had to contend with tort law, a branch of civil law concerning intentional and accidental harm of one party by another. The standard of negligence, which assigned punishment according to fault, was replaced by strict liability. Mirroring the expansion of protective regulation during the 1970s and '80s, namely with regard to the environment and the consumer, the shift to a strict liability standard resonated with new laws regulating artwork sales. From 1976 on, California dealers were fully responsible for any damage to consigned artworks, including damage caused by factors outside their control.[60]

Risk management also extended to an artwork's content. The supposed meaning of an artwork was subject to intense probing, with some artists going so far as to destroy their own work even when no legal threat was imminent. Initiated in 1975 by artists Jacob Silberman and Anthony Siani, who sued their colleague for painting them as muggers, *Silberman v. Georges* was one of the few cases to address how and when libel may be committed through painting. Of the case, dealer Allan Frumkin asked whether it would "come to the point where artists will have to ask their subjects for releases, as they do in the advertising business?"[61] Museums acted as if they were subject to strict liability, irrespective of what the law actually required. Fear of liability became a potent, if under-acknowledged, glue binding the otherwise unruly field of contemporary art.[62]

In 1967, University of Massachusetts officials removed large-scale paintings and drawings by Chuck Close from an exhibition installed on university grounds open to the public. The works featured girls and women depicted in various states of undress, accompanied by captions that seemed as if written by the subjects. In the first major case to revolve around how the nature of an artwork's location affects the viewing experience it produces, the Massachusetts district court initially found in Close's favor when the artist brought suit against the university, reasoning that the removal was arbitrary: "At most the exhibition seems to have displeased some persons who saw it, and to have given rise to some lively discussion."[63]Stung, perhaps, by how the district court dismissed its concerns as the scattered protests of a disillusioned few, the University of Massachusetts successfully appealed the lower court's decision.[64] In *Close v. Lederle*, the First Circuit reversed the lower court's decision, making no secret of its contempt for Close's works. Citing his use of "cheap titles" and characterizing the display itself as a form of "exposure" to an "unwilling audience," the higher court barely acknowledged Close's works as a legitimate form of expression, let alone as art.[65] While the reaction itself was hardly unusual, the First Circuit revisited the lower court's passing consideration as to whether the location of Close's works in the corridor was inappropriate, further noting how legal scholars observed how words that could be acceptable in the classroom or in a library book might not be acceptable if they appear on signs posted on campus trees. The First Circuit stressed how *location* was defined by both use and visibility; not only were Close's works displayed in a visible location, but that location was the only means of entering the student union, which made the public a "captive audience."[66] Battles over the physical location and context of art reflected how the U.S. government in the 1970s would dramatically increase its role in regulating the patterns of everyday life.

Few projects illustrated the predicament of competing audiences as vividly as the controversy over Richard Serra's *Tilted Arc* (1981), a forty-ton freestanding COR-TEN steel sculpture that the General Services Administration (GSA) commissioned for Federal Plaza, in front of the Jacob K. Javits Federal Building in New York City (fig. 9). Soon after its completion, the work attracted the ire of members of the public, including a federal judge and a congressman who asked the government to remove it. In what is arguably the best-known legal case involving a public artwork to date, a five-person panel appointed by the GSA voted to remove the work.[67] The extent to which Serra was compelled to justify *Tilted Arc* to multiple audiences before and during the GSA hearing emphasized just how intrinsic accountability was to any work involving government property. His arguments may have failed to persuade government and law officials who tended to judge Serra's claims according to their own morality systems. Yet for many of his advocates, Serra's cause was worth supporting because of the consistency he demonstrated in defending the integrity of the object—in this case, the artist's right to prohibit any distortion or misrepresentation of his or her work.

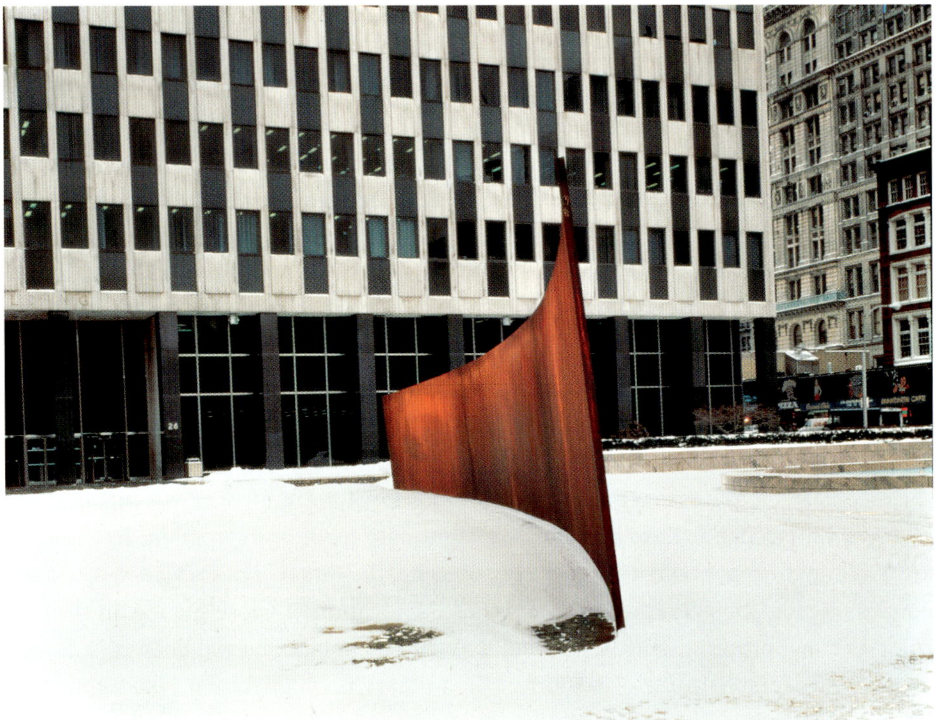

FIGURE 9
Richard Serra, *Tilted Arc*, 1981. Cor-Ten steel, 12 × 120 feet. © 2017 Richard Serra/Artists Rights Society (ARS), New York. Courtesy of Gagosian.

The war over space climaxed in 1990 when the Contemporary Arts Center in Cincinnati, Ohio, along with its director Dennis Barrie, stood trial in Hamilton County Municipal Court for seven photographs displayed as part of a larger exhibit of 174 photographs by Robert Mapplethorpe.[68] Popularly known as the Mapplethorpe trial, *City of Cincinnati v. Contemporary Arts Center* gained notoriety as the first attempt to prosecute a museum or art gallery under an obscenity statute in the United States. A key question was whether the artistic status of the offending seven photographs remained consistent; as architectural historian Mark Jarzombeck pointed out, the prosecution contended that whatever the status of the photographs "was *inside* of the museum, they were not art on the outside."[69]

THE CREDIBILITY ECONOMY

Struggles over the right to be present, especially in a public setting, were as much a part of the contemporary art milieu as the development of new artistic media. But shared predicaments did not make for equal treatment, as was vividly demonstrated by the almost contemporaneous experiences of Marc Morrel and Charlotte Moorman. In 1966, a New York gallerist, Stephen Radich, held a group exhibition that included an anti–

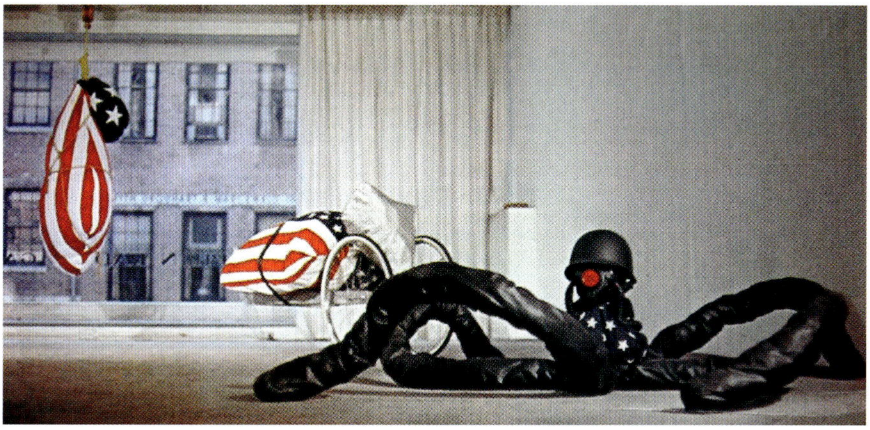

FIGURE 10
Installation view of Marc Morrel's works at the Stephen Radich Gallery, December 1966. Courtesy of Marc Morrel. © Marc Morrel.

Vietnam War work by Marc Morrel that made the flag look like a dead body hung from a noose (fig. 10).[70] In the first of the judicial decisions that would become known as *People v. Radich,* one of the most important and earliest legal cases to address the content of contemporary art, Radich was found guilty by the Criminal Court of the City of New York for "casting contempt" on the flag, a crime that during the Vietnam War years was committed so frequently in large cities as to practically be an everyday occurrence. Yet the Federal Flag Desecration Law in 1968 bestowed upon police and courts a remarkably broad set of powers to apprehend anyone who deliberately and publicly defaced or destroyed the U.S. flag. The decision was affirmed in 1968 by the New York State Court of Appeals, and again in 1971 by the U.S. Supreme Court. Radich was eventually vindicated in 1974, when the U.S. District Court for the Southern District of New York held that the dealer's conviction was unconstitutional. By that time, enough legal commentary had been published to convince a federal court that some forms of flag desecration in the name of art could be regarded as constitutionally protected symbolic protest.[71]

The law was much less forgiving of Charlotte Moorman, the cellist who performed *Opera Sextronique,* a four-part opera on February 9, 1967, at the Film-Makers' Cinematheque, a leading venue for avant-garde film and performance in New York City. Composed by Nam June Paik, the Korean artist widely celebrated for his association with Fluxus, an artistic movement known for emphasizing the process of creation over the completed product, the work instructed Moorman to perform in various states of nudity. Although both Paik and Moorman were arrested during the performance, only Moorman was found guilty of indecent exposure by the New York City Criminal Court. The general notoriety of the trial deeply impressed upon many artists how their audience now included the law and its agents.[72] Later anointed one of the ten worst judges in New York City, Judge Milton Shalleck gave Moorman a suspended sentence on account of her frality.[73] Commonly given to first-time offenders guilty of minor crimes, a suspended sentence in this case amounted to a period of penance imposed by Shalleck, whose unusually verbose opinion was riddled with deeply masculinist views of women typical of a legal system unwilling to recognize the agency of women (fig. 11).[74]

The Moorman trial illuminated what philosopher Miranda Fricker has described as a "credibility economy," where one's place in the world depends on how others perceive certain "social types."[75] In one of the most frequently cited art historical essays of the last half-century, the art historian Linda Nochlin argued that an institutional network so deeply entrenched in an oppressive gender hierarchy made it impossible for women to achieve even, equal footing with their male counterparts, "*no matter what* the potency of their so-called talent or genius [Nochlin's emphasis]."[76] Written in 1971, a year before Congress passed the Equal Rights Amendment, guaranteeing equal civil rights regardless of sex, the essay belonged to a groundswell of feminist action happening across multiple disciplines, fields, and localities. Yet Nochlin's essay indirectly reminded readers of how, despite the new vogue for meritocracy occasioned by sociologists like Daniel Bell, structural assumptions eclipsed the talents, achievements, and sometimes the lives of artists not born white, male, upper or middle class, and heteronormative.[77] A tragic case in point was the acquittal of sculptor Carl Andre for the murder of his wife, the artist Ana Mendieta, in 1988. On a summer night in 1985, Andre allegedly pushed Mendieta out the window of their thirty-fourth-floor home in Greenwich Village. Tried in New York's highest court, Andre was acquitted due to unreliable eyewitness testimony and a lack of evidence that at least one commentator suspected was an example of Mafia-like *omertà* among members of the New York art world elite.[78] "The cowardice of the art world has been staggering," wrote critic Ruby Rich.[79] Perhaps no one was as frank as the artist Howardena Pindell, who commented openly in Judd Tully's cover feature for the *New Art Examiner* that "if Ana had been an Anglo and if Carl had been black, the art world would have lynched him."[80] As Barbara Kruger stated in the aftermath of the notorious trial of Andre, the law

> determines who we are in the world and what our positions are to a large degree. Who's [*sic*] law is a client of and who it's not a client of. The whole thing about law is how things function in a symbolic space. How narrative is the motor of every social furtherance.[81]

Kruger suggested conceiving the law broadly as an established network of rules understood as regulating the actions of a given polity's members.

The Andre trial, which drew responses from all over the country, spelled out an escalating crisis of credibility. In whom could one trust, for example, amid the hypocrisy and racism underlying a spate of censorship cases involving visual artworks? When, in 1989, a painting of Mayor Harold Washington of Chicago was removed from a student art competition at the School of the Art Institute of Chicago at the behest of

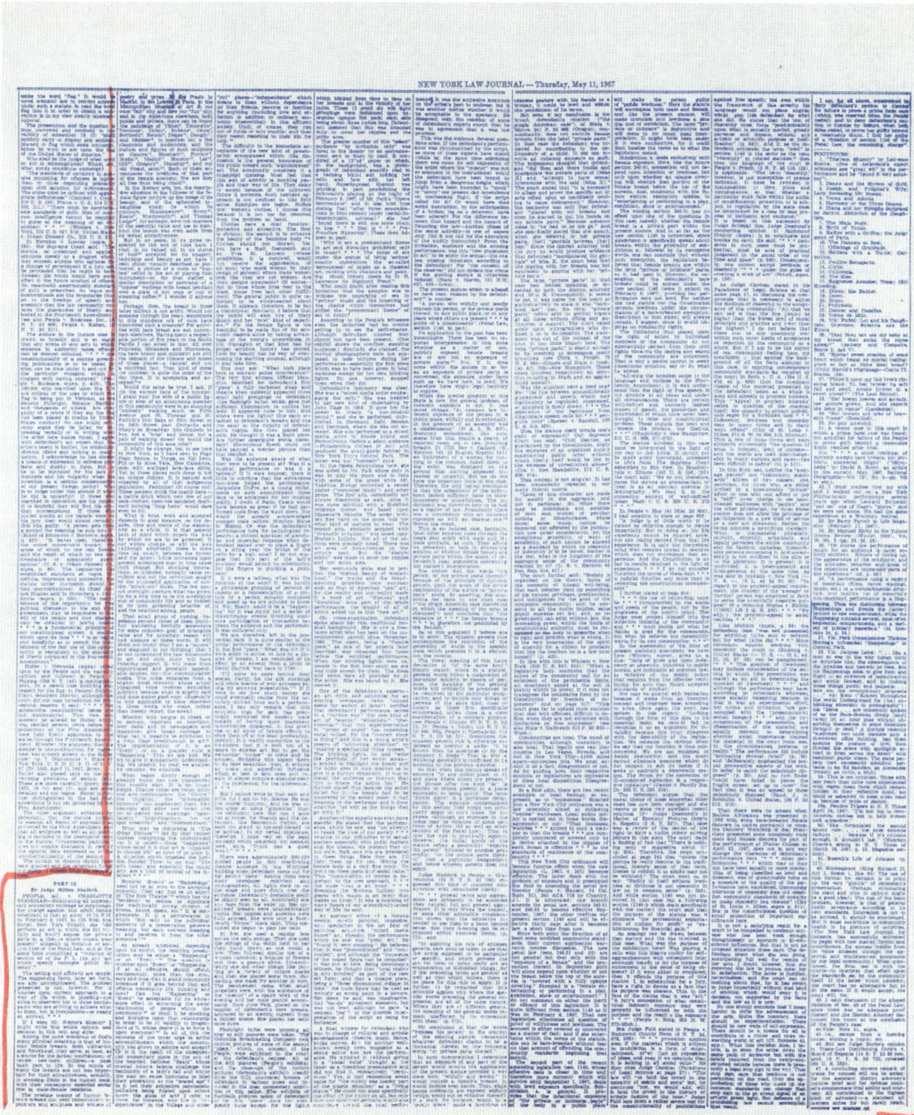

FIGURE 11

"Part 1E: People & C.V. Charlotte Moorman," New York Law Journal, May 11, 1967, 1967. Offset lithograph on paper, 24 ⅞ × 19 1⁄16 inches. Charles Deering McCormick Library of Special Collections, Northwestern University Libraries. © *New York Law Journal.*

African American city aldermen who saw the portrayal as racist, the highly publicized removal sparked an intense barrage of protests that cast serious doubt on the idea of "rights" and the liberal aspirations on which rights-based approaches to justice were founded. Pindell observed that although white artists were quick to condemn censorship of artworks by their white counterparts, most remained "profoundly unaware of, insensitive to, indifferent to, or outright hostile to the knowledge of the fact that artists of color are censored out of the art world system."[82] The art world, she implied, pivoted on unresolved asymmetries of power structured by reified perceptions of racial and sexual difference.

FIFTY SHADES OF GRAY: ON ILLEGALITY

Crime has had a special place in the history of avant-garde cultural production, with artists deliberately regarding law as the sine qua non of bourgeois conventions. Think, for instance, of Surrealists' fascination with violent crime and its potential to advance the cause of revolution and resist assimilation into bourgeois society in the early 1930s.[83] Yet the turn to illegality in the 1960s turned less on a romanticized view of artistic identity and more on reflecting a world defined by lawlessness, from the assassination of John F. Kennedy in 1963 to race riots that proliferated across the United States in the 1960s. In such a world, law itself had diminished credibility in the eyes of citizens directly exposed to police violence and political ineptitude. As noted by the filmmaker Jonas Mekas, who had been arrested and found guilty for showing Jack Smith's allegedly obscene film *Flaming Creatures,* "it is the community that should be measured against art."[84]

In some cases, lawbreaking helped flesh out that which existing legal structures had yet to properly articulate. Wanting to "validate" his work by confronting "operations of an authority outside myself," Jay Jaroslav revealed the compromised integrity of the very documents authorizing every individual's entry into, and exit from, social and civil life. Using his credentials as an MIT-employed scientist, he accessed and copied birth records of dead infants at Boston's City Hall and used them to obtain Social Security cards, driver's licenses, and passports. Eventually producing thirty-one legal identities in five years, Jaroslav thus created an identity chain that illustrates how birth certificates, perhaps the least secure form of identity, could be used as "breeder documents" to obtain other forms of documentary citizenship. Titling the resultant work *Extended Credentials* to reflect its extension of a previous work listing various emotional states and actions as résumé "credentials," Jaroslav never used the documents except as art (the only exception being perhaps his unwitting role as an advisor to contemporaries who may have wanted to create false identities to avoid the draft in the sunset years of the Vietnam War).[85] Yet *Extended Credentials* presaged not only concerns over the use of breeder documents in organized crime and by terrorists in the late 1970s, and in illegal immigration in the 1990s, but also how "identity theft," a phrase almost completely unknown before 2000, would pervade everyday life on mul-

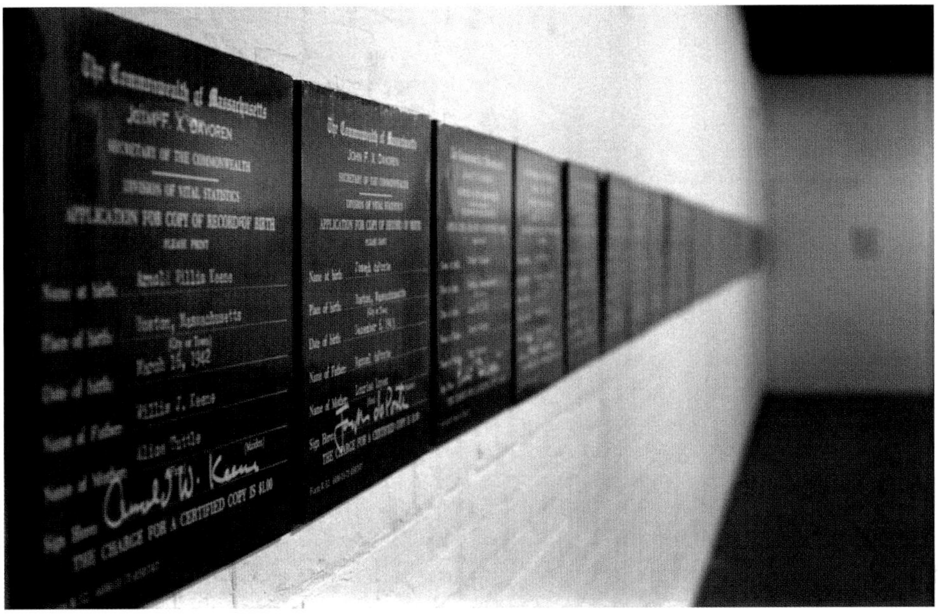

FIGURE 12
Installation detail of Jay Lee Jaroslav, *Extended Credentials,* 1967–72. © 1972 Jay Jaroslav. Courtesy of Trident Gallery, Gloucester, Massachusetts.

tiple scales, from legislation to casual conversation.[86] Although he intended to continue breeding identities, Jaroslav also knew he would eventually be apprehended, an awareness he built into his exhibitions by shrinkwrapping birth certificates so as to prove they had never been used except as artistic material (fig. 12).[87] Critic Kenneth Baker observed that *Extended Credentials* actually created a situation that forced the government to prove the artist's intent to defraud, a challenge prosecutors succeeded only partly in meeting when the artist was convicted of mail fraud, a serious federal felony, yet received a much lesser penalty than was typical.[88]

Illegal activity was more commonly a form of dissent also intended to convey moral and political responsibility. Among the most enthusiastic proponents of illegality as a morally necessary artistic strategy was the Guerilla Art Action Group, whose actions famously included urging the kidnapping of museum officials, for which Jean Toche was arrested by the FBI and forced by judicial order to undergo psychiatric treatment. The artist threatened the kidnapping in retaliation for what he claimed was the vandalism committed by the Museum of Modern Art, which had removed an inscription spray painted by Tony Shafrazi on *Guernica,* Pablo Picasso's devastating indictment of war's horrors. Toche later participated in "The People's Flag Show," the 1970 group show at the Judson Memorial Church in New York for which he, Faith Ringgold, and Jon Hendricks were arrested on charges of violating the flag anti-desecration laws

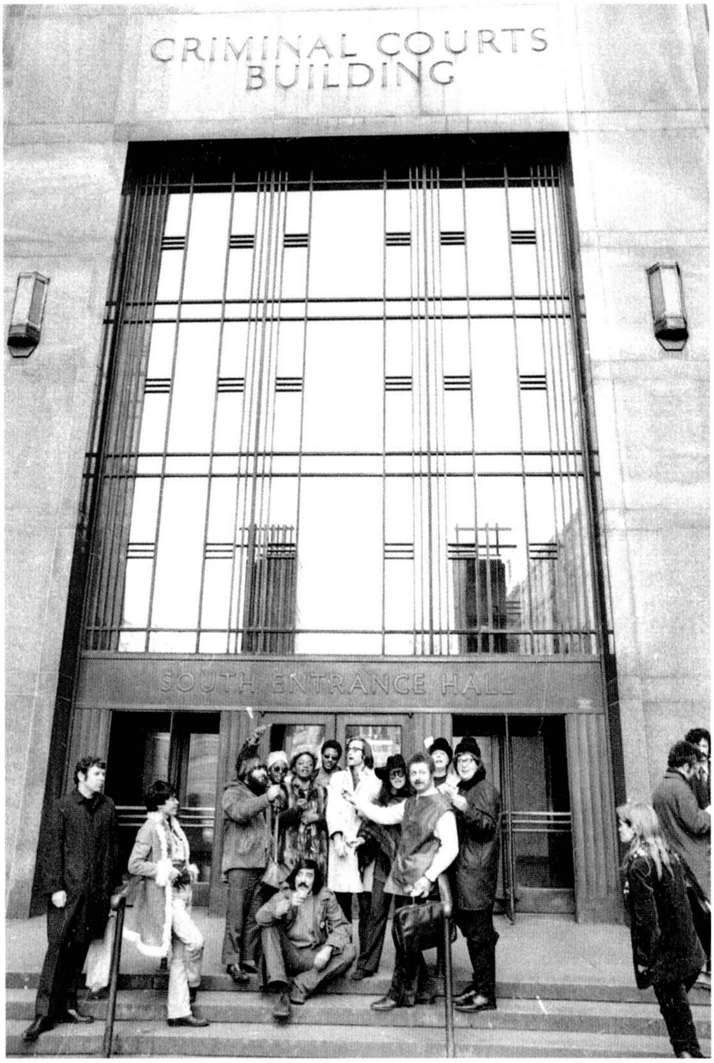

FIGURE 13
Jean Toche, Faith Ringgold, and Jon Hendricks with artist supporters (including Kate Millett, Fumio Yoshimura, Sandy Rellis, Alex Gross, Ann Arlen, and Joe DiGeorgio), burning miniature U.S. flags at the Criminal Courts Building following the first pretrial hearing, 100 Center Street, New York, December 1, 1970. Photo: Jan van Raay. © Jan van Raay.

underpinning cases like *People v. Radich*. Known as the "Judson Three," the artists asked for a jury trial, a costly and risky process most defendants are advised to avoid but a golden opportunity to publicly air differences between art and the law.[89] Citing *Radich,* which the court described somewhat passive-aggressively ("It thus appears that the State of New York may have the power to regulate and to punish acts of physical desecration of the flag"), it eventually ruled against the defendants.[90] Yet the trial and attendant hearings also provided an opportunity to bring the show to the people via outdoor performances, including the burning of miniature flags at the New York City Criminal Courts Building (fig. 13).

Prevailing views of artist criminality emphasize political resistance as the substrate of artistic production. Yet they risk glossing over how the actual politics of this production unfold through hiccups, incompletes, and hesitations that mirror the fallibility, and even perhaps the humanity, of regulation. Most illegal actions fell into the category of what artist Barry Le Va called "little crimes."[91] Le Va, whose arrangements of objects such as broken glass, ball bearings, shredded felt, and chalk powder often looked like evidence at a crime scene and were influenced by popular crime novels, implied a different set of motivations than those underpinning more notorious gestures of willful, spectacular, or radical illegality.[92] Ranging from petty theft to violations of health codes for the use of controlled materials, these "little crimes" were sometimes unintended, thus further demonstrating the discrepancy between artistic and legal standards of conduct but also how the social import of art partly turned on its unique ability to sensitize viewers to the pervasive irrationality of daily life. The notion of "little crimes" recalled earlier legal history in which crimes were divided according to severity, such as how punishments for theft depended on whether "grand" or "petit" larceny was committed. More recent is the separation of crimes into legal categories like felonies and misdemeanors, where the threshold separating the two, at least for crimes against property in the United States, is a surprisingly low $500. Frequently, little crimes are defined as situations so proximate to ordinary life that they cannot readily pass as art to a judge or jury generally unfamiliar with contemporary art.

For *Violations: Evidence of 153 Misdemeanors in Violation of Section 484 of the California Penal Code (Petty Theft)* (1971–72), Dennis Oppenheim stole 187 hubcaps from cars (fig. 14). These hubcaps were displayed on the floor of the Sonnabend Gallery in New York in 1972, accompanied by a video depicting them being pried from anonymous car wheels. Prior to the exhibition, he had photographed the hubcaps against a backdrop of San Quentin State Prison, which was the oldest prison in California and had one of the largest death rows in the country. Oppenheim described *Violations* as "fracturing" the law rather than breaking it, an important distinction that emphasized how the law is most viscerally affected not by its violation (which often results in more enforcement) but because it is thwarted, bent, and diverted in multiple ways.[93] Reproduced as a mailer sent by the Museum of Conceptual Art in San Francisco, the photographed hubcaps were potential evidence, not only of his crimes, but also of the lapse of vigilance by those to whom they belonged. Yet the bold display, both on the mailer and later on the floor of a publicly accessible space, also revealed how the protracted legal process—enacted in the name of fairness—opens up spaces for extra-legal behavior. Given the relatively modest cost of a hubcap and the decidedly high cost of arresting and trying Oppenheim, it was unlikely that the police would actually trace the hubcaps' lawful owners. In this way *Violations* implicated the law as its unwitting collaborator.

Artists who performed these "little crimes" worked within the space between the expectations of the viewer and the actual experience such crimes offered without devolving into pure sensationalism. For some, however, breaking the law was not itself

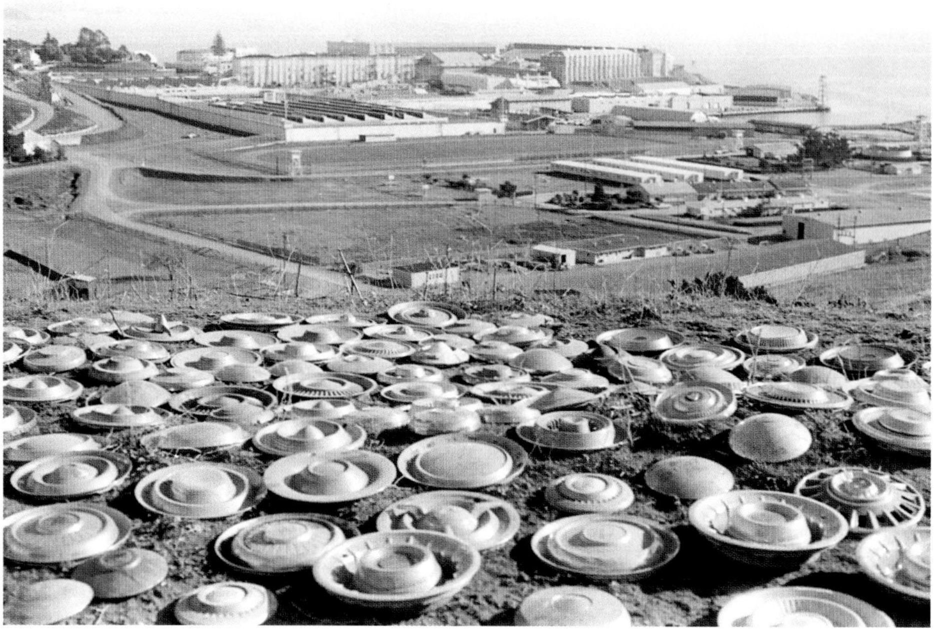

FIGURE 14
Dennis Oppenheim, *Violations: Evidence of 153 Misdemeanors in Violation of Section 484 of the California Penal Code (Petty Theft)*, 1971–72. Location: Bordering San Quentin State Prison, San Quentin, California. © Dennis Oppenheim. Courtesy of Dennis Oppenheim Estate.

a sufficient form of critique or challenge, as critic John Perreault pointed out in his review of "Illegal America," the first major exhibition to seriously consider contemporary U.S. art through the lens of the law.[94] Held at the Franklin Furnace in New York City in 1982, the exhibition was curated by Jeannette Ingberman, who later founded Exit Art, an alternative space that would become renowned for promoting female artists and artists of color. Focusing on artists who intentionally violated current law or alluded to such infringements, Ingberman saw illegality as a proactive attempt to address how everyday life was rife with risk: "The use of illegality is a commitment by the artist to deal with reality, [which carries] often dangerous risk," she wrote in the show's catalogue, which in fact could only be opened by an illegal act, tearing a dollar bill attached to its cover.[95] For Perreault, however, the exhibition repeated the "vital but perhaps dangerous romanticism that still sees the artist as divorced from society, impatient with seeking permission, beyond rules and regulation; in short, the artist as criminal."[96] In the post–Vietnam War years, the political and artistic value of illegality was less clear. Perreault tartly accused the show's participants of an uncritical dilettantism, noting how "it is probably exciting for a middle-class person to be arrested, or at least to experience the paranoia-rush of fearing arrest."[97] In such circumstances, "art does not survive as object, but as publicity."[98] Unconsciously echoing the legal maxim *de minimis non curat lex* ("Law does not concern itself with trifles"), Perreault added that most crimes committed in the name of artistic creation were "so inconsequential" as to compromise any political impact the artists may have intended their works to have.[99] In a worst-case scenario, celebrating illegality could lead to intellectual stupor and even complicity if one really believed that breaking a minor law was sufficient proof of a work's social or political relevance.

Yet if artistic integrity also meant committing to transparency, it required making law visible as a form shaped by multiple pressures. That Oppenheim was able to spirit away so many hubcaps without repercussion was due in part to limited police time and resources. Thus, *Violations* reads the law not as an absolute system of regulation but as itself subject to the rule of time. Along similar lines, Ann Messner traded the moral certitude that acts of overt resistance seem to promise for explorations into the ambiguous zones at the fringes of legality and morality. *Stealing* was a 1978 performance involving the petty theft of cheap shirts from the summer sale at a German department store (fig. 15). In full view of multiple surveillance cameras, Messner positioned herself near a pile of cheap shirts from which she initially took one surreptitiously, then others more boldly. The video recording the work suggests disbelief on Messner's part, with the repeated thefts undertaken to confirm the almost total lack of bystander reaction and, perhaps, how technology via the surveillance cameras has relieved viewers of any duty of vigilance.

"Breaking the law was not the point," Messner states.[100] Rather, *Stealing* reflects her interest in what she describes as the "gray zone of what's permissible in terms of material and how you get it, what you are allowed to work with, and questions of authorship within that."[101] Save for one suspicious matron who casts a baffled eye on Messner's shoplifting, *Stealing* proceeds uninterrupted; even the disapproving matron remains silent. The lack of response to a recognizably criminal act illustrates how indifference reflects a form of self-regulation by which the everyday maintains its even keel, especially in public spaces. *Stealing* illuminates how enforcing law can depend on the willingness of bystanders to violate norms of civility by accusing a stranger of wrongful activity. *Stealing* emphasizes how little crimes make legible disruptions otherwise neglected or forgotten in favor of more familiar narratives of resistance, rejection, and protest. In his contribution to "Illegal America," Vito Acconci observed how violating the law may have been "readymade advertising" for artists and institutions seeking to increase attendance but also tended to marginalize the violator. Such artists may have wanted "to be *in* the world" but "as a result of that 'illegality'" found themselves "out of the world."[102] Yet the "gray zone" of Messner's actions more specifically reflected how law actually functions in the real world, through the choices individuals and groups make as bystanders.

THE LENS OF ETHICS

More artists worked conspicuously *within* the boundaries set by statute, case decisions, or custom, not from any imagined duty to conform to a more powerful institution or

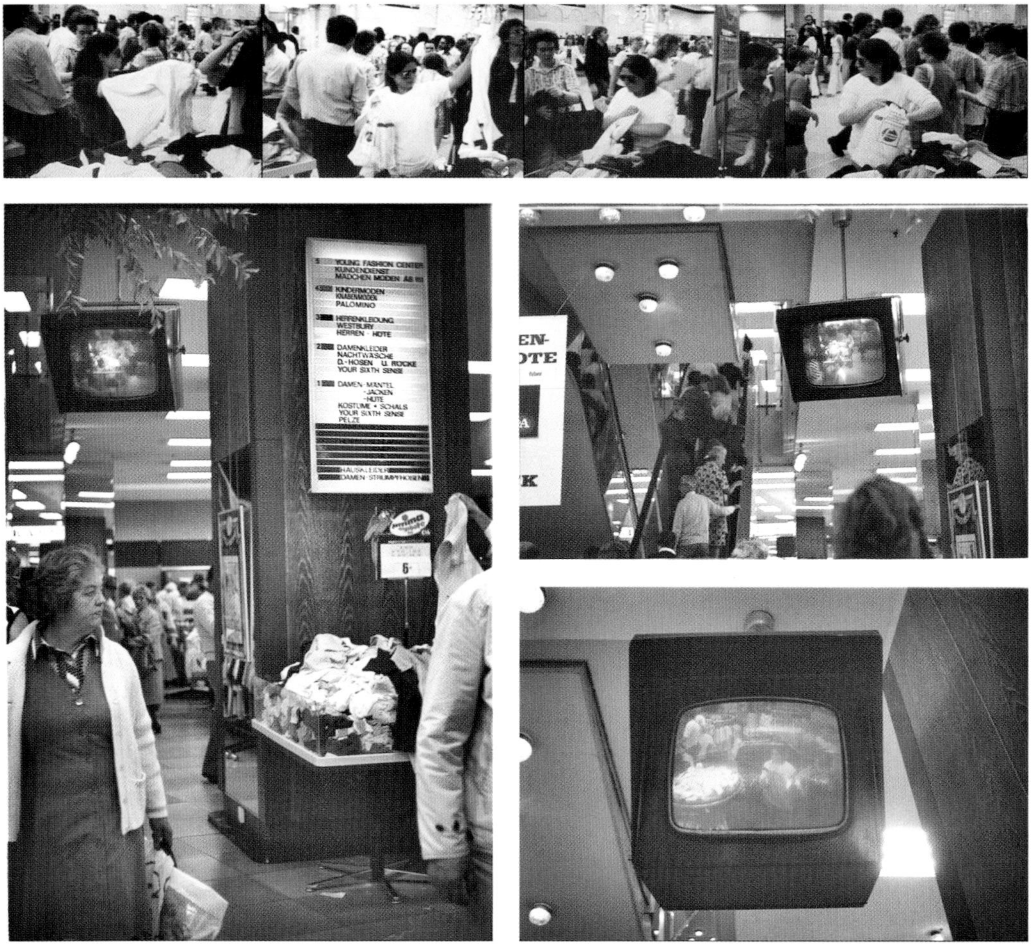

FIGURE 15
Ann Messner, *Stealing*, 1978. Summer end sale, C&A, Cologne Germany. Stills from film (digital transfer from Super 8), 3 feet, 33 inches. Photo stills: Peter Moennig. © Ann Messner.

the fear of possible retribution by a state unable to fully address the disjunction between law and justice, but so they could account for their own embedment in a densely interpersonal social structure. Even when working within the bounds of law, however, artists created ethically ambiguous situations that beckoned engagement from the legal community. An early and important example was Chris Burden's performance *Shoot* (1971), which consisted of the California artist asking a friend to shoot him in the arm with a rifle and the friend doing so (fig. 16). Law student Bruce Mitchell pointed out in the late 1970s how some examples of contemporary art, namely *Shoot*, turned on weighing one's rights as an artist against one's membership in a greater polity.[103] Mitchell wondered how artists could negotiate between their professional identities and their obligations as citizens, a distinction courts at the time were less inclined to respect, but

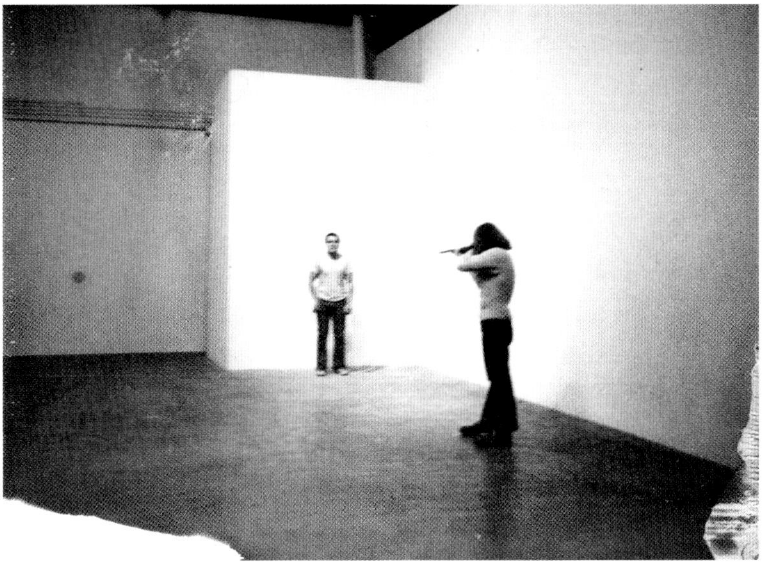

FIGURE 16
Chris Burden, *Shoot,* 1971. Performance at F-Space Gallery, Santa Ana, California. © 2017 Chris Burden/licensed by the Chris Burden Estate and Artists Rights Society (ARS), New York.

one that persisted nevertheless. Being a citizen meant being subject to certain laws, and the question of the artist's position in this regard was particularly foregrounded by the ethical dilemmas posed by certain forms of performance art involving potential hazards to the creator. Should Chris Burden be personally liable for injuries or damage caused as a result of *Shoot?*[104] Should the artist be entitled to some legal immunity? Mitchell proposed tasking artists to minimize the risk of harm to all concerned with the work.[105] In his view, artists were primarily defined as citizens whose status lay in being consistently accountable to a larger body of the law; in situations of conflict between artist's prerogative and citizen's duty, the latter necessarily prevailed.

Pondering ethics mattered as a means of reflecting on "what permits judgment, of what judgment itself authorizes," as Jacques Derrida noted in his widely read "Force of Law."[106] The question has special weight in common law jurisdictions such as the United States, where judicial precedent plays a substantial role in how law is administered and applied. Although legislatures make statutory law and executive branches make regulatory laws, it is up to courts to interpret those laws and even make laws of their own, particularly regarding contracts and one party's act that harms another. But Mitchell's response to *Shoot* also foreshadowed how judging artistic value would expand to include a reckoning with ethics. Performance art historian Kristine Stiles applauded Burden for avoiding an inevitable confrontation with the law by scuttling plans to enact *Shoot* at a university.[107] In sparing audiences any possible discomfort or distress caused by the sound of a fired bullet or the sight of someone being shot, Burden was being responsible. Less clear was how civility factored into this discussion.

Certainly Burden was aware that his actions involved legal risks. But whether such awareness was ethically exemplary is more difficult to determine than is implied by Stiles, whose reading of Burden's intentions also stems from the artist resigning from the faculty of UCLA in 2004 after the university refused to discipline one of his students who performed a version of Russian roulette in another instructor's class.[108] Critic Robert Horvitz observed that Burden may have followed correct procedure by securing participant consent and avoiding injuring others, "yet the manipulative, autocratic aspects of the work are obvious . . . to what extent are we justified in suspending our moral judgment when the material being worked is human? To what extent, if any, and under what conditions, does morality have a higher claim on our actions and reactions than esthetics?"[109] Decades later, another art historian, Frazer Ward, described *Shoot* as an instance of how "art" was invoked to sidestep difficult ethical questions about responsibility. Calling an incident "art" relieved the participants and the marksman of any social obligation they might otherwise feel as a result of watching someone being shot; as Ward points out, we still do not know the identities of the participants or the marksman, so casting individuals in the legal roles of witness and perpetrator remains elusive.[110] Moreover, the choice of venue (F-Space, an artist-run gallery) as well as the restricted audience implies an attempt to contain *Shoot* as a purely private act in that it took place on private property: whatever happens in the gallery stays in the gallery. That Burden may have intended *Shoot* to probe the limits of permissibility implies how art's roles now included asking whether certain situations should be recognized as legal claims in an ideal society. Despite the substantial differences separating art historical and legal reasoning, *Shoot* highlighted how the two might converge, in this case, through a mutual interest in addressing what behaviors should be condoned (or condemned) depending on whether Burden's legal status as a citizen takes precedence over his professional identity as an artist or vice versa.

Likewise, the ability to rationalize artistic activity through nonartistic means became part of the artist's toolbox. The ability to distinguish between honesty and fraudulence, and even between remediable and irreparable fraud, has been part of the story of American art in the twentieth century. Discussing how Marcel Duchamp famously invented the "readymade" in 1914, a new strategy for artistic creation so named for how the physical artwork consisted of common objects that were selected, modified, and presented in traditional venues of display, art historian Michael Leja writes how modernism opened the door to the risk of fraud: "When standards of achievement are constantly being overturned, the window for deception is thrown wide open."[111]

Not surprisingly, some artists justified their works as if they were policy decisions. Like an official running for reelection, Christo defended his and Jeanne-Claude's *Running Fence* on the grounds that it created jobs, including 65 full-time and 360 temporary jobs.[112] The utilitarian explanation was an intriguing rejoinder to Mitchell's puzzlement over Burden's performances. For if artists sounded more and more like politicians, economists, or even lawyers in explaining their works to audiences that could seem more like constituents, so too did lawyers and lawmakers more freely give way to their feelings toward certain works. Discussing artworks through the lens of ethics gave those trained to embrace the passive impersonal voice, and to silo the effects of emotion, a credible outlet to air what they could not otherwise express.

WHERE ART HISTORY AND ART LAW MEET

Mindful of how their own integrity hinged on working within the law as well as their bulging caseloads, judges repeatedly cited U.S. Supreme Court Justice Oliver Wendell Holmes, who famously instructed those "trained only in the law" to refrain from passing judgment on the worth of pictorial illustrations "outside of the narrowest and most obvious limits."[113] Yet what might be called the "legal sites" of art proliferated in the 1970s, '80s, and '90s, including the overlap between new forms of art and preexisting attitudes toward land, the expanding art market and its regulatory context, the unsettled status of artistic labor, the rising awareness of risk as a condition for artistic production and display, and the perceived social necessity of artworks that deliberately break the law. Navigating these sites required engaging with various boundaries where law was reproduced, including the divisions between the rule of law and the laws of the art world, between the imperatives of law and the market, and between legality and illegality.

The discursive encounter between art and law pivoted mainly around two ideas, the market and aesthetics. The rise of law and economics, or the economic analysis of law with its emphases on rational actors, efficiency, and cost-benefit analysis, strongly influenced the legal analysis of art. While some of this influence stemmed from the institutionalization of law and economics approaches in legal academia and, subsequently, the judiciary during the 1960s and early 1970s, it also derived from the accelerated expansion of the contemporary art market. From the late 1960s, which saw the creation of entities like Art Basel, the world's first contemporary art fair, to approximately 1973, when the OPEC oil crisis severely impacted the economies of countries that had large numbers of institutional and private collectors, the international art market expanded not only in terms of sales volume but also in the kinds of art shown, including conceptual art.[114] The expanded art market jumpstarted the formation of "art law," which was not so much a discrete legal subfield as it was a loose organizational rubric consisting of lawyers representing constituents of the art world (including dealers, museums, and artists) and law scholars interested in the problems of the art market, one of the most opaque and least regulated legal markets in any capitalist society. Robert Projansky and Jerald Ordover in New York counseled artists on myriad issues, including mediation of landlord-tenant disputes and advice on what to say when arrested.[115] Scott Hodes discussed the effects of law on the sale and circulation of art and antiquities in his book *The Law of Art & Antiques: A Primer for Artists and Collectors,* which sold briskly.[116]

The first scholar to seriously examine the legal history of visual art and its implications for various branches of contemporary law was Stanford law professor John Henry Merryman, who authored the first major compilation of legal cases and materials pertaining to visual art, a project he later expanded by collaborating with art historian Albert Elsen.[117] Since its initial publication in 1979, this compilation and later editions have become standard references for art law, discussing nearly every major legal case concerning visual art in the United States. Other books followed, many authored by lawyers with museum counsel experience, a reflection of institutional preoccupation with questions of liability.[118]

These, however, were exceptions in a discipline apparently fixated on maximizing transactional efficiency despite the emergence of critical legal studies (CLS) in the late 1970s and its examination of law as an ongoing struggle for hegemony. But even as law and economics became more firmly entrenched in legal academia during the 1970s, a resurgence of Marxist-oriented social art history approached the market as an ideological problem. The institutional setting of artworks was closely examined by major art theorists like Peter Bürger, who, in his 1974 book *Theory of the Avant-Garde,* offered a revisionist model of modern art history in which the avant-garde is defined not by criticizing its predecessors but by criticizing "art as an institution, and the course its development took in bourgeois society."[119] Contrary to traditional art history that emphasized judgments of artistic quality and were often deeply involved with the art market, the new social art history openly challenged the commodification of art and the institutions enabling this process, including the law.

Part of this antagonism may have been fueled by the frequency with which the legal establishment dismissed as costly encumbrances the noneconomic rights that artists claimed on moral grounds. Yet cases like *City of Cincinnati v. Contemporary Arts Center* eroded the credibility of law in the eyes of artists, art historians, and critics for whom the law was already suspect for being an instrument of demagogues bent on suppressing heretical liberal activity.[120] Despite having to work within the structures determined by statute and precedent, judges and prosecutors were vilified as philistines. Even defense attorneys, whose integrity depended on advocating the best possible outcome for their clients, were criticized for taming the sexual energy of Mapplethorpe's works through readings that insisted on their *beauty,* a word that has had surprising currency in legal decisions from the 1970s onward (fig. 17).[121] Initially used in planning and property law as a synonym for aesthetics, beauty fascinated legislators and judges who were simultaneously repelled by its unverifiability and intrigued by its potential to veil the imposition of personal tastes onto a general public.[122]

The fascination was commensurate with the suspicion that beauty aroused in contemporary art commentators. Take, for example, how some artists dismissed Mapplethorpe's works as "too beautiful to qualify for critical endorsement."[123] Reflecting "the banishing of beauty from the humanities" in the 1980s, these dismissals also reflected social art history's concern not only with class distinctions and the status of labor, but also with how aesthetics developed from, and in connection to, the structures of a given society.[124] Championed especially by a generation of art critics and historians keenly affected by the social, economic, and political reckonings massed

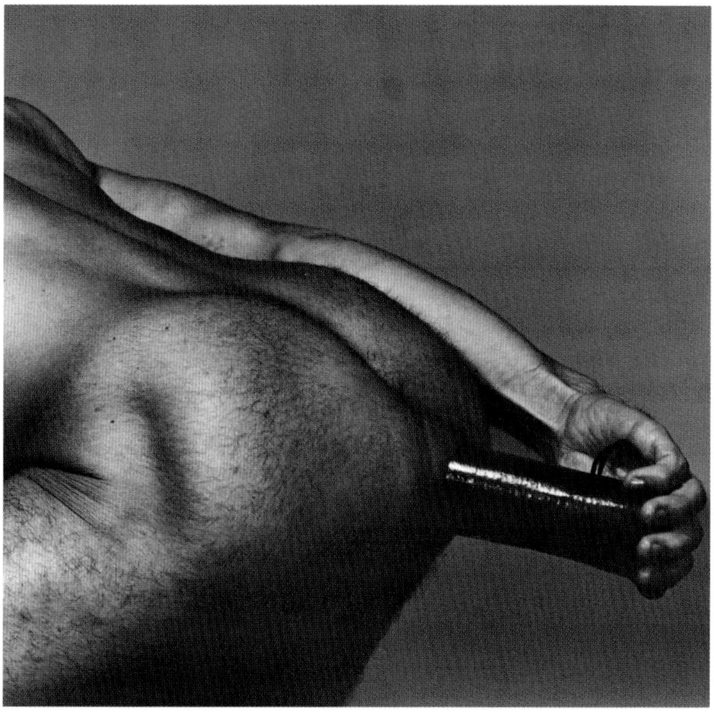

FIGURE 17
Robert Mapplethorpe, *John, N.Y.C.*, 1978. Selenium-toned gelatin silver print. Image: 7 11⁄16 × 7 11⁄16 inches. Jointly acquired by the Los Angeles County Museum of Art and the J. Paul Getty Trust; partial gift of the Robert Mapplethorpe Foundation; partial purchase with funds provided by the David Geffen Foundation and the J. Paul Getty Trust (M.2011.30.75.9). © Robert Mapplethorpe Foundation. Used by permission.

around the year 1968, the recuperation of social art history in the 1970s and '80s called for an accounting of artworks beyond deliberations of surface appearance, style, and iconography. In an unintentional coincidence with CLS interests in exposing the blind spots of liberal legal institutions, the art historian T.J. Clark claimed that social art history is as "concerned with what prevents representation as much as what allows it; one studies blindness as much as vision."[125]

Concurrent with how arguments like Clark's represented a new art historical establishment by the late 1980s, the artist Connie Samaras remarked that focusing on aesthetics reinforced what already operated as unlegislated law in the art world, where form was divorced from content in ways that excluded signs of identitarian and, particularly, queer difference.[126] The almost quixotic persistence with which the defense emphasized the aesthetic quality of Mapplethorpe's work strongly resonated with both prevailing juridical sentiment and lay opinion. But as legal scholar Christine Haight Fairley noted, "it becomes awkward to focus on the gradation of shadows and the play of values when the subject is one man urinating into another man's mouth."[127] Although decided by a higher court in another jurisdiction and thus only "persuasive authority" rather than binding precedent, *Miller v. United States* (1970) declared a group of photographs obscene because the judicial eye could not discern any sense of "composition," including attention paid to "background, surroundings or poses."[128] Despite the prosecution's efforts in the Mapplethorpe case to provoke class antagonism by portraying the experts as part of an elitist art world that sought to impose its own tastes on the public, the jury seemed convinced and decided in favor of the Contemporary Arts Center.[129]

What is perhaps most significant about this examination of the structural factors that affect artistic creation is how it facilitates critical thinking about art and the experiences it produces as a compass for the paths society might take, a stream of inquiry that productively joins with the thinking modeled by the law and humanities movement. Increasingly visible in Anglo-American law schools from the late 1980s on, considerations of law derived from the humanities or through its subjects endorsed more flexible approaches to legal judgment, including greater receptivity to visual analysis as a tool of legal interpretation and increased sensitivity to the role of visuality in everyday life.[130] As numerous scholars have argued over the past twenty years, there is no law without visual representation; Peter Goodrich in particular has made a compelling case for the social necessity of thinking about law as an iconographic system.[131] Elizabeth Porter has urged jurists to explicitly develop rules for visual analysis, lest they hasten their own obsolescence in an inescapably multimedia world.[132] Recognizing the need to consider the specificity of art in lockstep with legal structures, Amy Adler has eloquently pointed out how artworks do not readily conform to the kind of textual descriptions of "content" and "meaning" on which the law so heavily depends.[133] Instead, artworks pose a justified and necessary challenge to the law by forcing jurists to confront the magnitude of the law's reliance on the production of feelings, experiences, and other conditions not easily verbalized. Rebecca Tushnet, another legal scholar deeply attuned to the specific issues raised by visual material, has commented that "it's no more unreasonable to ask them to learn some art theory to resolve a case in which that theory provides useful analytical tools than it is to ask them to learn some economics to resolve an antitrust case."[134] Building on these arguments, which tacitly endorse an applied art history whose methods of visual analysis could be repurposed to serve questions arising in other fields, I argue that the everyday task of jurists to confront what is unfamiliar, alienating, and strange requires more than weaving the unfamiliar into the frameworks they understand best via analogy.

Any book about art and law must acknowledge the latter's practical impact on art historical writing. Heightened awareness of copyright has led to increased exchange between scholars and what might be called "image guardians," including museums, foundations, galleries, estates, and living artists for whom historicization can be a high-stakes situation, particularly where market interests and reputation are concerned. Unsurprisingly, denials of reproduction requests occur, sometimes as a bargain alternative to claiming defamation, which under U.S. law requires plaintiffs to prove the falsity of disputed statements with "convincing clarity."[135] More common are image and use-right fees that can be so high as to constitute deterrence.[136] The uncertainty, time, and stress that can attend this process are perhaps the greatest and least avoidable sunk costs of scholarship. Although fair use theoretically permits authors to reproduce images without permission of the copyright holder in the name of scholarship, the fear of being denied future access to sources and of liability, including the expense of any legal action, has resulted in scholars being contractually obligated by publishers to seek—and, in many cases, pay for—permission beyond what the law requires.[137] As this book discusses, more than one set of laws governs the production of art and art history.

ORGANIZATIONAL NOTES

Since this is a book about art that "messes with" the law, as well as law that calls into account various assumptions underwriting artistic production, I mobilize overlaps between art historical and legal analysis. Often this means applying ideas and arguments that originate in legal contexts to flesh out the specificity and complexity of the relationships that artworks trigger. I do not claim that art historical methods should necessarily be employed in legal cases or that legal thinking must be consistently incorporated into the art historical toolbox, only that there is something to be gained by putting the disciplines within striking distance of each other, particularly through close reading. James Boyd White, a pioneer of the law and literature movement, observed how close reading allows us to think about our participation in the formation of the world in which we live.[138] While close reading in an art historical context generally entails detailed visual analysis of a specific object, many of the works I discuss also require considerations of resource management, logistical organization, and how laws enable (or delimit) a work's creation, circulation, and reception. If sustained visual analysis has less prominence in this book than might be expected from an art historical discussion, it is also because I hope to convey something of the difficulty of contemporary art's imbrication within a juridical field marked by its striking ambivalence toward visual material.

In thinking about where art meets (or misses) law, I hope to add to the expansion of a discursive commons to which disciplinary fidelity matters less than the production of an intellectual friction capable of forming a community of readers and, potentially, actors. Neither an encyclopedia nor a chronicle, this book addresses selected case studies that illustrate relationship types especially pertinent to contemporary art's engagement with law. I am particularly drawn to art and art-related activity that takes the measure of law, not in order to advance a specific politics but to spawn forms of consciousness that might bring pressure to bear on politics in need of accounting.

Chapter 1 focuses on *The Artist's Reserved Rights Transfer and Sale Agreement,* a model sales contract coauthored by exhibition organizer, curator, and labor activist Seth Siegelaub and lawyer Robert Projansky. Representing a key moment of collaboration between art and the law, when a representative of the art world enlisted legal assistance to validate artists' intellectual property and economic interests, the agreement raised important questions about what it meant to survive as an artist in a society that explicitly favored the rights of buyers over those of creators. Chapter 2 discusses the significance of negotiation through the *Running Fence* (1976) of Christo and Jeanne-Claude. Erected in northern California, partly on land that was subject to new environmental protection laws, the work exemplified the question of legal aesthetics and the prominence of legal permission and negotiation to artistic creation.[139] That Christo and Jeanne-Claude largely succeeded in obtaining such permission was due to their expansive view of law as consisting not only of codified regulation but also of unwritten custom.

Chapter 3 addresses the productive potential of defiance through the works Gordon Matta-Clark produced in greater metropolitan New York by slicing or cutting into whole buildings, sometimes without legal permission. As contemporary art increasingly took shape around how artists could intervene directly in political and economic systems, the works and writings of Matta-Clark suggested how that purpose might include the ability to question the goals and operations of law. Defiance became a call to open up legal interpretation, and the works he produced in the mid-1970s invoked a more complex definition of property and space than what was legally available.

In the first four *One Year Performances* of Tehching Hsieh from 1978 to 1984, the artist subjected himself to conditions of extreme deprivation or banality over the course of a single year. Accompanying each performance were voluntary written pledges to uphold various behavioral restrictions, whose language and format strongly resembled those commonly used for legally binding contracts. Chapter 4 argues that Hsieh's obedience to these limitations, which required extraordinary persistence, fidelity, and reliability, was so extreme as to make the law seem inadequate as a system of moral principles.

Chapter 5 explores disengagement as a tactical response to law through Sally Mann's *Immediate Family,* the photography book published in 1992 featuring images of her children, sometimes in various states of undress. Appearing when the alliance cobbled between religious leaders, free marketers, and Southern Democrats disenchanted by federal civil rights and other reform legislation flexed its considerable political muscle by mobilizing family and constitutional law to serve its political bidding, the book and its images were subject to escalating ideological and moral speculation masquerading as a commitment to law. Against this backdrop, artistic integrity emerged as the sustained refusal to engage with attempts to undermine contemporary art's credibility.

Chapters 4 and 5 discuss how two common contemporary art practices—the photographic documentation of performance and the creation of photography through performance—raise questions of copyright, labor, property, and kinship. Integrity thus also meant recognizing the multiple, and sometimes conflicting, spheres of economic, legal, and artistic operation that artists increasingly occupied. Chapter 6 discusses the certificates of authenticity the artist Felix Gonzalez-Torres issued to buyers of his works starting in 1994. Inflected by Gonzalez-Torres's awareness of eroding privacy rights and their devastating effect on expressions of tolerance and intimacy, they proposed a different model of relationship formation than that embodied by struggles over the legality of artworks or by the suspicion and antagonism underwriting a post-1960s genealogy of artists using certificates and contracts in sales of their works.

In 2008, the U.S. District Court for the Northern District of Illinois weighed in on whether a display of live wildflowers constituted an artwork under VARA. The plaintiff, artist Chapman Kelley, protested the reduction of his display by the Chicago Park District as wrongful mutilation. The defendant argued that Kelley's work failed to qualify as an artwork under VARA because it was inherently subject to change and required maintenance. Presiding judge David Coar disagreed, writing that the "defendant's insistence that an artifact that changes over time, requires ongoing maintenance, or contains living matter cannot be considered a work of visual art protected by VARA is misplaced."[140] He justified his claim by citing Felix Gonzalez-Torres's *"Untitled" (Portrait of Ross in L.A.)*, a work commemorating his lover Ross Laycock, who died from AIDS in 1991 (fig. 18). The "portrait" consisted of a pile of individually wrapped candies whose weight equaled Laycock's. Viewers were invited to take a candy so that the weight of the pile diminished, mirroring Laycock's weight loss and eventual death. Coar observed that "although arguably no two viewers of *'Untitled' (Portrait of Ross in L.A.)* see the same work, there is no argument that its mutability precludes it from being described as a work of art."[141] Coar, who personally saw Gonzalez-Torres's work at the Art Institute in Chicago, commented how the open-endedness of VARA signaled a more expansive approach to artworks, including works that "a lay person would not necessarily consider as art."[142] Although he eventually decided that Kelley's flowers did not qualify for copyright protection because they lacked originality—a decision that a higher court eventually rejected—his reasoning illustrated how the framework within which legal judgments are made has been affected by direct encounters with artworks and by shifting approaches to artistic creation.[143]

Far from representing two antagonistic points at opposite ends of the intention spectrum, then, both art and law are similarly invested in considering visual materials that provoke extensive reflection on the nature of lived experience. Lawful or not, the encounters staged by many artists share a will to occupy, shape, or overlap the spaces ordered by legal constructs. How this shapes our perceptions of law helps us speculate how the law might better serve its own stated ideals of producing experiences of justice for all.

But in the period discussed in this book, artistic action entailed more than volition—it also meant recognizing the circumstances that enabled them to happen. "The legal decision-making process is in direct, everyday contact with the world of art, and thus the legal decision reflects a contemporary social assessment of problems in art," as law scholar Peter Karlen has observed.[144] I claim that reading artistic actions against the grain of law makes art's social implications more broadly legible. At the same time, having integrity meant letting audiences know of an artwork's social purpose without overstating its political impact or losing sight of how aesthetic decisions might compel audiences to see their everyday world differently—the act from which

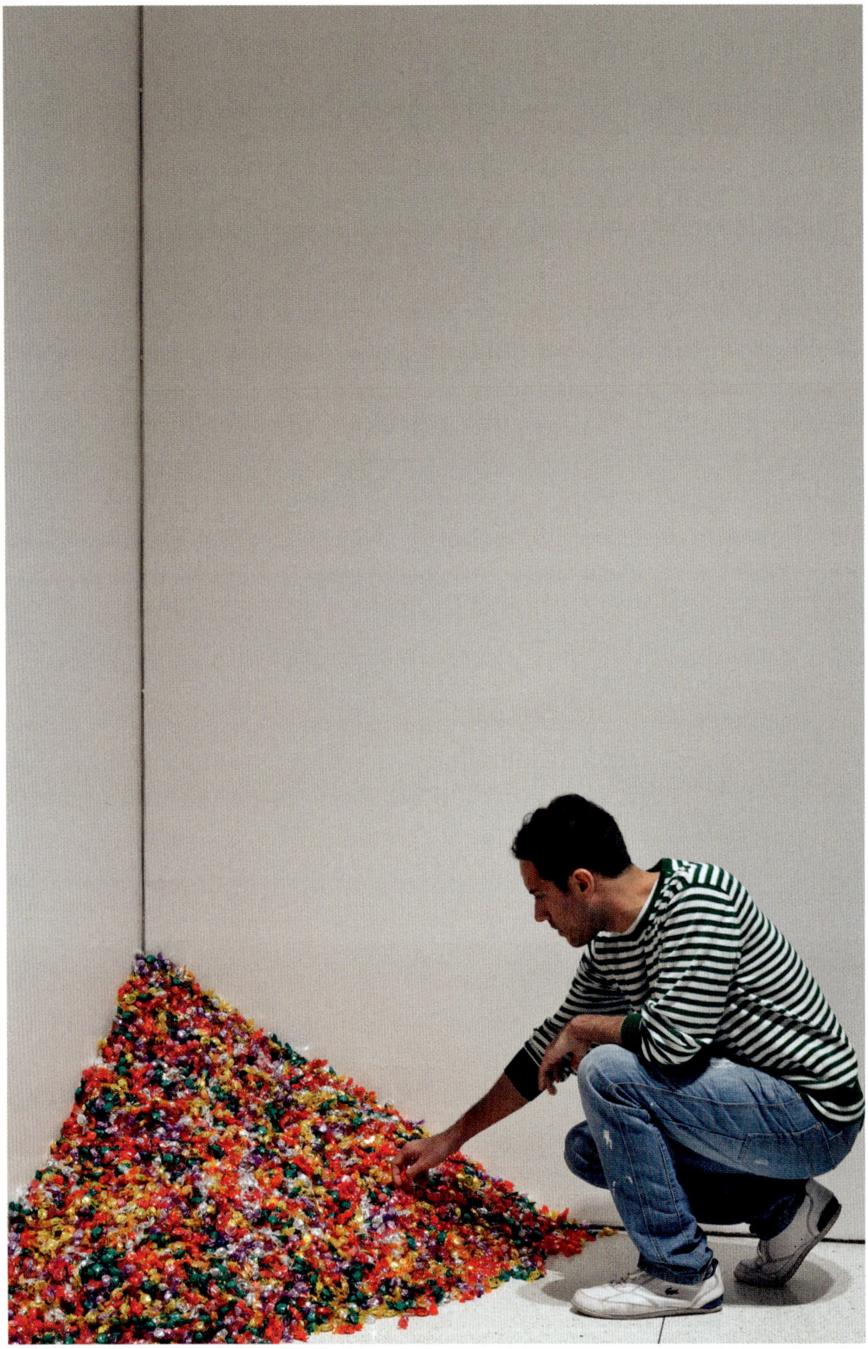

FIGURE 18
Felix Gonzalez-Torres, *"Untitled" (Portrait of Ross in L.A.)*, 1991. Candies individually wrapped in multicolored cellophane, endless supply. Dimensions variable. Ideal weight: 175 pounds. Installation view: "Feast: Radical Hospitality and Contemporary Art," Smart Museum at the University of Chicago, 2012. © Felix Gonzalez-Torres Foundation. Courtesy of Andrea Rosen Gallery, New York.

so much political work begins. In an interview published in 1991, Vito Acconci told Richard Prince, whose prolific career as a defendant in infringement lawsuits had the effect of making both the courtroom and the lawyer's office his studio, "I don't want to make laws and commandments. I do want to make places that function as models, models for activities, but models can be tampered with, and added to and subtracted from, and there's no punishment."[145] What those models looked like and how they unfolded against the unpredictability of extra-artistic life is the subject of the following chapters.

1

PARTNERS IN ADVOCACY

The Artist's Reserved Rights Transfer and Sale Agreement

IN MARCH 1971, the School of Visual Arts (SVA) in New York paid for the design and production of an eight-page fold-out poster (fig. 19). Designed by SVA alumnus Christos Gianakos, a graphic artist and typographic designer, the poster's most immediate feature was the large, boldface capital letters reading, "THE ARTIST'S RESERVED RIGHTS TRANSFER AND SALE AGREEMENT." Based on a mock-up, the letters echoed the all-capital block typography used in language-based conceptual artworks popular at the time. Yet the dense lines of small text grouped beneath the prominent header contained language far different than the terse instructions or pithy, aphorism-like statements for which conceptualism was known. No ordinary poster, it was but the first page of a universal declaration of artists' rights, a contract intended to be nothing less than "the standard form for the transfer and sale of all contemporary art."

Artists have long fought for what they felt was rightfully theirs, including proper attribution, compensation, and the right to bar others from copying their works.[1] But the concept of identifying

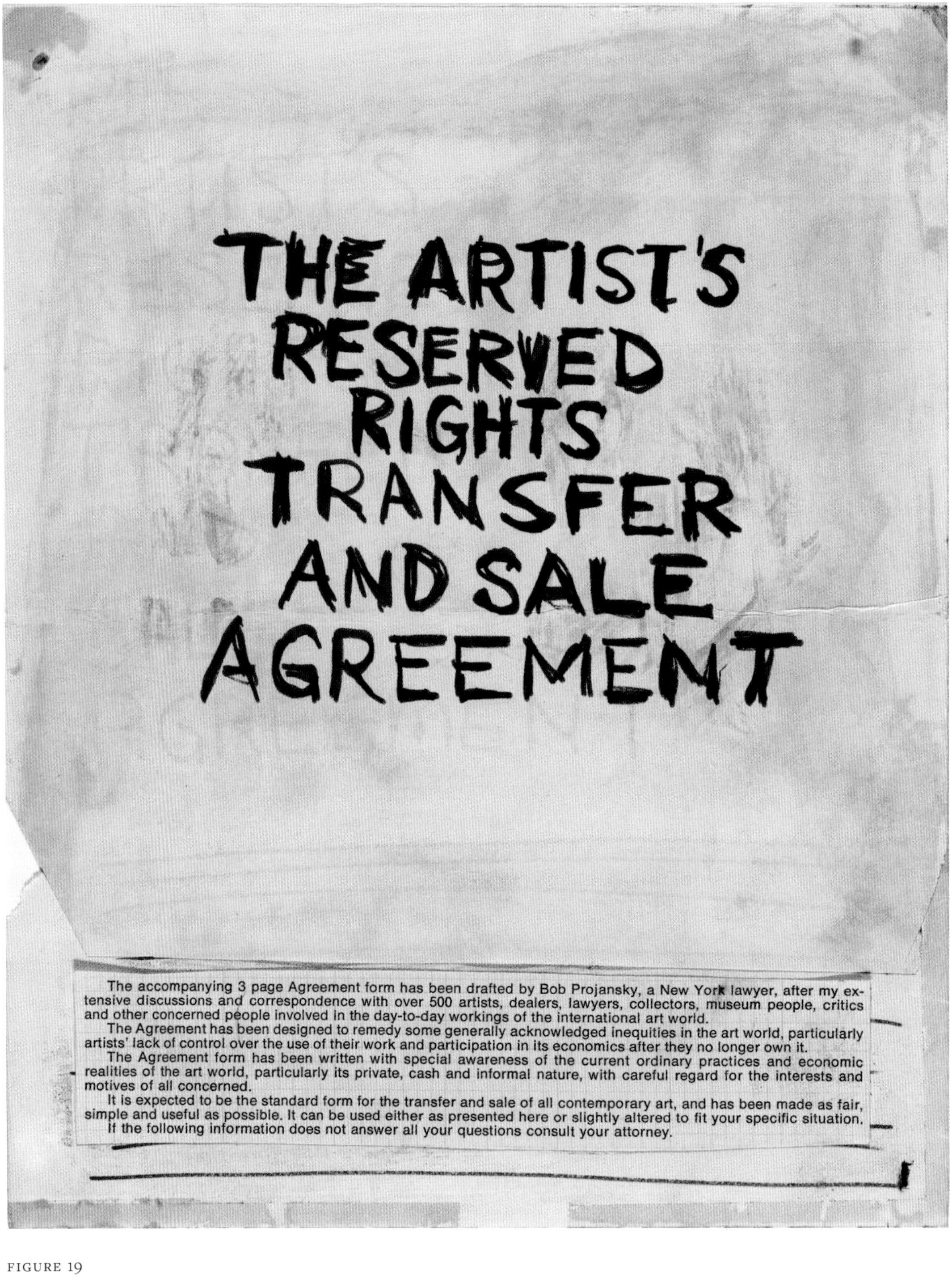

THE ARTIST'S RESERVED RIGHTS TRANSFER AND SALE AGREEMENT

The accompanying 3 page Agreement form has been drafted by Bob Projansky, a New York lawyer, after my extensive discussions and correspondence with over 500 artists, dealers, lawyers, collectors, museum people, critics and other concerned people involved in the day-to-day workings of the international art world.

The Agreement has been designed to remedy some generally acknowledged inequities in the art world, particularly artists' lack of control over the use of their work and participation in its economics after they no longer own it.

The Agreement form has been written with special awareness of the current ordinary practices and economic realities of the art world, particularly its private, cash and informal nature, with careful regard for the interests and motives of all concerned.

It is expected to be the standard form for the transfer and sale of all contemporary art, and has been made as fair, simple and useful as possible. It can be used either as presented here or slightly altered to fit your specific situation.

If the following information does not answer all your questions consult your attorney.

FIGURE 19

Mock-up draft of *The Artist's Reserved Rights Transfer and Sale Agreement* in English, c. 1971. Seth Siegelaub Papers [I.A.91], Museum of Modern Art. Digital image © Museum of Modern Art/Licensed by SCALA/Art Resource, New York. Courtesy of Stitching Egress Foundation, Amsterdam. © Stitching Egress Foundation 2017.

and claiming legal rights specifically for artists as a class is a phenomenon of the middle to late twentieth century, one radicalized in the wake of a general reconsideration of the social purpose and function of art. Beginning in the late 1960s, *artists' rights* became a popular umbrella term to describe what many artists believed was their fundamental right to earn a living from making and selling their work, as well as to protect their work.[2] Widely used in lockstep with numerous campaigns for social and legal reform taking place in the United States, artists' rights was a battle cry for artists addressing what they saw as a major imbalance of power between themselves and institutions, especially museums and the market. The first organization to systematically use the term *artists' rights* was the Art Workers' Coalition (AWC). A loose coalition of artists, writers, filmmakers, museum staff, and others associated with the art world, the AWC was founded in New York in 1969 after the artist Takis stole his own sculpture from its legal owner, the Museum of Modern Art, to protest its display in the group exhibition "Machine."[3] The AWC, which conspicuously excluded dealers, gained notoriety for the numerous demands it made for museums to be more expansive and inclusive in their admission and exhibition policies, and to apprise artists of their legal rights.[4] In order to situate art making within a larger struggle among laborers for economic and political validation, the group framed artists as workers and presented integrity as the capacity to collectively act upon a recognized duty to improve the lot of a particular community.

Yet the collectivism of groups like the AWC had little impact on transactional practice and institutional policy. Those buying contemporary art or serving as museum trustees were more likely to think along the lines of Milton Friedman, the economist and free-market champion who proclaimed that the "social responsibility of business" was to seek profit "so long as it stays within the rules of the game, which is to say, engages in open and free competition without deception and fraud."[5] AWC member Seth Siegelaub, the pioneering curator and dealer of conceptual art, tried to marry the AWC's collectivist politics to the ideal of free will embodied in contract law by a model agreement he co-drafted with Robert Projansky, a New York lawyer who occasionally attended AWC meetings.[6] As the hand-drawn letters of the contract mock-up broadcast so well, *The Artist's Reserved Rights Transfer and Sale Agreement* was an attempt by one of the New York art world's fiercest dreamers to rewrite the law of his chosen land. Yet it was less a work by Siegelaub than it was a collage of various conceptions of artwork, labor, and capital already present in the art and legal worlds. Although it failed to become the standard its authors hoped it would become, the agreement's creation and reception tried to expand the possibilities of action associated with being an artist, citizen, and worker. A major instance of collaboration accounting for both the structures of law and the claims of artists, *The Artist's Reserved Rights Transfer and Sale Agreement* called new attention to how artists might turn to the law to safeguard their interests, as well as to how the law might offer artists the language they needed to render their claims legible to lawyers accustomed to a different set of precedents and customs.

THE OPPOSITE OF AN ARTIST IS A PHYSICIST

In August 2017, the *New York Times* invited readers to identify their "opposite" jobs, based on data collected for a variety of occupations tracked by the U.S. Department of Labor. The opposite of "a fine artist, including painter, sculptor and illustrator," the official description used by the Labor Department for visual artists, is, apparently, a physicist.[7] According to the Occupational Information Network, a database launched by the Labor Department in 1998, physicists are characterized by their use of science and math, but also by their ability to "come up with a number of ideas about a topic" and to assess "how a system should work and how changes in conditions, operations, and the environment will affect outcomes," traits both conspicuously absent from the database's description of artists.[8] Although artists and physicists share complex problem solving as part of their respective skill sets, many of the "abilities" listed for artists are specifically physical in nature, including "arm-hand steadiness" and "finger dexterity," or the "ability to make precisely coordinated movements of the fingers of one or both hands to grasp, manipulate, or assemble very small objects."[9]

Pairing artists and physicists as opposites predictably rehearses familiar narratives that divide the impractical arts from the useful sciences while also negating many of the seminal artistic developments that, in fact, bring artists and physicists in closer orbit than the Labor Department presently allows. Still, the Labor Department's description also illustrates how both government and law perceive artistic creation as involving multiple labor categories. Since the early twentieth century, courts have recognized artists as professionals rather than as laborers.[10] In 1936, the Supreme Court of Louisiana included artists in its definition of a *profession* on the basis that artists relied more on intellectual than on manual labor: "There are certain callings which require both intellect and skill, but in such instances the pursuit is classified or listed as a 'profession'; i.e., artists, dentists, surgeons."[11]

Deciding who qualified as a professional artist was more challenging. Leaders of the Artists Equity Association, the first major professional artists' organization in the United States, established after World War II, stated that proof of professional recognition, namely inclusion in a "major exhibition" by a "recognized dealer," was a main criterion, with some members contending that a recognized educational credential should also be required.[12] In 1964, the New York State Legislature passed Article 7-B ("Joint Living Work-Quarters for Artists") of the New York State Multiple Dwelling Law, perhaps the first law to explicitly recognize artists as a desirable occupational class.[13] Yet it restricted "artist" to mean those working in "fine arts, such as painting and sculpture," thus excluding many of the law's possible subjects, including George Maciunas and other Fluxus artists who were creating "nonart" on the principle that anything might be art, including the performance of simple, repetitive tasks that most individuals could do.[14] The New York City Department of Cultural Affairs expanded the law's scope by requiring applicants to show their needs for space and "commitments to art" in order to establish "artist" status.[15]

Conversely, the judiciary determined professional status on the basis of an artist's income-producing capacities. Tax court judges, for example, permitted artists to deduct from their tax returns the expenses incurred in producing work only if they could prove that they were motivated by profit. In 1971, the Second Circuit upheld a decision by the U.S. Tax Court against a painter who had tried to deduct some of the expenses incurred in making his works.[16] A frustrated ex-lawyer who belatedly embraced the study of Abstract Expressionism in his mid-thirties, this late-blooming artist invested considerable time and money into his painting career, yet sold his paintings only intermittently, mostly to friends and relatives, and did not rely on sales for his economic survival, facts the U.S. Tax Court counted against him. Most damning of all was how this refugee from legal practice confessed his desire "to give mankind a better vision of beauty and to establish for himself a reputation as a great artist."[17] Having other motives besides economic profit violated what the court regarded as the definition of a professional. Anyone could style herself an artist, but as far as tax law was concerned, the moniker of "professional artist" applied only to individuals who depended on regular sales of their works for their livelihood.

Complicating the picture was the deliberate identification of visual art with underpaid or unpaid labor, one of the most pointed attempts to ingratiate art making to a lay public who might otherwise dismiss contemporary art as being removed from the alienation experienced by so many wage laborers in the 1960s.[18] Various interpretations of the artist-as-laborer (or "art worker") paradigm suggested that an artist's social credibility was contingent on being able to identify his or her work with that undertaken daily by those most disempowered by the systematic privileging of capital over labor. Such gestures of solidarity could seem inadequate and even disingenuous. Art historian Julia Bryan-Wilson has described Carl Andre, for example, as a self-identified art worker for whom "activism was an alibi for not making explicitly political art."[19] Some artists went so far as to ask whether the real measure of artistic integrity lay in one's willingness to relinquish the labels of "art" and "artists" and whatever social privilege or moral insurance they might provide. Jean Toche claimed that the Guerrilla Art Action Group was founded as a rejection of artists who would protest an institution's repressive policies yet still be happy to show their works in the same venue.[20]

The most extreme instances were attempts to liken mental activity to physical labor, in part to assuage the skepticism audiences had toward conceptual art. Wisconsin senator William Proxmire derided the National Endowment for the Arts for granting Leann Wilchusky a modest grant to produce one of her "Skyworks," experimental films made by having skydivers film the free fall of mile-length crepe streamers dropped from planes. Calling her work "artistic frou frou," the senator described Wilchusky's complex logistical coordination and planning efforts as patently unequal to the labor of three blue-collar workers: "While the $6,025 is relatively very small, it is the sum total of the taxes paid by three typical taxpayers," including "the worker who trudges through the factory gates at 7 every morning . . . the cleaning woman who ekes out a living scouring a floor in a Madison office building all night," and "the dairy farmer . . . who rises at 5:30 to milk his cows."[21]

In 1967, Sol LeWitt famously declared that ideas, "even if not made visual," are as much works of art "as any finished product," and Grace Glueck wrote that "for $15,000 or so, Ed Kienholz will sell you a "concept tableau." It is not a finished work of art but an idea for one. When you pay your money, only the idea is yours."[22] A contract accompanied each sale of a plaque and framed written description of a proposed work (fig. 20). Each contract verified the purchase and gave buyers the option to acquire other Kienholz works.[23] Like his contemporaries who sought to fold art making into familiar conceptions of labor, Kienholz—whose truck door read "Ed Kienholz, Expert"—insisted that buyers choosing to purchase the "finished *Tableau*" also compensate him for "all expenses that may be required for actual production," including "reasonable living expenses." Yet he expressly asked that his labor be valued as if he, too, qualified for "the combined hourly union wage scale for plumbers, electricians, and carpenters then prevailing in the Los Angeles area." Kienholz's language made a case for the value of artistic labor to a legal system that placed relatively little value on the labor invested in producing tangible artworks. Under the Tax Reform Act of 1969, for example, buyers donating artworks to qualified nonprofit organizations could deduct the works' full market value, whereas artists could deduct only the cost of materials used in making the works.[24]

The contracts translated Kienholz's thinking into the language of rights used in statutes and court decisions, and the scope and variety of rights reserved was remarkable. Not only would the artist be "the sole judge of the relationship" between the works belonging to a finished *Tableau*, a provision that theoretically gave him the right to deny that a *Tableau* was in fact complete, but Kienholz also reserved the right to freely reproduce the *Tableau* without securing the consent of the initial buyer.[25] Owners could sell their *Concept Tableaux*, but any option to purchase other works that might become a "finished *Tableau*" would be voided upon his death. Should Kienholz die before a *Tableau* was completed, the incomplete portion of the *Tableau* would remain in the artist's possession, with the buyer forfeiting any payments made in connection with said work. Kienholz professed indifference as to whether his contracts could be enforced, and indeed the aggressive pricing of the *Tableaux*, as well as the unusually broad category of rights, insinuated that the sale of works was perhaps hypothetical.[26] But the contracts' length, detail, and language ascribed to him an intention to legitimize the economic value of conceptual art beyond an insular art-world community.

Siegelaub, who knew of Kienholz's contract at the time he co-drafted *The Artist's Reserved Rights Transfer and Sale Agreement*, may have regarded it as a model through which to recast existing form contracts like the Artists' Equity Contract or the Sale of Photograph Contract as a codified bill of artists' rights.[27] But where Kienholz's contracts were likely to be read as both legally binding agreements and extensions of art-

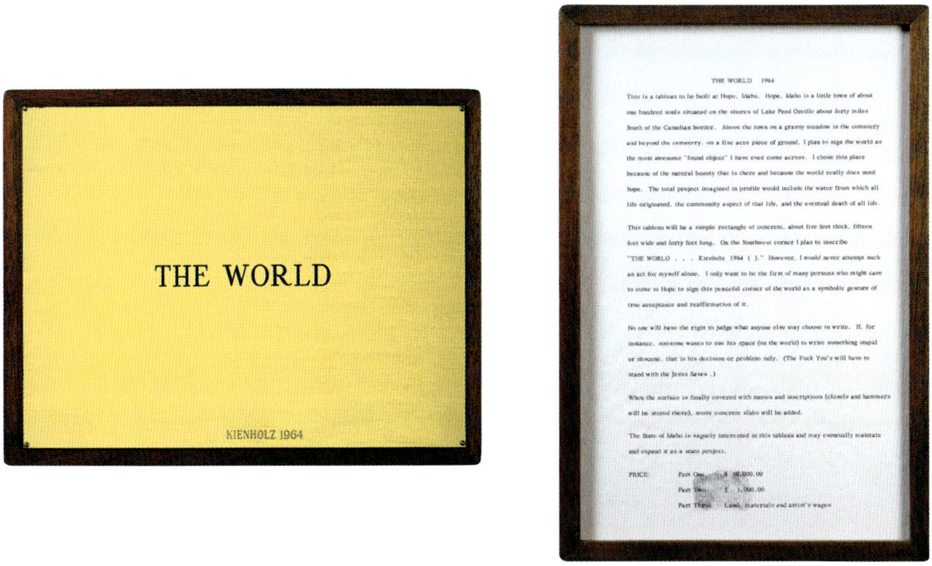

FIGURE 20
Ed Kienholz, *The World*, 1964. Concept tableau and plaque: 9 ¼ × 11 ¾ inches; framed concept: 13 ⅜ × 9 ¼ centimeters. © Kienholz. Courtesy of L.A. Louver, Venice, California.

works offered for sale, *The Artist's Reserved Rights Transfer and Sale Agreement* was an enforceable legal document meant to legitimate the labor of artists by establishing standards for an industry Projansky described to his fellow lawyers as being in desperate want of firm regulation "comparable to those in the medical or legal professions."[28] He wrote that "there is no branch of commerce in which the UCC and the Statute of Frauds seems more irrelevant than in the art market."[29] Even more than collective action, it was the length, formality, and specificity of the *Agreement* that made the strongest case for artistic creation as professional labor.

ART THROUGH PROPERTY

When Siegelaub began to discuss the idea of *The Artist's Reserved Rights Transfer and Sale Agreement* with his acquaintances in New York and Western Europe between 1969 and 1970, the contemporary art economy had expanded at an unprecedented pace.[30] Artworks became increasingly regarded as investment vehicles on a par, or even interchangeable, with more conventional instruments like real estate or securities.[31] Businesses likewise spent large sums on underwriting art exhibitions and building corporate collections.[32] The expanded scale of economic activity forced a shift in how artists understood their practice, and if, in 1966, conceptual artist Joseph Kosuth paid little attention to the "potential problems of ownership," by 1971 he and many other artists would spend considerable time determining how their works would be sold and represented.[33] One of the most creative in this regard was Hans Haacke, who tried to broker a compromise structure that would let collectors buy his work on an installment plan and take possession of the work after receipt of the first payment but transfer the title only when the last payment was received.[34]

Attention to property and its legal implications helped epitomize the emergence of a broad category of contemporary art created to intervene in various economic, political, and social structures. Fluxus, the international collective of multidisciplinary artists, was especially proactive. Likely influenced by his publishing activities, George Maciunas mobilized the idea of copyright from 1964 to implicitly raise the name *Fluxus* to trademark status.[35] His colleague Robert Watts, arguably one of the most law-aware artists of his generation, sought through a patent lawyer to legally bar commercial enterprises from using the term *Pop Art*.[36] Although unsuccessful, his efforts reflected a determination to preserve a distinct identity for visual art through the law. Yet, instead of barring outsiders from accessing their intellectual property per common corporate practice, Fluxus allowed others to perform their works so long as the group was credited.[37]

In asking members to effectively sign over their individual copyrights to him, Maciunas not only attempted to personally serve as Fluxus's permissions clearinghouse but may have inadvertently alerted them to the predicament existing copyright law posed to artists via concepts like "general publication," whereby exhibiting a work publicly might foreclose the creator's copyright permanently. Certainly, the early and mid-1960s saw an uptick of both academic interest in copyright in the visual arts and artists making their presence known to an extra-artistic audience through claims of infringement. Producers of ephemeral or intangible artworks that survived primarily through documentation became increasingly vigilant about defending their copyright, especially as the documentation itself became commercially valuable as artworks or quasi-artworks. Perpetually at financial loose ends, Gordon Matta-Clark, whose best-known works involved the physical destruction of buildings, relied on income earned from the sale of photographs, including large-format color images, slide sets, and what he called "process work," or texts and small black-and-white photographs.[38] Keenly aware of the growing demand and, consequently, of dealers eager to capitalize on his works, Matta-Clark vowed to ensure that "too many copies of my slides or negatives don't get distributed without due protection and remuneration [*sic*]. It must be clear that I give no one permission to copy slides of my work."[39]

The proprietary claims of artists sometimes vibrated antagonistically with those of buyers, which Siegelaub and Projansky tried to mitigate with the *Agreement*. Prior to its amendment by Congress in 1976, federal copyright law permitted owners of artworks to do as they pleased with their property, a point vigorously contested by AWC members.[40] As Siegelaub and Projansky acidly observed, "the sale of a work of art was like the sale of a pair of shoes. The buyer owned it absolutely, or could act as if he did."[41] Unlike some jurisdictions in Western Europe, which honored the 1928 Berne

Convention for the Protection of Literary and Artistic Works—granting artists a host of rights as the creators of copyrighted works, including the right "to object to any distortion, modification of, or other derogatory action" against a work that would damage the artist's reputation—U.S. law shifted onto artists the burden of having to defend their economic and noneconomic rights.[42] If artists wanted to protect their work from such destruction or other unauthorized changes, the responsibility was theirs alone.[43]

When *The Artist's Reserved Rights Transfer and Sale Agreement* was drafted, the prevailing legal standard concerning the integrity and intellectual property rights of artists was *Crimi v. Rutgers Presbyterian Church,* then the most significant U.S. legal case concerning the destruction of visual art. Decided in 1949, it barred well-known muralist Alfred Crimi from claiming damages from a church that had destroyed his work without his consent, holding that it was the artist's responsibility to contract in advance for any terms he or she wanted others to uphold.[44] Cases like *Crimi* and general common law held that artists selling their works intended to transfer their copyright interests as well as title to the purchased works to buyers, an assumption some artists internalized.[45] Efforts to protect artworks as the intellectual property of artists were largely unsuccessful. The Artists Equity Association was founded just before *Crimi* in 1947, in part to campaign for legislation that would specifically protect artists' intellectual property. Yet, as art historian David Sokol notes, suspicion toward organized labor, including artists, ran high in the "Red Scare" years between 1947 and 1957.[46] Politicians were reluctant to sponsor organizations that their colleagues and constituents might see as even vaguely pro-Communist. Only after John F. Kennedy's election as president in 1960 did politicians openly advocate legal reforms that would specifically benefit artists. On the campaign trail, Kennedy voiced his opinion that it was not enough to simply expand federal patronage of the arts: "I think we can do better than that, if only by alleviating the unfair tax burden borne by writers, painters, and other creative artists. They may exist on small incomes for years to perfect their skills, and then be plundered by the Treasury in a single year of plenty."[47]

PRAYERS FOR RELIEF

Judges and lawyers invested far more energy in protecting buyers, a zeal inflected by the codification of the consumer as a significant legal subject. Of the four basic rights enumerated by Kennedy in his famous Consumer Bill of Rights speech to Congress in 1962, the right to be informed resonated especially strongly with the buying and selling of art, as demonstrated by the frequency with which commentators described collectors as "consumers." This right holds that businesses should give consumers enough information for them to make informed decisions about their purchases. Beginning in the mid-1960s, the national consumer rights movement spearheaded by Ralph Nader further established the consumer as not only legally protected, but also morally unassailable. Emerging in the wake of a newfound recognition of the all-powerful consumer, then, was a legal culture of transaction that privileged buyers at the expense of sellers and, even more, of artists. Eager to capitalize on the interest expressed by first-time buyers, and not beholden to regulatory bodies, some dealers exploited new buyers' lack of knowledge by knowingly selling forged works.[48] The rising number of court cases initiated by collectors regarding artwork sales was a stark admission of how the gallery industry—among the most extreme forms of privatized industry—lacked regulation. Still, courts upheld buyers' claims in the name of commerce, thus reflecting general sentiment within the judiciary to consider the free market a universally ideal form of social organization.

An important example of how the law tried to contain the risk on behalf of buyers generally was the proposed amendment to the General Business Law of New York. Initiated between 1966 and 1968 by Louis Lefkowitz, the New York State attorney general and a master campaigner especially known for consumer advocacy, these revisions covered a range of relationships, including those between buyers and sellers of artworks, as well as those between sellers and artists. Some were intended to lessen the risk buyers assumed when purchasing artworks of dubious or unknown origin. Statements sellers made concerning authorship would no longer be mere opinion, but would be "accorded the dignity of a statement of fact."[49] But Lefkowitz, who transformed the office of attorney general to focus on representing citizens rather than government agencies, took an almost messianic interest in saving artists from dealer exploitation, going so far as to inform the New York State Legislature that dealer malfeasance alienated artists "from society."[50] Yet even at the level of everyday transactional practice, there was almost no guidance concerning the purported duty of dealers to promote and sell artists' works. "By mere inaction," a gallery could terminate any of its responsibilities.[51] Given such circumstances, Lefkowitz argued, the law should reframe dealer-artist relationships on the model of principal and agent, rather than vendor and vendee. In law, political science, and economics, such a relationship happens when a given entity (the principal) appoints another to act on its behalf (the agent). A vendor-vendee relationship is an arrangement in which an entity selling property (the vendor) transfers the full responsibility for the property to the vendee. Unlike the principal-agent relationship, in which the agent must promise to act in the principal's best interests, the vendor has no such obligation toward the vendee, who assumes the full duty of responsibility. Dealers would, accordingly, be required to uphold a higher standard of behavior under the rubric of the "duty of loyalty."[52] This higher standard would also provide artists protection they might not otherwise be able to procure through direct personal negotiation.

In 1967, Lefkowitz tried to introduce an Artists-Dealer Relationship Bill.[53] Such a law would have provided artists greater legal recourse in collecting proceeds of artwork sales from dealers and in recovering unsold works, the latter of which Lefkowitz called a larceny. Despite his personal rapport with Nelson Rockefeller, then New York governor, the bill was eventually vetoed, consequently leaving existing bodies of law intact and leaving artists and dealers to address any imbalances of power between themselves. Among dealers, Siegelaub was perhaps the most proactive in assuming the duties of care Lefkowitz hoped Rockefeller would sign into law. In an art world that critic Peter Plagens once deemed "a Woodstockian mud party of high-minded unprofessionalism," various forms of documentation became increasingly popular.[54] From the 1960s on, certificates of authenticity became especially visible as a hedge against forgeries.[55] Alvin Lane, a member of an art legislation advisory committee created by Lefkowitz, argued that the rise in forgery cases was largely the buyer's fault for not demanding proof: "The main offender is the collector."[56] Himself an avid collector of twentieth-century art, Lane further cautioned buyers to obtain certificates from artists directly, a lesson he had learned from personal experience after buying a cast of a Jean Arp sculpture that turned out to be a forgery.[57] Although Lane himself had provided the language for the certificate, which he then asked a dealer to have Arp sign, the certificate turned out to be counterfeit.

Determining who had the authority to draft these certificates, or what they in fact were, was less clear-cut. Article 12-F of the General Business Law of New York defines them as written or printed statements of fact or opinion "confirming, approving or attesting to the authenticity of the authorship of a work of fine art, which statement is subscribed by the authenticator and is capable of being used to the advantage or disadvantage of some person."[58] In 1968, the New York State Legislature passed the Arts and Cultural Affairs Law, which held that anyone who makes, utters, or issues a certificate of authenticity or any similar written instrument attesting to material facts that the work does not in fact possess is guilty of a Class A misdemeanor, a crime serious enough to result in punishment of the kind normally meted out for assault causing bodily injury or for violating a restraining order. The law thus saw certificates as a kind of warranty.[59] For many artists, the certificate of authenticity was the most powerful tool they had for protecting their property rights. Withholding certificates of authenticity became an effective means of leverage, even if it meant upsetting the delicate social balance of artist-dealer relationships.

But although withholding certificates of authenticity may have given artists some leverage in terms of extracting more timely payments from errant dealers or forgetful buyers, it had minimal credibility as a legal instrument. Although he worked under French law, which gave artists a number and quality of rights far more expansive than those accorded to their U.S. colleagues, the artist and lawyer Michel Claura made a point of telling Siegelaub why he drafted a purchase contract for his friend Daniel Buren: "It is not a certificate of authenticity, because, as you know, anyone can do such work."[60] A certificate could do very little to remedy the pressing question of what happens to an artwork after a completed sale. *The Artist's Reserved Rights Transfer and Sale Agreement* was created in hopes of providing artists the protection Siegelaub and Projansky felt was their due, which was not forthcoming from either courts or legislatures.

For artists like Jackie Winsor, Dorothea Rockburne, and Judy Pendleton, the *Agreement* was important not only as a theoretically convenient means of verbalizing their economic demands through the neutralizing language of contract law, but also as a means of legitimating their work when both female artistic labor and other work done by women was often considered negligible.[61] "The Contract [i.e., the *Agreement*] was a kind of shield in battle in the good war," said Winsor, referring to her "war" to secure recognition by insisting that others honor the integrity of her work regardless of ownership status.[62] Using the *Agreement* to retain some control over the artwork after its sale had real symbolic purchase at a time when not all women enjoyed full disposition of their property. Coverture, the common-law idea that married women had no legal existence apart from their husbands, still applied in many U.S. states well into the 1970s and, in some jurisdictions, legally permitted husbands to sell wives' property without their consent.[63] That artists like Winsor modified the *Agreement* to suit their requirements also suggested that the contract provided an opportunity for women to actively interpret the law for their own ends, an important counter in a time when less than 4 percent of all attorneys in the United States were women.[64]

"LET THEM EAT PRINTOUT!"

Siegelaub may have been too optimistic when he likened the *Agreement* to a time-saving appliance: "Just plug it in and watch it go—a perfect waffle every time!"[65] The promised ease encouraged artists to outsource the hard work of identifying the protections they needed to the contract. Indeed, Projansky and Siegelaub faithfully adhered to the standard laid out in *Crimi* by specifying, in meticulous detail, what they wanted for artists and from buyers. But the *Agreement* drew criticism from nearly every group Siegelaub claimed to have consulted, including dealers, collectors, lawyers, and even artists.[66] The fiercest disagreement pivoted around the resale clause, based on the concept of *droit de suite,* which dates to late nineteenth-century France and which legal scholar Monroe Price vigorously discussed in an article published in the *Yale Law Journal.* Although considered a leading advocate for artists' rights, particularly regarding compensation to artists for the use of their work, Price opined that *droit de suite* "rewards the wrong painters with probably inconsequential amounts of money at the wrong time in their lives."[67] But the strong reaction provoked by the *Agreement* showed how deeply enmeshed discussion of artists' rights had become with economic self-interest. It also made painfully clear the contest between, on one hand, the desire to maximize profit and, on the other, the culture of personal understanding and affinity that ostensibly went beyond mere profit seeking. Prospective buyers described the clause as a deferred excise tax, a characterization that strongly marked the subordination of art's inherent noneconomic worth to its economic value. In continental Europe, where the concept of moral rights had some legal standing, the *Agreement* had more support.[68] But in general only an extremely limited number of artists, many of whom were already so established as to be able to work without contractual guarantees, were able to use it without negative repercussions.[69] So unacceptable were the terms for many buyers and sellers that the very mention of the *Agreement* could terminate negotiation or dialogue altogether, a tactic used by the artist Cady Noland to signal her rejection of a gallery's terms.[70]

Invoking the law and all that it connoted might not work in a transactional environment where artworks, as Siegelaub and Projansky admitted, are bought and sold with regard to considerations other than profit.[71] Artists and lawyers whose opinion Siegelaub solicited expressed concern over the costs of record keeping involved with tracking each sale of the work, an issue repeatedly cited in earlier considerations of artists' resale rights.[72] Such record keeping was itself uncompensated labor for which the *Agreement* made no provision. Then there was the general aversion to collectivization, despite the visibility of organizations like the AWC. "There probably is no other professional group in this country that has a greater antipathy toward collectivating than the career artists," wrote Wayne La Com, a member of artists' rights group Artists for Economic Action.[73] The almost total rejection of the *Agreement* as a legal instrument inadvertently supported the claims of those demanding legislative rather than contractual relief.[74]

For many artists, the *Agreement* was a painful reminder of their embedment within a political, economic and legal system that continuously refused to acknowledge their works outside their exchange value. Some artists indeed seemed to think that the very idea of having to defend themselves "from exploitation in the sale and exchange of their art works" was "immoral."[75] Many artists made ephemeral artworks that did not yield a fixed, tangible object, and critic Lucy Lippard cited this as evidence of how contemporary art was increasingly defined by the "dematerialization of the art object."[76] Siegelaub remarked that ownership of such works was made impossible because "you never own the 'materials' of the work, but must be content with just the information about the existence of the 'materials.'"[77] He further claimed that the reliance on standardization by conceptual artists like Lawrence Weiner was intended to make it "impossible to own (or make) a genuinely unique object."[78] Certainly, from a legal standpoint the idea of "dematerialization" compromised the assumptions, and even the authority, of judges and lawmakers, not only because it reified the dream Lippard and her contemporaries had of an art "free of art-world commodity status," but also because of how conceptual art challenged the idea-versus-expression paradigm so central to U.S. copyright law.[79] Only when fixed in a tangible medium could an idea qualify for legal protection.[80] The split between intention and execution embedded in the amended Copyright Act of 1976 had already put pressure to bear on artwork ownership.

Nevertheless, some artists for whom integrity meant refusing, as much as possible, the legal status of artworks as property-as-commodity continued to disdain *The Artist's Reserved Rights Transfer and Sale Agreement* as a capitulating gesture to a system that legitimated artworks purely as commodities. As Siegelaub later noted, Weiner objected to the *Agreement* "because he felt that, by trying to protect his work, or give it rights, I had changed it into a piece of merchandise—a capitalist commodity—and that was that."[81] Yet Weiner regarded the *Agreement* as a possible strategy. Writing to Siegelaub in the early 1970s, he noted that "advanced capitalism turns all relations to paper: first the money, then the art . . . it is the genius of the brgoisie [*sic*] to be able to buy anything."[82] The time had come to shift tactics and flood the collectors with what they wanted: "Let them eat printout!"[83]

THE LIFE OF ARTWORKS

If dematerialization exemplifies the breakdown of the art-law relationship, longevity signifies its possible recuperation. Artists, buyers, sellers, and the law were all interested in the life of the artwork. Concerned about the reproduction of his works and whether he would have access to them for use in future exhibitions, Robert Barry wrote to one of his European dealers in 1971 that the "resale part is less important" than "*the artist's control over his work after it's sold*" (emphasis by Barry).[84] Although he did not require buyers to sign the *Agreement*, whose practicality and enforceability he doubted, he asked collectors to provide "verbal assurances that they will try to comply" with its terms.

Interest in safeguarding what might be called the "futures" of an artwork stemmed from three major considerations. First, buying an artwork was no longer a matter of a single purchase, but was rather a durational process. For instance, a provisional agreement between the Italian collector Giuseppe Panza and the artist Michael Asher from 1974 indicated that the sale of an Asher began with the buyer paying the artist one-half of the work's total purchase price.[85] In exchange, Panza would receive from Asher a written statement declaring that he was the exclusive owner of the work represented by the plans given him. Once Panza executed the plans, Asher would then certify the work's completion. Second, starting in the late 1960s, the expansion of the commercial art market was increasingly based on financial speculation. A growing number of investors expressed interest in art as a form of investment whose rate of return could potentially compete with that of more conventional investments. Art funds based on potential rates of return multiplied, and these considerations could determine a given artwork's future.[86] Third, the future-oriented nature of the market was borne out by the growing interest that lawyers and artists took in moral rights.

The idea that an artwork would continue to exist beyond the life of its creator was a powerful concept, especially when it was hypothetically possible to control at least part of that future. Indeed, this idea propelled numerous campaigns waged on behalf of the umbrella concept of "artists' rights," which became, in the 1970s, pseudo-legal shorthand referring to a particular set of rights concerned with the production and circulation of artwork, including the right to prevent a work from unjustified mutilation or destruction, the right of reproduction, and the right to claim a share of resale profits. Artworks could "die" through mutilation or destruction or continue to live on through reproductions. The discourse of artists' rights may have emphasized the authorial claims of artists for the benefit of a legal regime that recognized the claims of authors generally, but the main focus was to prolong the lives of works.

The law, too, was committed to thinking about the life of the artwork, particularly in the branch of the law from which no artist, buyer, or seller was exempt: taxation. In 1973, the Seventh Circuit defined artworks as both material and nonmaterial entities having multiple, concurrent lives of varying durations. In *John R. Thompson Co. v. United States,* a restaurant owner tried to claim a business-loss deduction for paintings he had acquired and used to decorate one of his restaurants.[87] A lower court had previously ruled that the artworks were capital assets, not business assets, thus disallowing the deduction, a decision the Seventh Circuit upheld. The verdict was less significant than how the court defined the paintings in terms of what it described as their physical, economic, and useful lives. The Seventh Circuit recognized the artwork's physical life as a function of its condition: an owner could claim depreciation only to the extent that the artwork had suffered "physical decay." Such a definition implied that the artwork had a linear, and potentially finite, life in contrast to what the court described as the economic life of the artwork, which was theoretically indefinite but perpetually unstable. Although often tied to the condition of the artwork, the economic life could be independent of its physical life; a deteriorating work might command a high market value due to its scarcity. An added wrinkle was whether the status of the artwork should change upon the death of its creator; in the late 1970s, artists' rights advocates sought to have artworks reclassified as capital upon the death of their creators so that artists' heirs would not have to pay the much higher unearned-income tax rates on inherited works.[88] "The irony of an artist not to be able to afford being alive or dead can be creativ[e]ly altered by the passing of your bill," wrote Robert Rauschenberg to Congress.[89]

Most controversial of all was "useful life." This phrase, coined by the Treasury Department in 1954 to refer to "the period over which the asset may reasonably be expected to be useful to the taxpayer in his trade or business or in the production of his income," was almost never used in connection with artworks.[90] Yet, in *John R. Thompson Co. v. United States,* the Seventh Circuit admitted that artworks might have a "useful life" if they were proven to be an integral part of a business, or in this case, to contribute to the image for which the restaurant was known by its customers. The useful life depended on the user and whether he or she continued to use the artworks for the purpose to which they had initially been put. Here the restaurant owner claimed that the useful life of his paintings ended when he closed the original restaurant where they were originally shown. The court rejected this argument by pointing out that he had actively contemplated reinstalling the works in another restaurant, thus prolonging their useful life.

The Artist's Reserved Rights Transfer and Sale Agreement internalized the notions of an artwork's physical and economic lives. It contained a "Non-Destruction" provision forbidding collectors from destroying, damaging, or altering the artwork as well as a "Repairs" clause that required collectors to alert artists should the work be damaged.

The *Agreement* emphasized the artwork's economic future, not only through the hotly debated resale clause requiring collectors to pay 15 percent of a work's appreciated value, but also through a rent-fee clause that entitled artists to collect half of any exhibition loan fees paid to collectors.

The idea of artworks having multiple lives had real potential to bridge the divisions between artists, buyers, and sellers, all of whom had vested interests in extending these lives. Advertising copywriter Eugene Schwartz, who was also a major contemporary art collector, suggested that the *Agreement* should reflect the risk assumed by the buyer, given that collectors are often responsible for artworks rising in value. Should the value of an artwork decline, its maker would compensate the buyer not with cash, but by applying half the economic loss suffered by the buyer to the purchase of a new artwork by the same artist.[91] Schwartz, who would memorably describe collecting as "the only socially commendable form of greed," argued that such a reverse resale clause would only be fair "to the collector who loved the artist's work."[92] However disingenuous collector "love" might be, it may have been a means for Siegelaub to emotionally pressure buyers into regarding ownership as more than a financial investment or the acquisition of certain property rights. What would have been the result if Siegelaub and Projansky had reworded the language of the *Agreement* so that it challenged collectors to prove to artists the sincerity of their "love" by accepting certain responsibilities?[93]

The fact that the *Agreement* failed to systemically overhaul the daily transactional culture made it clear that only government action, preferably something as strong as defining artworks as patents or trademarks, would be effective.[94] Nevertheless, it succeeded in attracting the attention of the legal and political establishments on a scale well beyond that of many forms of protest and critique. Not since Brancusi's *Bird in Space* had any event thrust contemporary art into legal and policy debate more forcefully than the *Agreement.* While politicians and judges often ignored protests for artists' rights, which tended to fade into a larger background of resistance against government policy vis-à-vis the Vietnam War and civil rights, lawyers took the *Agreement* seriously, even if only to find fault with its logic.[95] New books appeared on the subject of art law, containing sample contracts intended for artists negotiating artwork sales, museum donations, reproduction rights, and loft leases.[96] A subcommittee of the American Bar Association, the major professional organization for lawyers in the United States, debated the contract's merits, concluding that its core resale provision could be enforced only through federal law.[97] The resale provision in particular attracted nationwide interest, including articles in major newspapers and magazines about the possibility of "artist royalties," a featured segment on the influential PBS news program *The MacNeil/Lehrer Report,* and a documentary film.[98]

LEGISLATION AS ARTISTIC PRACTICE

In 1973, the auction house Sotheby's Parke Berne in New York organized the sale of the Robert and Ethel Scull Collection. Dedicated exclusively to contemporary art, the

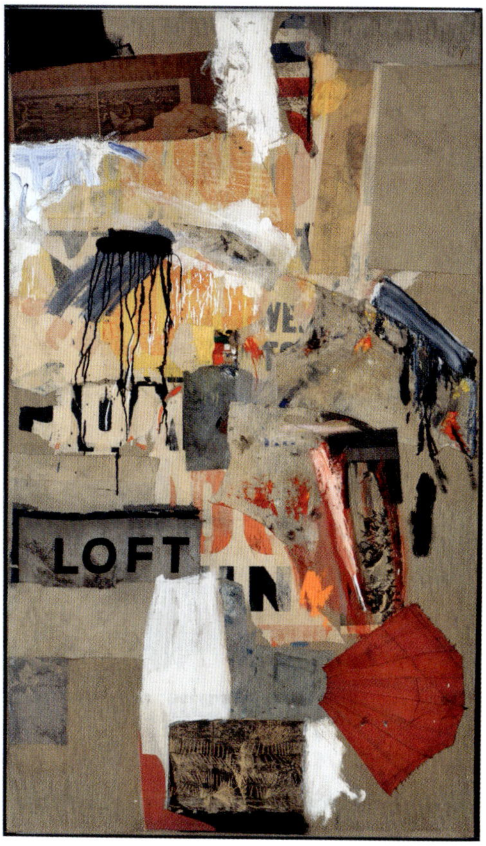

FIGURE 21
Robert Rauschenberg, *Double Feature,* 1959. Combine: oil, paper, printed paper, printed reproductions, and fabric on canvas, 90 ¾ × 52 inches. Kunstmuseum Basel. On deposit from Peter and Irene Ludwig Foundation, Aachen. © Robert Rauschenberg Foundation.

Scull sale set a new benchmark for art prices as works like Rauschenberg's *Double Feature* (1959) sold for what was then the astronomical sum of $90,000 (fig. 21).[99] E.J. Vaughn coproduced and filmed a documentary of the auction whose best-known sequence depicted Rauschenberg confronting Scull, who had originally paid $2,500 for *Double Feature.* The artist declared, "I've been working my ass for you to make all this profit!" To which the collector retorted, "Well, I've been working for you too."[100] Rauschenberg then shoved the collector. Although the confrontation felt staged to some viewers, or at least "conditioned by the presence of the news media and film crew," the indignation of the artist, who demanded that Scull buy his future works for the same prices they fetched in the auction, was genuine.[101] Scull aggravated Rauschenberg further, not only by refusing to acknowledge his creative labors, but also by emphasizing instead his own efforts to ensure and maximize economic investment.[102] The collector's rationalization mirrored what Karl Marx has described of interest-bearing capital that deceptively comes across as generative while suppressing the actual processes involved in its creation.[103] For the artist, the artwork was primarily defined by the conceptual and physical labor involved in artistic production; for collectors, the artwork was a generative source of income. Tax law appeared to side with artists. In the same year as the Scull auction, painter Mark Tobey successfully appealed an Internal Revenue Service ruling that held that income derived from painting sales counted as a "use" of property rather than earned income and was therefore not entitled to benefit from the foreign-source-income exclusion rule.[104] The U.S. Tax Court disagreed, holding that artwork sales were earned income derived from the artist's "expenditure of time, energy and skill," thus acknowledging Tobey's labor as a form of service rather than as a use of capital.[105]

Following the celebrated Scull auction, Rauschenberg campaigned for artist-specific legislation. His main focus was resale royalty laws that would not only make the resale clause of *The Artist's Reserved Rights Transfer and Sale Agreement* more generally enforceable, but also require legislatures and courts to acknowledge visual artists on a par with other professions entitled to royalty payments, including authors of literary, musical, and theatrical works.[106] Another priority was the Artists' Tax Equity Act of 1979, proposed legislation that sought to put artists "on equal footing" with collectors who donated artworks to charity by allowing artists as well as collectors to deduct the full market value of artworks donated to charitable organizations.[107] Although never enacted as law, the act attempted to amend the "hobby loss" rule permitting deductions for profit-seeking activities while barring them for activities undertaken as hobbies. Current law stated that artists would qualify for the more favorable treatment if they made a profit in two of the preceding five years, a condition Rauschenberg and his lawmaker supporters claimed was unfair to artists, who frequently had to struggle for longer periods before reaping any kind of profit. The act instead stipulated that the "hobby rule" be revised to two years out of ten.

Given how artists' rights campaigns figured as claims to representation in what often appeared as an insular dialogue between law, business, and government, it was small wonder that Rauschenberg enlisted an accountant in his lobbying efforts. Rubin Gorewitz, the unofficial accountant of the New York art world, used his intimate knowledge of artists and their finances to help draft and promote legislation benefiting visual artists. Writing for both art and mainstream publications and frequently quoted by members of Congress, Gorewitz found it "incongruous" that "such care is taken with the inanimate art object—while the human artist is treated as disposable . . . so much money is spent on eulogies and death anniversary celebrations, but what is being done to help the artist stay alive and productive?"[108] Recognizing that it was in the area of tax law that the status of visual artists was most precarious, Gorewitz lobbied federal and state lawmakers to revise federal tax laws to benefit artists.[109] Even before the Scull auction, he drafted a bill with the assistance of critic and video artist Douglas Davis that would permit artists donating their works to nonprofit institutions to deduct their full market value from their tax returns. That the bill was introduced for congressional consideration was an encouraging sign of growing national interest in legislation specifically affecting the visual arts.[110]

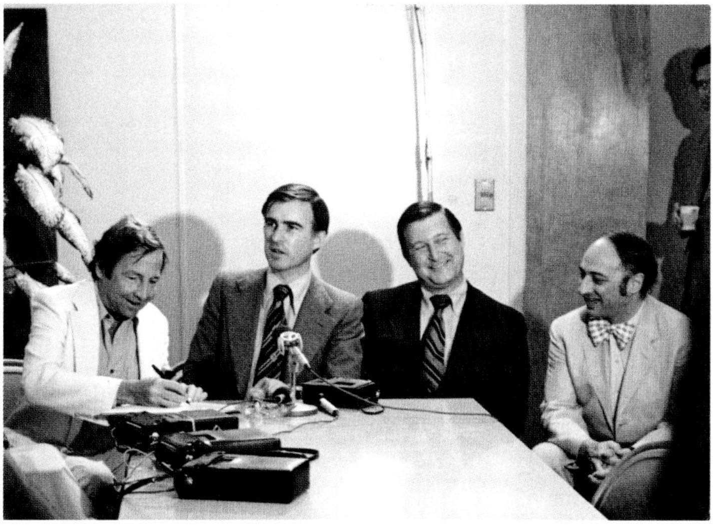

FIGURE 22
Robert Rauschenberg at the signing of the California Resale Royalty Act in 1976. Pictured, from left: Rauschenberg, Governor Jerry Brown, State Assemblyman Alan Sieroty, and accountant Rubin Gorewitz. Photograph Collection, Robert Rauschenberg Foundation Archives, New York. Photo: Harriet Zeitlin. © Harriet Zeitlin.

The greatest success Gorewitz and Rauschenberg had was in facilitating the passage of the California Resale Royalty Act (CRRA) by the California State Legislature in 1976 (fig. 22).[111] Likening visual artists to authors and composers, the CRRA became the first law to acknowledge how the economic rights of artists were inextricably connected to an understanding of their noneconomic rights, a belief underpinning the bill U.S. senator Ted Kennedy introduced in 1986 that eventually became the foundation of VARA.[112] The first resale rights law in the United States, the CRRA required sellers to pay artists 5 percent of the resale price for works sold for more than $1,000 and at a profit. Gorewitz worked with various artist associations, including the Artists' Equity Association, which enjoyed new life in the mid-1960s, and the California-based Artists for Economic Action (AFEA), formed initially to urge lawmakers to grant citizens a tax deduction for the purchase of artworks. AFEA's president, artist Ron Blumberg, had successfully interested California State assemblyman (and lawyer) Alan Sieroty in supporting arts legislation, and the proposal Gorewitz sent Blumberg influenced the arguments Sieroty made in favor of the bill that became the CRRA.[113] The CRRA, in turn, affected the passing of the Artists' Authorship Rights Act in 1983 by the New York State Legislature, one of the first laws in the United States to protect artists whose works were altered without their consent.[114]

Not all of Gorewitz's ideas were implemented, including his suggestion that resale provisions be written into uniform, official certificates of authenticity issued and tracked by a nonprofit organization or government agency. It was a tactical way of maximizing the enforceability of resale payments as it capitalized on the intense demand for certificates of authenticity from collectors anxious to protect their investments. The certificates Gorewitz proposed would be standard for all sales of art in the

United States and would include a record of past ownership and exhibition as well as obligate the work's creator to assist with artwork restoration. Such benefits, Gorewitz claimed, were worth more than the 5 percent resale royalty fee.[115]

"Getting involved with art really messed up my life," Gorewitz jokingly said to Rauschenberg, who returned the sentiment.[116] The accountant's mock-complaint illuminated the merging of the fields of art, economics, and law, which sometimes resulted in unexpected alliances. Even Scull became a supporter of resale rights for artists through interacting with Rauschenberg; Gorewitz claimed that the collector wanted to "lead a whole delegation to Washington."[117] Similarly, lawyers and lawmakers became more comfortable with artists as professionals, lobbyists, and sources of information. As Sieroty noted, lawmakers looked to artists and arts organizations for suggestions about what laws would be most useful.[118] The contiguity of fields catalyzed new relationships between art and the law that often played out through individual relationships between exhibition organizers and lawyers (Siegelaub and Projansky), accountants and artists (Gorewitz and Rauschenberg), or artists and lawmakers (Blumberg and Sieroty). Being an artist was a deeply social enterprise that required considerable ability to ventriloquize thoughts and feelings by engaging with other professions; doing art meant knowing law.

COLLECTING AS SOCIAL INVESTMENT

In "The Wrath of Rauschenberg," the most comprehensive legal analysis of the claims Rauschenberg so vigorously supported after his public confrontation with Scull, John Henry Merryman argued how it was emotion, namely regret and wrath, that did the real work motivating broader discussions of labor, value, and the market.[119] Rauschenberg's "market aversion," Merryman remarked, took "form as an expression of regret that works of art . . . are bought and sold—'commodification' is the currently stylish epithet."[120] That the artist was able to help convince the California State Legislature to pass the CRRA was also due to a screening of Vaughn and Schott's documentary of the Scull auction, a trenchant representation that pressed against a perspective of economics that neglected or even denied any subjective dimension to the sale of artworks.[121] But while Rauschenberg's rage, regret, and chagrin communicated the depth of his and others' commitment to a particular view of economic justice based on abstract conceptions of fairness, it was not enough. Merryman found resale rights laws wanting on economic grounds, implying that the cost of requiring owners' compliance outweighed the financial benefits to artists.

Certainly, the compliance model of artists' rights was only slightly more successful than *The Artist's Reserved Rights Transfer and Sale Agreement* in securing the royalties Gorewitz and Rauschenberg thought artists deserved.[122] Quoting from Tom Camp's study of auction sales in New York from 1973 to 1977, Merryman observed that only five artists accounted for almost a third of all recorded resales, Rauschenberg foremost among them.[123] Gorewitz had actually developed a version of the *Agreement* to address collector concerns about the supposed financial burden incurred by having to share resale profits with the artist. Called the *Artist Residuum Transposal* (A.R.T.), it stipulated that in exchange for a certificate of authenticity, the seller would pay a royalty of 15 percent of the difference between the purchase and sale prices. Gorewitz argued that the royalty would actually reduce the total capital gains tax that collectors would have to pay.[124] Responding to collectors like Scull, who publicly admitted at a symposium at New York University in October 1974 that artists should be entitled to fees whenever their works were shown or reproduced and that they should receive resale royalties of "about 1 or 2 percent" (the same percentage assigned to patent royalties), Gorewitz modified the proposal he circulated to lawyers, lawmakers, and artists' groups, lowering the resale profit percentage from 15 to 5 percent.[125]

Some artists tried to make the resale provision less about economics and more about art by recasting it as part of the work. At least that was the impression Hans Haacke gave when he, as one of the few artists able to successfully use *The Artist's Reserved Rights Transfer and Sale Agreement,* called it a "partnership between the maker of the work and the person who eventually owns it."[126] It was unclear what Haacke meant, beyond suggesting how the sale of an artwork was merely the beginning and not the end of a relationship. The term *partnership* legally refers to a model of business whose parties agree to share in the business's profits and liabilities. When a collector buys a work, he or she is retroactively compensating the artist for the cost of its creation, including, in many cases, the personal and physical risks directly incurred by the artist. The purchase price also covers the right to claim a majority share of any resale profits. Seen in this way, the resale provision could be reframed as one partner (the collector) allocating to the other partner (the artist) a minority share of profit. Still another possibility suggested by Haacke's language is to reframe artwork sales as a form of royalty financing, whereby an artist sells a work significantly below its fair market value in exchange for a guaranteed share of resale profits. The share could perhaps be negotiated as a discounted percentage of the difference between the overall sale price and the current or projected market value of the work. Should the total resale price be over a certain amount, the resale share or percentage could be capped. Another arrangement would be to have the collector annually pay a percentage of any rise in the assessed market value of the work for a fixed term.

Perhaps most convincing was the rationale of Jackie Winsor, who used the *Agreement* in fifteen sales in the 1970s, including sales of work to Oberlin College and the collector Charles Carpenter. For her it was a measure of whether her collectors defined worth beyond her works' current or future exchange values. Testifying before Congress in 1987 on behalf of the bill that would later become VARA, she argued that profit distribution after resale made tangible the "respect" she deemed central to any relationship between artists and collectors: "Given the care which I take with each piece . . . the escalated price tag (a form of monitory respect), provides a stronger guarantee for the physical integrity of the sculpture."[127] Winsor later added that a collector's willingness to sign the *Agreement* was for her a proof of their trustworthiness: when collectors "engaged with me on that level . . . I had such a sense of their integrity that it almost didn't matter if they signed or not."[128] Winsor's belief suggests how the *Agreement* might have served as the grounds for a model of ethical collecting. Not unlike socially responsible investing, a concept that also gained momentum in the late 1970s, ethical collecting might apply to buyers interested in art investment for both profit and promotion of the social good. Thus, rather than define resale rights through the language of royalties, the provision could be reframed as a contribution to the arts as a social responsibility, an idea that in the 1970s was very much part of art-world culture via the skyrocketing of government support for the arts from $1.7 million in 1965 to $55 million in 1975.[129] But the idea of collecting as social investment would also mean emphasizing artworks as public-minded contributions toward improving society, as opposed to Siegelaub's call for collectors to recognize artists as workers and professionals, a demand many collectors suspected to be little more than a thinly veiled plea for income redistribution.

In sum, *The Artist's Reserved Rights Transfer and Sale Agreement* emphasized not only the economics of art, but also how law was indispensible for artists seeking to broker an identity as a genuine political and social force. Subsequent decades would expand upon this primacy, with law functioning as art's foil, support, and catalyst. Above all, the *Agreement* showed how law might act as contemporary art's silent partner, provoking artists and artworks to speculate deeply about the place and function of culture in a civil society.

2

CIRCLING THE LAW

Christo and Jeanne-Claude's *Running Fence*

FROM A DISTANCE, *Running Fence* resembles a thin band of white material, running across largely treeless, sparsely populated, hilly land (fig. 23). Intermittently punctuating the land are a loose constellation of trees and, in the distance, scattered clusters of low buildings. The white band runs throughout, its color sharply contrasted by the brownish-green grass. The starkness of the white against the ground strongly recalls the image of the white picket fence, an association that coincides with how the band appears to function as a boundary, dividing one half of the trees or the buildings from the other. At closer range, we see the white band less in terms of its function and more through its constituent materials. What previously looked durable and even solid is now revealed as pliable and even ephemeral. Sheets of what initially read as plastic or fabric are secured into the ground at regular intervals, but they billow in the wind, the strain evident through bulging ripples of fabric. The bottom edge of each panel looks as if it could easily be ripped from its delicate moorings.

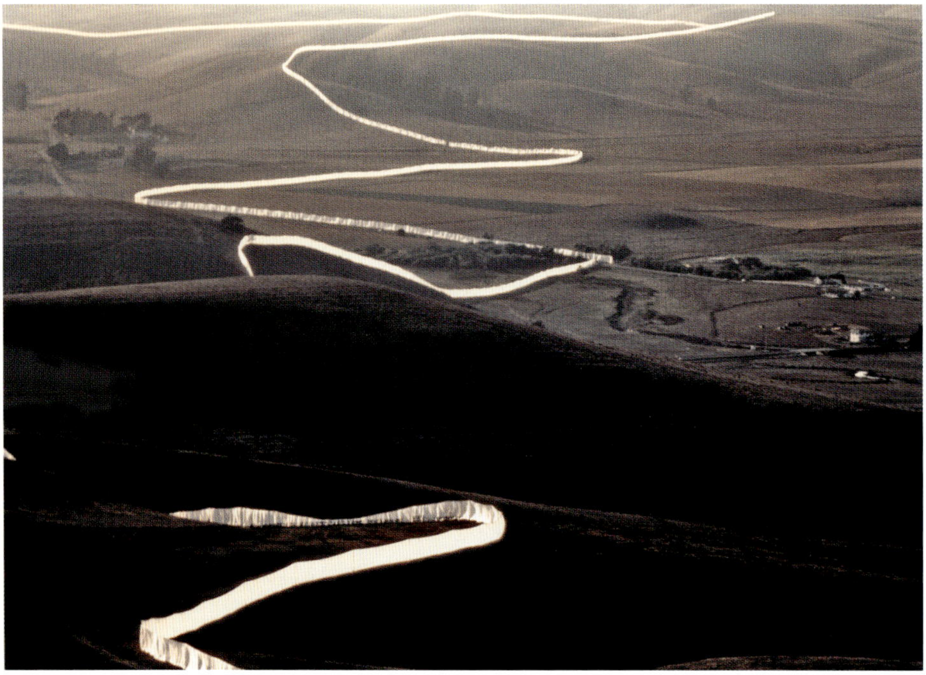

FIGURE 23
Christo and Jeanne-Claude, *Running Fence, Sonoma and Marin Counties, California, 1972–76*, September 10–20, 1976. Smithsonian American Art Museum. Photo: Bruce Lauritzen. © 1976, Christo.

Long celebrated for creating larger-than-life works, Christo and Jeanne-Claude are perhaps most remarkable for how they made legible the conflicts produced by multiple categories of law, including environmental law newly passed by federal and state governments and long-standing customs among neighbors. Begun in 1972 and completed in 1976, *Running Fence* spanned 24.5 miles over public and private property in Sonoma and Marin counties in Northern California. The process of its creation, specifically the efforts to obtain permission from courts, governments, and landowners, vividly illustrated how the complex of property was constructed from claims of entitlement and obligation. Christo described *Running Fence,* the first artwork in U.S. history to require an Environmental Impact Report—a document required by law when a designated government agency judges a proposed action to have potential significant effect on the environment—as having a "necessary" relationship with law.[1]

But let us return to the photograph. Not only because it emblematizes the role photography played in galvanizing public support for a work that triggered a level of scrutiny more commonly reserved for political candidates, but because of how succinctly it revealed the duality underpinning the complications *Running Fence* encompassed. Seen from a distance, the land appeared continuous and, presumably, unified. As the work rolled into the foreground, it brought with it a vision of land brought to order by its division into adjacent, but separate, parts owned by discrete entities. As Christo observed during the work's construction, "the subdivision is a very important part of American society, especially in California where everything is subdivided."[2] Once raw earth, the land is most legible as real property, a particular legal subset of property defined by the cultivation or improvement of the land.

Having to contend between two competing ideas of what land could be, the artists were required to navigate different systems of regulation. This played itself out in the extraordinarily complicated process of obtaining the requisite permissions from local residents to start construction. Understanding how law was conveyed through social norms and other uncodified rituals and local expectations concerning land and land ownership was as critical to the completion of *Running Fence* as the deployment of existing legal structures to realize a work whose medium was as much logistics as it was cloth and metal. Indeed, the making of *Running Fence* stressed how the law most often worked outside legislation and litigation, and instead through business and casual personal communication where language, timing, and even tone of voice could affect the outcome.

CORPORATE LAW FOR ARTISTS

The sheer size of Christo and Jeanne-Claude's works so dramatically increased the chances of possible injury to workers and audiences that creating them became an issue of risk management and, eventually, of how artistic creation meant involuntarily assuming a certain measure of legal responsibility toward the viewer. Existing business law offered Christo and Jeanne-Claude both a means of fundraising and protection. Scott Hodes, the Chicago corporate lawyer who had represented the artists since meeting them at a party in New York in 1964, set up a corporation, a legal entity allowing collectors to purchase works of art while limiting their liability to the amount invested.[3] Collectors were not responsible for debts or judgments against the corporation, while the artists were protected from any possible liability should damage or harm occur during the construction, display, and, perhaps most importantly, the dismantling of the work.

In his biography of Christo and Jeanne-Claude, Burt Chernow writes that Christo sought to erect a fence of his own in an area with rolling hills largely devoid of trees, yet with a freeway, and with different types of fences.[4] In the summer of 1973, the artists settled on a route in Northern California that ran perpendicular to the Continental Divide without intersecting it. The location of the route coincided with what Christo later stated was a long-standing fascination with the idea of the West, and particularly California, which he described as "the most American state in the[ir] way of living."[5] His interest mirrored that of artists associated with the earthworks movement, which emerged almost simultaneously with Christo's initial forays into wrapped objects. As art historian Suzaan Boettger argues, the decision of many artists associated with earthworks or land art to work in the western states was inflected by how the idea of the frontier—a geographical reference to a zone where no state exercises complete political control and that also tends to be either sparsely inhabited or uninhabited—had been romanticized in literature and art. An exemplary case was Northern California native Michael Heizer, who openly confessed his dislike of what he saw as the "degenerating" East, an indication of his growing disillusionment with the parochialism of the New York art world.[6]

Calvin Tomkins, possibly the most eloquent and enthusiastic chronicler of *Running Fence*'s creation, stated that Christo and Jeanne-Claude had opportunities to erect the work on private property controlled by a single owner in Mexico or South Africa, where they would have encountered no legal interference.[7] Places where a single landowner could own a large tract were less interesting to Christo and Jeanne-Claude, however, than "a community with a fantastically acute and very nervous relation to the land."[8] In many respects a precursor for *Running Fence*, *Valley Curtain* (1970–72) was a 1,500-foot-long curtain of orange nylon attached to a steel cable suspended between two mountains (fig. 24).[9] Erected in Rifle, Colorado, it temporarily occupied land owned by two individuals who eventually agreed to let Christo and Jeanne-Claude use their property.[10] Considerable effort was made to avoid crossing federal land, which would have required the artists to negotiate with federal agencies, from whom permissions were far less forthcoming than they were from local governments. Jan van der Marck, the founding director of the Museum of Contemporary Art Chicago (MCA Chicago) who became *Valley Curtain*'s project director, expressed relief that no such negotiation would be needed.[11] Traversing both private and public lands, *Running Fence* more forcefully pushed the issue of scale, in a manner reminiscent of land artists whose projects' scales of execution had cast into extreme relief the question of whether there were limits as to what could be done in land art on and with lawfully occupied property.

For *Running Fence*, one of the first things Christo and Jeanne-Claude did was to establish, or rather prolong, the life of a corporation they had previously established in connection with *Valley Curtain*.[12] Renamed the Running Fence Corporation in October 1973, the corporation's officers were Christo as treasurer and director and Jan van der Marck as vice president. The choice of van der Marck was especially strategic given his "sterling reputation" in international art circles and the radicality of his curatorial thinking, which included inviting Christo and Jeanne-Claude to wrap the exterior of the MCA Chicago building in 1969.[13] Citing the difficulty of getting museums to pay project expenses to artists, due to the tax liability consequently assumed by these institutions, Jeanne-Claude later observed that the corporation was an ideal means to accrue funds without the risk of being taxed; because their corporations always incurred losses, no taxes would be owed.[14]

That Christo and Jeanne-Claude paid for all costs involved in *Running Fence*'s construction was central to its success, as it preempted the challenges directed against them in earlier projects ("Who is paying for this insane idea?" as one viewer wrote to van der Marck of the wrapped MCA Chicago).[15] The artists asked various parties,

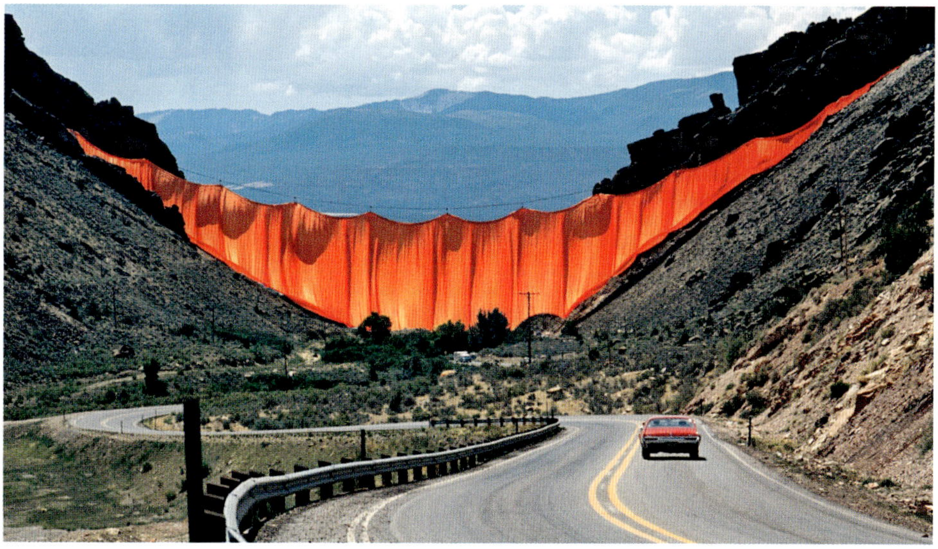

FIGURE 24
Christo and Jeanne-Claude, *Valley Curtain, Rifle, Colorado, 1970–72*, 1972. Photo: Wolfgang Volz/laif/Redux Pictures. © 1972, Christo.

almost all of them European, to effectively buy "shares" that also doubled as options or futures contracts. Per written agreement, sometimes called a "Co-Sponsorship Agreement," a buyer would purchase a certain percentage of the total cost of a Christo work minus a discount. The work being sold was left unspecified, except for the provision that the payment could be applied to works made in a certain period, for example 1958–72; in one proposed agreement, a $20,000 loan or "purchase" would represent 60 percent of a work sold at $33,500 but whose retail value was 40 percent higher.[16] The agreement was strictly nontransferable, and the lender had the option of commissioning a new work or edition through the Running Fence Corporation. Should the corporation fail to repay the loan within a certain period, usually a calendar year, it would give the lender Christo artworks worth double the amount of the original loan. All lenders would receive from the artist a small Christo artwork of his or her choice.

But the corporation did not fully absolve Christo and Jeanne-Claude of all risk. Some of the loan agreements they drafted unwittingly exposed them to certain conditions. On July 23, 1975, the two artists signed an agreement with Ephraim Ilin, the founder of Modarco (abbreviation for Modern Art Collection), one of the many incorporated art dealerships created in the wake of an expanding art market. Established in 1971 as a subsidiary of a Geneva bank and as a publicly traded firm, Modarco was among the most visible of the new art investment funds of the early to mid-1970s.[17] Though not usually in the habit of lending to artists, Modarco did so in exchange for Christo collages and drawings valued at U.S. $100,000, with the additional provision that the works would be valued at $300,000 should the loan not be repaid within a calendar year.[18] Proceeds from any sale would be split equally between the company and the artist. Ostensibly to encourage Modarco to advance the loan, the artists added that they would give the firm additional works if they directly received money from a sale. In this, the Running Fence Corporation differed from other artists' uses of the corporation, such as *Income (Outflow) Piece,* Dan Graham's unrealized proposal of 1969 that would have allowed buyers of Graham's works to become shareholders in a public corporation. Buyers would then receive as dividends a share of the artist's income. Such a work insinuated on Graham's part a desire to use existing legal and financial apparatuses—the corporation and the public offer—to emphasize in concrete terms the value of artists and artworks.

THE FENCE IN LAW AND CULTURE

Incorporation helped embolden Christo and Jeanne-Claude to embark on a project whose logistical difficulty was complicated by its reference to one of the most enduring symbols of property in American culture, the fence. The legal history of fences is defined by the profound ambivalence surrounding the rights and obligations of property owners. Traditionally, the fence was used to protect one's livestock as well as prevent the livestock of others from encroaching on one's land. So engrained was this convention that local officials called "fence viewers" were charged with making sure that neighbors upheld their obligations to one another by taking good care of the fence separating their lands. Fence proverbs abounded in legal decisions concerning boundary disputes, where fences were said to "run" properly or improperly on one's land.[19] In the middle to late nineteenth century, fence-related disputes reflected changes in the way land was used, particularly in California, as land formerly used for grazing was now put to more explicitly agricultural purposes. Thus, by the early twentieth century the standard of "fencing out," which emphasized the exclusionary role of fences, shifted toward a new standard of "fencing in," which stressed the fence as a means of enclosure.[20] For the residents of rural Northern California, fences were high-budget items for dairy farmers and ranchers who not only had to build fences to protect their animals but also bore responsibility for their repair and eventual replacement.

In California, extra-legal custom defined fences as much as case law and legislation did. As legal scholar Ralph Ellickson has pointed out in his magisterial discussion of the problems caused by escaped cattle in Shasta County, California, as an example of how governance can take place on an extra-legal basis, most activity concerning fences was regulated by long-standing norms and customs rather than by law.[21] Fences configure physical land as a shared resource, access to which depends on the relationships between those living in close physical proximity to one another. The conspicuous absence of lawsuits concerning fences suggests an awareness of this interdependence.

The preparatory drawings of Christo undermine any effort to stabilize the definition of a fence (fig. 25). Seen closely, his fence might resemble a wall and thus seem more

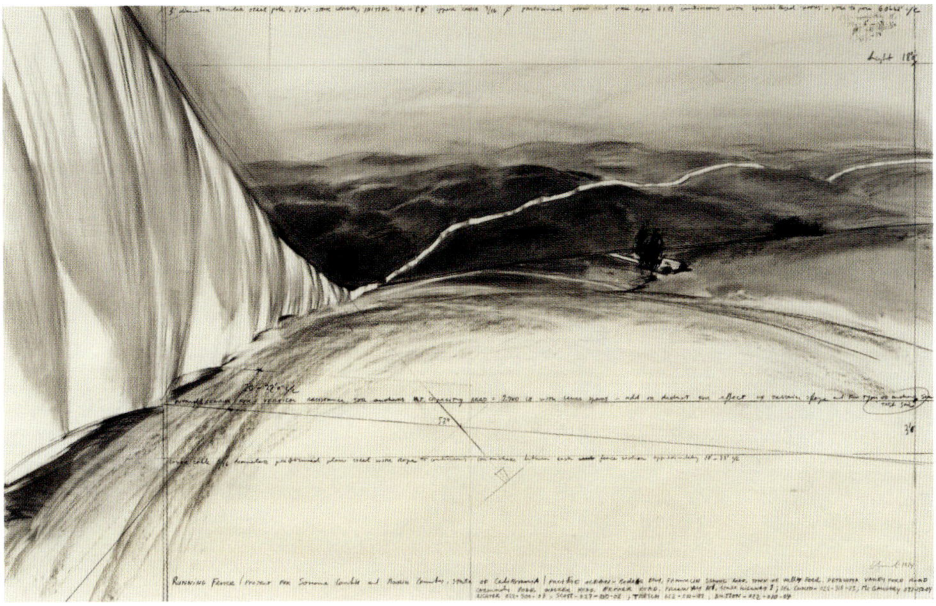

FIGURE 25
Christo, *Running Fence (Project for Sonoma County and Marin County, State of California)*, 1974. Pencil and charcoal on paper, 42 × 65 inches. © 1974, Christo.

like a traditional boundary dividing one space from another. Yet, from a distance, the fence would appear as a thin band more aligned with the symbolic lines used to transform space into place on a political map. Such variations implicitly called attention to the aesthetic dimensions of fences and, more broadly, to how aesthetic considerations factor into written law. As early as 1897, the Supreme Court of California held that a fence was a boundary marker that had to be on an actual division line between two distinct physical properties.[22] A "lawful fence," moreover, was defined as a fence "good, strong, substantial and sufficient to prevent ingress and egress of livestock."[23] In 1913, the California State Legislature passed "spite fence" laws generally disallowing the erection of fences exceeding ten feet. Christo and Jeanne-Claude envisioned how *Running Fence* might compromise its own capacity to function as a fence. Not only did it not enclose a specific area, it consisted of large fabric panels highly susceptible to the elements (fig. 26). In Sonoma and Marin counties, barbed wire and steel posts were standard materials for agricultural fencing.[24] Steel posts—although much taller than those used for agricultural purposes—also anchored the work into the ground, but the enormous sheets of white cloth appeared to invite contact as readily as barbed wire fences deflected the same. The latter, claims historian John Jackson, is most effective when it eliminates existing spaces, by closing roads and by discouraging openings.[25]

As Christo and Jeanne-Claude developed the concept of *Running Fence*, Christo's drawings of the projected final work were studiously devoid of images that suggested

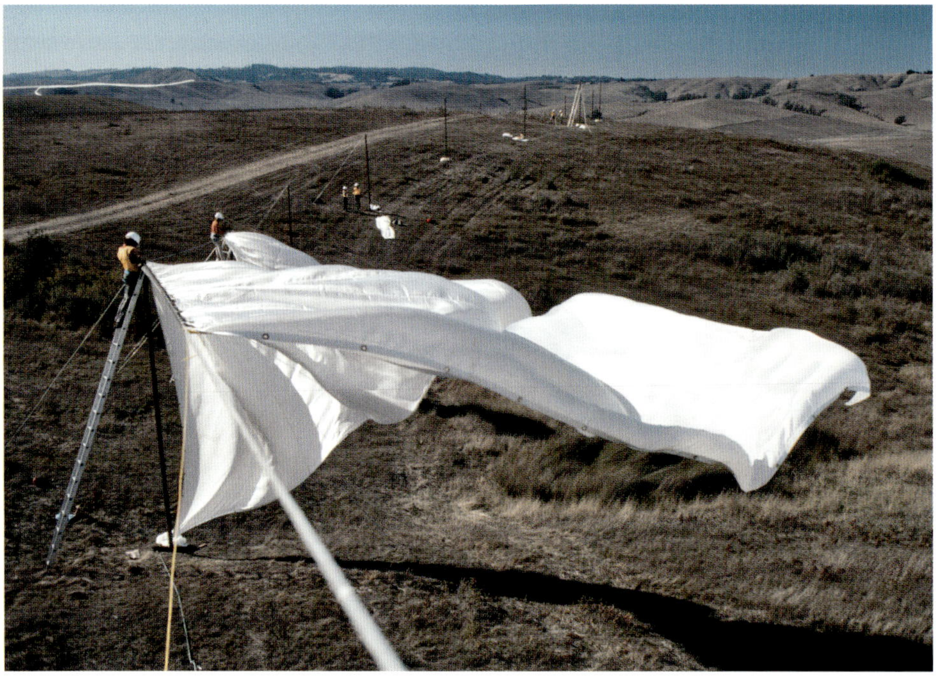

FIGURE 26
Christo and Jeanne-Claude, *Running Fence, Sonoma and Marin Counties, California, 1972–76,* fighting the wind, September 8–10, 1976. Smithsonian American Art Museum, Photo: Wolfgang Volz. © 1976, Christo.

obstacles or waste. Similar to a cartographer working for a developer, he carefully shaded, colored, and illustrated to make the proposed work as attractive as possible while still providing enough information about the preexisting landscape to make the work seem believable. Early drawings and collages of *Running Fence* were initially called "The Divide," presumably after the Continental Divide of the Americas that separates neighboring drainage basins. Jeanne-Claude later claimed to have discouraged further use of this title because she perceived the word *divide* as having too many negative connotations.[26] Jeanne-Claude may have been apprehensive of *Running Fence* being read in terms of an iconography of division, or against Christo's own biography as a former citizen of the Communist bloc. Christo then described the work as a "barrier," albeit an "open barrier that runs through the country, the town, etc."[27] At least one of his drawings supported this claim; rendered against the paper, the white looked solid, as if the fence were made of concrete or stone rather than fabric (fig. 27). It differed sharply from the forbidding wall of oil barrels that gave new meaning to the already loaded title of *Iron Curtain,* a work consisting of eighty-nine oil barrels precariously stacked on top of one another, filling the narrow gap flanked by two buildings and creating a wall measuring approximately 13.7 feet (fig. 28). In contrast, the semi-sheer woven nylon Christo and Jeanne-Claude used for *Running Fence* appeared to

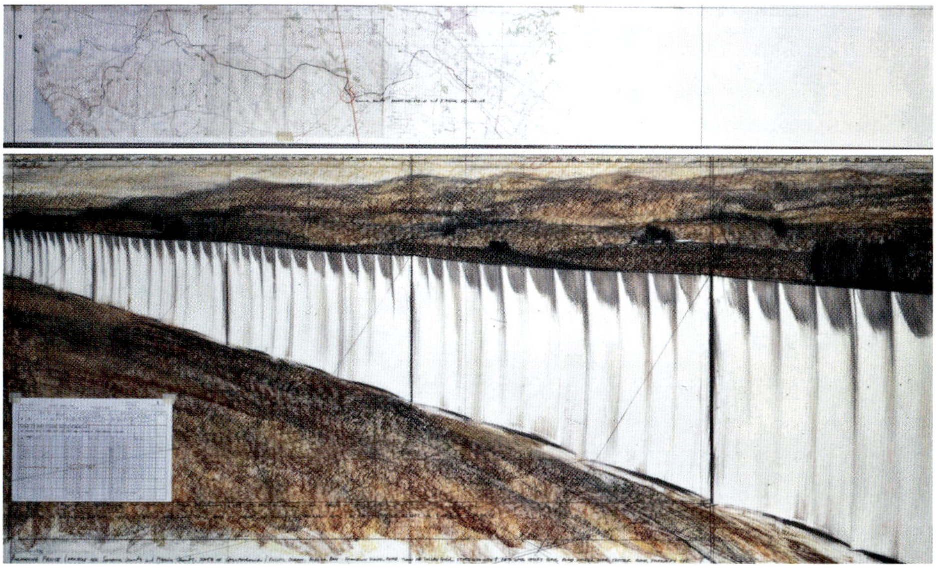

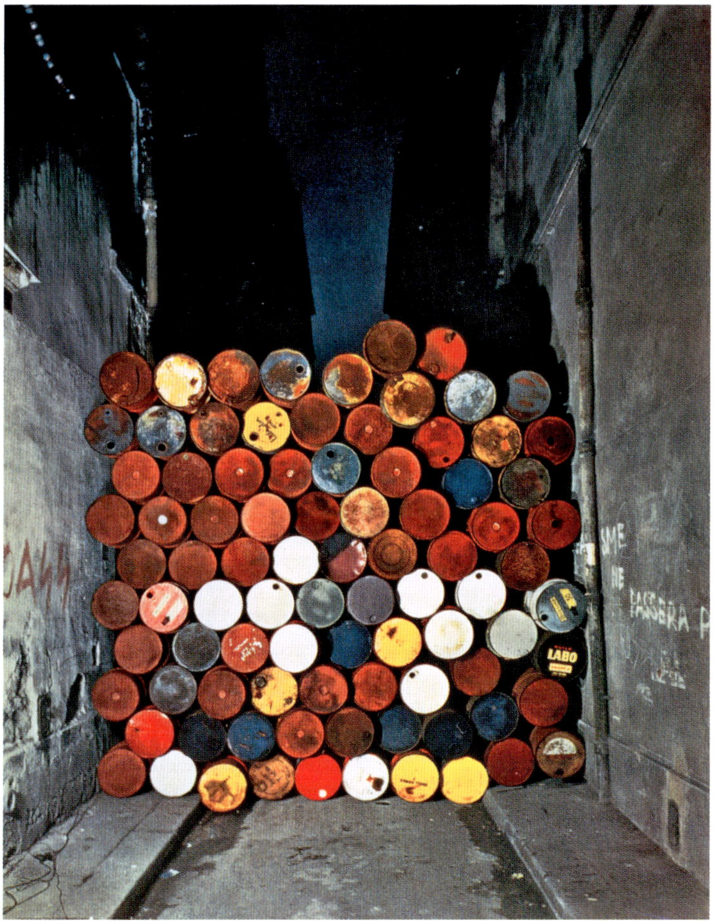

FIGURE 27
Christo, *Running Fence, Project for Sonoma County and Marin County, State of California,* 1976. Pencil, charcoal, pastel, topographic map, technical data, and tape, 15 × 96 inches and 42 × 96 inches.

FIGURE 28
Christo and Jeanne-Claude, *Wall of Oil Barrels—Iron Curtain, Rue Visconti, Paris,* June 27, 1962. Photo: Jean-Dominique Lajoux.

flutter in the wind, barely held together by a delicate armature of metal pins and poles, an experience that Christo described as a matter of "passing through": "If there is an obstruction, if it's steel, or wood or concrete, there is no way to go through."[28]

Despite exceeding the general height allowed by law for fences, the dimensions of *Running Fence* were mitigated by the fabric looking as if it could easily be burned, torn, or punctured. Further affirming the supposed vulnerability of the work—or, to borrow Christo's language, its "fragility"—was the decision to make the work white, a color conspicuously unlike the vivid orange used for *Valley Curtain.* The white of *Running Fence* seemed calculated to provoke in viewers a desire to mark or deface the blank fabric surfaces.[29] Indeed, after parts of the work were erected, the white fabric panels were a particularly attractive target for vandals, some of whom regarded the blank sheets as an opportunity to communicate such messages as "Dada is God."[30]

Opponents of the work claimed that it impinged on their rights. The grounds upon which they justified their objections were squarely rooted in considering the land a virtual public commons that imparted to them a duty to protect the area from unwanted use by strangers. Thus, although his work was often construed through Robert Frost's celebrated 1914 poem "Mending Wall," which prominently featured the proverb "Good fences make good neighbors," *Running Fence* did exactly the opposite of what Frost depicted. Instead of erecting a boundary intended to deliver peace and privacy to those living on either side, Christo and Jeanne-Claude provoked conflict that, in turn, demonstrated how even land subject to the most complex divisions could be claimed by anyone, so long as he or she declared an interest in how it was used or what it looked like.

The very ambiguity generated by the apparent contradiction between the work's title and the presumed experience of the work was central to the conflicts produced by *Running Fence.* These conflicts paradoxically reaffirmed the existence of a real community based on interaction. What, then, are the unspoken norms of property ownership and when do we feel justified, even obligated, to support restrictions on how others choose to use their land? When does private entitlement become a matter of public scrutiny?

CUSTOMS OF THE COUNTRY

In a 1973 interview that took place during the first stages of the work's creation, Christo asserted that part of the reason for situating the work in Northern California was to deal with as many different constituents and kinds of land as possible:

> It involves—it is very big in size, it is about twenty-five miles. It involves many private properties and cities, it will pass through a small town. It involves a huge amount of contracts, permits, liability insurance and I think it will be one of the most exciting parts of the project. But of course, with these things, we create fantastic relations, me going to negotiate with farmers, cowboys, and people of the city.[31]

The reality, however, proved exceedingly different. When the artists arrived in Northern California in October 1973 to investigate the nature of the land on which they would build *Running Fence,* the Petaluma Chamber of Commerce forewarned them that while obtaining government permits would be relatively simple, getting the ranchers' permission would not.[32] The fifty-seven-minute 1978 film that Charlotte Zerwin and Albert and David Maysles made of the work's construction shows one bystander labeling the artists "big city slickers." There were palpable differences between these European urban expatriates and the residents of Sonoma and Marin counties.

Interestingly, the question of calibrating their requests according to preexisting customs and standards was an issue with which Christo and Jeanne-Claude had the most trouble, because they were perhaps too familiar with the significance of such customs—especially Christo, whose own biography was a veritable series of cultural displacements and adjustments. A case in point was when they, at Hodes's suggestion, offered each of the landowners who chose to grant access and use of a restricted area of their property for the duration of *Running Fence*'s construction and deinstallation the gift of a television, a refrigerator, or a freezer.[33] If these offers were ignored, it was not only because the landowners already owned these appliances, but because the land was more than a commodity: theirs was a world based on kinship, custom, and personal relationships rather than the accelerated creation and accumulation of capital. Christo, Jeanne-Claude, and Hodes appeared to rethink their tactics when the artists promised to gift Marin County with a biokinetics machine meant to convert animal waste into animal feed.[34]

How, then, does a stranger become a neighbor? In this part of the country, most interactions that would ordinarily involve some kind of formal regulation tended to be undertaken or resolved according to long-entrenched customs or norms. After first meeting those whose properties *Running Fence* needed to cross, Christo and Jeanne-Claude met approximately two hundred other property owners in a group dinner at the Sonoma County Fairgrounds building on January 20, 1974. Even after explaining what *Running Fence* would entail, there was little response from the landowners, a matter the artists confronted by deciding to approach on an individual basis the owners whose lands the work was likely to cross. Initial calls went largely unanswered, so Christo and Jeanne-Claude traveled to meet the landowners beginning in June of that year.

In presenting the idea of *Running Fence* to the landowners, the artists emphasized that the latter possessed the authority to permit or exclude *Running Fence.* Artist renditions in the form of drawings, sketches, and written descriptions were critical. Many illustrated a white fence-like structure blending seamlessly with the landscape, while detractors made unflattering comparisons ("toilet paper" was especially popular). Christo tried to acknowledge the latent concerns about the work's scale by producing numerous drawings anticipating what *Running Fence* might look like from the perspective of an individual viewer or, in one case, a driver (fig. 29). To further establish credibility as well as anticipate the general scale of *Running Fence,* Christo pointedly screened the Maysles' award-winning documentary of *Valley Curtain,* which at least

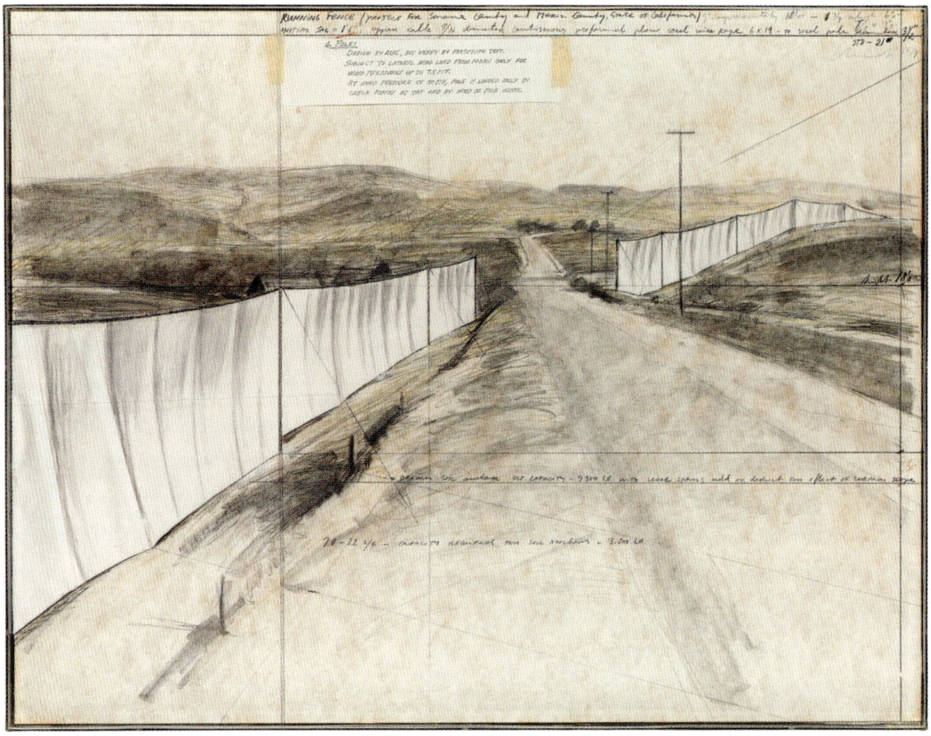

FIGURE 29
Christo, *Running Fence (Project for Sonoma County and Marin County, State of California)*, 1974. Pencil, pastel, charcoal, wax crayon, tape, and ballpoint pen. © 1974, Christo.

one skeptic-turned-supporter later identified as a reason for their conversion.[35] Critics of *Running Fence* pointed out that the film did not show the destruction of the work, nor the tense relationship between the artist and his contractors.[36] Sonoma County supervisors intuited likewise and eventually disallowed the film from being shown at one hearing in March 1975.[37]

Only when the property owners were offered cash did Christo and Jeanne-Claude begin to make significant progress in securing the necessary permissions, a sign that they were still considered outside the local social sphere. As Ellickson observed of residents living in rural areas, resolving intra-neighbor disputes with cash was considered "distasteful," which implies that such resolutions were appropriate only when involving non-neighbors or strangers.[38] Christo and Jeanne-Claude recast this situation as a matter of guest-versus-host, amply reflected by Jeanne-Claude's interpersonal skills and emphasis on civility. But the relationship was formalized by the signed agreements. Each of the agreements, issued to each of the fifty-five landowners, stressed the importance of the owners' individual consent, a particularly sensitive issue for many of the ranchers, who resented the way in which corporate ranches affected their own practices.[39] The emphasis was in sharp contrast to the wording of the agreements issued during *Valley Curtain;* there, lessor and lessee were depicted more as partners on comparable footing, each defined by his or her responsibilities.

Conversely, the *Running Fence* agreements were phrased to emphasize owners' rights, almost making those involved with the work appear as guests whose collective presence entirely depended on the owners' consent. Referring to the borrowed land as a "strip," the easement agreement minimizes the extent of occupation by stating that "the sole purpose" will be to allow the Running Fence Corporation to build on the strip, as well as have access to it during the term of the lease. It provides, however, that such access will occur with "least damage and inconvenience" to the landowner.[40] The agreement cleverly begins by deferring to the landowner ("Grantor shall have the right to use the Strip for purposes not inconsistent with Grantee's full enjoyment of the rights granted"), yet ends by imposing substantial restrictions on that use by prohibiting the landowner not only from building any structure, but also from operating any drill or well during the Corporation's occupation.[41] The easement then lists a number of promises regarding the assumption of liability.[42] In sum, the agreement was much more cautiously organized than that executed in the course of building *Valley Curtain,* where transactions were much more straightforward, in part because one of the landowners actually donated their land without asking any rent whatsoever.[43]

Even though Christo and Jeanne-Claude obtained the permits they needed by a process far more formal than a handshake or a verbal agreement, they partly understood the customs by which such transactions normally took place, as evidenced by their offering to the landowners the raw materials from which *Running Fence* would be made. In reference to the ranchers, whose backgrounds and concerns closely resembled those of the majority of the landowners whose permission Christo and Jeanne-Claude sought, Ellickson observed that voluntary in-kind contributions comparable to an exchange of gifts determined most inter-neighbor transactions. Christo recalled how excited the ranchers became when they saw the army-surplus poles that would be used to hold the fence upright: the ranchers "would come and look and touch. They could see real value."[44] Amplifying the excitement was how the ranchers could envision using these materials, including two-thousand-plus panels of nylon, a similar number of twenty-one-foot-high steel poles, some ninety miles of steel cable, and over three hundred thousand steel hooks. At a March 1975 hearing before the Sonoma County Board of Supervisors, a rancher from neighboring Marin County testified: "I can't wait for Christo to come and go so I can use his pipes and cable. I have a sheep and dairy operation and you know how the price of posts are today. I think when it's all over with, you'll agree with me; you'll be glad they came to Marin County."[45]

Lester Bruhn, another rancher whose land Christo and Jeanne-Claude temporarily occupied, similarly commented of the fabric, "They say it makes nice curtains or bedspreads. Well, we could also sell it."[46] Seen in terms of its raw material, *Running Fence* made economic sense, at least to those whose lands the work would directly occupy.

SCALES OF LAW

Central to the debates around *Running Fence* were the various perceptions of what it actually was, an issue complicated by the fact that the work had yet to be constructed and that no one, not even Christo and Jeanne-Claude, could predict the result. The very idea of building a structure so large as to conflate the different scales associated with the sizes of the home, the neighborhood, the town, the region, and even the state pushed to the limits individualistic conceptions of property based on the idea of ownership. Similarly, *Running Fence* called attention to the anxiety of courts and legislatures toward any physical object perceived to be excessively tall or large.

Christo had long been fascinated with vastness and its capacity to destabilize perception; in 1969 he expressed his admiration for the Great Wall of China, claiming that "its power derives from sheer expanse; it no longer makes sense because it has become alienated from its historic, geographical, and strategic contexts."[47] His remarks loop him into a broader conversation about land art, which the critic Elizabeth Baker memorably implied was an art of entitlement writ large. In 1976, she wrote that it did "not seem strange to Americans perfectly accustomed to altering the landscape endlessly, usually for an economic motive, that other Americans, even artists, should also do something to the face of the earth."[48] She saw land art as significantly defined by what Americans regarded as their right to mine, till, carve, and even demolish the land as they saw fit: "It is increasingly clear that from the beginning we have also had a national attitude that the land was there to be *used*."[49]

Christo and Jeanne-Claude also perceived scale as a function of the number and kinds of people involved in a work's construction and reception. "To take on a whole structure of people, a hundred people say, that is what matters—not the physical scale," said Christo in an interview published in August 1975.[50] Thinking about scale in this way, he added, was critical to ensuring the long-term viability of the so-called "art world" of some ten thousand people bound together by their common acceptance of a given set of conventions.[51] For this world to survive, the priority was not to attract larger audiences to museums, but to "get out of this scale of 10,000 people and set up a dialogue with other people—not to get people to understand or to love art, but do it . . . [not] always with the same people, who go to performances, galleries, and concerts . . . [but with] people who are not interested in art."[52] He suggested that *Running Fence* be construed in the light of site-specific works that fulfill, in the words of Robert Morris, "a service function rather than that of object production."[53]

But unlike the kinds of site-specific projects to which Morris was referring, *Running Fence* was very pointedly defined by its own status as a physical object, or rather objects. Part of the artists' intention was to build something so monumental as to make it impossible to think of selling or buying the work. Monumentality, for Christo and Jeanne-Claude, meant producing an experience that could be shared by any number of viewers but that also indicated when a given work could no longer belong to a single owner, presumably because of the viewing experience it offers.[54] What might be considered excessive length and height in a gallery or museum context were expedient ways of making sure that the work could not be easily transported in the manner expected of salable goods or, in Christo's term, "commodities."[55] In addition, resituating the panels, posts, and cables elsewhere would destroy the work, given the lengths to which Christo and Jeanne-Claude went to identify the land on which *Running Fence* was to run. This aspect effectively denied the work of its value as a transferable commodity, although it meant that photographs of the work would then gain economic value as the only tangible, lasting evidence of the work's existence.[56] Others saw the completed work itself as property with real value, cutting snippets of hooks and poles as presumed souvenirs.[57]

Christo and Jeanne-Claude's aspirations for the social, and possibly even political, implications of *Running Fence* intersected with the law's penchant for analogy and categorization. A physical object exceeding a particular size was recognized as a billboard, a structure, or a land development. When researching what permits they would have to acquire, the artists' contractors were told by a zoning official that a proposed fence over six feet high would be deemed a "structure" and therefore likely to be subjected to more stringent regulation, particularly in light of new federal and state laws concerning environmental protection.[58] In order to lessen the possibility that agencies would view the work as a structure subject to government regulation, Christo and Jeanne-Claude emphasized the nature of *Running Fence* as a "short-life work of modern art" in their draft permit application to the North Central Coast Conservation Commission, one of the first government agencies they faced.[59] To improve the chances that *Running Fence* would be seen primarily as an artwork, Peter Selz, the work's project director, lobbied museum directors for a show of Christo's work.[60]

Likewise, Christo showed at hearings numerous hand-drawn, large-format projections of the completed *Running Fence*. The emphatic presence of the hand in the coloring and sketching shows the work not just as a set of points on a map, but as an aesthetic object. By asserting to politicians, judges, and government employees that *Running Fence* was exclusively art, Christo and Jeanne-Claude inadvertently tested the authority of artists to define their work for others. The steady stream of questions Christo received suggested the limitations of that authority, especially as only a handful of those from whom permission was sought knew of land art. At the March 1975 Sonoma Board of Supervisors public hearing, a bewildered rancher asked how something so large could be art, insisting that "a curtain ten feet long and eighteen feet high is not art; it's not art if it's twenty-four *miles* long" (rancher's emphasis) (fig. 30).[61] The length was not unreasonably long for a fence in that particular part of the country, but the height far exceeded what the law deemed acceptable for a fence. The rancher's incredulity may have stemmed from general uncertainty as to whether *Running Fence*—or artwork of that scale and situation—was necessary.

In fact, some residents described the work as a *nuisance*, a legal term that in California referred to an unreasonable, unlawful, or otherwise unjustifiable use of property

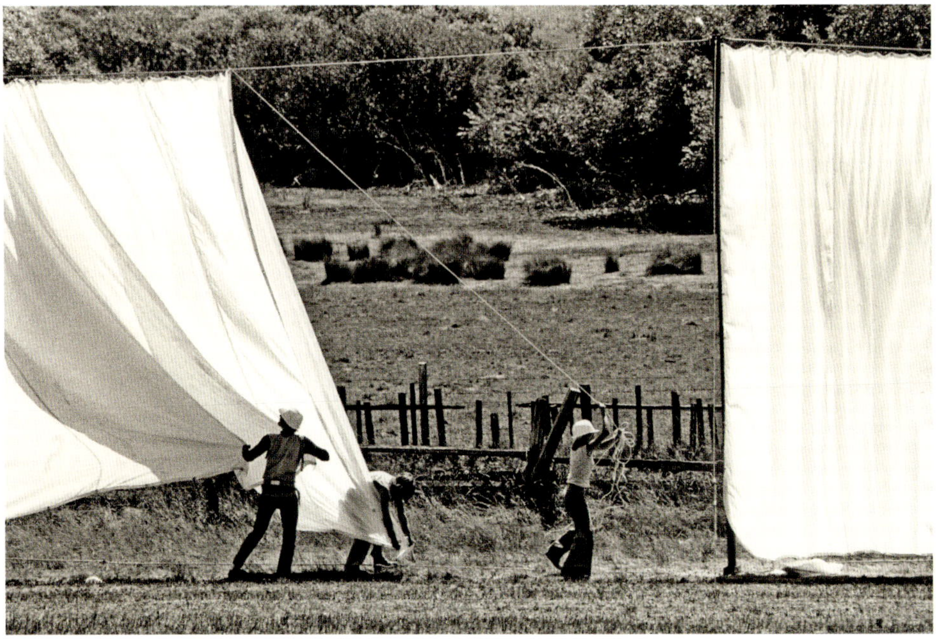

FIGURE 30
Christo and Jeanne-Claude, *Running Fence, Sonoma and Marin Counties, California, 1972–76,* hooking and pulling panels together, September 8–10, 1976. Smithsonian American Art Museum. Photo: Wolfgang Volz. © 1976, Christo.

that interferes with the rights of others. In early 1975, Lois Raymond, who lived within sight of the work's projected route and became cochair of the Committee to Stop the Running Fence, claimed that the work's dimensions were completely out of proportion with those of private residences, because at no point could homeowners escape from seeing the work. Many pointed out the likelihood of cars clogging the narrow roads, as well as the likelihood of air pollution caused by audiences coming to see the work by airplane. Some residents objected that those coming by car might park by the side of the road in order to inspect the work more closely, consequently raising the likelihood of crowds trespassing on both the land on which parts of *Running Fence* stood and adjacent lots.

These possibilities raised two related issues concerning the physical scale of the work. One was whether the likelihood of crowds trespassing on private property that had nothing to do with *Running Fence* outweighed the personal rights of other individuals to permit the work to occupy their own property. The other, which was only tacitly raised in the debates for and against the work's construction, was whether those ranchers who permitted the work to occupy their respective properties were, in fact, bad neighbors. Ownership reemerged in this situation as a case of competing rights, between those who agreed to let Christo and Jeanne-Claude erect parts of *Running Fence* on their land and those living nearby, as well as between the artists and their

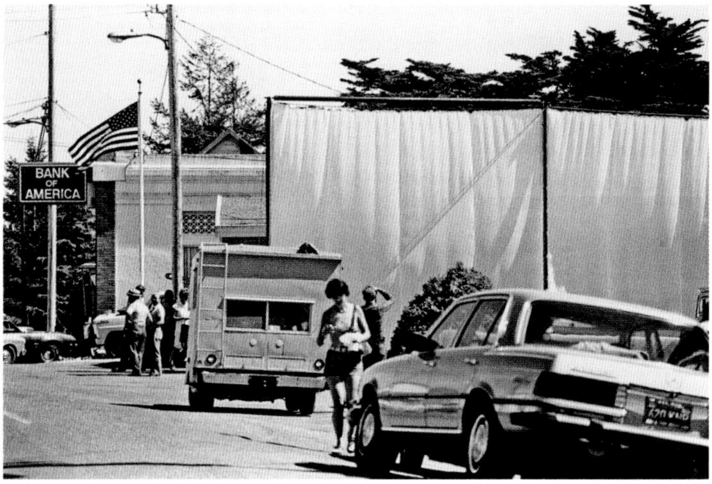

FIGURE 31
Christo and Jeanne-Claude, *Running Fence, Sonoma and Marin Counties, California, 1972–76, Segment 7: Valley Ford where the fence ends by the Post Office*, September 10–20, 1976, 15¾ × 23¼ inches. Smithsonian American Art Museum. Photo: Wolfgang Volz. © 1976, Christo.

closest audience. At the heart of the objections was a tacit fear as to whether the artists, through *Running Fence*, were trying to compress the scales at which the individual homeowner, the neighborhood, and the community operated into the overarching idea of a public. Several complaints specifically named Christo as the culprit, as if he were solely and personally responsible for erecting the work.

Photographs taken during the construction of *Running Fence* unwittingly support these anxieties. Similar to Christo's drawings, many of which show the work from the perspective of the viewer, several photos show bodies near the panels as if to dispel suspicions of the work being out of touch with human scale (fig. 31). Conversely, photos taken from an aerial perspective capture how the work appears to mimic the lines indicating routes on a map, which in turn recalls how many maps are scaled to human hands (fig. 32). Pulsing through these images is a tension between the scale of the human (the imagined user of maps) and the map itself on which human bodies are not marked at all. In photos taken during and after construction, *Running Fence* calls attention to itself in a manner somewhat different from that assumed by its objectors who regarded land art or "earth art" as so intently demanding a kind of attention to itself as to be a form of territorial possession. In contrast, the photos show the work operating at a less intense valence; in them *Running Fence* registers neither as a form of intrusion nor as the primary focus of attention. Even close-up photographs show the work as making sense only when its dependence on the ground is made known (fig. 33).

The dimensions of the work, and more importantly the projected amount of money and material to be spent in its construction, prompted Marin and Sonoma county citizens to compare *Running Fence* to a land development project.[62] At least one of the regulatory agencies from which Christo and Jeanne-Claude were required to obtain a permit agreed, especially as some of Christo and Jeanne-Claude's negotiation tactics, which included enlisting political and art-world personalities to call local commissioners

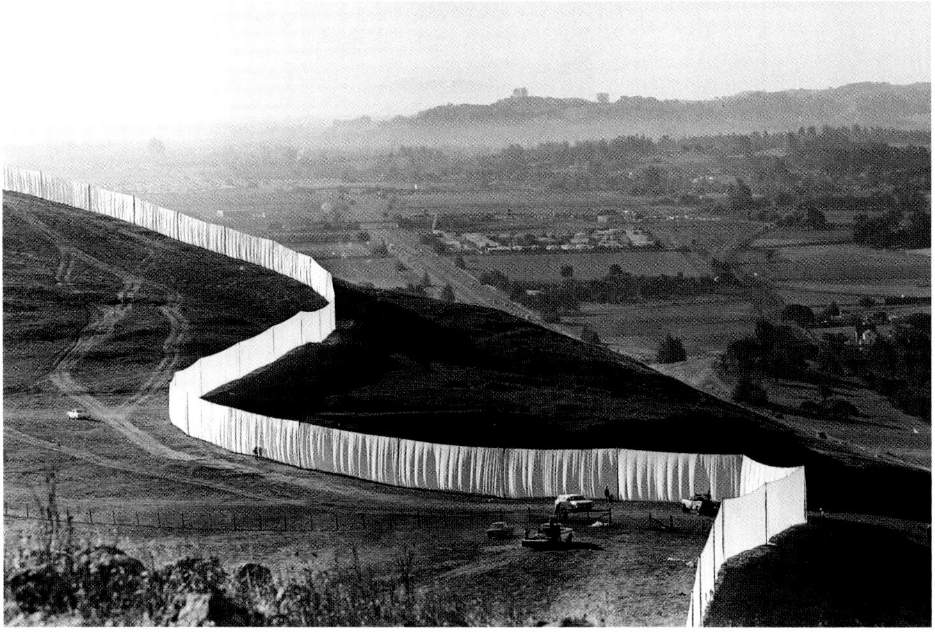

FIGURE 32
Detail of Christo and Jeanne-Claude, *Running Fence, Sonoma and Marin Counties,* 1976. Photo: Ernest Murphy.

and inviting them to receptions, were comparable to those used by land developers seeking permission to construct their projects.[63] Reviewing the artists' request to take *Running Fence* into the waters off the Marin County coast, the California Coastal Commission used their own words as evidence that the work was, in fact, a development. If indeed "the process of developing, planning, implementing . . . is the most important artistic aspect" of *Running Fence,* then there appeared to be no difference between any land developer and an artist.[64] The commission concluded that it must treat *Running Fence* "as it would every other proposed development, and not accord it special treatment."[65]

County agencies were mollified by what they saw as the possibility of shared community gain from the building and display of *Running Fence.* As was noted by at least one state agency, the Sonoma County Board of Supervisors voted four to one to grant a permit to Christo and Jeanne-Claude because of the economic gains the work promised for the county, including temporary employment numbering in the hundreds and considerable income resulting from tourists coming to see the work.[66] The proposed work itself became an argument for less regulation; not interfering with the construction would not only make investment easier, it would also create jobs and stimulate the economy, factors of considerable importance in this economically depressed part of California.

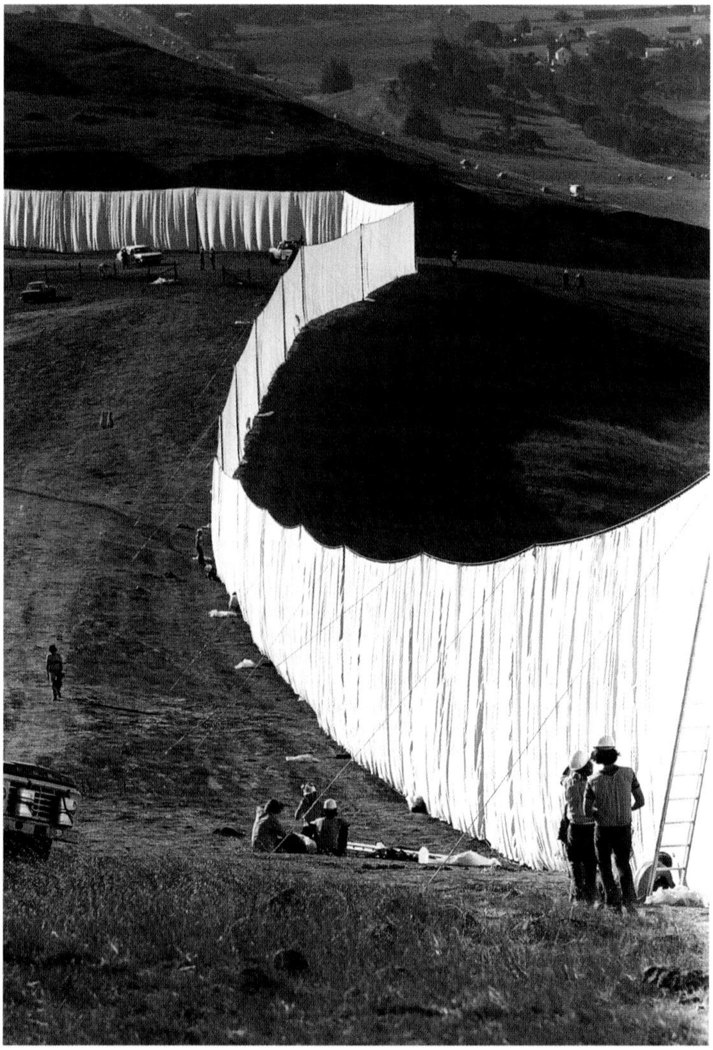

FIGURE 33
Detail of Christo and Jeanne-Claude, *Running Fence, Sonoma and Marin Counties,* 1976. Photo: Ernest Murphy. © 1976, Christo. Photo use by permission of Ernest Murphy.

On one hand, the proposal of *Running Fence* brought forth a multiplicity of viewpoints that under other circumstances might not be expressed. On the other, the proposal could also be seen as a co-optation analogous to how large businesses work, where the scale of operation is so overwhelming as to preclude the possibility of resistance or critique. This latter concern lay at the heart of the many objections levied against the work, that what was being presumably championed in the socially benign name of art was far too close to the structures lawmakers and politicians were publicly charged with overseeing. Christo and Jeanne-Claude professed satisfaction with the controversy their work provoked, mentioning that the debates for and against its erection resembled those surrounding the construction of a new town, or a highway, yet the parallels drawn between *Running Fence* and land development worked against their quest for permission.[67]

By approaching Sonoma County authorities for a permit to erect *Running Fence,* the artists also faced some of the fiercest skeptics of private construction in the country. In 1968, a private real estate developer building an exclusive residential enclave over a vast stretch of Sonoma County coastline had conceded only 120 acres for the construction of a public park. Although the development was initially accepted by the Board of Supervisors, it was soon bitterly contested by local citizens who held that public access to the coastline was an inviolable right. Among the most vocal of these protesters was Bill Kortum, the only Sonoma County supervisor to vote against Christo and Jeanne-Claude's petition. To him, the hearing over the art project was nothing short of a civil war between land developers and environmentalists who wanted to preserve the area's agricultural character.[68] Fears that *Running Fence* was an elaborate profit-making scheme intended to enrich the artists at the possible expense of Sonoma and Marin county residents were endemic, a symptom of what in that region had been a long-entrenched protectionism against corporate developers.[69] In that spirit, local citizens including Kortum and Virginia Hechtman had banded together to protest the anticipated threat to public access to the coast, efforts that resulted in the formation of advocacy group COAAST, or Californians Organized to Acquire Access to State Tidelands.[70]

The analogy between *Running Fence* and corporate development was supported by the size of each fabric panel, which from afar looked to some like a billboard (fig. 34). A species of public display figuring prominently in the expansion of nuisance law, the billboard was a major barometer gauging courts' views of when and how police power could be exercised on aesthetic grounds throughout the first half of the twentieth century. As early as 1911, courts permitted police and legislatures to regulate billboards because of their constituent materials, shape, and size. Generally long, tall, and made of a continuous sheet of wood, metal, plastic, or even paper, the billboard was regarded by courts as big enough to shield criminals from public view, yet not sturdy enough to avoid becoming a community hazard in times of inclement weather.[71] As an advertisement intended to project a given message to a large group of people, courts saw the billboard as having a distinct front, but also an equally prominent back, behind which people might be tempted to unlawfully dispose of their trash.

U.S. courts increasingly moved away from the general rule set forth in the 1932 case *Perlmutter v. Greene.* In that situation, the New York Court of Appeals had allowed police or legislatures to restrict property rights for aesthetic concerns so long as some issue of public safety, health, or morals was involved.[72] Numerous legislatures throughout the United States consequently placed considerable limits on the size and position of billboards and the frequency with which they could be erected, while others restricted the proximity at which a billboard could be erected to an area of scenic or historical importance.[73] In his classic article on zoning and aesthetics, legal scholar

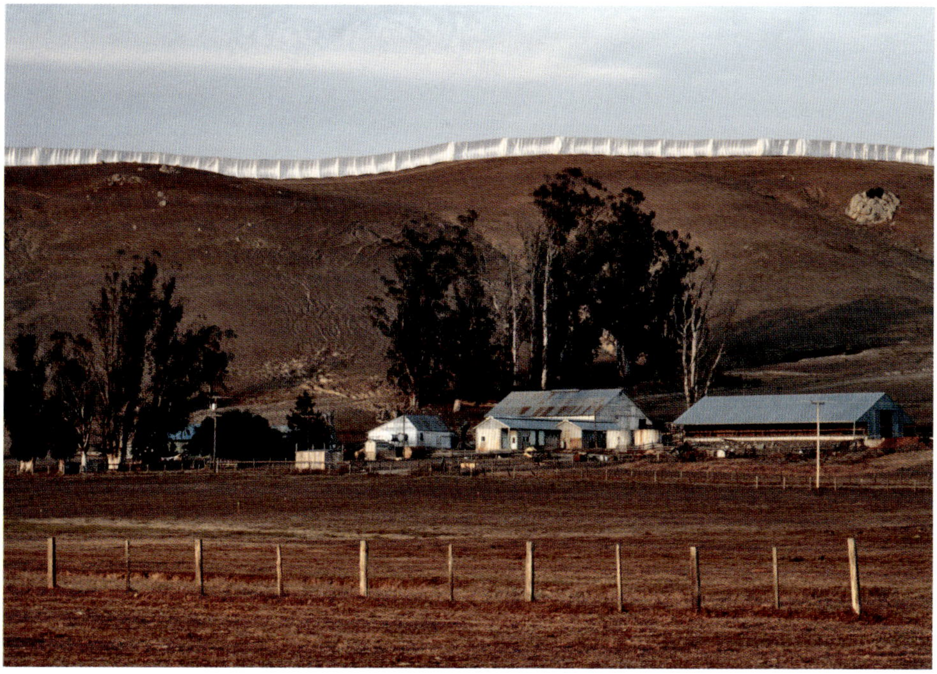

FIGURE 34
Christo and Jeanne-Claude, *Running Fence, Sonoma and Marin Counties, California, 1972–76, Segment 17*, September 10–20, 1976. Smithsonian American Art Museum. Photo: Wolfgang Volz. © 1976, Christo.

J.J. Dukeminier suggested in 1955 that courts had gone too far in allowing such restrictions, instead proposing that they should be applied only to prevent "serious" damage to the immediate surroundings.[74] The trend seemed to move in the other direction by the early 1970s, yet courts still accepted that the idea of public welfare encompassed aesthetic issues arising from what the average citizen could see as well as hear and smell.[75]

But the materials Christo and Jeanne-Claude proposed using, and the construction process itself, made it difficult to classify their work exclusively as a development. Despite using steel posts that were taller and thicker than those used for actual fences, the work itself was not continuous, stopping intermittently to let cars and animals pass (fig. 35), an important aspect that deflected possible accusations that the work was a malicious attempt to prevent neighbors from "reasonable enjoyment" of their own property.[76] The choice of white for *Running Fence* seems tactical; there is an association not only with the proverbial white picket fence, but also with the idea of keeping within preexisting conventions—in short, of being proper.

Although *Running Fence* was not a legal nuisance, it upset some who regarded its size and scale as symptoms of an ethically suspect indifference to the work's immediate surroundings. Addressing the deceptively utopian premises of what he called "non-size," a

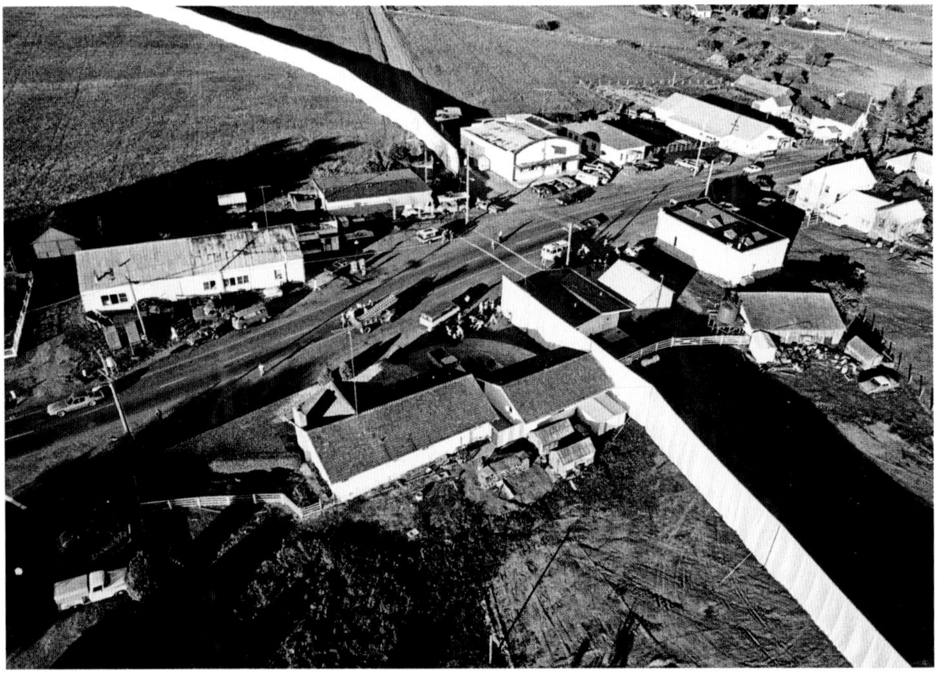

FIGURE 35
Christo and Jeanne-Claude, *Running Fence, Sonoma and Marin Counties, California, 1972–76, Segments 8 and 7: Valley Ford,* from helicopter, September 10–20, 1976. Smithsonian American Art Museum. Photo: Wolfgang Volz. © 1976, Christo.

characteristic ascribed to the critical mass of artworks so long or so large as to have no reliable point of comparison, artist Douglas Davis criticized *Running Fence* for what he took as its disregard of context. That its size required the involvement of so many people highlighted the importance of process and social relationships, yet that very size also encouraged prospective viewers to bypass consideration of the immediate, local grounds on which the work physically stood in favor of more abstract, general ideas about the land. Perhaps more troubling still, in Davis's view, was what he saw as the teleology encompassed by the process of construction—that for all its emphasis on process, the end result was simply "to produce a Christo."[77] The problem was the ease with which Christo and Jeanne-Claude, and the process of constructing *Running Fence,* seemed to dismiss outright the distinction between art and life. The distinction mattered, Davis argued, if only to remind ourselves that situating artworks outside the gallery necessarily meant having to compromise with the social ecology already in place in a particular area.

THE ENVIRONMENT: TAKING SIDES

Building *Running Fence* was not simply a matter of temporarily using someone else's property, but required significant commitment from those whose legal responsibility it was to maintain equilibrium between private interests and those of the community at large.[78] For officials like Michael Fischer, executive director of the North Central Region of the Coastal Zone Conservation Commission from 1973 to 1976, this duty meant reifying a particular kind of scale whereby "man's built works should be subordinate to the natural land forms, and that man should not dominate the earth, but instead be part of it."[79] The art-versus-life distinction mattered, for although *Running Fence* might be "benign and temporary," other examples of land art were "utterly antithetical to the philosophy and spirit" of government agencies entrusted to protect nature by putting humans and human development in their place.[80]

Being able to define *Running Fence* as an artwork became even more necessary given how courts and legislatures in the late 1960s and early '70s separated land into two conceptual streams. The first was land as property. As the long, contentious process of obtaining permission from individual landowners indicated, this category was less a classification than a responsibility to consider the precarious intersection of ownership rights and public interest. The second category was land as environment, which both federal and California law in the 1970s increasingly defined as an inherently public space whose proposed use meant assuming a duty to care. It included the physical surroundings and the general welfare of those presently inhabiting the land as well as those who might use the land in the future.

Valley Curtain gave Christo and Jeanne-Claude a foretaste of what objections environmental activists might raise. Recognizing the political necessity of at least entertaining such concerns, Christo and van der Marck met at length with the Colorado Open Space Council, a private nonprofit initially formed in the wake of the federal Wilderness Act, passed by Congress in 1964 to protect those areas "where the earth and its community of life are untrammeled by man, where man himself is a visitor who does not remain."[81] While many members of the group remained unconvinced of the work's appropriateness, they nevertheless considered it minor compared to "the dangers of air pollution, underground atomic explosions and the 1976 Winter Olympics."[82]

California had some of the toughest pro-environmental legislation in the country. Incidents such as the February 1969 oil spill near Santa Barbara, then the largest in U.S. history, and accelerated rates of pollution and land development sparked increased environmental activism. Sonoma County, where most of *Running Fence* would be built, saw the rise of several environmentalist groups after high-profile corporations tried to install nuclear reactors on seismically unstable land or develop private enclaves that would bar public access to the coast. Environmentalist concerns were given a special boost by the National Environmental Policy Act (NEPA). Signed into law on January 1, 1970, it required every federal agency to consider environmental issues in their decision-making processes. NEPA also signaled the beginning of the end of what in the late 1960s had been the proliferation of land art; as Suzaan Boettger has pointed out, Heizer could execute *Double Negative* without having to secure government permission because it took place before NEPA was passed.[83]

Among the fifty states, California was one of the earliest and most enthusiastic proponents of NEPA, legislating its own version, the California Environmental Quality Act (CEQA), in September of that same year. The speed with which the state enacted CEQA also led to a number of glaring procedural holes, namely when relevant state agencies were to determine projects whose effects would require the submission of an Environmental Impact Report (EIR).[84] Such a report was to describe the environmental impact of the proposed action, any adverse or irreversible effects, measures designed to minimize the impact and effects, as well as alternatives to the proposed action.[85] Although this was not mentioned or anticipated in CEQA, the EIR—"the heart of CEQA"—almost always required extended professional engineering and scientific analysis, which was expensive and time consuming.[86] CEQA, moreover, coincided with a series of major changes in environmental regulation, including the passage of the California Coastal Zone Conservation Act in 1972. Also known as Proposition 20, the act established a statewide commission as well as six regional commissions that wielded extraordinary power over coastal development.[87] The ambiguity of CEQA's original wording provoked considerable litigation, the first instance of which was *Friends of Mammoth v. Board of Supervisors of Moro County.* Decided by the Supreme Court of California in September 1972, it expanded the purview of CEQA to include both public and private projects. Anxious to uphold the relatively new law, the *Mammoth* court read the California legislation as requiring an EIR "not only when a proposed project will have a significant environmental effect, but also when it 'may' or 'could.'"[88]

Although the *Mammoth* court's expansion of CEQA became widely cited in other environmental litigation, it contained a pointed dissent by one judge who argued that the California legislature did not intend the EIR requirement to be applied to projects undertaken by private individuals or entities.[89] Certainly, other authorities in California were much more leery of expanding the provisions of CEQA. In April 1973, Sonoma County granted the Environmental Protection Committee the power to determine whether a "private project which would ordinarily be expected to have a significant effect on the environment will have no significant effect on the environment due to circumstances peculiar to the specific private project." The wording offered flexibility by essentially giving those proposing projects—most likely real estate developers with strong support—the opportunity to make their case to the committee. Yet, in a move calculated to appease environmentalist demands, the ordinance then directed the committee to indicate that an EIR is required if it finds that the project "may" have a significant effect on the environment.[90]

Despite considerable resistance to what some critics saw as an undue burden on property rights, California as a whole moved toward more intensive regulation along the lines set by *Mammoth.* At the end of 1974, the Supreme Court of California significantly expanded the circumstances under which EIRs were required in *No Oil, Inc. v. City of Los Angeles.* Emphasizing how CEQA applied to projects that "may" have a significant effect on the environment, the court also gave wide latitude to the term *significant*, declaring that it should not be limited to projects that might have an "important" or "momentuous" effect, but followed *Mammoth* by extending the term's interpretation if it meant affording "the fullest possible protection to the environment within the reasonable scope of the statutory language."[91] Yet, as the lone dissent noted, the court did future jurists a disservice by declining to propose a test for determining "what constitutes a 'significant effect' on the environment."[92] The confusion over "significant effects" reflected an ongoing battle between environmentalists and their opponents over such proposed legislation as the Coastal Plan, which would significantly limit the kinds of developments allowed in the name of protecting the coast.

Running Fence put this struggle in decisively allegorical terms in a way that clarified the interests at stake. Equally as challenging as negotiating easement agreements with various landowners was securing permission from county and state authorities, beginning in November 1974. Initially, the process of securing permits was remarkably smooth. Authorities in both Marin and Sonoma counties granted Christo and Jeanne-Claude permits to erect their work in February and March 1975. Almost concurrently, they succeeded in obtaining a noncommercial lease to use the tide and submerged lands in the ocean from the California State Lands Commission, an agency charged with protecting natural and cultural resources as well as access rights. Christo and Jeanne-Claude crafted this petition around claims that the beach and waters they hoped to use were largely unused, hence obviating the public-access question. Their legal team further stressed that the land would be restored to the condition in which the artists found it: "No trace of the project will remain after [the work's] removal."[93] Shortly thereafter, in April, the North Central Coast Regional Commission granted Christo and Jeanne-Claude a permit to extend *Running Fence* into the waters of Dillon Beach.[94]

In recommending that the artists be granted their permit, the North Central Coast Regional Commission emphasized that they assumed complete financial responsibility for any failure in restoring the land to its original condition.[95] This unwittingly insinuated that one could use even protected land so long as one could pay for that right, particularly when the use in question had been previously reviewed. By putting the artists' petition on the consent calendar, an action designed to save committees time by designating certain issues as noncontroversial, Margaret Azevedo, chair of the North Central Coast Commission, made it clear that permission should be granted as a matter of course. In a memorandum explaining her decision, she urged colleagues to dismiss as "totally irrelevant" questions regarding the costs and status of the work.[96]

The relative ease with which Christo and Jeanne-Claude secured their permits roused their opponents, as indicated by COAAST reversing its initial decision not to take a position on *Running Fence*.[97] That the passage of the Coastal Plan was far from certain played a key role in the reversal, as the group acknowledged in an April 8, 1975, letter to the North Central Coast Regional Commission.[98] Strategically, the publicity surrounding *Running Fence* would be useful in calling attention to the environmentalist cause. COAAST then appealed the permit by taking its case to the California

Coastal Commission, which duly granted the group a hearing for June 4, 1975.[99] To refute the assurances the artists and their supporters made, COAAST retained Joel Hedgpeth, a locally celebrated marine biologist. Christo and Jeanne-Claude's legal team tried to justify the work on the basis that they were only interested in the art, a strategy that failed precisely because it did little to deter authorities from seeing its material scope.

The Coastal Commission resoundingly voted against issuing the permit. In a letter to Christo, commission director Joseph Bodovitz tersely stated that the artists failed to meet "the burden of proof that the proposed development would be consistent with the objectives of the California Coastal Zone Conservation Act."[100] The accompanying staff recommendation saw the coastal area in question as being in need of an especially high level of care ("fragile, generally unspoiled, and relatively isolated"), while insinuating that *Running Fence* would be a magnet for interlopers and even defilers ("Into this area the applicant proposes to bring a corps of consultants . . . and large but unpredictable number of spectators").[101] The Coastal Commission all but made rebuttal impossible by repeatedly mentioning that it was impossible to predict how many people the work would in fact attract to the protected area, but also envisioning a worst-case scenario (clogging of major coastal access roads and interference with recreational travel). So pessimistic was the commission's outlook that it regarded as inevitable the possible consequences of the risks posed by *Running Fence,* finding "no legal basis for excusing long-term environmental damage on grounds the cause of it was on display for only two weeks."[102]

Part of the Coastal Commission's protectionism came from its own understanding of water as being itself land, an aspect inadvertently underscored by Christo's own preparatory drawings showing poles driven into the seabed (fig. 36). Another possible reason was Bodovitz's personal disapproval of what he suggested was the special treatment of *Running Fence* on account of its artistic status.[103] About two weeks later, the Sonoma County Superior Court admitted for hearing the protests of the Committee to Stop the Running Fence, which had been formed on February 27, 1975. Led by Lois Raymond, the group enumerated the usual concerns: excessive traffic caused by curiosity seekers, the related risk of crowds and crowd control, the possibility that the work might encumber wildlife, and sight pollution. Leaning heavily on the *Mammoth* and *No Oil* precedents, which warned that a negative finding of significant environmental impact may not be used to avoid the preparation of an EIR, the court decided in favor of *Running Fence*'s opponents, ruling that the work was "a project which strongly suggests the likelihood . . . of significant and adverse environmental impacts."[104]

That the Sonoma County Superior Court strongly favored the arguments raised by the Committee to Stop the Running Fence was demonstrated by how it seemed to conflate remote possibility with impending likelihood. Even the submitted permit application, the conditions of the permit, and the precautions undertaken by the Running Fence Corporation were all construed as "substantial evidence" that the work "may

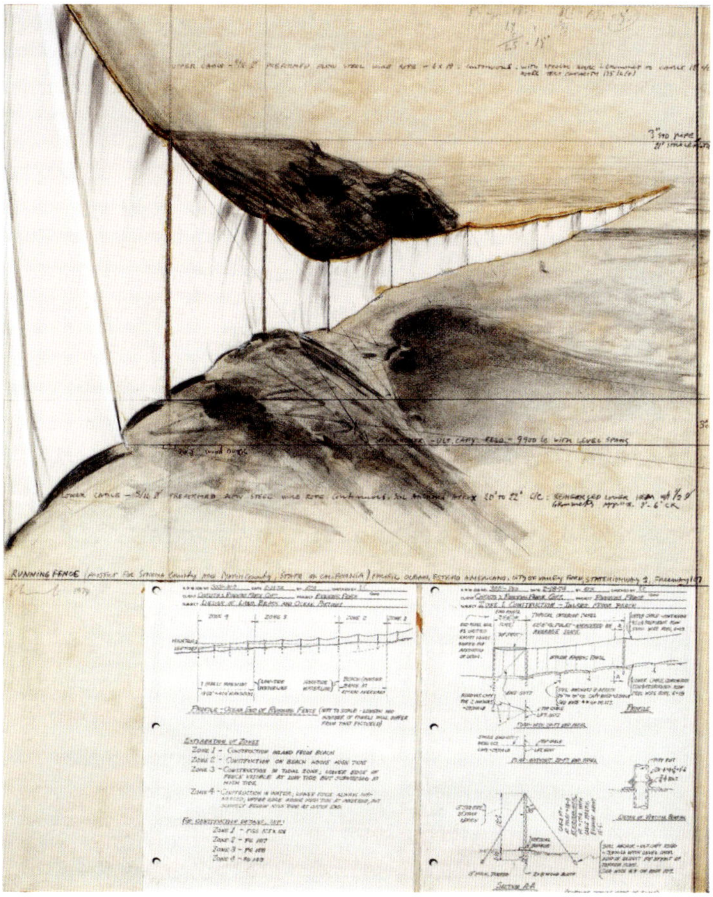

FIGURE 36
Christo, *Running Fence (Project for Marin County and Sonoma County, State of California)*, 1974. Pencil, fabric, charcoal, paper collage, ballpoint pen, staples, glue on paper on cardboard, 71.5 × 55.5 centimeters. © 1974, Christo.

have a significant adverse effect environmentally."[105] Presiding over the court was John Golden, a judge brought in from neighboring Lake County in order to maintain the court's impartiality, as *Running Fence* did not cross Lake County. Although his usual jurisdiction would be unaffected by the work's erection, Golden still ruled for the Committee to Stop the Running Fence, quickly deciding two days after the June 17 hearing that avoiding or mitigating adverse environmental impact was an issue best decided after an EIR was submitted. Golden lowered the trigger point for the EIR requirement so that even proposed relief measures accepted by agencies empowered with deciding whether an EIR was required were still not enough to avoid the duty of providing such.

The ruling was the strongest setback yet for Christo and Jeanne-Claude. It effectively stopped construction on *Running Fence* until the artists could have a time-consuming and costly EIR prepared and reviewed. Although they quickly appealed to the California Court of Appeal to block the Sonoma County Superior Court from taking any further action to stop construction on *Running Fence*, the artists went ahead and commissioned an EIR at the sizable cost of $39,000 (in 1975 dollars) as a preemptive measure and possibly to acknowledge the relatively tight environmental protection laws. The report they submitted was even more elaborate and detailed than other examples, in part because after projects like *Valley Curtain* and the wrapping of MCA Chicago, Christo and Jeanne-Claude were well aware of the value of paperwork overkill and the strategy of overwhelming skeptics with as many details as possible.

On September 17, 1975, the California Court of Appeal decided in favor of the Running Fence Corporation, holding that the lower court had erred in ordering the Sonoma County Board of Supervisors to withhold permission until the corporation submitted an EIR before proceeding further with the erection of *Running Fence*. Citing CEQA, which granted each public agency the right to decide for itself whether a given action constituted a significant effect on the environment, the higher court stated that the lower court had no standing to reject the decisions of those agencies empowered to decide upon whether an EIR was necessary, in this case Sonoma County's Environmental Protection Committee, Board of Zoning Adjustments, and Board of Supervisors. That the Board of Supervisors had adopted less stringent standards for determining when an EIR was needed was not for the lower court to rule on; its primary responsibility was to adhere to the county code: "The determination of the effect or impact on the environment relates to the project in the form in which it is applied for and approved, not as it might otherwise have been constructed or conducted."[106] The higher court capped its opinion with unusually strong language, declaring that "the conclusion of the local agency . . . is unassailable."[107]

While the higher court largely justified its decision on grounds of preserving jurisdictional borders per county and state codes, it also interpreted precedent in favor of the Running Fence Corporation. It read the *No Oil* case, for example, as saying that even though temporary projects might sufficiently affect the environment to require an EIR, there first had to be "substantial evidence to suggest that possibility."[108] Mindful of the considerable outlay of time, money, and effort needed in commissioning and processing an EIR, the court remarked that determining when relevant substantial evidence existed should be done on a case-by-case basis. *Running Fence*, for instance, was an exception because there was "no substantial evidence here that the project will have other than a negligible and temporary effect on the environment."[109] The court likened the work to legal exemptions to the EIR rule, "including carnivals, sales of Christmas trees, etc."[110] The higher court further insinuated that the lower court was unduly swayed by the volume and intensity of public opinion:

> We reject the inference that the existence of factual controversy, uncertainty, conflicting assertions, argument, or public controversy can of themselves nullify the adoption of a negative declaration and require the preparation of an EIR when there is no substantial evidence in the record that the project as designed and approved will fall within the requirements of the act.[111]

In a footnote, the higher court practically reprimanded the lower court, adding somewhat caustically that "we, therefore, do not attempt to extract the wheat of environmental protest from the chaff of aesthetic displeasure in the voluminous clippings presented by the protestants."[112]

Following the court's decision, the Marin County Board of Supervisors agreed to extend Christo and Jeanne-Claude's permit in September of that year so that *Running Fence* could be completed in the fall of 1976. The next, and most important, challenge would be the December 3, 1975, hearing in front of the Sonoma County Board of Zoning Adjustments. Given that the majority of the work would be physically situated in Sonoma County, getting approval at this hearing would conclusively determine whether *Running Fence* would be constructed at all.

LAW SITS ON THE *FENCE*

An important subtext running throughout the hearings and consequent litigation were the twin concepts of use and harm. Early debates over *Running Fence* turned on the question of its potential to be used in a practical context. Ranchers supporting the work's construction made clear their views concerning the anticipated use of the work once deinstalled and dismantled into its constituent material parts; such parts had value because they conferred future economic benefit through reuse or sale. Others mentioned the jobs and tourist dollars likely to result from the work's construction. In contrast, critics who refused to acknowledge *Running Fence* as art insinuated that it was so absolutely useless that it could not even be classified within a category basically defined by the absence of practical utility. Christo himself denied that the project had any specific purpose, calling the work "unusable."[113] Such characterization was a judicious move, for in distancing *Running Fence* from the notion of use so encumbered by issues of cost, benefit, and impact, Christo deflected attention away from comparisons likening the work to corporate development.

The conflict over *Running Fence*'s apparent use, or usefulness, soon overlapped with broader conventions concerning the use of particular kinds of land. The late 1960s to early '70s saw considerable activity among federal and, especially, California courts and legislatures seeking to regulate the types and frequency of actions that could take place on various categories of land, a general predilection that puts into context the arguments made for and against *Running Fence*. One of the laws most often cited by protesters was the so-called Williamson Act. Officially known as the California Land Conservation Act of 1965, it exempted owners of farmland and open-space land from paying property taxes for ten years so long as they agreed not to develop the land or use it for any other purpose. The only exceptions were certain recreational uses. In anticipation of the December 3, 1975, hearing before the Sonoma County Board of Supervisors that would decide whether *Running Fence* would be built at all, local homeowner Ronald Raymond claimed that the work violated the Williamson Act by obstructing public views of rural areas designated as open spaces.[114] At the hearing, another resident stated it was not enough for the artist to claim nonviolation of the act by simply refraining from charging the public for admission to see the work.[115]

The centerpiece of the hearing was the 450-page draft EIR that Christo submitted to the Sonoma County Board of Zoning Adjustments. It meticulously described all aspects of *Running Fence*'s construction, including a full explanation of its objectives, materials, and stages, its legal history to date, and the social, economic, biological, and physical conditions of its projected route. One of its appendices even listed types of birds known to migrate near that route. The EIR repeatedly downplayed the anticipated impact *Running Fence* would have on the natural environment. Despite its immense size, the number of people potentially affected as either residents or visitors, and a fairly complex process of construction and deinstallation, *Running Fence* was continually characterized as a delicate structure; near the very beginning of the EIR, Christo described the fence as having the "special beauties of impermanence. The fabric is a light-conductor for the sunlight, and it will give shape to the wind. It will go over the hills and into the sea, like a ribbon of light."[116] The description supported the report's insistence that the work would inflict no harm to the environment, an important consideration given the acute sensitivity of local politicians to how environmentalist concerns affected their own chances of remaining in office.

But as Ronald Raymond's criticism alleged, the matter of harm was inextricably tied to questions of use linked to the identity of the alleged user. In a November 1975 letter to the Sonoma County Board of Zoning Adjustments, Raymond asserted that because Christo and Jeanne-Claude were undertaking the construction as a corporation, *Running Fence* must necessarily be seen as a commercial venture in violation of the Williamson Act.[117] The December 1975 hearing initially read as a conflict between the rights of a few private landowners and those ascribed to the public good. Certainly, many ranchers came to support Christo and Jeanne-Claude's plans as a means of defending what they saw as the sacrosanct right of all landowners to do as they pleased with their own property, a concern that resonated widely among rural landowners whose land was subject to regulation by the California Coastal Commission.[118] Yet the hearing was more symptomatic of the precarious balancing test between different kinds of property rights and the agitation such tests provoked. If hearing attendees were visibly upset, it was because *Running Fence* obviated divisions established by long-standing assumptions regarding property. Eventually, the Board of Zoning Adjustments accepted the EIR. Following the hearing, the county's Board of Supervisors granted Christo and Jeanne-Claude an extension to use the properties over which they and their lawyers had negotiated easement agreements. The State Lands Commission also extended their lease agreement in February 1976, noting in particular the temporary nature of the work.[119]

In the deliberations over whether to reissue the lease, Joel Hedgpeth suggested that Christo and Jeanne-Claude stop the fence on "top of a hill and build a big circle. I think that would be much more interesting." In this way, *Running Fence* directed others to consider the land as an aesthetic proposition. Mervyn Dynally, lieutenant governor of California and a commissioner for the State Lands Commission, sharply deflected Hedgpeth's argument that Christo and Jeanne-Claude's work would bar access to the beach: the "public" to which Hedgpeth was referring was not "the poor" or tourists, but "a very exclusive group of people who want to preserve the beach for themselves."[120] Dynally added that *Running Fence* did the opposite: not only would it not undermine property rights or public access to the beach, "it would make it open to the public," an issue that would prove decisive in a later stage of the case.[121] Here, "the public" referred to those who were "proper" citizens and not "hippies" who would consider the beach a temporary home. At the same time, how the word *public* was defined varied. In April 1976, the North Central Coast Regional Commission approved Christo and Jeanne-Claude's petition to renew their permit to stake part of *Running Fence* in a small section of tidal and offshore land. Construction began at the end of the month.[122]

DEEDS OF ENTITLEMENT

The hearing for the appeal before the California Coastal Commission was planned for September 23, 1976, after the expected completion date of *Running Fence.* Christo and Jeanne-Claude could have decided to reroute the work so as to avoid having to obtain permission from the Coastal Commission, but their determination to exercise their right of creation overcame their patience and, perhaps, their prudence (fig. 37). By this time there could be no further delay, lest the imminent onset of the rainy fall season make both construction and display impossible. Not completing the work by the end of 1976 would, moreover, force Christo and Jeanne-Claude to restart the process of negotiating easement agreements and acquiring permits, which were valid only until the end of the calendar year. Their impatience was translated in no uncertain terms by their lawyers, who declared any prohibition on *Running Fence* as "unconscionable abuse."

Up to this point, Christo and Jeanne-Claude had operated within the law by repeating again and again that their actions would not violate its parameters. But this most recent denial seemed to illustrate the inability of current models of regulation to sufficiently acknowledge what the artists saw as their legitimate rights. Many observers sympathetic to the artists saw these rights as a freedom-of-expression matter, describing the protests against *Running Fence* and the various legal obstructions as tantamount to censorship.[123] Yet for Christo and Jeanne-Claude, the rights at stake were more entwined with the concepts of ownership and authorship.

In April 1975, the *San Francisco Examiner and Chronicle* reported Christo as "fiercely" asserting that "it is my right to do anything with that money."[124] Courts seemed to agree. In September 1975, the California Court of Appeal recognized the energy and capital invested in building *Running Fence.* Since he "had tailored his project and is willing to accept conditions which the appropriate agency finds will render the project such that it will not have a substantial adverse effect on the environment," there should be no reason to "further delay the project in the absence of evidence that the

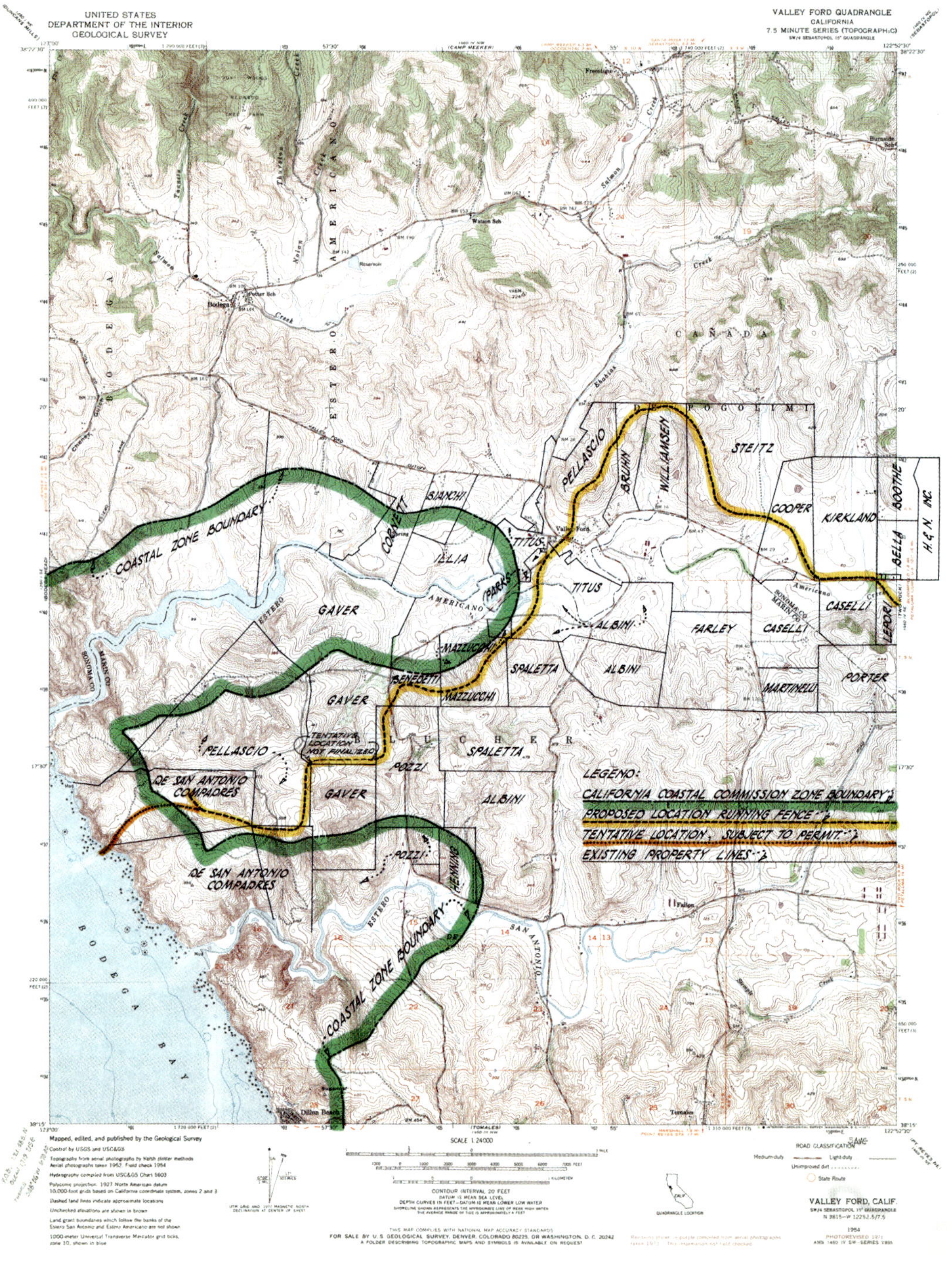

FIGURE 37

Christo and Jeanne-Claude, *Running Fence, Sonoma and Marin Counties, California, 1972–76, Valley Ford Quadrangle, CA.* Topographic map with proposed *Running Fence,* 1954, revised 1971, undated inscriptions, ink and felt-tip pen on color printed paper, Smithsonian American Art Museum. © 1971, Christo.

project as designed and projected and approved will have a substantial adverse effect as a matter of law."[125] But Christo and Jeanne-Claude had still not received permission by the end of 1975 to install the last section of *Running Fence* in the waters controlled by the Coastal Commission. The work's associate project director, Lynn Hershman, stated that Christo and Jeanne-Cluade had no intention of doing anything illegal and, in fact, did not know that installing the last part of the fence would be against the law.[126] Tomkins claimed that Christo and Jeanne-Claude deliberately weighed the advantages and disadvantages of proceeding with construction, permit or no permit.[127] He quoted Christo as suggesting the issue was nothing less than an assertion of his own right to creation: "If I go to jail and people ask why I am there, I will say I am building my fence."[128]

The artists' truculence coincided with a considerable amount of tactical maneuvering on the part of their lawyers. Originally scheduled to vote on Christo and Jeanne-Claude's appeal in the last week of June 1976, the Coastal Commission was requested by the artist's legal team to postpone the vote until August.[129] Reluctant to delay the vote any longer than necessary, especially since its authority would expire should the proposed Coastal Plan fail to pass the vote, the Coastal Commission later offered Christo and Jeanne-Claude's legal team a choice of two dates, August 11 or September 23.[130] The latter date was chosen on July 28, more than a month after the commission was slated to pass final judgment on Christo and Jeanne-Claude's appeal.[131] The postponement effectively created a window of time in which the artists could build and remove their work in its entirety. Should the vote take place in late June when the work had yet to be substantially completed, there would be no such chance, particularly if the commission denied the appeal. Any injunction issued as a result of the denial would take some time to be processed, an aspect of legal bureaucracy Hodes and local attorney Edwin Anderson knew very well. Paul Kayfetz, whom the artists hired to be their lead attorney on environmental issues, assured the Coastal Commission that his clients would not take the work into the water without permission.[132] But Bodovitz remained suspicious of the artists' intentions, and the commission consequently sought a temporary restraining order through the state attorney general in order to immediately stop any possible construction in the water.[133]

Running Fence extended into the Pacific Ocean, thus triggering legal action by the attorney general's office (fig. 38). No stranger to law as politics, Hodes, together with Anderson, successfully persuaded Judge David Menary of the Marin County Superior Court to delay the injunction so that the offending parts of *Running Fence* could be properly taken out of the water.[134] Hodes later recalled that Menary was not hostile to the work; addressing the representatives of the attorney general's office, the judge himself suggested that two weeks would be sufficient time for Christo and Jeanne-Claude to remove the offending portion of the work.[135] Knowing that *Running Fence* was temporary, Hodes and Anderson did not press the judge further; two weeks would be more than enough time for the artists to feel that their work was complete. Christo

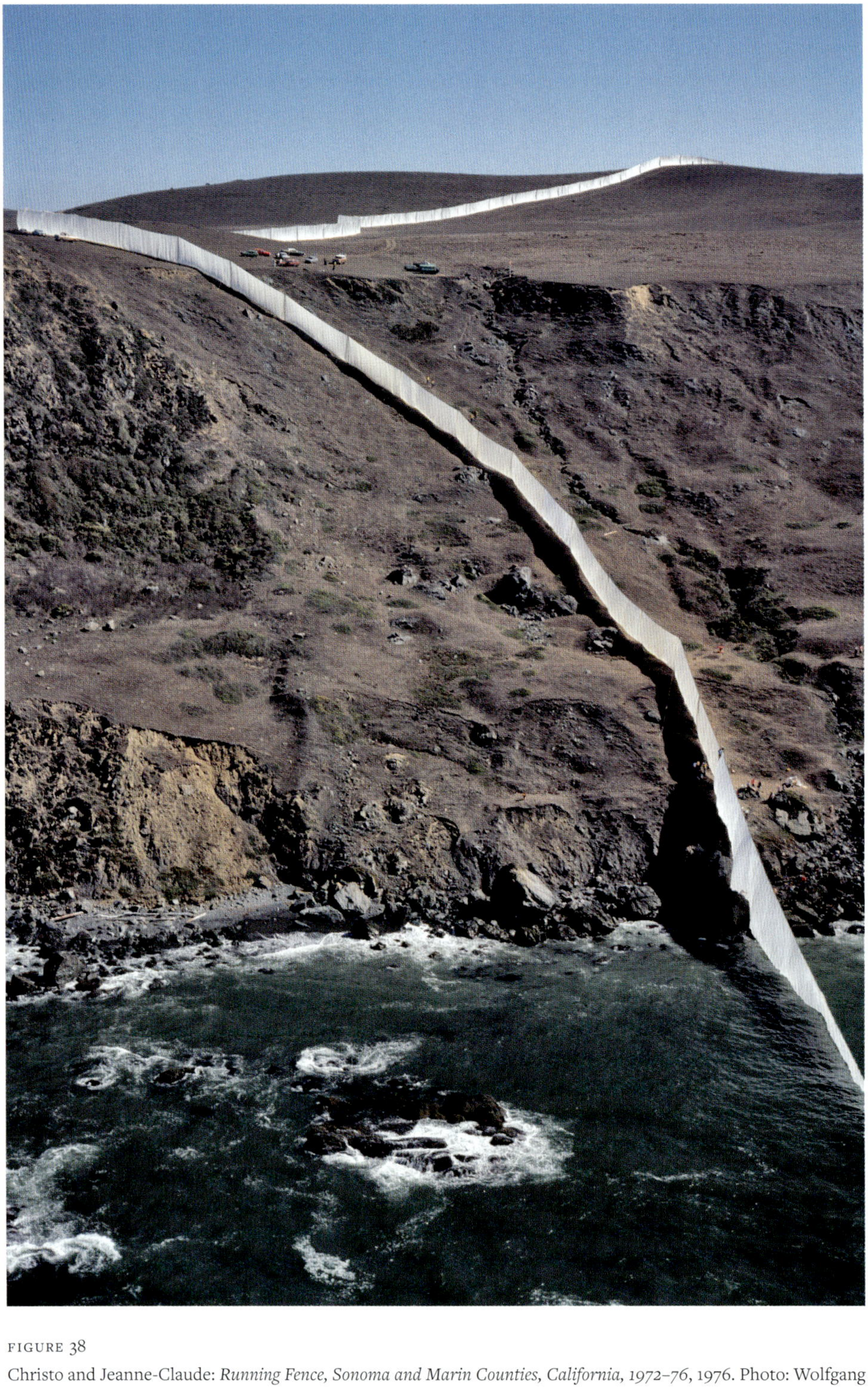

FIGURE 38
Christo and Jeanne-Claude: *Running Fence, Sonoma and Marin Counties, California, 1972–76*, 1976. Photo: Wolfgang Volz/laif/Redux Pictures. © 1976, Christo.

and Jeanne-Claude exercised their own grasp of property rights by barring the media from entering the private land on which they had temporary egress.[136]

Completed on September 10, *Running Fence* was removed after two weeks, except for the portion anchored to offshore land, which was taken down almost immediately. Although the State Lands Commission had previously granted Christo and Jeanne-Claude a lease to use the seabed off the California coast, and although its chair was a nonvoting member of the Coastal Commission, the latter agency overwhelmingly voted seven to one against the Running Fence Corporation on September 23, 1976. Despite knowing that *Running Fence* had already been completed and removed, the Coastal Commission nonetheless asked the attorney general to press charges against the corporation. One of the artists' own lawyers was taken aback that Christo and Jeanne-Claude, who were otherwise so diligent in conforming to legal structures, would suddenly repudiate that diligence to pursue their own interests. Kayfetz refused to join Anderson to stop a court order forcing the removal of the work, claiming that he felt Christo and Jeanne-Claude "had not told me the truth and had embarrassed me in front of the coastal commission."[137]

Although a friend of the artists, prominent art critic Alfred Frankenstein protested their actions, not because they were illegal, but because they betrayed what to him was the conceptual integrity of their method of working. Until they decided to take *Running Fence* into the water, the artists' success in being able to erect their work on land depended on their reification of an individualist, capitalist view of property still very much endorsed by California law. Their scrupulous, even obsessive, deference to both legal and extra-legal rules, going so far as to draft an EIR before it was legally required, mirrored all that was expected of good Americans. Rather than replay the predictable scenario of a rebellious artist fighting against the rule of law, Frankenstein claimed that the whole point was to use the "machinery of American law" on behalf of an idea it would not ordinarily consider.[138]

Christo responded that "legality is essential to the American system" but implied that legality was, nonetheless, not always consistent with his goals. Indeed, Tomkins described Christo and Jeanne-Claude's anxiety as nothing less than a symptom of what the artists viewed as an ethical imperative. Making sure the work was fully constructed was a matter of upholding one's "good name."[139] The artists saw themselves not as lawbreakers, but as rational actors responding to their own understanding of which property rights were most important, particularly given the potential of extreme sunk costs should *Running Fence* be incomplete.[140] In a letter to Tomkins, Lynn Hershman interpreted the decision to take *Running Fence* into the water as having "effected a reversal of the legal system."[141] Instead of allowing the law to completely structure their actions, Christo and Jeanne-Claude deemed it permissible to work outside its structures once they no longer suited their own purposes.

For some, *Running Fence* constituted such an infringement of what they saw as their own rights that any means justified its removal, even if they were illegal. As the artists succeeded in obtaining the permits they needed to legally execute their work, threats made against the physical work and even against those involved in its construction escalated. A little over a month before the work's completion, vandals attacked trucks used in the construction. The culprits later claimed to have planted bombs along the projected route of the fence.[142] That the violence of these responses was incommensurate with the potential harms ascribed to the work suggests that they were less about the work than about what some residents might see as the failure of state and city authorities to thoroughly consider their objections. No less indicative of the property status of *Running Fence* was Christo's alleged response to those seeking to block construction: "Put guards on every corner, and if they come around, shoot at them."[143] The ferocity of this remark conveyed Christo and Jeanne-Claude's investment not only in the idea of one's right to private property, but also in the right to defend it; in this light, the aggression reflected the fullness of Christo and Jeanne-Claude's own embrace of one of the most cardinal values of the American free market.

When Christo further justified his and Jeanne-Claude's actions by commenting that *Running Fence* was more about the law because they violated it ("If there is no illegal part, the project is less reflective of the system"), he may have been closer to the truth than he realized.[144] About ten days after the Coastal Commission again denied Christo and Jeanne-Claude's petition to take the work into the sea, Governor Jerry Brown signed into law the 1976 Coastal Law, a bill that guaranteed continued regulation of the coastal area by making the Coastal Commission permanent. Already under significant taxpayer pressure due to increased property assessments, the elected members of the Sonoma County Board of Supervisors demanded that Christo and Jeanne-Claude insure county land for $1.5 million.[145] The Coastal Commission saw differently, however, stating that it was not enough to prove an ability to compensate the state for any damage caused. The liability to which Christo and Jeanne-Claude exposed themselves implied that ownership was not only having the right to freely use one's property, but also having to assume responsibility for what takes place on or because of it.

The long process to secure the necessary permissions emphasized just how conceptually unstable the notions of land and property were. Moreover, the concessions Christo and Jeanne-Claude made as a result demonstrated how realizing one's entitlements meant recognizing one's own belonging to a larger community, however fragmented or at odds that community might be. As one rancher commented, *Running Fence* was "not a game or a stunt or even art—you go down there to a hearing because you really want to say something. There's a vertigo thing that in order to be a citizen you've got to be a part of that art."[146] *Running Fence* catalyzed a sense of entitlement within its viewers, overlaid by an equally powerful need to think about the duties and costs incurred by exercising that entitlement.

At the same time, the debates over *Running Fence* turned on just how much of a defense art—or, rather, aesthetic effect—could provide in the face of countervailing attitudes that regarded art as simply another form of property. Yet, as the work gained support from local audiences, governments and courts took the work more seriously as a socially necessary experience. Populist appeal eventually morphed into what might be called the "experience defense," whereby an initiative is legitimated not by what it looks like, its popularity, or even the tangible economic benefits it might yield, but by its historical singularity. Potential and actual inconveniences could be overlooked because they too were part of the "experience." More than almost any other artist, Christo and Jeanne-Claude demonstrated just how powerful the experience defense could be, as abundantly reflected in the many large-scale projects they successfully executed after *Running Fence.*

3

CLAIMS FOR DEFIANCE

Gordon Matta-Clark's Domains

A **WAREHOUSE ON THE NEW YORK CITY** waterfront appears to project itself from a nondescript monotony into open space (fig. 39). Indelibly marking one side of the building is a dark half-moon so awkwardly proportioned and situated as to divert attention from the neglected façade to the question of the hand. By *hand* I do not mean provenance, for the image is firmly embedded in chronicles of contemporary art history as one of the better-known representations of *Day's End*, Gordon Matta-Clark's memorable, and some might say triumphant, expropriation of neglected city property. A mammoth warehouse Matta-Clark physically cut in five places during the summer of 1975, it was among the most ambitious of his "cut" buildings. Produced illegally after the artist broke into the city-owned warehouse, *Day's End* was also a rejoinder to a system of property dashed to pieces by a toxic combination of municipal ineptitude and federal indifference. "Ford to City: Drop Dead," read an unforgettable *New York Daily News* headline that cast President Gerald Ford's refusal to aid New York as callous abandonment. Taken by Matta-Clark in the winter of

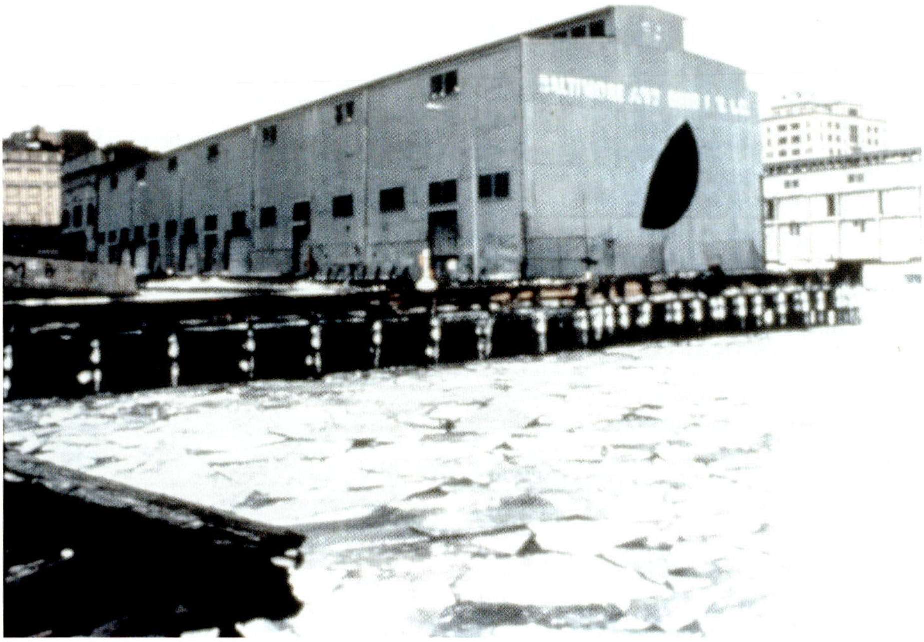

FIGURE 39
Gordon Matta-Clark, *Day's End* (*Pier 52*) (*Exterior with Ice*), 1975. © Estate of Gordon Matta-Clark/Artists Rights Society (ARS), New York. Courtesy of the Estate of Gordon Matta-Clark and David Zwirner, New York/London/Hong Kong.

1975, months after city authorities forced the artist to abandon the work, the photograph was not so much a last fond look as a parting shot against a legal system he saw fit to doubt, and also defy. He wrote to art historian Wolfgang Becker that "the building was surrounded by ice, all locked up. The city had placed a guard house in front of it and built clumsy railings around the areas that I removed from the dock floors."[1] In the photograph, the building is set just far back enough to invoke visual rhyming between the sharp endpoints of Matta-Clark's cut and the ice shards that might have been a metaphor for a city fragmented along social and economic divisions sharper and more perilous than any floe edge. Yet, even in such circumstances, the enduring image of the sail-shaped mark—too lopsided and oddly scaled to be anything but Matta-Clark's handiwork—persisted in reminding viewers that intervention was possible. One could still have a hand in shaping the world, even if on a much lesser scale than a cut into the side of a pier warehouse.

Confronting a locus where property law and its enforcement bore heavily on artistic everyday life, Matta-Clark turned to sliver lots, abandoned piers, buildings slated for demolition, and other spaces with compromised ties to the property regime. While his friends Christo and Jeanne-Claude made high art out of permission acquisition, Matta-Clark mined aesthetic and social opportunities in the foreclosures of property and criminal law.[2] Although not acts of rebellion, the works of Matta-Clark ranged from noncompliance with conventional uses of property to open disregard for the authority ascribed to the idea of property within the public imagination, as well as for the authority of government officials as expressed through the key property right of exclusion. Far too ambitious, however, to be content with producing anarchic signs of presumptive rebellion, Matta-Clark's engagements with property point to his interest in law as a function of failure and contradiction: "If you like the law, yet at the same time recognize that the ultimate law cannot possibly exist, then wouldn't it be better to talk about the impossibility of law than run around being a lawyer practicing the law?"[3] Against this statement, the defiance of Matta-Clark in three of his best-known works, *Day's End*, *Splitting*, and *Reality Properties: Fake Estates*, seemed purposed to provoke others into questioning what law could be and to initiate exchange between art and law on matters consequential for both approaches to living. Although the actions he took to realize his works used property in legally impermissible and even economically counterproductive ways, they also opened up, sometimes literally, different possibilities for thinking about property beyond entrenched binaries pitting safety against danger, right against wrong, or the criminal against the law-abiding.

"SOMEWHERE OUTSIDE THE LAW"

In the universe of block-letter phrases Matta-Clark wrote to flesh out his thinking, "SOMEWHERE OUTSIDE THE LAW" may be the most instructively cryptic. Found in his "Proposal for Anarchitecture" (1974), it alluded to a groundswell of interest in speculating on possibilities unacknowledged by current legal theory or practice.[4] It coincided with broad interest in the possibility of extra-legal or sub-legal spaces at a time when, as legal scholar Gregory Alexander has noted, the debate over the moral position of land ownership intensified dramatically.[5] Architectural historian Felicity Scott has discussed how critics, artists, and architects active in the United States during the 1970s paid close attention to spaces that were foreign to or disowned by lawmakers, including outer space, penal colonies, and communes. These types of extra-legal or sub-legal spaces appeared less beholden to the rule of law, which some artists and intellectuals perceived as an inflexible justification for an extensive system of regulation mainly intended to protect the interests of property owners. Scott cites "open land" communes, established in Northern California in the late 1960s, as an attempt to refigure human relationships to the land in hopes that they would lead to more harmonious and less violent forms of social interaction.[6] True to their name, these communes were imagined as sanctuaries from the demands of the law; the legal owner of one such property described himself as "a patriarch who doesn't govern, a landlord who doesn't charge."[7]

Matta-Clark encountered a very different property regime than the one faced by Christo and Jeanne-Claude in rural California. New York City was marked by a depleted tax base, abandoned buildings, and a crime rate so high as to prompt Matta-Clark to wryly observe that while "an empty street in Europe is a De Chirico, in New York it is a mugging."[8] The system of property was thus so disrupted as to require inhabitants to experiment with other ways of spatial occupation, from squatting to artist cooperatives of the kind pioneered by George Maciunas and his Fluxus colleagues. Conventional approaches reproducing the logics of exclusion and exchange value that underscore legal conceptions of property seemed woefully out of place. In a 1971 letter to Harold Stern, the assistant commissioner of the Real Estate Department of New York City, Matta-Clark asked to rent a building that was condemned and awaiting demolition, arguing that even buildings left for dead could be "put to use during this waiting period."[9] He tried to convince Stern that the worth of a structure was not exclusively tied to its physical condition or to a particular use, but was also based in its very existence in a given period. "A building is really a moment in time through which I carry my ideas," he later remarked.[10]

In 1973, Matta-Clark purchased residual land, left over from surveying errors, at public auction. Casually known as "sliver properties" or "gutterspaces," and often the result of expressway construction, which affected how local streets were reconfigured, such parcels of land were left for dead by the commercial market for being too small or irregular in shape to develop. Owned by the New York City Department of General Services (now part of the Department of Citywide Administrative Services), the branch of city government responsible for managing, leasing, and buying real property on behalf of the city, such land was sold at auction, together with land seized from private owners who were unable, or in some cases unwilling, to pay the associated property taxes.

Art historian Pamela Lee has characterized Matta-Clark's engagements with property as a Bataillean form of willfully profligate expenditure, enacted in large part to deplete property of its value, and specifically of its capacity for wealth creation.[11] She describes the parcels bought by the artist as examples of a "radical uselessness."[12] Physically inaccessible, and thus outside the usual expectations accompanying the purchase of land, the sliver lots were not unlike artworks in the sense that they were legally defined as having no specific utilitarian purpose.[13] But as Matta-Clark stated, "Property is all so pervasive. Everyone's notion of ownership is determined by the use factor."[14] Sliver-lot buyers were ingenious, using their purchases as storage spaces, private gardens, or miniature dog runs.[15] Others eagerly bid on these lots in hopes that they might become valuable in the future.[16] As one owner stated, "Maybe an adjacent property owner—He'll want to build on it, and he'll discover he doesn't own it. . . . Someday, someone will need it."[17] These buyers often recognized the lots not as singular, self-contained entities, but as units in a larger, interconnected system of property in which activity occurring on one lot was likely to affect the value of adjacent plots. For example, speculators purchased slivers of land directly in the path of someone's garage, thereby virtually holding the garage owner hostage until she bought out the speculator or paid a fee to guarantee access. More egregious still were those who put up milk or ice vending machines on their sliver lots, hoping that the loud noises of the machines would force neighbors to pay them to stop.

For Matta-Clark, buying the sliver lots was a critical preemptive step to exempt them from market pressures, a defense against what he condemned as a "hygienic obsession in the name of redevelopment."[18] At the same time, he was keen to reverse what geographer Nicholas Blomley has described as the tendency to consider property as objects rather than relationships.[19] Shortly after Matta-Clark purchased his lots, he made a video with his friends, video artist Jaime Davidovich and filmmaker Betsy Sussler, documenting his attempt to find each of his purchases in the New York borough of Queens. Sometimes referred to as *Land Queens* or *Queens Project* (1974), this fourteen-minute black-and-white video shows Matta-Clark having to meet other property owners.[20] Another scene shows Matta-Clark knocking on the door of a house adjacent to one of his lots. A person who appears to be a young man opens the door and looks at the map the artist holds, in a scene of temporary community.

Throughout *Land Queens,* Matta-Clark is consistently excluded from his own property. "Why arc you taking pictures?" one suspicious homeowner asked of the artist, to which a neighbor responded, "Oh, he bought [the lot] back there." Unimpressed, the first homeowner retorted that Matta-Clark "didn't buy mine," thereby suggesting that ownership was insufficient to guarantee access to the thing owned. Hence, those who rejected Matta-Clark and his camera deprived him of his chance to fully exercise all his ownership claims, in turn reframing property as a function of limits or lack: What do you *not* possess? Was *Land Queens* a reflection of what might be called "counter-property"? Eventually Matta-Clark's attempts to identify and document his holdings through photography and video became the basis for creating a property interest that helped compensate for the artist's exclusion from his purchases, namely through the posthumous creation of assembled collages of documentation

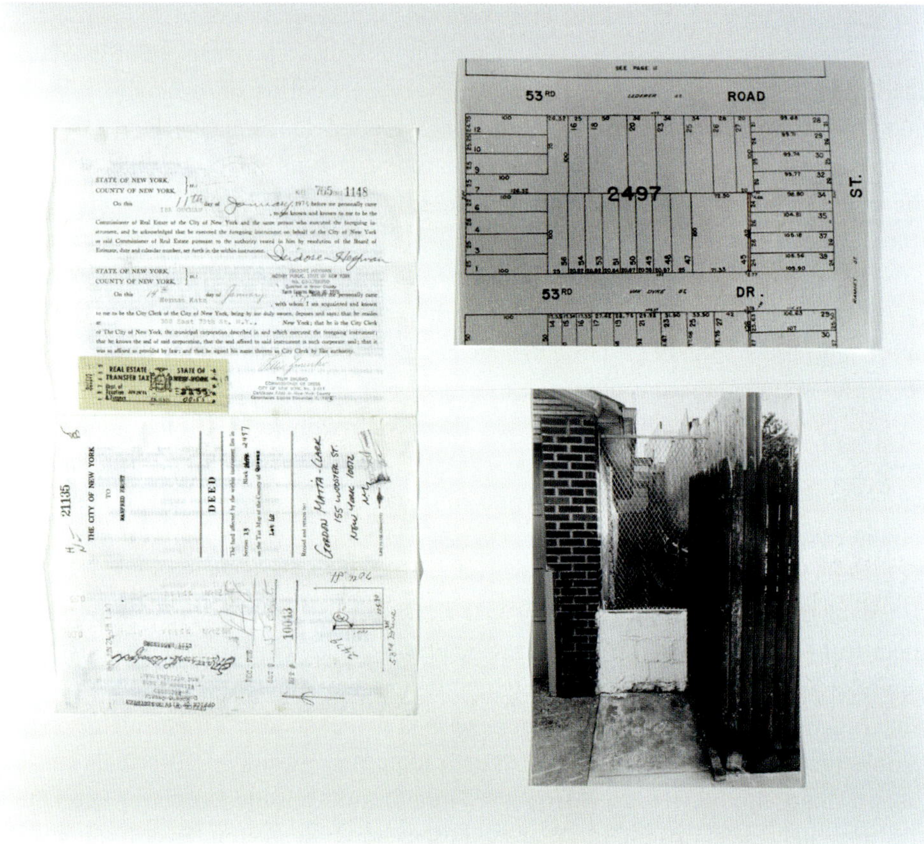

FIGURE 40

Gordon Matta-Clark, *Reality Properties: Fake Estates, Little Alley Block 2497, Lot 42*, 1974 (posthumous assembly, 1992). Photographic collage, property deed, site map, and photograph. Framed photograph collage: 10 × 87 3/16 × 1 3/8 inches; framed photograph and documents: 20 5/8 × 22 5/16 × 1 3/8 inches. Photo: Solomon R. Guggenheim Foundation/Art Resource, New York. © Estate of Gordon Matta-Clark/Artists Rights Society (ARS), New York.

initially titled *Reality Position: Fake Estates* and now known as *Reality Properties: Fake Estates* (fig. 40).[21]

The year *Land Queens* was filmed, Matta-Clark famously cut into a two-story residential house slated for destruction (fig. 41). Built in the 1930s on a lot in Englewood, New Jersey, it belonged to Matta-Clark's dealers Holly and Horace Solomon, who granted the artist permission to "work" on the house. Although the house legally belonged to the Solomons, who could do with their property as they wished, *Splitting* recast the principle of absolute ownership as a question rather than a statement. Should owners be able to do with their property as they see fit, including willful mutilation or destruction? Photographs of the work provoked viewers to ask whether there were, or should be, limits to what owners could do to their property. Critic Maud Lavin challenged Matta-Clark's stated intention of producing works that rebelled against

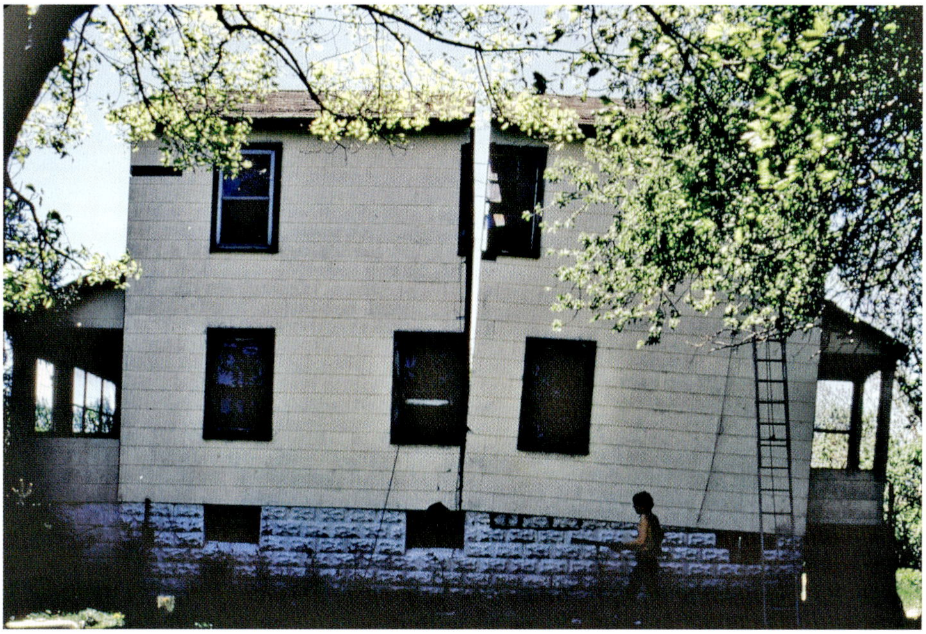

FIGURE 41
Gordon Matta-Clark, *Splitting*, 1974. Color photograph, 68 × 99 centimeters. © Estate of Gordon Matta-Clark/ Artists Rights Society (ARS), New York. Courtesy of the Estate of Gordon Matta-Clark and David Zwirner, New York/London/Hong Kong.

"an ever less viable state of privacy, private property and isolation."[22] She contended that his cuts were acts of possession that only confirmed and extended the notion of private ownership.[23] Each cut of Matta-Clark's work celebrated the Solomons' ability to more fully exercise their ownership rights by allowing Matta-Clark to create personal property from the land they owned. Not only did they let him cut into the house, they also permitted him to claim the result as his work and thus his personal property. If the Solomons had not granted Matta-Clark permission, *Splitting* might be regarded legally as a conversion, or an action voluntarily taken by one party (Matta-Clark) that was inconsistent with the ownership rights of another (the Solomons).

Part of Matta-Clark's artistic vocabulary since 1971, cutting into buildings initially read less as destruction than as repurposed construction. Yet the cuts he made for *Splitting* severed the house from the law altogether by rendering the structure utterly noncompliant with building codes. *Splitting* accordingly reads as an attempt by Matta-Clark to create a space outside the law, where property had to be rescued from the measures of value most commonly assigned to it; land and buildings were worth more than money. Visually, however, his cuts demonstrated how the representation of an action can so forcefully call its ethics into question as to transform perceptions of its legality. Although generally sympathetic to Matta-Clark's projects, Margot Wellington, vice president of the Downtown Brooklyn Development Association, sent him a recent

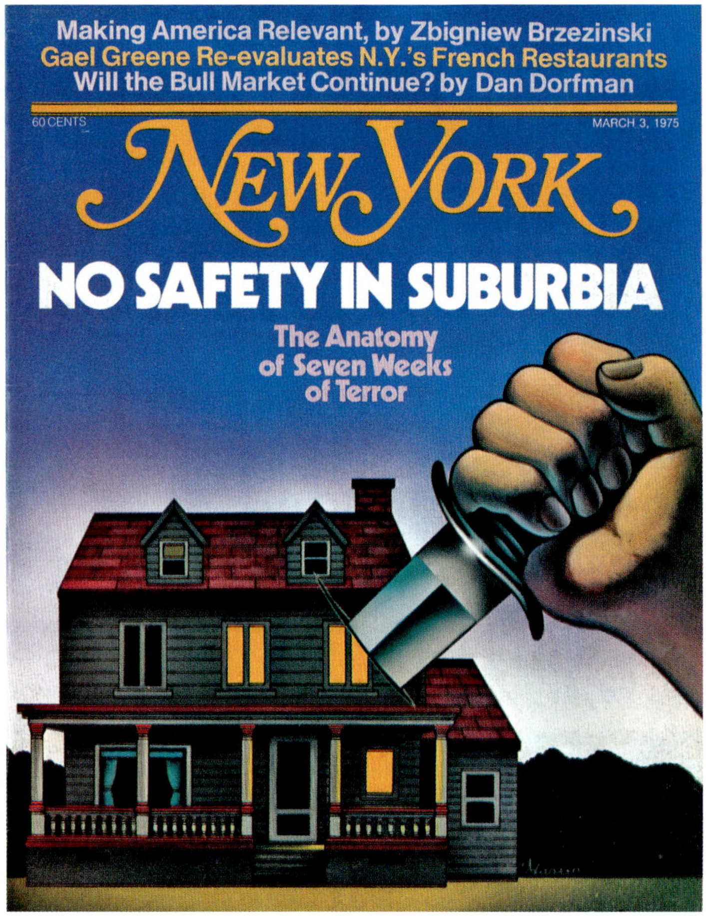

FIGURE 42
Haruo Miyauchi, cover of *New York* magazine, March 3, 1975. Courtesy of the Estate of Haruo Miyauchi and *New York* magazine. © The Estate of Haruo Miyauchi and *New York* magazine.

cover of *New York* magazine titled "No Safety in Suburbia: The Anatomy of Seven Weeks of Terror." Rendered by Haruo Miyauchi of the influential graphic design collective Push Pin Studios in his distinctive vocabulary culled from Surrealist, Pop, and even Primitivist sources, the cover showed a giant, disembodied human hand stabbing a detached frame house reminiscent of the one used in *Splitting* (fig. 42). To Wellington, who was instrumental in saving city landmarks like Grand Central Terminal from destruction, the image may have been her letting Matta-Clark know that any blow to the home was likely to be seen as a form of unjustified threat or assault, intent notwithstanding. Certainly, Matta-Clark struck many viewers as guilty of violating cherished principles like the "castle doctrine." Recognized in Anglo-American common law since the seventeenth century, this doctrine recognizes one's home as one's "safest refuge," where homeowners may legally use force to defend themselves from intruders in certain circumstances. Some viewers accordingly compared the work to "out and out rape," one of the most personally invasive of crimes.[24] Matta-Clark conceded that little could be done about this entrenchment in a culture that regarded most forms of destruction as having unavoidably criminal overtones, confessing that "there is no way to deal formally with the environment with[out] committing rape!"[25]

The comparison of *Splitting* to rape, a crime typified by the absence of victim consent, alluded to how the work was created without permission or input from the neighbors. The severed house was fully visible to those living nearby, a potentially unwelcome reminder of how wealthy speculators saw the neighborhood as ripe for plunder. Moreover, the noise produced in its construction may have violated the nuisance code of New Jersey state law prohibiting "unreasonably or unnecessarily loud" sounds.[26] Here the law complicates what art history valorizes as a form of direct action and a singular artistic gesture by shifting attention toward the costs borne by anonymous others. As if to downplay the pejorative connotations of his cuts, Matta-Clark would shift to calling his works "re-distributed building works" by late summer of 1975.[27] Later he dubbed them "redevelopment" projects, perhaps to assuage the worries of potential collaborators, donors, and government officials and satisfy their preferences for socially useful art, even though the very idea of redevelopment ran counter to the values he professed to uphold.[28]

WHEN POSSESSION WAS NINE-TENTHS OF THE ART

Motivating the artist's engagement with property was the well-known common-law dictum "Possession is nine-tenths of the law," a reference to how the person in actual possession of the property is presumed to be the rightful owner. The stakes of such possession were especially acute for land in an urban context, which, unlike land in rural areas governed by long-standing custom, was usually regulated by written law. To Matta-Clark, "nine-tenths legal property structure" was almost a mantra. But instead of ownership representing the end goal, possession to him meant breaking down abstract ideas of property in favor of a literal reading of the "real" in "real property," whereby possession and ownership entailed a series of experiential agitations and logistical difficulties. In an undated essay, he wrote: "There's so much in our society that purposely intends denial: deny entry, deny passage, deny participation, etc. We would all still be living in towers and castles, if we hadn't broken down some of the social and economic barriers, inhibitions and restraints. My work directly reflects this."[29] More obliquely, the antipathy he encountered hinted at what the Guggenheim's rejection of a Hans Haacke work—*Shapolsky et al. Manhattan Real Estate Holdings, a Real-Time Social System, as of May 1, 1971*—made explicit: the tendency of wrongdoers to exploit privacy to justify nondisclosure of the activities most in need of public scrutiny. Matta-Clark's rejection of privacy became more concrete in 1975 after his trip to Milan, Italy, where he professed interest in converting buildings into social spaces so that real property could be "finally responsive to the express will of its occupants" and not necessarily its owners.[30]

Many commentators portray the artist as wanting to challenge a particularly American view of property, one inextricably bound to idealizations of personal privacy. Matta-Clark certainly seemed to relish cutting into wall and floors—structural features "that had been staunch defenders of other people's privacy or isolation."[31] But he was less against privacy than what it potentially encompassed, such as the exclusion of others, unethical concealment, withdrawal from participating in community formation, and the cultivation of fear justified in the name of risk management. Among the primary rights associated with property, the right to exclude theoretically allowed voluntary self-isolation in the name of autonomy. In cutting open houses, office buildings, and later a building on a pier, Matta-Clark made it all but impossible for these structures to effectively function as vehicles of exclusion. The size and scale of the incisions guaranteed that the structures would always be subject to imminent entry (fig. 43). The location of Matta-Clark's works in derelict or disenfranchised places suggested that his idea of the public specifically included both those who experienced exclusion as a result of others' exercise of property rights and those for whom property ownership was an unobtainable privilege.

Matta-Clark's interest in rejecting the right of exclusion stems from what in the New York art world was a sustained interest in thinking about the relationship between permission and exclusion. In *Claim*, Vito Acconci had no compunction about enforcing exclusion through violence (fig. 44). Viewers passing by 93 Grand Street could hear his statements on a monitor placed next to the stairway door at street level, which recorded his activity as well as his warnings to curious visitors who may have wanted to descend the stairs. As the performance progressed, "eventually he threatened to kill anyone who encroached on his territory."[32] A few days after performing *Claim*, Acconci said: "I am thinking in terms like these: habitation-invasion-containment-placing-cover-intrusion-insinuation."[33] *Claim* took place not long before Charles Bronson would loom large on movie screens as the vigilante par excellence, the hero defending his turf from murderous interlopers. This was New York City circa 1971, a time and place that, while not quite lawless, was ruled by violence, including bombings throughout the city. The law could not adequately protect private property, so the burden shifted to owners and occupants. But just how far this shift could go remained troublingly open.

Christo remarked that Matta-Clark was committed to "buying, renting, taking, using, owning, cutting a place—all that revived the space."[34] Provisionally called "Visit to Humphrey Street House," the black-and-white film Matta-Clark made of visitors coming to *Splitting* illustrates the work as an experience activated by physical engagement (fig. 45). After a long take of the journey from Manhattan to New Jersey through the Holland Tunnel, the film shows numerous scenes of the Humphrey Street house's immediate surroundings. It then brings viewers to the roof, treating them to vast expanses of sky and neighboring homes. A person grasps a door frame, ostensibly to steady himself, but also, perhaps, to confirm what he is seeing. Others stand at either edge of the split roof, running their hands cautiously over the jagged edges. The work is portrayed as a loosely related series of vantage points that emphasize both the visual precariousness of Matta-Clark's cuts and the durability of the house.

Splitting reinforces the boundary as the primary lens through which considerations of space must pass. At the sixteen-minute mark, the camera makes one of its startling cuts,

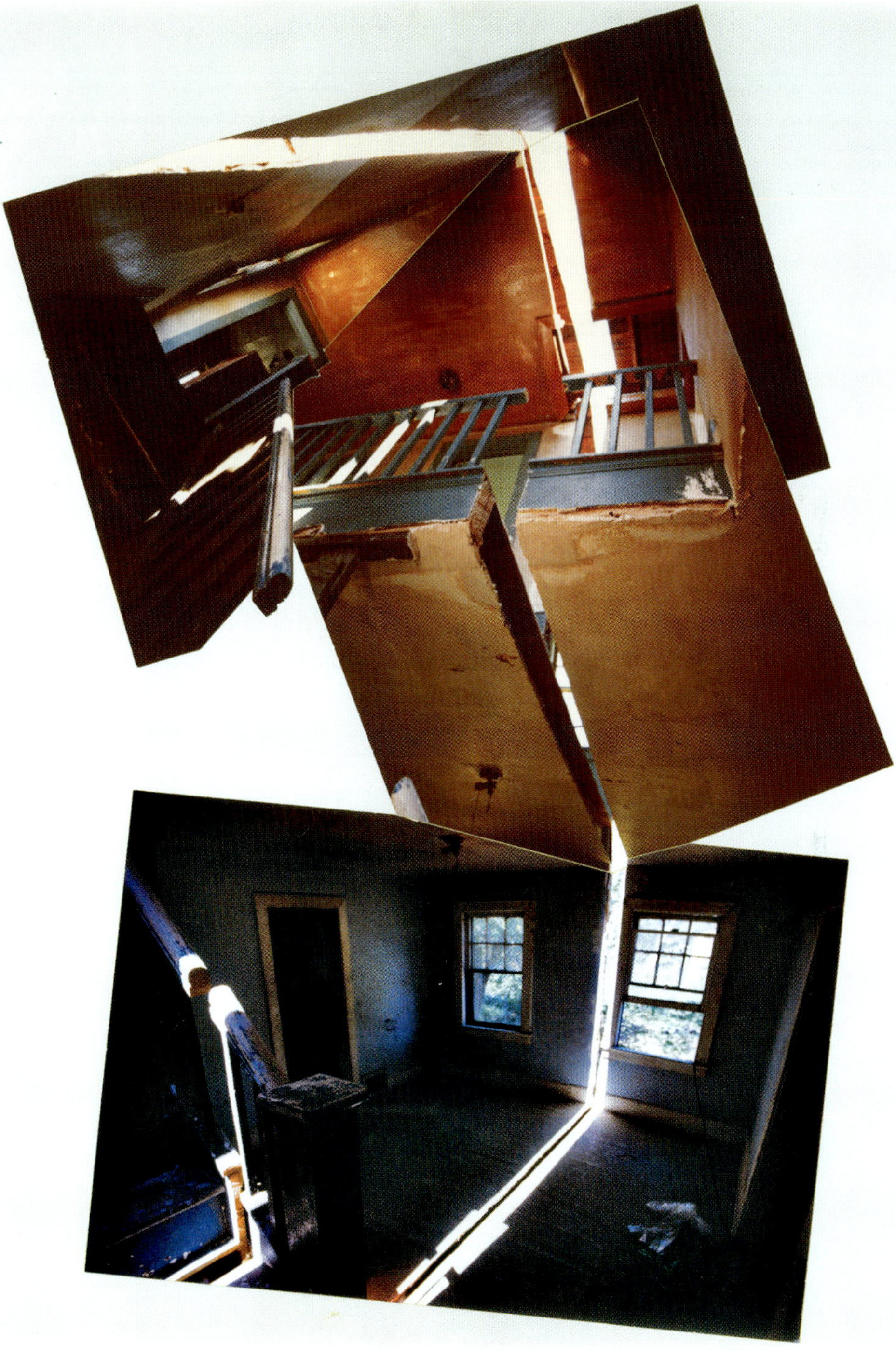

FIGURE 43

Gordon Matta-Clark, *Splitting*, 1974. Chromogenic prints mounted on board, 40 × 30 inches. Image copyright: Metropolitan Museum of Art. Image source: Art Resource, New York. © Estate of Gordon Matta-Clark/Artists Rights Society (ARS), New York.

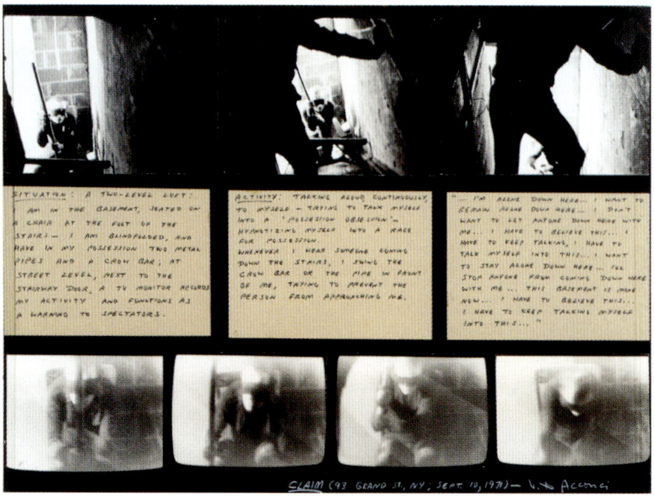

FIGURE 44

Vito Acconci, *Claim (93 Grand Street, New York, 10 September 1971)*, 1971. Seven gelatin silver prints and handwritten text, 30½ × 32 inches. Milwaukee Art Museum, Purchase, Richard and Ethel Herzfeld Foundation Acquisition Fund M1993.18. Photo credit: Rhona Hoffman Gallery, Chicago. © 2018 Vito Acconci/Artists Rights Society (ARS), New York.

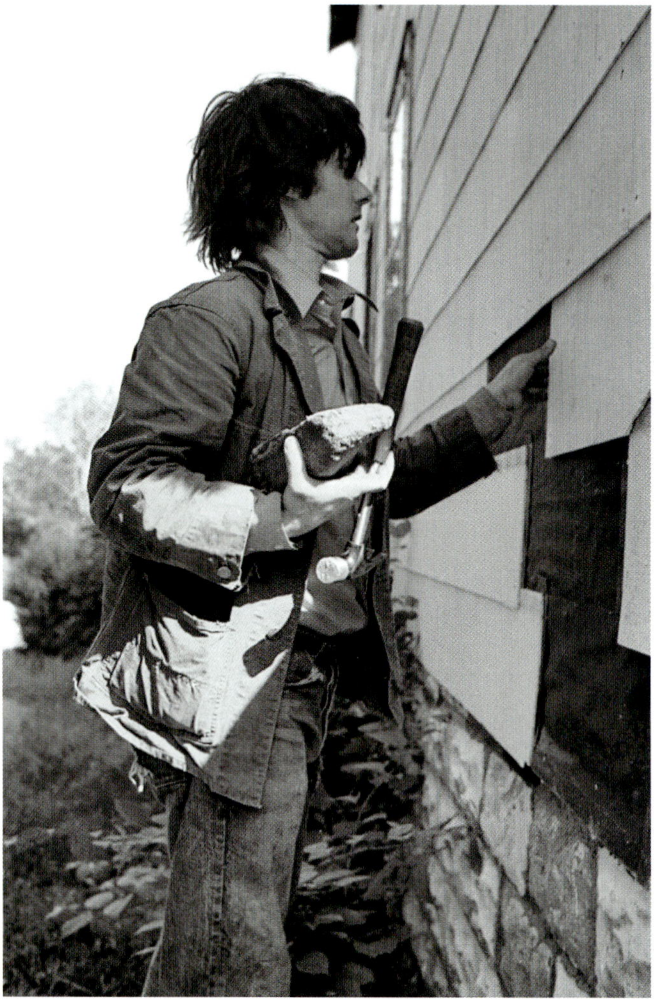

FIGURE 45

Gordon Matta-Clark, still from *Splitting*, 1974. © Estate of Gordon Matta-Clark/Artists Rights Society (ARS), New York. Courtesy of the Estate of Gordon Matta-Clark and David Zwirner, New York/London/Hong Kong.

this time to a scene of white and black children happily playing a pickup game of basketball. Compared to the mostly white group of daytrippers to New Jersey, the scene—to which Matta-Clark would return at least twice—delineates an instance of integration strikingly at odds with the stark racial lines separating whites from blacks that defined many suburbs in the 1970s. But the very act of creating *Splitting* registers as a stark boundary dividing valuable from valueless property. Such a work was possible only because the market had already abandoned the house and its surrounding neighborhood.

Few artists were more keyed into the limitations and potential of law's fictions than Matta-Clark, a condition he made clear in his documentation process. Wielding his camera "like he used a buzz saw," according to his friend Joseph Kosuth, the photographs Matta-Clark took of his sliver lots reveal especially well the abstraction and elusiveness of real property.[35] The multiple shots he sometimes took of a given lot impart a breathless futility distinctly at odds with the staid deeds and maps solemnly promising certitude to the bearer. City auction listings of gutterspaces showed only a single frontal shot for each lot; photography was supplemental, with the real work of verification done by figures and addresses. That Matta-Clark died without assembling the photographs adds another layer of complexity to his exploration of property. One wonders if Matta-Clark purposely kept the photographs unbound so as to allow future viewers—users—to experience for themselves something of the connection he had with the ground. To piece the photographs together, viewers must look down upon, rather than frontally at, the images that one imagines would read more strongly as tangible fragments than as flat scenes best seen from a distance (fig. 46). Yet, even after the pieces have been assembled, the depicted plot remains curiously unreal, suspended in the interface between somatic, affective, and cognitive perception that makes viewer

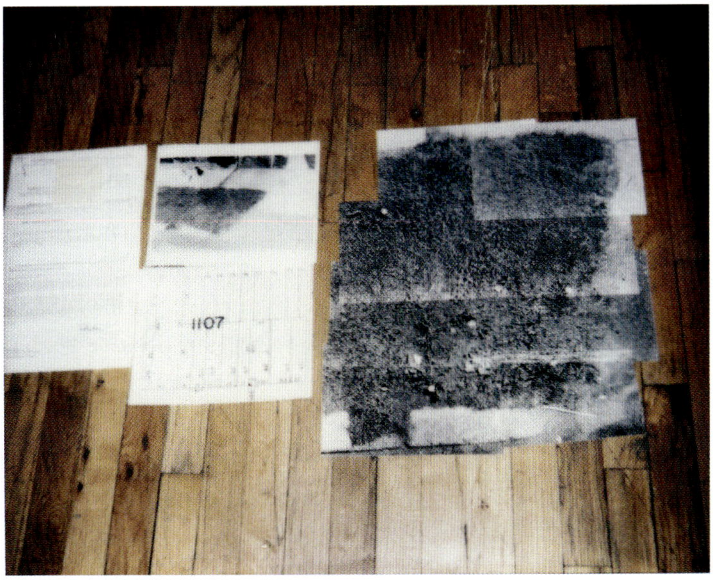

FIGURE 46
Gordon Matta-Clark, *Reality Position: Fake Estate, Block 1107 Lot 146 at 96th St, Queens, 1973*, 1973. Holly Solomon Gallery Records, c. 1948–2003. Archives of American Art, Smithsonian Institution. © Estate of Gordon Matta-Clark/Artists Rights Society (ARS), New York.

experience so difficult to describe or appropriate. Possession may be nine-tenths of the law, but the remaining tenth consists of what remains firmly out of reach.

ART FOR THE TAKING

Matta-Clark's efforts recall the influential philosopher Robert Nozick's discussion of John Locke's proposition that one may legitimately acquire property rights by combining one's labor with resources held "in common" only if "there is enough and as good left in common for others."[36] In *Day's End,* the commons Matta-Clark imagined was based on assumptions consonant with those underpinning government-administered public spaces (fig. 47). In 1971, the empty, unused Pier 18 became a new stage for Willoughby Sharp, whom the critic Alfred Frankenstein had dubbed, somewhat facetiously, "the guru of conceptual art" and who invited artists like Matta-Clark to do with the pier as they liked.[37] The freedoms Sharp permitted the artists may have led Matta-Clark to believe that the piers were possible sites for artistic intervention. As the artist later declared, "because these buildings were outside society and not part of anybody's protective property motive, they were free to all."[38]

A few months before he started to work on *Day's End,* Matta-Clark tried to rent Pier 52 from the city, possibly at the behest of his lawyer, Jerald Ordover. By the late 1960s, Ordover was de facto consigliere to the New York art world, representing an extraordinarily wide range of artists and gallerists.[39] His clients included Leo Castelli, whose gallery he represented for decades; Charlotte Moorman, who turned to Ordover for legal advice about performing nude on stage for Nam June Paik's *Opera Sextronique;* Lawrence Weiner, for whom the attorney served as a one-man copyright registry office; and Carl Andre, whose release from police custody he would secure after Ana Mendieta's death in 1985.[40] Ordover suggested to Matta-Clark that renting the pier legally might help him win financial support from Holly Solomon.[41] But obtaining permission in a context marked by increasing risk aversion proved challenging. In January 1975, Matta-Clark approached Controlled Demolition, a building demolition company, to secure in-kind support for one of his works.[42] He tried to downplay the subject of destruction, writing that "although the work destroys to a degree, it is done with some refinement to allow others to experience and understand architecture as they rarely do." Senior management of Controlled Demolition responded positively to the artist's initial request, and especially to documentation of *Splitting,* but balked at the "awesome" legal involvements that only complicated the firm's preexisting "public liability responsibilities."[43] The fear that potential liability might outweigh any positive publicity from a collaboration with Matta-Clark may explain why so many of his letters requesting support from companies and developers were rejected.

Eventually he gave up. "I had no faith in any kind of permission," the artist told Liza Béar.[44] Because the city never granted artists permission to do anything "on a large scale," the sole option was to simply "occupy and possess."[45] New York City was then in such a state of near lawlessness that creating a law of one's own, even if it ran

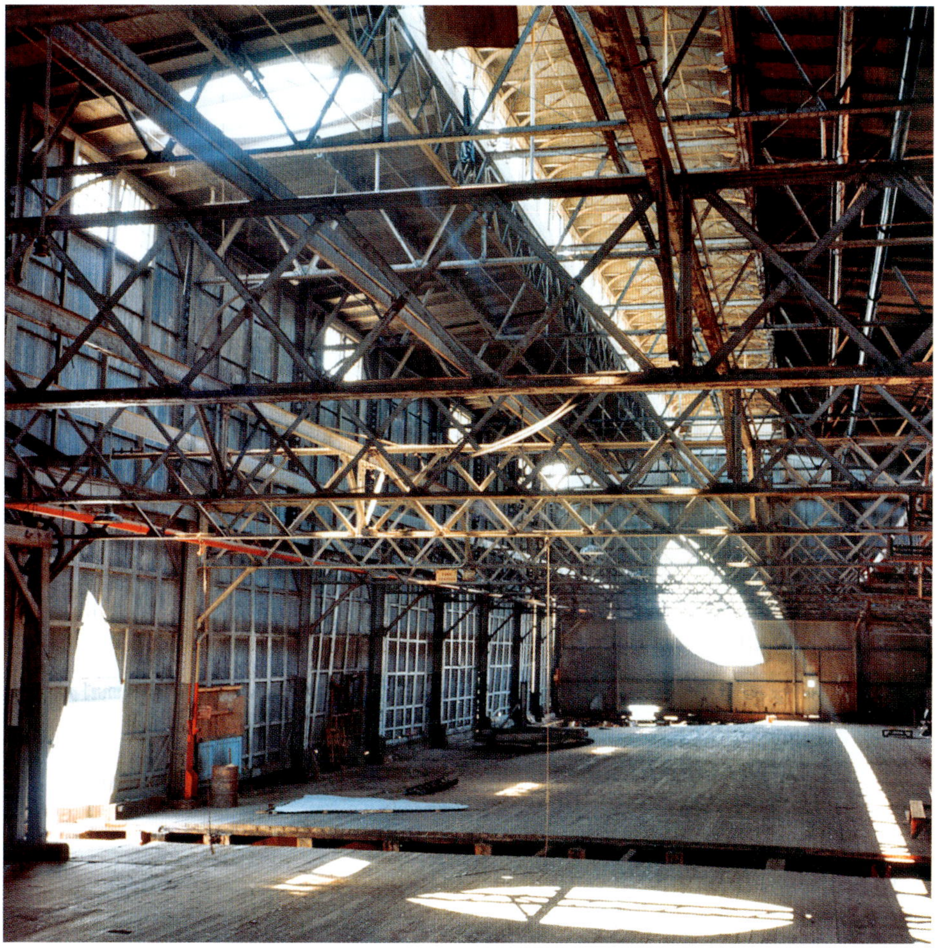

FIGURE 47
Gordon Matta-Clark, *Day's End, Pier 52, Gansevoort Street and West Street,* 1975. © Estate of Gordon Matta-Clark/Artists Rights Society (ARS), New York. Courtesy of the Estate of Gordon Matta-Clark and David Zwirner, New York/London/Hong Kong.

counter to the views of legislatures and judges, seemed not only necessary but even reasonable. City government, which owned the pier and its surrounding lands, posted signs on the road leading to the pier warning passersby about muggers.[46] Although the signs may have been placed to indicate to the general public that the pier was under city jurisdiction, Matta-Clark seemed to consider them signs of a "disinterested abandonment," by which the city abdicated its ownership rights, such that the buildings and land comprising the property in question were no longer subject to another party's right to exclude others.[47] Cutting into the pier was for him an inverse taking. A legal doctrine referring to government acquisition of private property through its seizure or destruction, a "taking" required governments to compensate owners.

Matta-Clark justified his use of public property as defending the pier from the "squadrons of pigeons as well as the waterfront homosexual S&M trysting community," a remark that pointedly mimicked, and even mocked, the legal establishment's own exclusionary logic as to who qualified as proper members of the public.[48] Artist Gerard Hovagimyan, who assisted Matta-Clark with the creation of *Day's End,* noted that dock inspectors' fear of that very community ensured uninterrupted construction throughout the summer of 1975.[49] Indeed, Matta-Clark's defiance of property norms resulted in the production of spaces that a vilified queer community used in nonnormative and nonpejorative ways. As chronicled so eloquently by the photographer Alvin Baltrop, the pier looks less like a forbidden no-man's-land and more like a domestic space (fig. 48). The cuts yielded opportunities for psychological as well as carnal intimacy.

To produce *Day's End,* Matta-Clark committed the crimes of trespass, breaking and entering, and criminal mischief in the second degree, the latter a more serious crime defined by New York State Penal Law as intentional damage of another's property exceeding $1,500. Classified as a felony, it carried a potential sentence of up to seven years in prison.[50] He minimized the legal import of his actions to friends, explaining that he "simply appropriated the pier by keeping my crew of henchmen boarding and barbwiring up all alternative entrances for the front door in which I substituted my own lock and bolt."[51] Having spent nearly two months constructing the work under physical conditions that could only be described as extreme, he displayed a playful yet thinly veiled territorialism in calling his coworkers (whom he paid from a foundation grant he had received) "henchmen."[52] A guard, moreover, was hired to watch over the work three days a week from September to November of 1975. Shot through the project is a certain glee in being able to take from a city bureaucracy that had continuously frustrated him, whether by denying him permission to rent space or by refusing to provide information about the land below the city.[53]

In his "Art Delinquency Notes" of 1974, artist Tony Rickaby described vandalism, a crime identified since the seventeenth century as the reckless destruction of property, as "a symbolic threat to a society which places high value on property and culture."[54] But the tone of Matta-Clark's language pointed more toward sociologist Stanley Cohen's description of the intangible pleasures of vandalism:

> Vandalism is just right. It is the ideal form of rule-breaking both in *expressive* (expressing certain values) and *instrumental* terms (solving certain structural problems). It is satisfying and provides just the right amount of risk. If one is looking for toughness, excitement, action and a sense of control . . . then school and work do not provide the right arenas.[55]

The above excerpt demonstrates the emotional value of vandalism to the perpetrator, one Matta-Clark seemed to understand when he described his works to a curator as a form of "liberation."[56] Echoing Cohen's views on vandalism, legal scholars Eduardo Moisés Peñalver and Sonia Katyal argue the importance of what they call "property

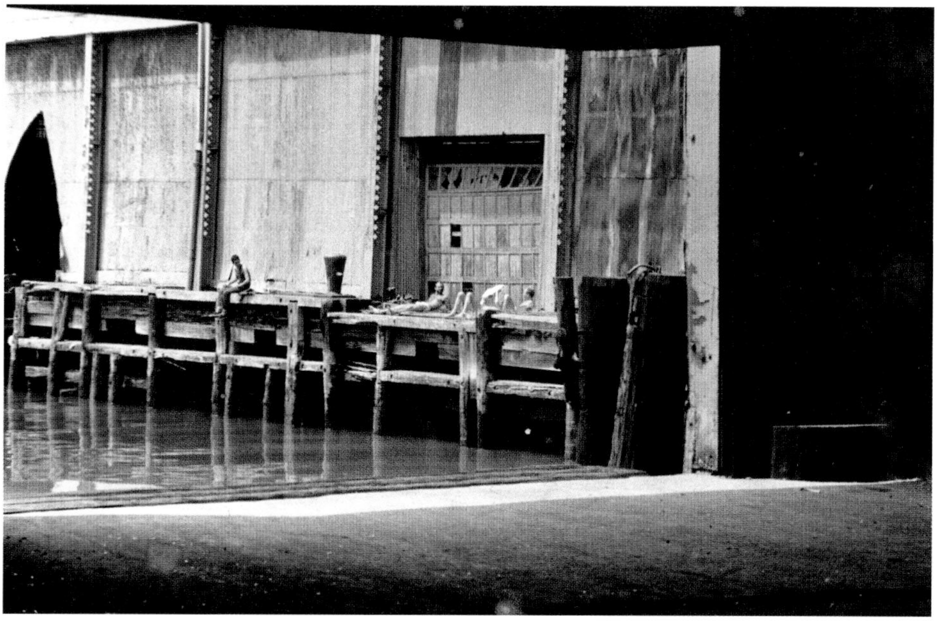

FIGURE 48
Alvin Baltrop, *The Piers (Men Sunbathing on Dock)*, 1976–77. Gelatin silver print, 6½ × 4½ inches. Courtesy of the Alvin Baltrop Trust. © 2010, Alvin Baltrop Trust and Third Streaming.

outlaws" in the shaping of property law, a body of regulation whose vested commitments to stability often fail to reflect the lived realities of the people whom such laws affect most.[57] Such outlaws commit infractions ranging from squatting to civil disobedience, which in many cases have proved more effective than conventional, lawful measures in changing various kinds of regulation. Matta-Clark dwelled not only on obligations that people owe one another, but also on whether the obligations to respect boundaries set and endorsed by the state, in law, should in fact be respected.

Ordover later claimed that the city became aware of the work after two of Matta-Clark's friends applied for a film permit to document it.[58] The artist himself speculated that it was an article in *Soho Weekly News* that alerted the authorities, whom he said came to Pier 52 one week before *Day's End* opened.[59] The dockmaster chained the work shut, but "a lot of people took it on themselves to break in and so keep the work in some kind of public domain."[60] With a potential lawsuit looming, friends and supporters of Matta-Clark tried to argue that the work was a "generous donation of a work of art to a decaying city."[61] In a high-profile *Village Voice* feature, David Bourdon likened it to an improvement project so as to minimize the description of *Day's End* as the result of breaking and entering, a misdemeanor.[62] Language more commonly associated with an upscale real estate listing or perhaps a guidebook entry for a stately home was used to describe the experience *Day's End* offered: "The interior of the

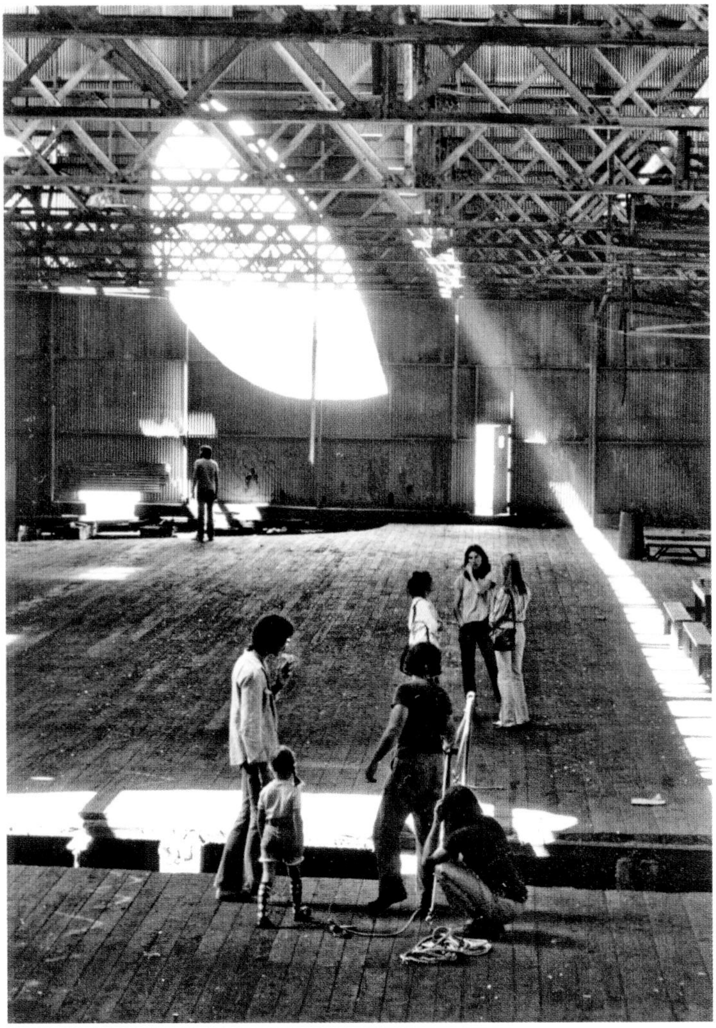

FIGURE 49
Gordon Matta-Clark, interior view of *Day's End*, 1975. © Estate of Gordon Matta-Clark/Artists Rights Society (ARS), New York. Courtesy of the Estate of Gordon Matta-Clark and David Zwirner, New York/London/Hong Kong.

covered pier is a spectacular open space," a "gloomily romantic place" boasting a "vast, cathedral-like setting."[63] Photographs emphasized that the pier was no longer a decaying wreck, but a site consecrated by streaming light. Similarly absent was any indication of the danger involved in the creation and experience of the work (fig. 49).

The engagement with property in *Day's End* compelled Matta-Clark to negotiate a complex relationship between the persona of the vigilante and the reality of working under politically and economically circumscribed conditions. It was perhaps even more important that the work not be seen exclusively through the optic of illegality. "I think the space and situation that's there is perfectly valid on its own. It doesn't need any kind of reinforcing through notoriety," he told Béar.[64] Certainly, Matta-Clark had persistent doubts about the risk inherent in making work that broke the law. This

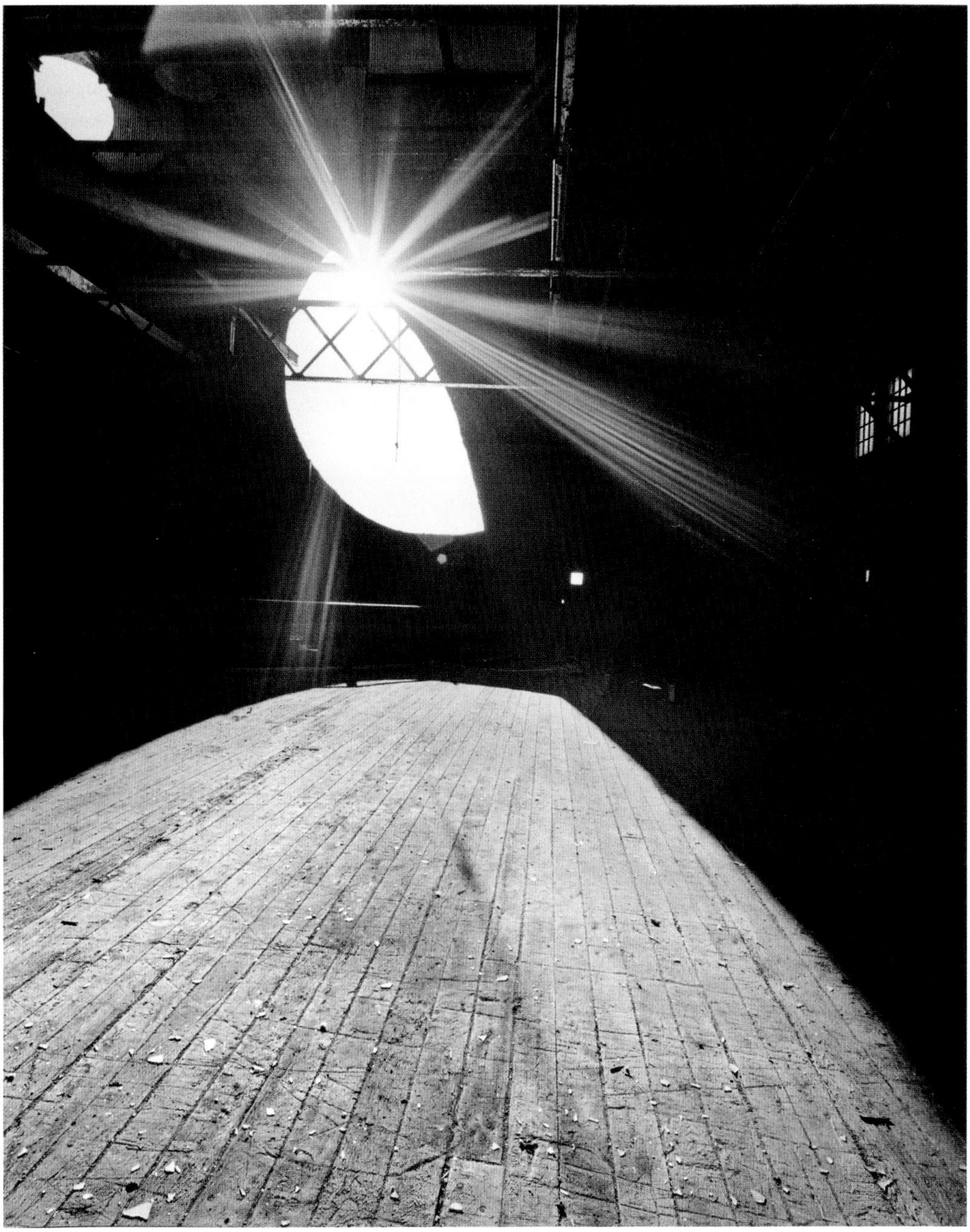

FIGURE 50
Harry Shunk, *Gordon Matta-Clark, Day's End, Pier 52, New York, 1975 September 9*. Photo: Harry Shunk. © J. Paul Getty Trust. Getty Research Institute, Los Angeles (2014.R.20).

was not because of the potential for punishment, but rather because the illegality of the actions might take precedence over all other considerations, particularly for general audiences already predisposed to discount artists as inconsequential renegades or even as a nuisance class. As he wrote to Ordover several months before beginning work on *Day's End:* "My real problem is that my ongoing challenge to the [nine-tenths] legal property structure (people's sense of privacy and prudery as well) may continue to make me a somewhat criminal type."[65] The anxiety his words suggest betray a fear that his works would not be taken as seriously if they only illustrated the segregation of art from the real world.

As with *Splitting,* there is something intentionally epic about *Day's End.* Photographs showing the cut from a distance outside the warehouse remind viewers of the pier as an actual physical site, and perhaps even as a living site with a few good years remaining. Matta-Clark's vaguely sail-shaped perforation of the building resembles a silhouette cutout against its sun-dappled wall. Seen from within the building, the cut offers another use for the building in connection to, but also in lieu of, its original practical functions. Light streams through the cut, channeling sunlight into the ordinarily dark interior (fig. 50). It draws attention away from the building's practical purpose as a shelter and repository to emphasize the building as an aesthetic object. For Matta-Clark, an artist in reference to whom the phrase "grand gesture" seems an understatement, the origin of the work reads more like an allegory than an anecdote, intended to galvanize its audiences into taking similar forms of direct action. Legal scholar Carol Rose analyzes how some of the most influential scholars and theorists of property have relied on decidedly narrative explanations to convince their audiences to "exercise a little imagination" and get them—us—"to take a chance on cooperating too, for the sake of a larger good."[66] Seen in this light, *Day's End* becomes a morality tale meant for a public much too accustomed to the pursuit of self-interest, and perhaps even for a city government looking for a reason to care more actively about the public interest.

MATTA-CLARK RESPONDS TO THE LAW

Less than two weeks after Bourdon's article was published, the police contacted Ordover. The attorney met Detective Gagliardo of the Sixth Precinct, who was in charge of investigating the break-in on behalf of the New York City Economic Development Agency. Ordover provided Gagliardo information about Matta-Clark's status as an artist, and likewise stressed to Matta-Clark the need to cooperate with the agency, which had the sole power to cancel the investigation. By this time, Matta-Clark had moved to Paris and was thus "comfortably out of the long . . . reach of the law."[67] But to Ordover, cooperation was necessary lest the artist be branded a "fugitive" and possibly even extradited.[68] Gagliardo asked Matta-Clark to submit a written statement explaining what he did and why, a request Ordover counseled the artist to take seriously by responding with “a sincere statement which will reek with cooperation,” but not so cooperative that police could use it as a “confession before the world.”[69]

Matta-Clark did not respond for several weeks, despite Ordover’s pleas.[70] Finally, in December 1975, he sent the lawyer a written statement that read as both a gesture of self-defense and a deliberate provocation to those empowered with interpreting and enforcing the law. Far from the conciliatory path Ordover advised Matta-Clark to take, the artist’s response was polemical and very much worth examining as a rare instance of an artist directly addressing the agents of the law in their own language, or something very close to it. The document reads almost as if he relished the prospect of a trial, which he described to Ordover as “the best relevant pop-theater,” and which in practical terms would have cost the city as much in time and aggravation as it did Matta-Clark in his fruitless application for a permit.[71] The first paragraph notes that the pier was already in such bad condition that “there is no reason to believe” any property owner might lay claim to it. Neglect and abandonment of the urban environment has only been met with “bureaucratic and juridic ambivalence and inaction.” The pier suffered from “base mismanagement” and had devolved into a “veritable muggers’ playground.” *Day’s End,* he argued, comprised a more optimal use of resources than neglect masquerading as nonuse, a claim that further suggested how his actions constituted a nonmarket mechanism for addressing the negative externalities of failed city administration. Matta-Clark’s legal transgression reads as an indictment of the excess of regulation partly responsible for New York City’s dire financial straits. He all but demands to be thanked, describing *Day’s End* in his letter as a “generous human act” that “is not only defendable but would make a valuable contribution to the people of New York.”[72]

Playing the roles of both dedicated public servant and private property owner, Matta-Clark tried to appeal to the ideals of both personal autonomy and public interest ingrained in the law. The first role was to deflect possible accusations of *Day’s End* as a source of unjustifiable harm, the usual rationale invoked in trespassing cases. The second tapped directly into a venerable history of regulation aimed at encouraging citizens to demonstrate their productivity and social belonging by putting unused property to some viable use. Matta-Clark demanded that citizens, and artists in particular, be given the opportunity to accomplish what the state and its institutions had failed to do. He even went so far as to castigate anyone who might dare to condemn his works. In so doing, such persons (or institutions) attacked not only freedom, but Western culture generally: “The value of art is so closely related to occidental beliefs in individual rights of free expression that one can accurately speak of the state of art as a measure of the state of freedom in our society.”[73] Addressed to police, the statement implicitly challenged the legal institution to prove that law was not inconsistent with life. But Matta-Clark’s response also signaled a distinct shift in his thinking that revealed the legally fraught nature of property destruction. Consistent not only with previous efforts to minimize waste and maximize value but also with contemporaneous legal decisions barring owners from destroying their own property for fear of wasting resources, the artist emphasized *Day's End* as an act of value preservation.[74] Unintentionally echoing moral rights justifications for preserving artworks, namely that there is a public interest in protecting significant cultural resources, Matta-Clark further claimed that his work had general social and cultural value that made it a public resource worthy of preservation. With its well-placed apertures seemingly calculated to show the warehouse interior in the most favorable light, *Day's End* lent itself to stunning photographic representation that harmonized strategically with juridical sympathy for aesthetic beauty. Incidentally, the best argument for preserving *Day's End*, at least to courts concerned with maximizing economic value, may have been the prices its documentation commanded and the artist's vigilance in monitoring the same. As if to presage the Copyright Act of 1976, the artist declared, "I must take special steps to insure that too many copies of my slides or negatives don't get distributed without due protection and remuneration."[75] Matta-Clark, who relied on the sale of such documentation for his livelihood, fully understood how the structures of intellectual property were integral to the growth of his market.

The New York City Economic Development Agency, the branch of city government charged with overseeing waterfront property, remained unconvinced and shut the work down for reasons of public safety. Cited ad nauseam in capitalist and socialist regimes alike, public safety is difficult to argue against or, more importantly, *with*. Certainly, it was impossible to contest, particularly in mid-1970s New York. The "authorities" made his work "safe" by erecting railings on a bridge and closing off the surface entrances.[76] As Matta-Clark would write with some bitterness, "This contradiction between vandalizing my work—making it fit (safe) for public circulation while totally closing it off from the public, make[s] its history a remarkable portrait of bureaucratic absurdity."[77] In a time when police were in notoriously short supply in a crime-infested city, it struck Matta-Clark that policing his intervention wasted taxpayer resources. City authorities exerted themselves on behalf of protecting the public, but their actual object was reducing the risk of their own liability.

Criminologist Jeff Ferrell argues that human interaction can devolve into a state of dichotomy between illegal and legal behavior.[78] Although Ferrell writes hypothetically, this notion of dichotomy is particularly apt in light of 1970s New York, given how local governments pursued even minor violations of their property interests. The deep recession led to severe cuts in other forms of protection, including law enforcement and social services, but had little bearing on government vigilance in apprehending those who violated its property interests. In addition, the discourse on safety had expanded to an unprecedented degree in the mid-1970s. Laws designed to prevent physical harm, consumer protection laws, and occupational safety laws proliferated in large quantity, including the Occupational Safety and Health Act of 1970, which empowered the federal government to enforce safety and health standards for workers. Safety rhetoric became so established that it was routinely cited by governments seeking to justify even measures likely to minimize the very public they purported to serve.[79]

The risks Matta-Clark took figure as efforts to push back against the deadening rhetoric of public safety and the general earnestness of the managed society that city government officials considered vital. Anticipating, perhaps, the specter Ferrell would later raise of a world defined by safety discourse, Matta-Clark formed communities around the conditions of risk and danger that the law tried to erase or at least minimize. In his influential 1976 treatise on safety, William Lowrance argued that safety was a judgment question; an object, activity, or structure is safe if its attendant risks are judged to be acceptable.[80] Matta-Clark leaves it up to the viewer to decide whether to enter *Day's End* or *Splitting* and how extensively she interacts with it. In any other circumstance, the disrupted structure would have called for hard hats and other protective gear. But in Matta-Clark's *Splitting* film, visitors show little trepidation. The building cuts are a source of pleasure derived from both the social nature of the event and the novelty of engaging with the physical surroundings. The future suggested by *Splitting* involved a world no longer governed by fear or a need to constantly manage risk as defined by a state interested in using the concept of risk to manage its citizenry, in the name of public safety.

For the artist, there is the risk that someone may sue for any injury suffered on the property, a risk Matta-Clark addressed by going so far as to take out a two-week liability policy in one instance.[81] He insisted on personally undertaking the manual labor needed to create the work while recognizing how "contrary" it was to other ways of working, including the increasingly common practice of outsourcing the fabrication of large-scale works.[82] His willingness to undertake fabrication and its accompanying dangers, even when it was common artistic convention to authorize others to do so, suggests another definition of integrity, one commensurate with an individual's appetite for risk and that pivoted on confronting not how much one might gain, but rather how much one was willing to lose. The second condition, danger, rests on an extremely heightened sense of self. It is a condition that makes one face the possibility of death or injury, and not as part of a carefully managed experience. Uninterested in making life predictable, Matta-Clark brought his audiences literally to a precipice by putting them in the position of having to answer for their own occupation of space. If the label of "avant-garde" still conferred a leadership role on visual artists, Matta-Clark's works and statements implied that it meant having to raise various situations to the surface of legal awareness, or at least to get audiences thinking about what directions law should take.

THE LOT OF FREE SPACE

A young woman stands in what looks like someone's pleasant jumble of a study (fig. 51). She wears an expression that suggests satisfaction, or at least contentment. Her right arm is draped casually over a guitar case opened to reveal a pair of large bolt cutters inside. She is Ann Messner, a few years after her pilfering escapades in Germany (described in the Introduction). Although she stands over the tool in a cluttered space filled with boxes, cases, and equipment, the image conveys the air of commemoration.

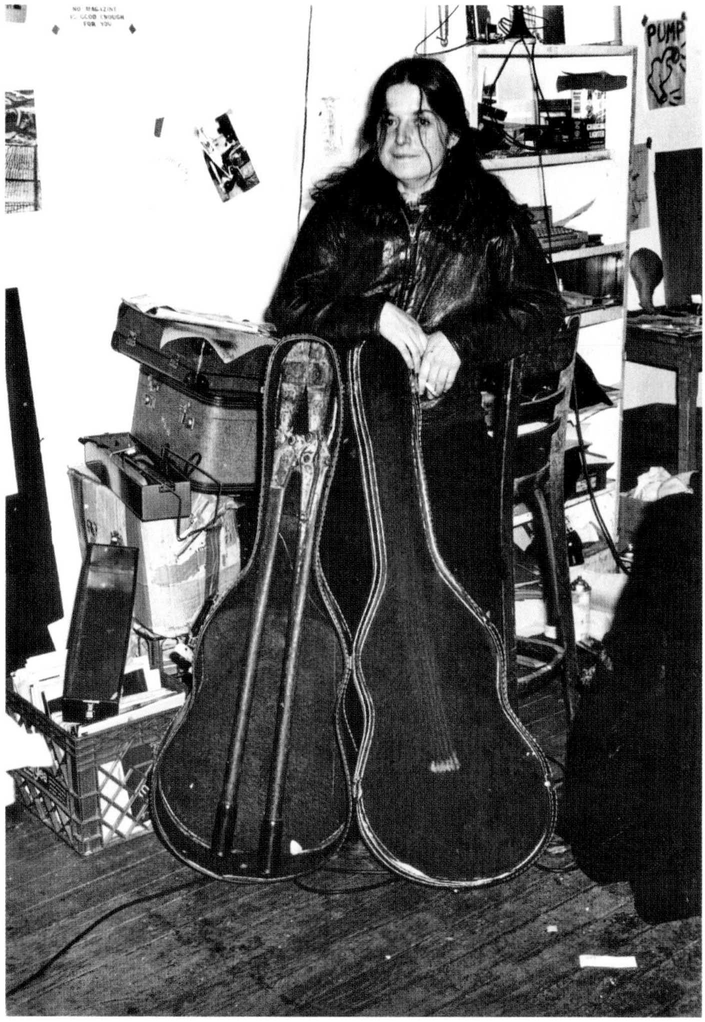

FIGURE 51
Ann Messner with bolt cutters used to enter 125 Delancey Street, the Real Estate Show, Lower East Side, New York, 1980. Photo: Peter Moennig. Courtesy of Ann Messner. © Ann Messner.

If the bolt cutters were accorded the treatment of a relic, it was because of how they symbolized one of the most notorious occupations of government property since *Day's End*.[83] Frustrated by bureaucratic nonresponse to multiple requests for a building in which to show their work, a dedicated band of artists cut the lock barring access to 123 Delancey Street in the Lower East Side of New York. There they held "The Real Estate Show," a group exhibition of works intended to call attention to the problems of social displacement shrouded by the myths of abundance and quality: "The illusion of free available space—Freiraum—promoted throughout modern art and represented in the American society by the misconception of equal opportunities for everyone does not work."[84] The show was backed by Colab, a loose organization of artists, including those formerly in Matta-Clark's employ as assistants. Messner recounts Colab as having

> a collective disregard for institutional structures and traditional modes of practice. Out of the cultural malaise caused by Vietnam, the tragic assassinations of quixotic public figures, the images of kids being hosed and in the case of Kent State gunned down, the indiscriminate blazing of the inner city already in desperate need of repair, very little that remained standing seemed at all respectable. Just as with the neglected neighborhoods, particularly in New York where we chose to live, reality had fallen apart exposing distressing hypocrisy. And not surprisingly our relationship as artists to culture took on the form of refusal and deconstruction.[85]

When Messner and her colleagues approached Colab for funding, already there was significant trepidation regarding possible legal implications. Some, like Coleen Fitzgibbon, felt that the organization "shouldn't be doing anything illegal during this period where the state was getting more aggressive."[86] Others feared jeopardizing future chances of obtaining public funding.[87] Still they went through with their plan, which, like *Day's End,* resembled an inverse taking, whereby public property was expropriated for private aims. Yet here the occupation of Messner and her colleagues was a collective no-confidence vote in the law and its presumptive ability to uphold justice. As the original notice for the show stated, it was undertaken to commemorate the memory of Elizabeth Mangum, an African American woman killed by police while resisting eviction in Flatbush, New York.

In many ways, Messner and her colleagues rose to the call Jimmy Carter sounded in his famous "malaise" speech given only a few months earlier. Delivered to assuage what Carter dubbed a "crisis of confidence" amid rising inflation, an unprecedented energy crisis borne of overdependence on imported oil, and high unemployment, the speech was a well-intentioned but ultimately doomed attempt to urge citizens to reverse the trend whereby "human identity is no longer defined by what one does, but by what one owns."[88] New York City government may have threatened to sue Matta-Clark because he had the audacity to question the integrity of the real property regime. Yet if the cuts into Pier 52 were for him another means of creation, such generative activity would soon be reabsorbed into the market. As artist and critic Gary Indiana lamented on the occasion of Matta-Clark's first retrospective, the "baldly mercantile" interest that galleries displayed in urban detritus reflected how "the Reagan Years have left artists with little to do besides amuse the idle rich and decorate executive offices."[89]

"The Real Estate Show" was never intended to inscribe one set of property rights over another. An announcement proclaimed the show as an "extra-legal" action, meaning that it "illuminated no legal issues, calls for no 'rights'. It is preemptive and insurrectionary."[90] The symbolic cast of the bolt cutters emphasized how the show's organizers intended to free the space from the system of property that justified the authority of the state, even when that authority was misplaced or abused. Despite Colab's fears of an "aggressive state," none of the artists involved in "The Real Estate Show" were arrested. Messner later claimed that the publicity attracted by the illegal break-in unnerved city officials who feared having to account for their managerial failures, particularly in the Lower East Side.[91] Instead, after protracted negotiation, which the city refused permission to document, the artists were given another building, which became ABC No Rio, an important center for socially engaged art and activism. Like *Splitting* and *Day's End*, "The Real Estate Show" tried to facilitate a future in which individual voices might be amplified. The hopes Messner later expressed "as a citizen of a country with such overzealous military and economic interests" for an expanded civil movement in Western Europe also applied to why defiance still mattered as a form of productive political and legal engagement: that it might enable citizens "to finally determine their own future" despite government ineptitude or negligence.[92] As the next chapter shows, what self-determination actually looked like could vary as much as the people on whose behalf governments purported to act, yet whom they failed to adequately recognize.

4

RADICAL OBEDIENCE

Tehching Hsieh's *One Year Performances*

FROM 123 DELANCEY, it takes about twenty minutes to walk to the north entrance of the New York City Criminal Courts Building on 100 Centre Street. Here, on a spring day in 1982, a young man named Tehching Hsieh was photographed after being released from custody following an arrest for assault and battery (fig. 52). Thc incident occurred during his undertaking of *One Year Performance 1981–1982*, a work the thirty-year-old artist began in September 1981. Known informally as *Outdoor Piece,* it consisted of him living outdoors for an entire calendar year without entering any built structure. The photograph here shows him centered in the composition, one hand in a pocket and his rucksack casually laid at his feet, as if to suggest that posing for the camera marked only a brief respite in his continuous journey. In the background is a long granite wall that has been cropped in such a way as to omit the courthouse's true height of seventeen stories. Nonetheless, we can still read the legend that runs across the top like a frieze: "THE ONLY TRUE PRINCIPLE OF HUMANITY IS JUSTICE. JUSTICE IS DENIED NO ONE."

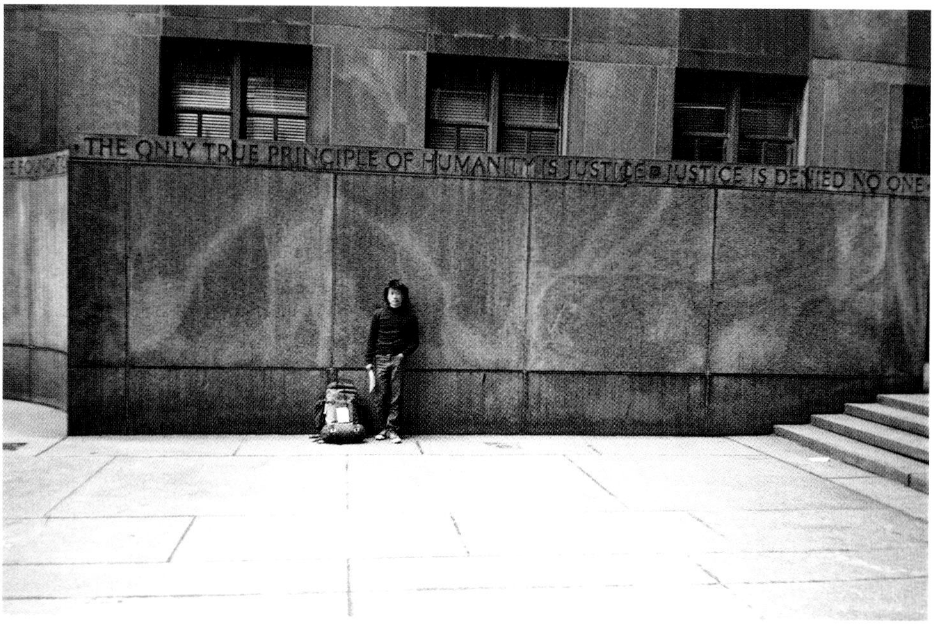

FIGURE 52
Tehching Hsieh, *One Year Performance 1981–1982*. "Life Image." © 1981 Tehching Hsieh. Courtesy of the artist and Sean Kelly, New York.

When published in 2008 in *Out of Now: The Lifeworks of Tehching Hsieh,* the most comprehensive catalogue of his works to date, the photograph was cropped on the right by the book's designer, an intriguing truncation whose unintentional effect was to emphasize "justice is." The phrase recalls a running joke among Asian Americans, Hispanic Americans, and African Americans accused of crimes who ask whether "justice" is more accurately rephrased as "just us," a telling pun that lays bare the realities of a justice system often prejudiced against nonwhite suspects.[1] As an incomplete sentence, "justice is" becomes an open question to viewers who must consider the effect of identity on an individual's relationship to the law, a connection frankly highlighted by Hsieh's standing directly in front of the courthouse wall. The physical distance between the text above and the artist standing his ground below suggests a profound disjunction between the rhetoric of American democracy and the experience of being subject to its regulations. By including the legend above, Hsieh corrals the law within the picture frame, a tacit reminder that the law is also subject to framing by others.

Completed between 1978 and 1983, the first four of Hsieh's *One Year Performances* involved extremely regulated living situations demanding intense levels of physical and psychological endurance. They included living in a small cage like a prisoner (*One Year Performance 1978–1979*, informally called *Cage Piece*); living entirely out of doors

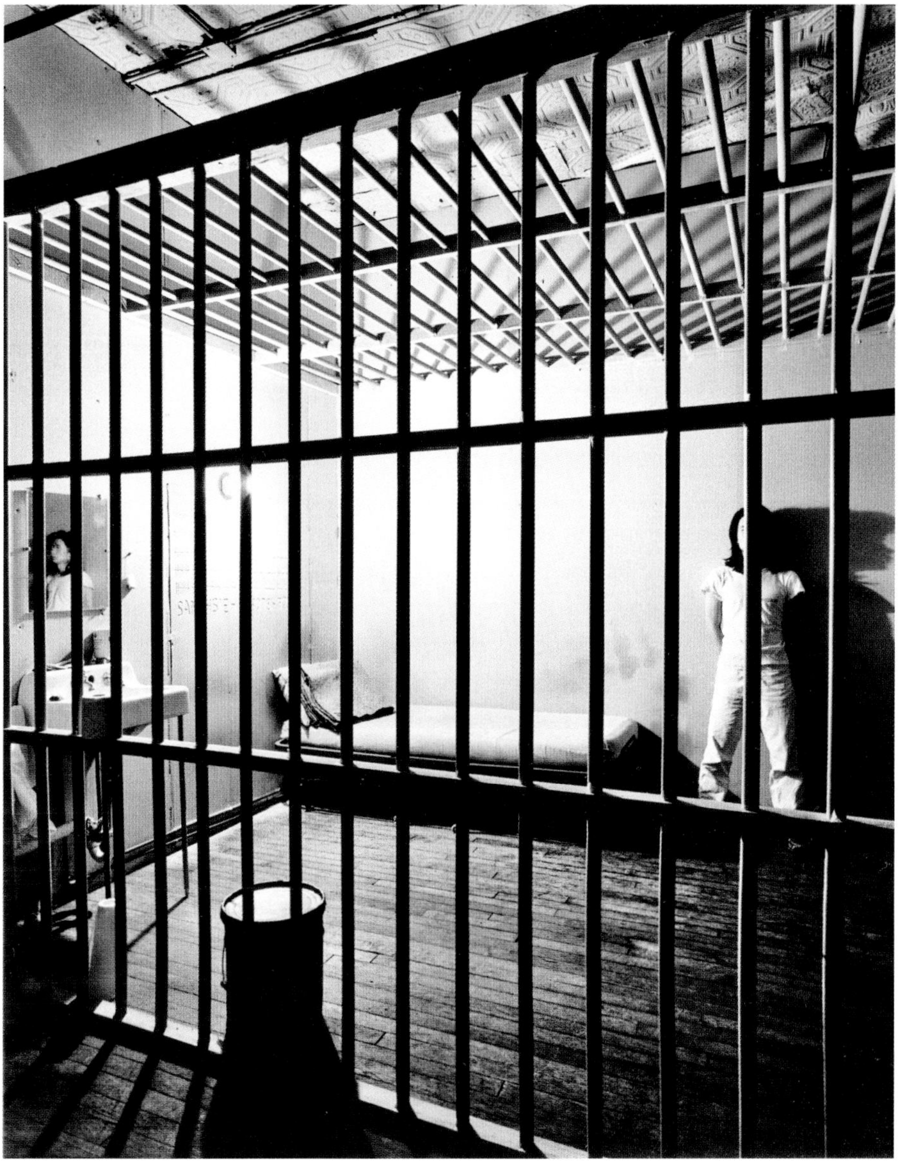

FIGURE 53
Harry Shunk, *Tehching "Sam" Hsieh, One Year Performance, New York, 1979 October 8*. Photo: Harry Shunk.
© J. Paul Getty Trust. Getty Research Institute, Los Angeles (2014.R.20).

without entering any natural or constructed dwelling (*Outdoor Piece*); feeding a card into a time clock every hour (*One Year Performance 1980–1981*, or *Time Clock Piece*); and, perhaps most psychologically challenging, cohabiting with but not touching another individual, the artist Linda Montano, despite being tied to her with an eight-foot preshrunk nylon rope (*Art/Life: One Year Performance 1983–1984*, or *Rope Piece*).

Each of these works was accompanied by a typed statement composed by Hsieh indicating the scope and limits of his actions. These he signed, dated, and distributed prior to beginning each performance, and their language primes them to be read as if they were contracts, a framing Hsieh strongly implied when he remarked that the "language of the law was appropriate to support my ideas."[2] The contract, a legally binding agreement regulating the interaction between one party and another, offers a useful conceptual framework through which to consider Hsieh's first four *One Year Performances,* given the formal congruence between his written statements and contracts as well as how diligently Hsieh fulfilled the terms outlined in each statement. In fact, so vigilant was Hsieh about discharging these duties that his projects bring to mind the legal definition of *performance,* the accomplishment of an obligation set forth in a contract.[3]

Hsieh's steadfast adherence to his written statements nevertheless reads as a form of competition, of wanting to beat the law at its own game by structuring a world through rules so unforgiving as to render obedience a form of sustained punishment. Rather than propose hypothetical instructions or perform feats of endurance as incidents of spectacle, Hsieh created for himself an entire system of living that reinforced his own claims to self-determination, legal and social status notwithstanding. In *Cage Piece* and *Time Clock Piece,* he declares his very autonomy by being his own warden, the one in full command of the terms and conditions of his regulated state of living (fig. 53).[4] In *Rope Piece,* he placed no restrictions on the number of people he and Montano met or on the content of those interactions.[5] Yet the duration of the interaction was limited to that of a social call; viewers could enter the world of Montano and Hsieh, but only on their specific terms.[6] As the artist stated, "I was the one who built rules, executed them and broke them as well."[7] The unbending strictness of these rules and Hsieh's corresponding obedience to them grafted personal integrity onto professional integrity in ways that made the force of actual statutory and judicial law seem pale by comparison.

THE AESTHETICS OF TRANSPARENCY

In May 1978, four years after he entered the United States from Taiwan illegally, Hsieh created *Wanted by U.S. Immigration Service,* a mock wanted poster affixed to various places in downtown New York (fig. 54).[8] Resembling standard intake forms used to process foreign nationals, *Wanted by U.S. Immigration Service* gave new meaning to a history of works using various types of documentation to address how identity became increasingly defined through legally sanctioned forms and techniques of identification. Biometric technologies proliferated in the 1970s, especially as prisons, banks, military offices, and government agents sought to tighten access to physical spaces in the name of security.[9] Having one's documents in order—having to prove one's right to stay—was an indelible part of life for any foreign national and even more so for those who were *illegal aliens,* a quasi-legal term used by the U.S. government and

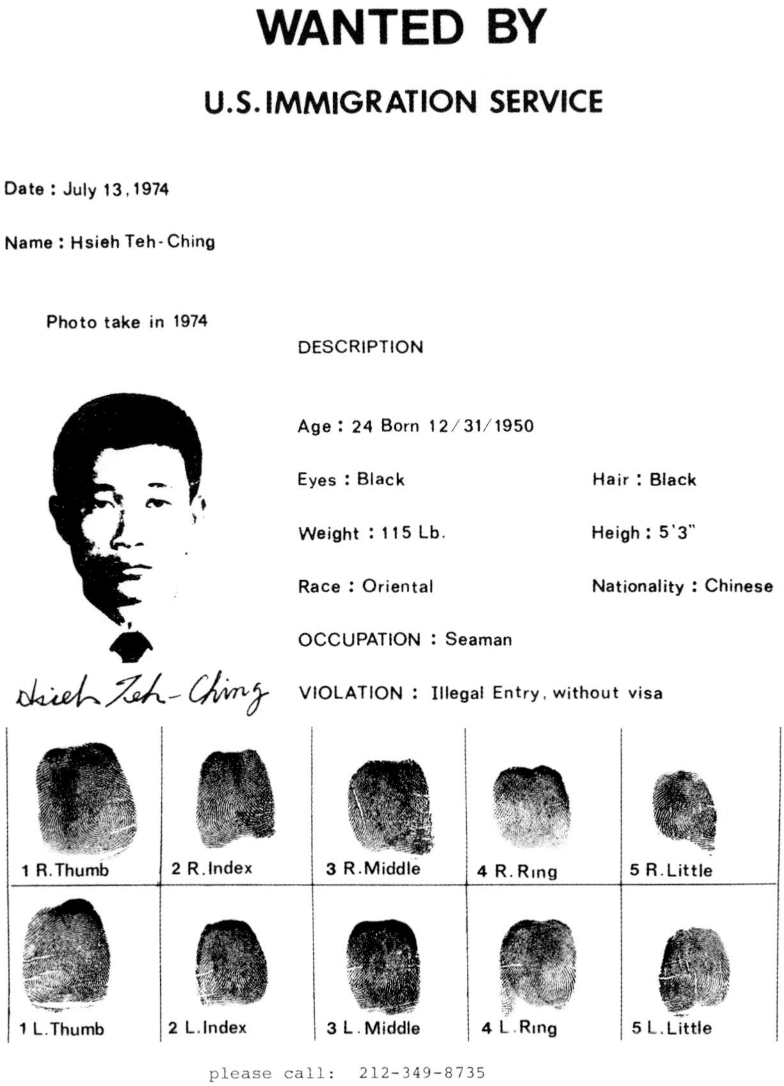

WANTED BY

U.S. IMMIGRATION SERVICE

Date : July 13, 1974

Name : Hsieh Teh-Ching

Photo take in 1974

DESCRIPTION

Age : 24 Born 12/31/1950

Eyes : Black

Hair : Black

Weight : 115 Lb.

Heigh : 5'3"

Race : Oriental

Nationality : Chinese

OCCUPATION : Seaman

Hsieh Teh-Ching

VIOLATION : Illegal Entry, without visa

1 R.Thumb
2 R.Index
3 R.Middle
4 R.Ring
5 R.Little

1 L.Thumb
2 L.Index
3 L.Middle
4 L.Ring
5 L.Little

please call: 212-349-8735

FIGURE 54
Tehching Hsieh, *Wanted by U.S. Immigration Service*, 1978. © 1978 Tehching Hsieh. Courtesy of the artist and Sean Kelly, New York.

federal agencies to indicate what courts called "undocumented aliens," or individuals entering the United States without proper documentation or permission.[10] To avoid arrest and deportation, Hsieh used "Sam" as a pseudonym.

Shown in the exhibition "Illegal America," *Wanted by U.S. Immigration Service* throws into stark relief Hsieh's own cultural and national background as defined by immigration law: "Culture shock and the language gap deepened my experience as an illegal immigrant."[11] Hsieh wrote to curator Jeannette Ingberman of his depression living as an illegal immigrant in the United States: "I was always thinking [that the] immigration service wanted me."[12] When Hsieh came to the United States, the distinctions between citizens and noncitizens, and between criminals and noncriminals, were deeply inscribed in his everyday life. During his first few years in New York, he worked as a dishwasher and cleaner at a Chinese restaurant that immigration officials periodically targeted while hunting for illegal aliens.[13] The hunt was overcast by a parallel sense of new racial pressures brought to bear as the devastation wreaked by the Vietnam War led to an influx of refugees from Indochina. Together with the rapidly increasing numbers of Mexicans seeking greater economic opportunities in the United States, this contributed to a shift in immigration, with more Asian and Latin American nationals than Europeans entering the country for permanent settlement. By 1976, the Immigration and Naturalization Service had detained or arrested over a million illegal migrants, thus prompting the creation of the Immigration Reform and Control Act in 1982. Intended to "close the back door to immigration," the act criminalized the hiring of illegal aliens.[14] From its introduction to when it became law in 1986, many courts became so anti-immigration as to openly endorse racist practices. Even lawful permanent residents, particularly elderly Asian Americans on public assistance, were "returned" to their countries of ethnic origin.[15] Hsieh's disclosure through art reads as a form of extreme self-reporting that created the distance necessary from which to consider this context.

Such disclosure sharply contrasts with the intensification of surveillance under martial law in Taiwan, inflected by Taiwanese anxiety over growing international acceptance of the People's Republic of China.[16] Hsieh would later suggest that his coming to the United States was born of a need to be somewhere that allowed "the liberty to do certain things."[17] Yet, on another level, the public dissemination of the wanted poster reflected how privacy was largely a fantasy, an abstraction to make concrete the notion of the "public interest" on whose behalf governments claimed to act. Voluntary, preemptive disclosure was perhaps the only way of preempting the subjection of everyone—illegal aliens and citizens alike—to an ever-growing bureaucracy from which attempted escape was futile.

Wanted by U.S. Immigration Service resonated with artistic efforts to model the kind of behavior some artists felt was conspicuously missing from the very institutions empowered to uphold ideal standards of conduct. Against numerous acts of state subterfuge, such as President Richard Nixon's ill-fated attempts in 1972 to cover up the illegal break-in of Democratic National Committee headquarters at the Watergate complex in Washington, D.C., transparency through acts of personal disclosure became an important artistic tactic. Between 1976 and 1977, Chris Burden produced his multipart work *Full Financial Disclosure*, including a short television commercial during which the artist announced his intent to "to be the first artist to publicly make a full financial disclosure," followed by images of his tax returns. A concurrent exhibi-

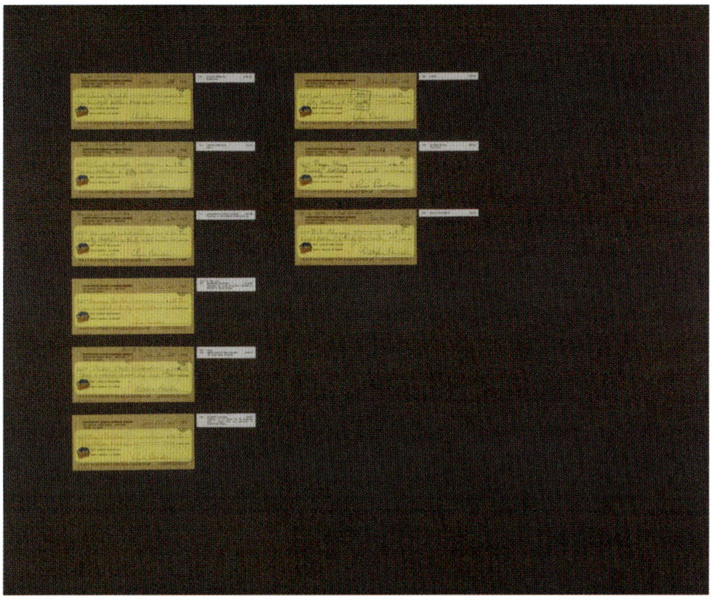

FIGURE 55
Chris Burden, Detail of *Full Financial Disclosure*, 1977. Work on paper, 30.2 × 36.2 inches. © 2017 Chris Burden/licensed by the Chris Burden Estate and Artists Rights Society (ARS), New York.

tion displayed Burden's canceled checks and tax returns for the year (fig. 55). Later describing *Full Financial Disclosure* as parody, Burden's earnest recitation of intent and facts mimicked the self-righteousness underpinning attempts to hold federal authorities accountable for their behaviors.[18]

Full Financial Disclosure took place when Congress discussed the Full Financial Disclosure Act, a bill introduced in January 1977 that would require federal employees to disclose their income and financial transactions with the government. Although never passed into law, the bill's introduction suggested that some lawmakers firmly believed that government employees, particularly those in positions of authority, should be held particularly accountable.[19] Burden suggested that his work developed out of a veiled exhaustion with the excessive calls for financial transparency and even as a form of defense: "I've come clean as to where I got all my money, where it went, and how much I made, okay? I'm clean."[20] Unlike his government counterparts being made to involuntarily account for their actions, Burden voluntarily offers himself as a model for the kind of transparency newly demanded of government by the law, paying for the commercial himself using a substantial proportion of his meager personal income. Burden's self-sufficiency recalled the way some artists strove to prevent external interests from determining how and where they could undertake their work by foregoing public grants or private sponsorship. Christo and Jeanne-Claude sold futures in their works to support their mammoth installations without donor backing, while Hsieh and Montano installed art, cleaned apartments, and undertook repair and carpentry work to support themselves.[21]

By freely and even brazenly revealing so much personal information, including his real name, Hsieh incurred far more personal risk than Burden. The disclosure potentially exposed him to Taiwanese state surveillance; the deeply anti-Communist state was known to monitor its citizens abroad for any fraternization with mainland Chinese.[22] Yet the act of creating the poster suggested that Hsieh was reclaiming personal information from the state. It recalls coincident demands that artist Bruce Conner made of San Jose State University to return fingerprints it took when he was in the university's employ: "My fingerprints have a value in themselves as works of art. Unless they are sold or leased under agreement with me then they cannot be represented without my permission."[23] Having long signed his works with thumbprints partly to guard against forgeries, Conner emphasized his point by collaborating with Palo Alto police to produce fingerprints he included in a limited-edition artwork.[24] Privacy was allegedly not at issue, even though the Supreme Court had legitimized fingerprinting in general on grounds that it did not probe "into an individual's private life and thoughts."[25] As Conner put it, "Everything I am is public, but I want what belongs to me. If anything belongs to me, it's my hand."[26] In framing his protest as a property law question, Conner deftly complicated the rapidly escalating debate over whether the "fundamental" right to privacy might outweigh the state's interest in ensuring public safety.

The questions Hsieh's poster raises come into sharper focus when brought together with the New York City Police Department rapsheet that doubled as an exhibition booklet for a show of Andy Warhol paintings at the Sonnabend Gallery in Paris in 1967 (fig. 56). An important precedent for Hsieh and other artists who used legal documentation and forms developed for legal administration and enforcement as artistic material, Warhol's booklet casts artistic representation as a source for thinking about the implications of legal change. A replica of a police publication issued by the NYPD for the apprehension of thirteen most-wanted criminals, the booklet rehabilitated the images Warhol used for *Thirteen Most Wanted Men,* his thirteen silkscreened mug shots commissioned as murals for the façade of the Queens Museum. Removed by officials a few days before the opening of the 1964 World's Fair in New York, the murals highlighted legal as well as political tensions.[27] Although Warhol authorized the effacement of his own work, the removal wove together urgent questions regarding artists' intellectual property and freedom of expression with legislative and judicial tensions concerning privacy rights.[28] Warhol had obtained the mug shots from a publicly available publication, issued in the wake of significant recent criminal law decisions like *Kolb v. O'Connor,* a 1957 case holding that even a "minute possibility" that a person's arrest record might prevent or solve a future or present crime outweighed the "conjectural harm" that might result from the record's dissemination.[29] Legislators' concerns regarding the easy accessibility of personal records, including arrest records of innocent individuals, swung the pendulum in the other direction.[30] Supreme Court Justice William Rehnquist may have put it best when he proposed that legal decisions regarding privacy be analyzed "not only in terms of the values they would advance, but in terms

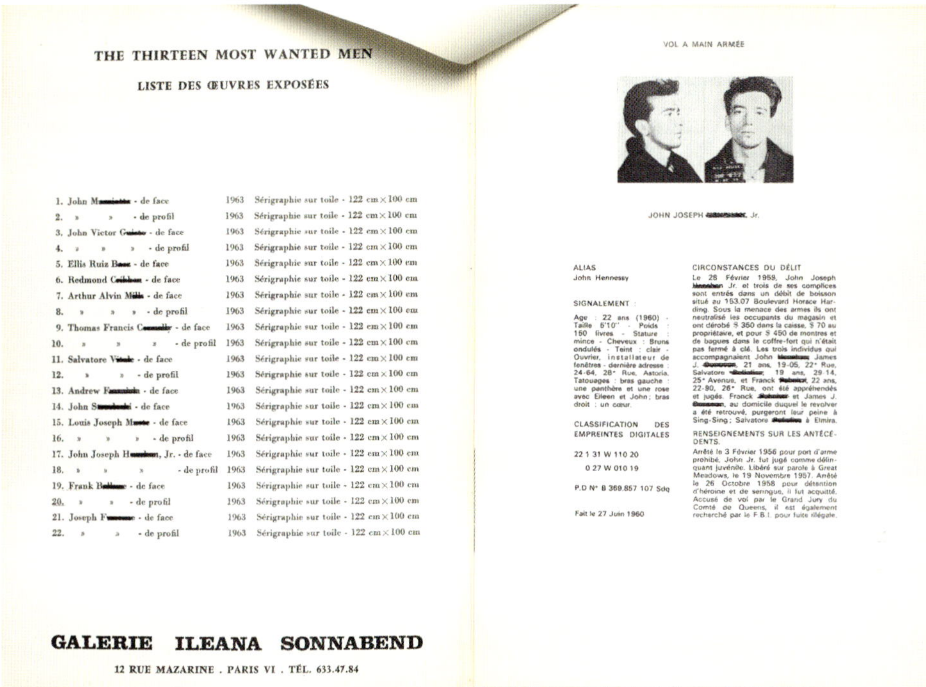

FIGURE 56
Andy Warhol, illustration in *The Thirteen Most Wanted Men: Dossier No. 2357*, 1967. Dossier with printed paper checklist, offset lithograph, and criminal rapsheet. Museum purchase, Reva and David Logan Collection of Illustrated Books, Reva and David Logan Fund, Fine Arts Museum of San Francisco. © 2018, Andy Warhol Foundation for the Visual Arts, Inc./Licensed by Artists Rights Society (ARS), New York.

of the values they would displace," including the value of having an orderly society through police enforcement.[31] A further layer of complication was juridical debate as to whether the mug-shot format was inherently prejudicial toward its subjects.[32]

In the Sonnabend Gallery booklet, proper names identifying specific individuals were struck through, presumably a nod to the fugitives' privacy interests. The names, however, remained legible, as opposed to erased per redaction. For the point was not to capitulate to American privacy rhetoric or even to recognize the wanted men as rights-bearing subjects, but rather to acknowledge their personhood and its subsequent construction via the visual templates of law.

Hsieh, who respected what he called Warhol's "criticality," pushed the latter's thinking further by framing self-representation—self-portraiture—as a function of data management.[33] Created about a decade after Warhol's booklet, when the rate of information production led to increased government regulation, *Wanted by U.S. Immigration Service* addressed the wanted poster category of portraiture, defined by the purging of subjectivity. Yet it reads as an act of reclamation as well as disclosure. Information concealed from a public that legislators might describe as "unauthorized persons," information used to feed a growing database of suspicion, was thus made available to all. At the same time, the free disclosure of Hsieh's metrics only emphasizes the unknowability of his private thoughts. An example of how law sustained its regulatory hold through nonlegislated forms, the wanted poster is a type of signage used by law enforcement officials to apprehend criminals. It denotes the reach of state control by making personal data widely known without having to first obtain the subject's consent. However, as Rachel Hall suggests in her study of wanted posters in the United States, the form and scope of the poster also advertises the state's limitations by documenting the existence of subjects that have escaped its reach.[34] A form of depiction based on its ability to persuade viewers to look outside it, the wanted poster delegates the surveillance function of the law to ordinary viewers. Like the suspect lineup or neighborhood watch advertisements, the wanted poster belongs to a class of depictions whose usefulness depends on how well it can get private citizens to perform the role of the state on its behalf.

Looking at *Wanted by U.S. Immigration Service* through Warhol makes clearer how adeptly Hsieh channeled a deadpan aura, a connection that both folded him into a larger conversation about contemporary art and amplified its rhetorical force. Adamantly dispassionate, the description of Hsieh's physical characteristics permits viewers to look back at the poster as an example of how the force of law is reflected by its uncanny ability to both identify and render anonymous the individuals over which it holds jurisdiction. The work makes transparent the empiricist reimagining of the body typical of wanted posters, as well as how state perceptions of identity depend on reinscribing individual selves into a stratified framework based on constructed rubrics of citizen, criminal, and alien. Above all, it provokes viewers to comprehend the limitations of Hsieh's legal situation in order to fully explore what those limitations allow.

That law and legal subjects continued to interest Hsieh can be inferred from the articles he cut and pasted in notebooks during his year performing *Rope Piece*. His clippings include reports of a person who had no legal existence because of a lack of documentation, as well as articles about the right to die, the challenges of prison life, the struggle of black Americans to gain full citizenship rights, and workplace sexism.[35] Yet he has also explicitly stated that "law is not the reason nor foundation" of his works.[36] Still, by understanding just how much law depended not only on the communication of meaning in written form, but on the use and repetition of specific forms, Hsieh constructively claimed a place within the American body politic, even if his claim would be officially recognized only decades later, when he became a U.S. citizen in 1994. So attuned was Hsieh to the workings of U.S. law that it occasionally seemed as if he could predict its course: *Wanted by U.S. Immigration Service* appeared tailor-made to meet one of the most stringent requirements of the Immigration Reform and Control Act of 1986. The largest amnesty program for illegal aliens in U.S. history, it required applicants to prove they had entered the country illegally before 1982. Federal law required citizenship applicants to pass a civics test demonstrating basic knowledge of history and government, but Hsieh's detailed comprehension of the law's enactment through specific visual and verbal protocols more than proved his bona fides as a citizen. That the written statements for the *One Year Performances* looked and sounded as if they could actually be contracts resonated profoundly with how U.S. law acknowledged the right of illegal aliens to enter into contracts. At the time of the first four *One Year Performances,* illegal aliens were permitted to form valid contracts that could be upheld in a court of law.[37] A type of document legitimated by the demonstration of mutual consent, the contract, under both the Fourteenth Amendment and section 1981 of the U.S. Code, guarantees that "all parties within the jurisdiction of the United States shall have the same right in every State and Territory to make and enforce contracts."[38] Contract law was one of the few opportunities for an illegal alien—otherwise so vulnerable to multiple forms of legal and illegal power—to exert genuine agency. In this regard, Hsieh's authority resulted partly from his ability to convert a disadvantageous legal status into a source of ethical advantage.

FROM CONCEPTUALISM TO CONTRACT

The typewritten texts accompanying the *One Year Performances* each follow roughly the same format. The date is flush right at the top of a sheet of white, U.S. letter-size paper (fig. 57). Below the date appear several sentences under the general header "*STATEMENT.*" The first sentence begins with the identification of the author (for example, in the case of *Cage Piece,* "I, Sam Hsieh"), followed by a description of his general intentions ("plan to do a one year performance piece") and the conditions under which the performance will be undertaken ("I shall seal myself in my studio, in solitary confinement inside a cell-room").[39] The artist signs each statement, and his studio address is centered at the bottom of the page.

According to Hsieh, his statements were written without reference to any existing models. But the form and language of each trails a well-established tradition of instruction-based conceptual artworks dating back to Marcel Duchamp and Tristan Tzara's "To Make a Dadaist Poem" (1920).[40] In the 1960s, experiments in musical notation by John Cage and the artists associated with Fluxus catalyzed the production of instruction-based works, ranging from Yoko Ono's proposal pieces, brief instructions that set forth mental or physical tasks to be carried out by the reader; to the "Wall Drawings" of Sol LeWitt (fig. 58), based solely on written directions and diagrams; to the "Activity Booklets" of Allan Kaprow describing predetermined actions drawn from the routines of everyday life, such as speaking to friends over the telephone. In each case, the artist charged an unidentified audience with performing a given action. Instruction-based works have often been described as examples of what art historian Benjamin Buchloh famously called the aesthetic of administration, a phrase illustrating how conceptual artists in the 1960s and '70s actively incorporated into their works the methods, forms, and materials associated with bureaucracy.

September 30, 1978

STATEMENT

I, Sam Hsieh, plan to do a one year performance piece,
to begin on September 30, 1978.

I shall seal myself in my studio, in solitary confinement
inside a cell-room measuring 11'6" X 9' X 8'.

I shall NOT converse, read, write, listen to the radio or
watch television, until I unseal myself on September 29, 1979.

I shall have food every day.

My friend, Cheng Wei Kuong, will facilitate this piece by
taking charge of my food, clothing and refuse.

Sam Hsieh

Sam Hsieh

111 Hudson Street, 2nd/Fl. New York 10013

FIGURE 57
Tehching Hsieh, *One Year Performance 1978–1979*. Statement. © 1978 Tehching Hsieh. Courtesy of the artist and Sean Kelly, New York.

A particular characteristic was using what Buchloh called "legalistic language," terms or words that might in fact be used in actual legal documents and whose presence was a symptom of how artists explored the workings of institutions in the name of critique: "The definition of the aesthetic becomes on the one hand a matter of linguistic convention and [on] the other the function of both a legal contract and an institutional discourse."[41] If conceptualism should figure prominently in discussions of art and the law, it is because so many of its practitioners called audiences to recognize the contingency of artworks in relation to the visual culture of the law and the

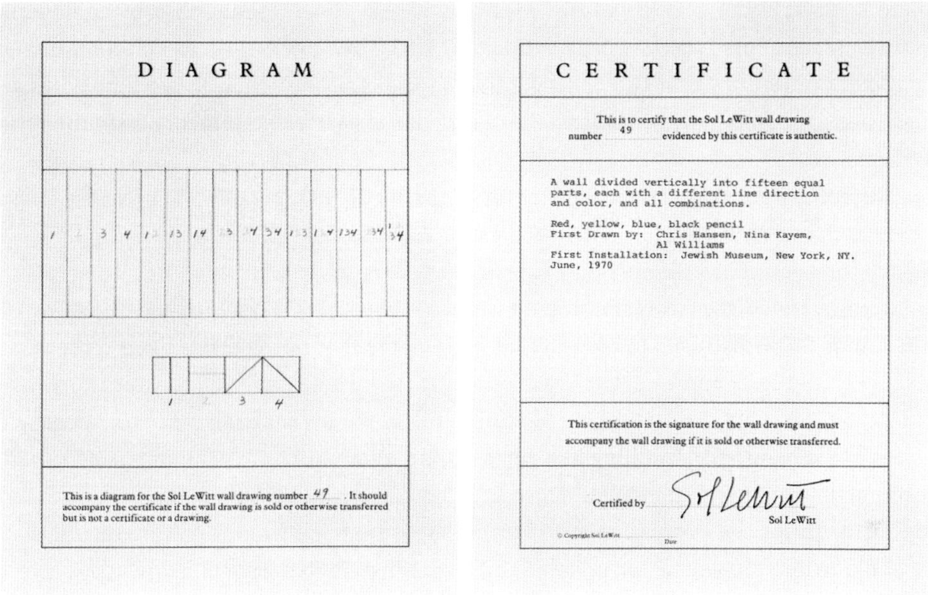

FIGURE 58
Sol LeWitt, proposal for wall drawing, 1970. © 2016 LeWitt Estate/Artists Rights Society (ARS), New York.

bureaucracies designed to uphold them. Vito Acconci later observed that creating a performance work was like "performing a contract," yet the same could hold for owners of instruction-based works.[42] Instructions for LeWitt's drawings, for instance, are not invitations but are in fact orders that must be fulfilled to produce a LeWitt. They are not legal notices per se, but the obligation imposed upon the bearer approximates the force of a contract.

In contrast to artists who typically obligated others to perform the carefully prescribed actions outlined in their work, Hsieh's self-imposed rules implicate him as a promissor, in legal terms someone who voluntarily pledges to fulfill a promise made to another party as part of a contract. Individual sentences in the artist's statements turn on Hsieh granting or denying himself access or permission. In *Cage Piece,* the second sentence explains what Hsieh will do ("I shall seal myself in my studio . . ."), while the third sets forth limits to his activities ("I shall NOT converse, read, write, listen to the radio or watch television . . ."). Hsieh mitigates the force of that denial in the fourth sentence with a brief permission ("I shall have food every day"), then concludes by delegating responsibility for "facilitat[ing]" the work to a named party ("My friend, Cheng Wei Kuong"). The repetition of "I" in beginning a sentence, particularly its use in the first statement, in which "I" is immediately followed by the artist's name, mimics the language used for all legal documents that require the affirmation of personal identity, such as a will. The combination of "I" and one's given name is used so often as to become ritual in the eyes of the law, an aspect Hsieh emphasized by calling his written statements "vow[s]."[43] The direct language of Hsieh's written statements was markedly different from the "exaggerated formalism" of which lawyers and jurists have been accused.[44] Nevertheless, the clarity of the written statements, including the conspicuous placement of words, resonates with the law's position on warranties. It recalls, for instance, how the Civil Court of the City of New York, in the 1971 case *Weisz v. Parke-Bernet Galleries, Inc.*, criticized as inadequate the "understated manner" with which the auction house warranty appeared in its catalogue.[45]

Legally, Hsieh's written statements were not contracts. There was no "meeting of the minds," a phrase used in contract law to indicate that both parties to an agreement are aware of the commitments they are making to one another. Neither was there *consideration,* the legal term referring to something of value that each party to a contract gives in exchange for fulfilling the terms of an agreement. Yet the language of the statements conveyed an express sense of obligation to an outside party, even if Hsieh never identifies the party save for what might be inferred from targeting mailings to "people in the art world" or posters and flyers distributed near his downtown New York studio on Hudson Street.[46]

The exception was *Rope Piece,* Hsieh's fourth *One Year Performance,* which took place after Montano, who read about *Cage Piece* in *High Performance,* met Hsieh through the artist Martha Wilson.[47] Hsieh too had been searching for a partner to whom to be tied.[48] Following their meeting, both artists agreed to undertake a performance that would require them to be literally tied together for a full year (fig. 59). Independent of Hsieh, Montano had been thinking about a comparable work as early as 1975. As described in a statement titled "Living Art: Time Spent Artfully Alone or Not Alone," such a work would consist of artists or nonartists living together "in a marathon fashion" after having the terms of cohabitation set by a "mutually workable contract."[49] Such a contract would declare any "time together and activity performed" as ART (capitalized by Montano).[50] Dated February 1983, not long after she met Hsieh, the statement for *Rope Piece* resembled an unusually specific prenuptial agreement, dividing all foreseeable responsibilities between the two artists. These included managing each day's schedule, documenting the performance, finding and/or making food, and earning money.

In a classic work on performance and agency, José Muñoz proposed the strategy of disidentification, whereby the performer refuses either complete assimilation into or resistance against what he calls "dominant ideology," a category to which the law might belong.[51] By adhering to a set of self-made rules as if any violation could in fact have real legal consequences, Hsieh's performance brings to mind the legal definition of performance, or the accomplishment of an obligation set forth in a contract. Yet it falls provocatively short as a gesture of compliance, for Hsieh's adherence comprised a form of authority not easily dispelled.

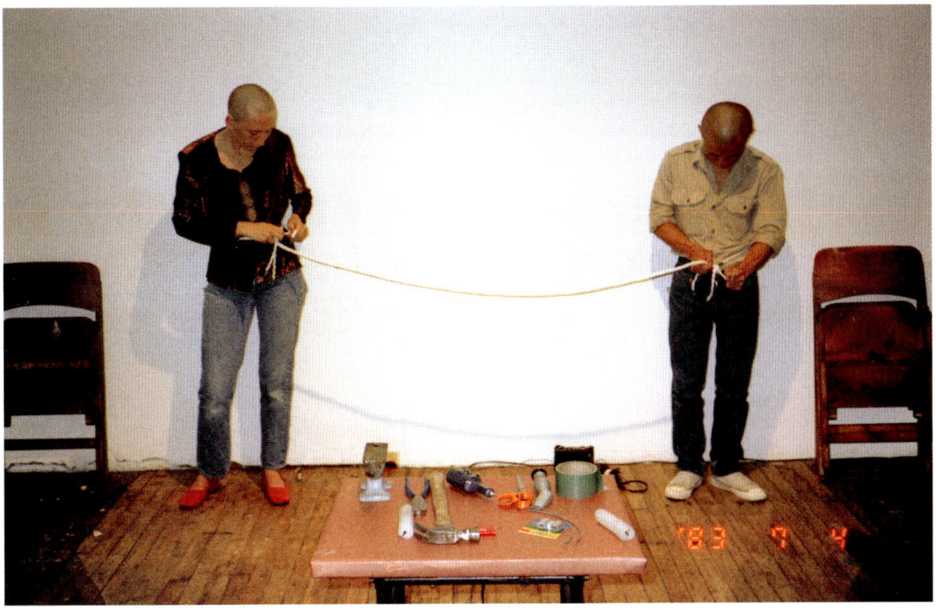

FIGURE 59
Tehching Hsieh and Linda Montano, *One Year Performance 1983–1984*. "365 Daily Image." © Tehching Hsieh, Linda Montano. Courtesy of the artists and Sean Kelly, New York.

Hsieh tried to communicate his ideas in the *One Year Performances* as clearly as possible, since the statements were directed to a generic reader.[52] Clear communication was particularly necessary because the statements were often the only explanation of what Hsieh was doing. Drafted in English with particularly important words first identified in Chinese and English, Hsieh's syntax and vocabulary are simple enough to be widely accessible.[53] In the statement for *Outdoor Piece,* he declares that he will "stay OUTDOORS," then describes that condition as the refusal "to go inside" (fig. 60). The next sentence explicitly defines the ambiguous condition of being "inside" as the occupation of any built structure, whether synthetic or natural, temporary or permanent (caves and tents are included, as well as buildings and various modes of mechanized transport). Anticipating the harsh New York winters, he then qualifies his promise in the next sentence, "I shall have a sleeping bag."

The succinctly composed statements accord with the standard of *plain meaning,* a legal term that refers to the judicial practice of interpreting text from the perspective of a lay reader. The plain meaning rule requires wording that does not have more than one likely interpretation, to ensure that a lay adult reader can easily understand a given document.[54] In the late 1970s, plain meaning became a key issue as consumer rights groups helped bring about state and federal initiatives to promote its use

September 26, 1981

STATEMENT

I, Tehching Hsieh, plan to do a one year performance piece.

I shall stay OUTDOORS for one year, never go inside.

I shall not go in to a building, subway, train, car,
airplane, ship, cave, tent.

I shall have a sleeping bag.

The performance shall begin on September 26, 1981 at
2 P.M. and continue until September 26, 1982 at 2 P.M.

Tehching Hsieh

New York City

FIGURE 60
Tehching Hsieh, *One Year Performance 1981–1982*. Statement. © 1981 Tehching Hsieh. Courtesy of the artist and Sean Kelly, New York.

in consumer contracts.[55] While there was no set readability test, the length of sentences, complexity of grammar and syntax, and difficulty of vocabulary were considered important criteria.[56] Hsieh's language also revealed almost nothing about his origins or background. The exception is a minor grammatical lapse in the second sentence of the written statement for *Outdoor Piece* ("I shall stay outdoors for one year, [and] never go inside"). The studied neutrality of Hsieh's words and syntax reads as strategic, for while Lady Justice may be blind, who and what she chose to hear depended very much on how messages were delivered. Even those of uncertain legal status could be heard so long as certain protocols and standards of communication were met.

Likewise, the clarity and concision of Hsieh's brief statements recall what was then juridical emphasis on intelligibility in deciding the validity of contracts. As the Court of Appeals for the Second Circuit held in an important 1977 decision, a contract had to articulate its provisions clearly ("It exhausts credulity to think that they or any other layman reading these legalistic words would have known or even suspected that they amounted to [such] an agreement"). Moreover, the contract's terms had to be easy to identify and not "buried in a multitude of words."[57] This ruling represented a decisive shift in the law from the 1960s, when the same court discounted the relevance of a contract's visual appearance in assessing its efficacy.[58] Hsieh maximized the readability of his texts by using generous spacing after each sentence. His selective use of capitalization ("I shall NOT converse, read, write, listen to the radio or watch television," in *Cage Piece,* for example) notably, if unintentionally, conformed to the standard of conspicuity set forth in the Uniform Commercial Code governing the sale of goods, which requires that any disclaimer in an agreement be "so written that a reasonable person against whom it is to operate ought to have noticed it. A printed heading in capitals is conspicuous. Language in the body of a form is 'conspicuous' if it is in larger or other contrasting type or color."[59]

BURDENS OF PROOF

The strong resemblance between the language and format of Hsieh's written statements for the *One Year Performances* and those of legal documents likewise may have assuaged the incredulity some viewers expressed regarding his work, which was performed largely out of the public eye. The full-year length of the artist's performances made it hard for some viewers to believe that he actually completed the work according to the letter. Before visiting Hsieh in his studio during the course of *Cage Piece,* critic Kay Larson confessed to assuming that the performance took place only on the days that the artist's space was open to the public.[60] Abundant photographs of his *One Year Performances* suggest that written documentation was insufficient as the sole proof of Hsieh's dutiful undertaking of his "contractual" obligations. As art historian Kathy O'Dell has argued, if a performance is best seen as a contractual structure joining an artist with an audience, it was photography that provided "pseudolegal" proof that such an agreement was in fact executed.[61] For *Cage Piece,* the artist even went so far as to hire Robert Projansky and a notary to ensure that he adhered to the terms he had set for himself.[62] Hsieh's upstairs neighbor, the artist Claire Fergusson, who also witnessed the work from beginning to end, remembers a lawyer signing slips of paper printed with the artist's name and serial number, which were then affixed to every joint in the cell (fig. 61).[63] On the final day of the performance, Hsieh walked out of the cage and shook hands with Projansky in front of an audience of seventy people. The ceremonial quality of the artist's entrance and exit from the cage suggested the

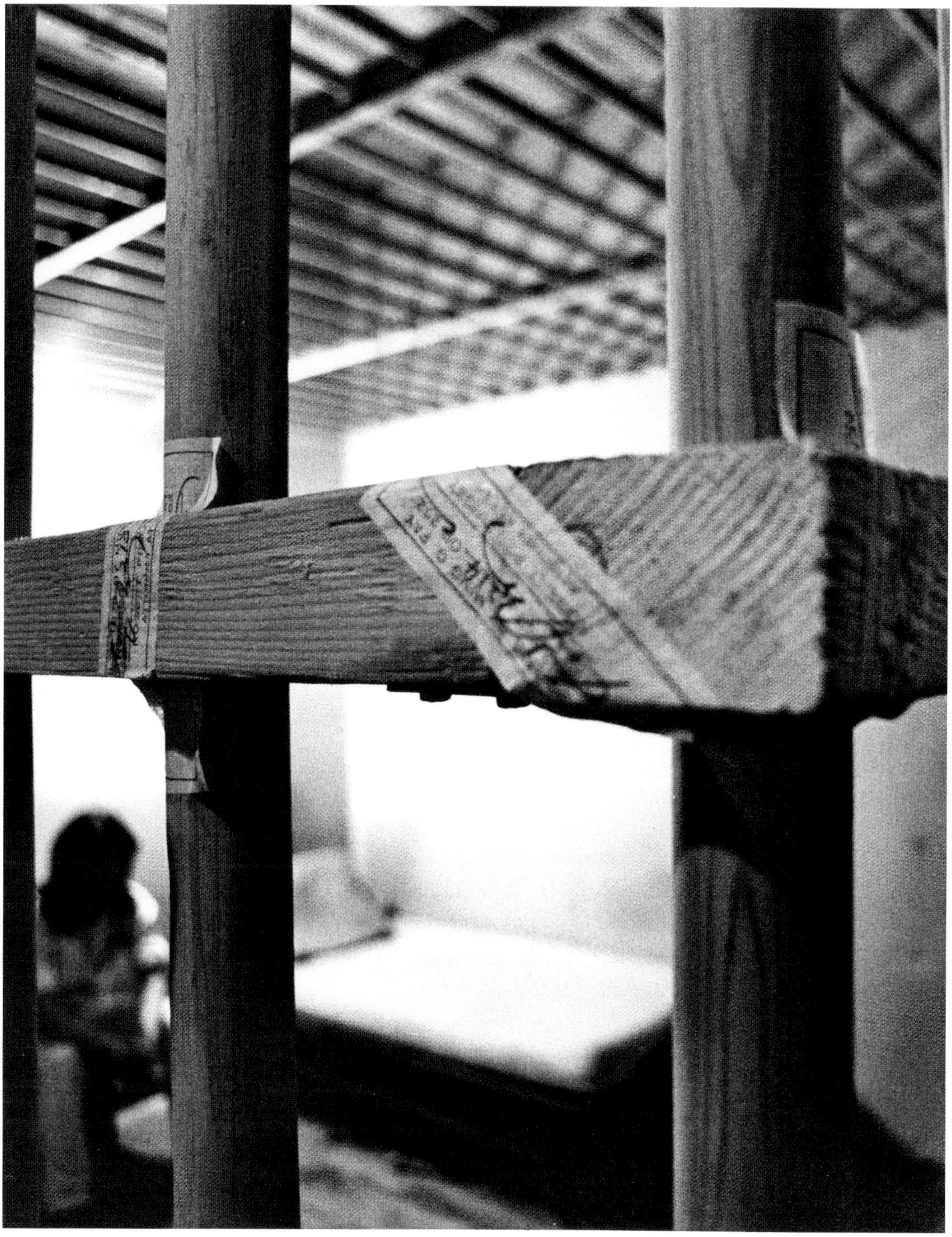

FIGURE 61
Harry Shunk, Tehching "Sam" Hsieh, *One Year Performance, New York, 1979 October 8*. Photo: Harry Shunk. © J. Paul Getty Trust. Getty Research Institute, Los Angeles (2014.R.20).

seriousness with which he took his charge. Certainly the presence of an actual lawyer to ensure that Hsieh adhered to his own terms has helped mitigate doubt regarding Hsieh's fidelity to his statements of intent.[64]

Ritual offered another source of accountability. At the end of *Time Clock Piece,* seventy people gathered to watch Hsieh, who "stood solemnly for 30 seconds, took four steps forward and punched in."[65] *Outdoor Piece* began with an even larger audience, a veritable crowd of 150 gathered in Tribeca Park. The event lacked the scripted quality of its predecessors, only involving Hsieh talking with onlookers, many of whom were not affiliated with the art world.[66] Attended by sixty-some viewers, the opening event for *Rope Piece* mobilized the order and physical repetition intrinsic to ritual actions.[67] The safeguards Montano and Hsieh implemented to visibly show how difficult untying themselves would be included a padlock engraved with both artists' initials, an object whose purpose was more symbolic than practical. Compared to the events marking the beginning and end of *Cage Piece,* those of *Rope Piece* reflect a shift toward thinking of how obligations and their enforcement could be managed through extra-legal means. The duties assumed by Projansky in *Cage Piece,* of making sure that the proper seals and restraints were in place, were now personally assumed in *Rope Piece* by Hsieh and Montano. It also spoke volumes that Hsieh and Montano chose not to enter into contracts that would clearly divide responsibilities for food procurement and pet care, despite the advice of friends and even Montano's earlier thinking.[68]

As performance studies scholar Peggy Phelan observed, performance art "becomes itself through disappearance."[69] Documentation may corroborate the testimony of the performer and the audience, but it can only attest to a fraction of a durational work. Yet photographs extend the life of performance by directing the attention of later audiences toward details less likely observed. On the last day of *Cage Piece,* longtime friend and associate Cheng Wei Kuong took a black-and-white photograph showing part of a sheetrock wall in Hsieh's cell covered with uneven rows of tally marks inscribed by the artist with a nail clipper (fig. 62). The portion of wall fit neatly within the camera's viewfinder, excluding all other information save for a legend, at bottom, that reads "Sam Hsieh 93078–92979," indicating the duration of the performance (from September 30, 1978, to September 29, 1979). The photograph was one of many Cheng took during *Cage Piece,* most of which focused on the cage-like cell of pine dowels in which Hsieh resided over the course of the performance. Many images draw attention to how much of daily existence is about being subject to physical and psychological enclosures: windows blocked by wrought iron bars, razor wire around construction sites, doors requiring that one be 'buzzed in.'"[70] Flattened curves of the "9" and "2" in the artist's signature line are telling traces of the significant time and effort Hsieh must have invested in carving each daily mark and stress the materiality of his physical presence in the cell. Cropped so that Hsieh's signature runs along its bottom edge, the photograph shows a set of numbers indicating both the duration of the performance and his diligence in visualizing the passage of time.

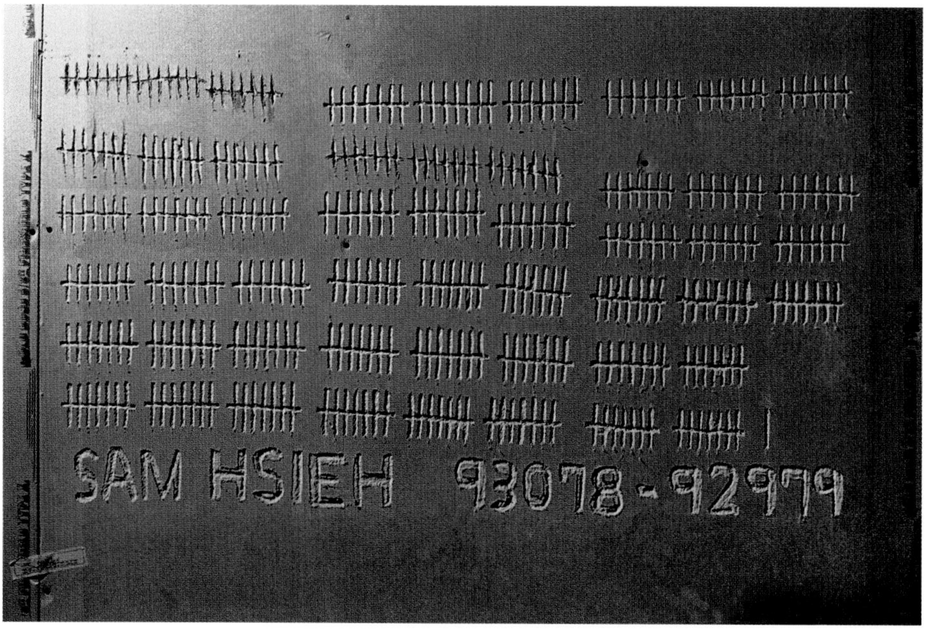

FIGURE 62
Tehching Hsieh, *One Year Performance 1978–1979*. "366 Daily Scratches." © 1979 Tehching Hsieh. Courtesy of the artist and Sean Kelly, New York.

The central role of time resonates with the primacy of time in law's administration. Telling on this front is a criminal justice system in which cases are resolved not by trial but by deals struck quickly between the prosecution and defense, lest courts become too encumbered to function. In this light, the insistence on a trial expressed by artists like Burden has the thrust of resistance. The photographed markings of *Cage Piece* recall those made by prisoners doing time, but Hsieh may have been running out of it as well: the outlaw is defined by the time he has left before he is caught, imprisoned, and deported.[71] Hsieh noted he was simply "killing time," a statement that could allude to the seemingly interminable delay accompanying the processing of paperwork, including the lengthy process of gaining permanent residency or citizenship in the United States.[72] The force of law resides in the organization of time, a point Hsieh would carry forward in *Time Clock Piece,* his next work.

PERFORMING "GOOD FAITH"

How much weight does an artist's word carry? Just before starting *Outdoor Piece,* Hsieh told conceptual artist and critic Barry Kahn that "it is not possible for someone to witness, follow me all the time. If I did [*Outdoor Piece*] before I did the cage piece, people might not believe me, but now they believe me."[73] Posters advertising *Outdoor Piece* included Hsieh's general location, yet the absence of a specific address made it presumably more difficult to believe that he in fact lived outside for a whole year. Each performance was preemptive evidence of Hsieh's ability to successfully complete future works, even when there were no witnesses. The cumulative effect of Hsieh's *One Year Performances* demonstrated the importance of precedent in establishing credibility.

It was with *Time Clock Piece* that Hsieh seemed most intent on proving his trustworthiness—or, more specifically, suppressing signs of untrustworthiness (fig. 63). For this performance, the artist set out to "punch a Time Clock in my studio every hour on the hour for one year." Hsieh's diligence in keeping time reads as an extreme demonstration of his trustworthiness for audiences deeply skeptical of language. By the time he began *Time Clock Piece,* in 1980, the history of conceptual art was rife with works that underscored the malleability of language. For many viewers it was difficult, if not impossible, to take any written statement by an artist at face value without also wondering whether it was meant to be ironic, a response, perhaps, to the law's insistence on regulation. The challenge for viewers was how literally they should consider similarities between Hsieh's statements and the idea, if not the function, of the contract.

A productive lens through which to read Hsieh's work is the legal concept of good faith, or the duty of those entering into a contract to deal with each other fairly and honestly.[74] Another important concept in contract law, "good faith" resonates with the material ends to which Hsieh went to ensure that he met his stated obligations. In the case of *Cage Piece,* for example, Hsieh had paper seals pasted on the wooden dowels that formed the bars of his cage. The fragility of the paper ensured that any attempt on the artist's part to escape would have been duly recorded. In performing *Time Clock Piece,* Hsieh used twelve alarm clocks as well as a wristwatch to minimize the possibility of missing a punch of the clock. To decrease the risk of falling asleep at night, the artist placed his watch in front of a microphone secured to a loudspeaker that amplified the sound of its alarm. While measures such as these were no guarantee that Hsieh would make his hourly commitments, they indicated a level of care and concern that might be considered sufficient for good-faith purposes.[75]

Hsieh honored what legal scholar Roger Summers called "the spirit of the deal" by generating what he called an "Explanation of Procedure" for *Time Clock Piece* that set out three steps he would undertake "to avoid any suspicion of cheating." Hsieh had a witness sign each of the daily time cards and oversee any "repair or adjustment" of the clock; documented each punch with a sixteen-millimeter movie camera set up in his studio for the duration of the project; and commenced the performance with a shaved head, allowing his hair to grow back naturally "to help illustrate the time process" (fig. 64). Similar methods of enforcement were instituted for the faithful execution of *Rope Piece.* He and Montano bound themselves to one another using sailor's knots that were then sealed with lead pieces signed by two witnesses, Pauline Oliveros and Paul Grassfield.[76] Eight feet long and made of nylon, the rope was both flexible and long enough to allow the two artists a certain measure of respective freedom, but not

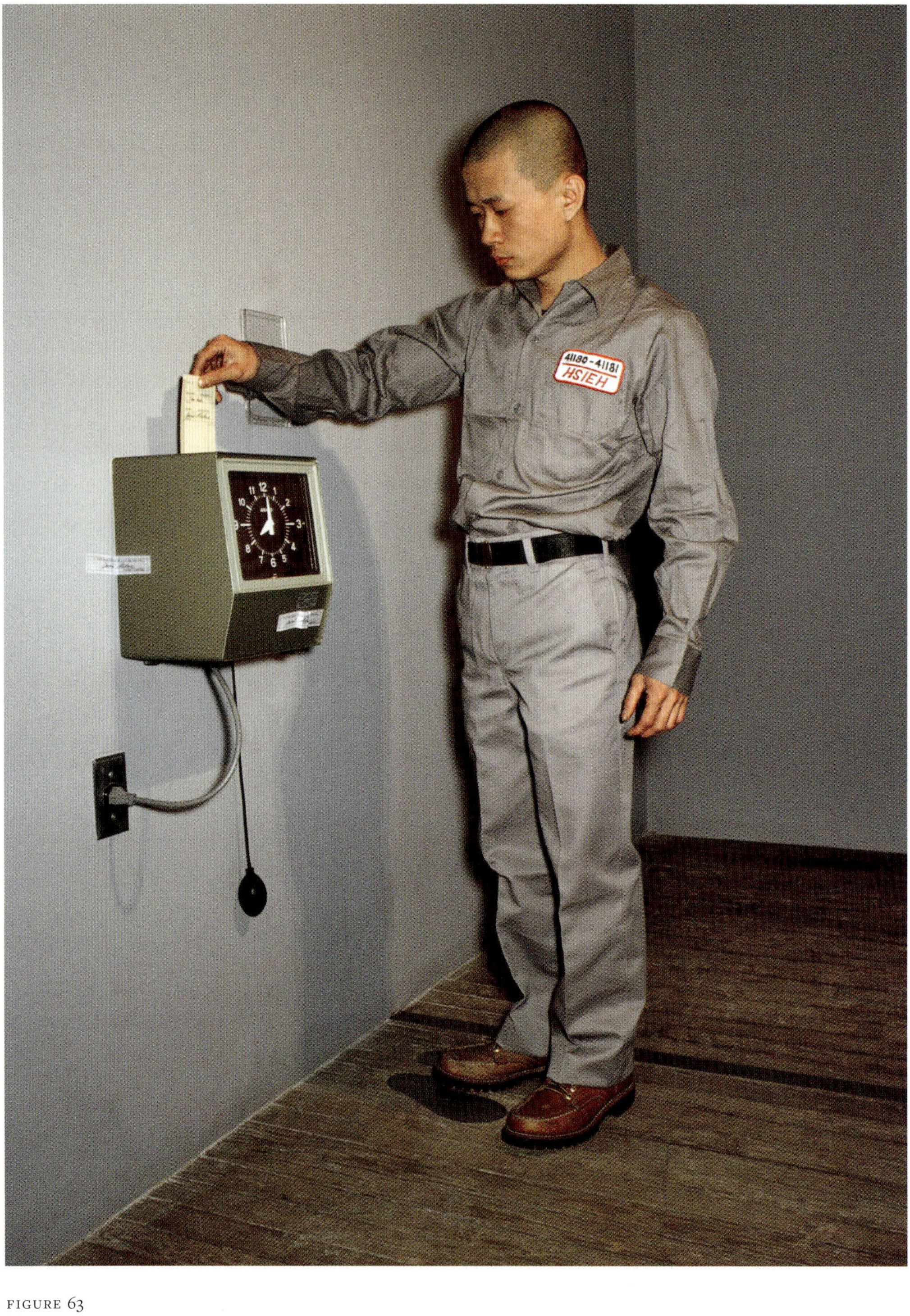

FIGURE 63
Tehching Hsieh, *One Year Performance 1980–1981*. "Punching the Time Clock." © 1981 Tehching Hsieh. Courtesy of the artist and Sean Kelly, New York. Photo: Michael Shen.

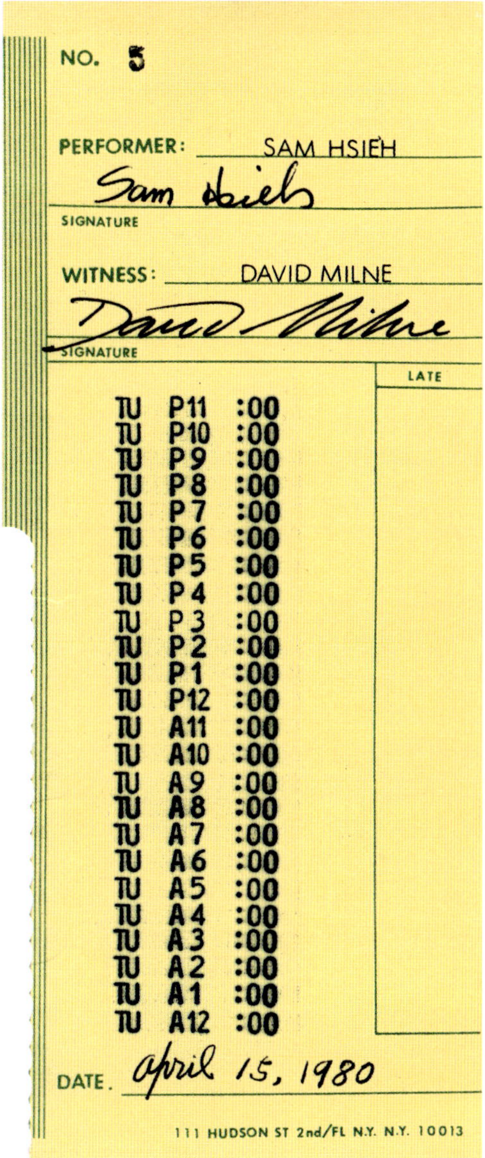
NO. 5

PERFORMER: SAM HSIEH

SIGNATURE

WITNESS: DAVID MILNE

SIGNATURE

LATE

TU P11 :00
TU P10 :00
TU P9 :00
TU P8 :00
TU P7 :00
TU P6 :00
TU P5 :00
TU P4 :00
TU P3 :00
TU P2 :00
TU P1 :00
TU P12 :00
TU A11 :00
TU A10 :00
TU A9 :00
TU A8 :00
TU A7 :00
TU A6 :00
TU A5 :00
TU A4 :00
TU A3 :00
TU A2 :00
TU A1 :00
TU A12 :00

DATE. april 15, 1980

111 HUDSON ST 2nd/FL N.Y. N.Y. 10013

FIGURE 64
Tehching Hsieh, *One Year Performance 1980–1981*. "Time Card: April 15, 1980." © Tehching Hsieh. Courtesy of Sean Kelly, New York.

so long that they could live independently. The fact that the rope was tied to both individuals at the waist left their hands free but also reinforced the full-body nature of their connection.

As time passed, however, the rope became a yoke of sorts. Notes Montano took while tied to Hsieh divulge her considerable frustration and anxiety ("I feel like a prisoner," "He is trying to destroy me, punish me," "He plays Pac Man for hours"), even mentioning having almost killed Hsieh "twice."[77] For his part, Hsieh pasted articles about anger management, Opus Dei, pot use, and instructions on braiding what looked like a noose.[78] Less than a month before the end of *Rope Piece,* Montano showed a friend an article in *Life* magazine about a girl who had learned Harry Houdini's trick of freeing himself from ropes while underwater.[79]

What prevented them from cutting ties may have been the opening ritual of tying the rope in front of sixty viewers. Drawing from the distinction legal philosopher Roscoe Pound made between "law on the books" and "law in action," legal theorists Jack Balkin and Sanford Levinson contend that law works only when it becomes "enacted behavior" in front of an audience.[80] For some viewers, the nature and duration of the action suggested that the artists were performing according to a preexisting set of rules. "It's like a wedding . . . they're officially tied together," commented one witness to the process.[81] In describing the action as "official," witnesses to the start of *Rope Piece* indicated that they perceived Hsieh and Montano to have undertaken their actions with the gravity demanded by ceremonies undertaken at the behest of the law. The knots binding Hsieh and Montano remained intact until the rope was cut on the final day of the performance.[82]

The true gauge of accountability was whether Hsieh treated the conditions of his statements as if they were enforceable or, at the very least, whether nonfulfillment would trigger any form of punishment or consequences. Art historian Max Liljefors has asserted that Hsieh's performances reproduced, and therefore exposed, the contradictory nature of the law as a source of legitimation that is also profoundly malleable, its tenets frequently subject to what the philosopher Giorgio Agamben describes as "mere writing," without any power to enforce itself.[83] There was no pressing reason why Hsieh should obey the self-imposed draconian limitations on his own movements, but this was hardly the point. What mattered was whether the artist took these restrictions seriously. Hsieh expressed his resoluteness in many ways, expressing regret, for example, when he overslept during *Time Clock Piece* ("I felt bad about the times I missed") and attempting to make amends by scrupulously recording the times when he forgot to punch his sheet (out of a total 8,760 required punches, he missed 133).[84] Kathleen Ann Hughes, one of Hsieh's most dedicated chroniclers, observed that Hsieh missed only 1.5 percent of the total, adding that in ten instances it was because he had punched in early.[85] Another journalist claimed that Hsieh "has never forgiven himself for sleeping through" the punch-ins.[86] For *Cage Piece,* the only reported violation of his self-imposed quarantine was when he wrote to Cheng for some medicine to relieve a bad headache.[87] Montano stated that during the course of *Rope Piece,* she and Hsieh recorded how they violated their no-touch rule about one hundred times.[88]

Still more compelling proof was Hsieh's distress when confronted with the prospect of having to involuntarily violate one of his own rules. In February 1982, while drinking tea on the corner of a private doorstep at 34 Hubert Street in Tribeca in lower Manhattan, Hsieh was attacked by the building's owner, who allegedly threw an iron rod and the backpack containing the camera the artist used for documenting *Outdoor*

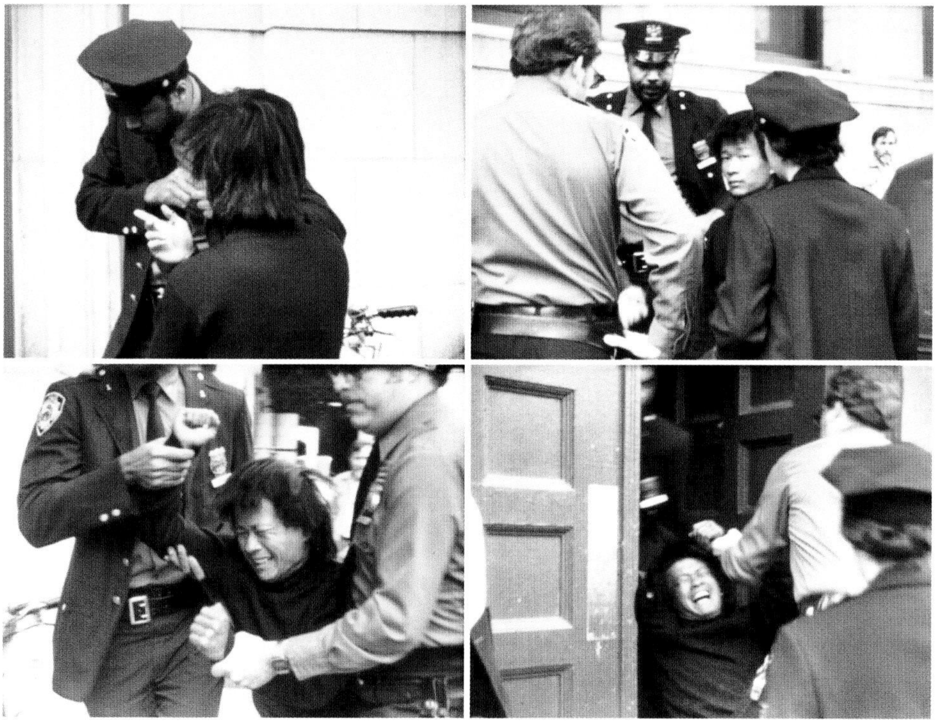

FIGURE 65
Tehching Hsieh, *One Year Performance 1981–1982*. "Arrested." © 1981 Tehching Hsieh. Courtesy of the artist and Sean Kelly, New York.

Piece.[89] Hsieh defended himself with the set of nunchucks he carried for protection, resulting in charges of possession of a criminal weapon and second-degree assault, a serious crime defined as the infliction of significant bodily harm having a moderate to severe impact on a person's ability to live a normal life.[90] Video footage taken by Claire Fergusson shows an increasingly agitated Hsieh as New York City police surround, grab, and haul him into a precinct station (fig. 65). As he is dragged into the station, where he would sit for fifteen hours, the lens focuses squarely on his open mouth and tightly shut eyes.[91] In one shot, Hsieh is bounded by the closed door on the left and the right shoulder of the policeman standing in the extreme right foreground. These images show how Hsieh's refusal to violate the terms of his performance double as evidence of law's own performativity. The authority of law is conveyed through the bodily gestures and dress of the police, as well as by the futility with which Hsieh attempts to resist arrest. Consider how in one image a policeman occupies nearly half of the frame, his hands planted firmly on his hips. Dressed in full official regalia, another policeman looks down on Hsieh, while a third officer stands directly in front of the artist, creating within the picture a shallow space within which the latter is trapped. The lower left-hand photograph shows Hsieh being dragged by the wrists by police whose faces are entirely or partly cut off by the frame.

The force with which Hsieh resisted being pulled inside the station may have convinced legal officers of the sincerity of his intentions. During the initial hearing for Hsieh's case, Judge Martin Erdmann allowed the artist to remain outside the courtroom.[92] Once a storied criminal defender for the Legal Aid Society, the largest provider of legal aid to indigent populations in New York City, Erdmann may have felt sympathy for Hsieh, whose living situation perhaps reminded him of his former clients.[93] The case was eventually dismissed, the serious charge of second-degree assault having been reduced to the very minor charge of disorderly conduct.[94] Hsieh accepted his conviction and punishment in stride: "If they [the police or the judge] ask me to go inside the court building, I will. I understand reality. It's the law."[95] His remark was not so much an expression of defeat or resignation as a voluntary recognition of the context, or rather the system, within which he worked. Ironically, Hsieh was able to fund *Outdoor Piece* by subletting his loft.[96] His landlord status later proved to be one of his most powerful legal defenses following his 1982 arrest, enabling him to effectively refute any accusations of permanent vagrancy.[97]

PROPERTY MAKES THE PERSON

Outdoor Piece thus also intervened in the property-and-personhood equation by toggling between autonomy and nonautonomy. Perhaps the most telling example was *Outdoor Piece,* whose conception and performance overlapped with contemporary debates about the criminalization of homelessness. In the early 1980s, some courts attempted to resurrect the anti-vagrancy laws that higher courts had previously rejected as anti-constitutional in cases like *Fenster v. Leary* in 1967 and *Papachristou v. Jacksonville* in 1972.[98] Since the late 1970s, however, legislatures and governments have taken numerous measures to contain rising numbers of homeless men and women, including statutes allowing for the involuntary detention of "endangered" persons. One such example was the Protective Services for Adults Law, enacted in 1981 by the New York State Legislature not long after Hsieh began *Outdoor Piece.*[99] Increasingly, the definition of *homelessness* turned less on the absence of a permanent abode than on the location of habitation. As claimed by Ellen Baxter and Kim Hopper in the first major study of homelessness in New York City in the 1980s, *Private Lives/Public Spaces: Homeless Adults on the Streets of New York,* the status of being homeless was defined by the public nature of the spaces they inhabited: doorways, train stations, bus terminals, public plazas, and subways.[100] The many photographs Hsieh took of himself performing conventionally private actions like sleeping or bathing outdoors further suggested the extent to which the homeless body was subject to public scrutiny. Although the photographs for *Outdoor Piece* look as if they were taken by a companion or third party, nearly all were taken by the artist himself using a tripod, save for a few that were taken on Hsieh's behalf "by chance."[101] The studied remove at which Hsieh keeps the viewer from entering the space he occupies strongly resonates with surveillance photography of the kind used to track the location and activities of individuals under suspicion. Viewers are placed at a sufficient distance from Hsieh's body to downplay any suggestion of a personal connection between the artist and his audience. *Outdoor Piece* was intermittently witnessed by many, but usually from a distance and not in any prolonged or memorable way.[102]

When Jeannette Ingberman researched Hsieh for possible inclusion in the exhibition "Illegal America," among her notes was "Diary of a Homeless Man," a well-publicized article by labor economist John Coleman published in the February 21, 1983, issue of *New York* magazine. Published shortly after *Outdoor Piece* ended, the article detailed Coleman's experiment living on the streets. The economist was struck by how often he was excluded from various spaces, ranging from Penn Station to the pavement: "Again and again we were told to finish and get out."[103] Mirroring Coleman's experiences was Hsieh's own sense of shame regarding passersby who saw him as a "bum," an individual not only lacking in personal possessions but also having no rightful claim to permanently occupy any particular space.[104] The artist was scrupulous in paying for his food and even for an assistant, yet the many photographs documenting his use of public utilities—from bathing in the water of a fire hydrant to sleeping on park benches—read like an inversion of the legal practice of takings, when a government appropriates private property for public use.

Then there are images that unfurl altogether different scenarios. One of the most remarkable photographs of *Outdoor Piece* shows Hsieh sitting on an ornate upholstered armchair that might once have graced a banker's office or a judge's chambers (fig. 66). The image does not beckon the eye so much as it keeps the viewer's body at arm's length. Its space has the false intimacy of a studio portrait, in this case a family portrait of one. Yet there is something of the still life too, with Hsieh ensconced in a chair that looks just solid enough to support his physical weight and metaphorical burdens. Not for long, of course—next to the chair is its upturned mate, with its slashed seat and exposed entrails. A casualty of the office trenches, the hapless chair emphasizes the mortality of things and bodies. *Outdoor Piece* is daily life stripped to its core purpose of survival. But there are different ways of surviving, and here Hsieh appears to have domesticated a sliver of the inhabitable urban wilderness the word *outdoor* so plainly suggests. For Hsieh, *Outdoor Piece* was "about feeling at home outside. Really, it's about freedom."[105] Photographs like this recuperate a measure of agency not ordinarily ascribed to the homeless, with their ambiguous legal status. But if such images never quite settle into an allegory of rehabilitation that cathartically rescues the homeless figure from abjection, it is because they remain purposely suspended between the world Hsieh creates for himself and a parallel world from which he is excluded or in which he is diminished or ignored.

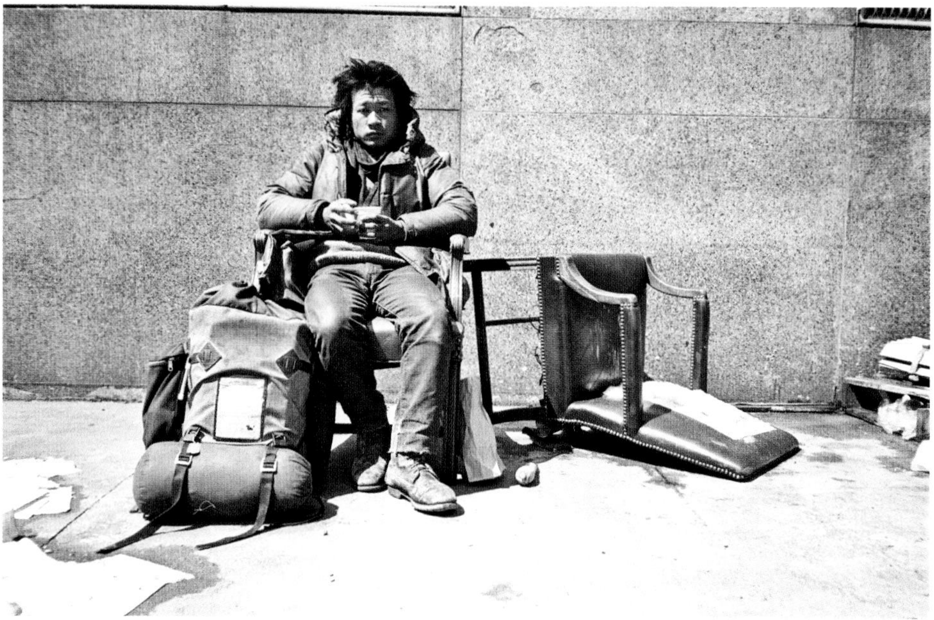

FIGURE 66
Tehching Hsieh, *One Year Performance 1981–1982*. "Life Image." © 1982 Tehching Hsieh. Courtesy of the artist and Sean Kelly, New York.

THE DYNAMICS OF COLLABORATION

Posing a special challenge to the property and personhood relationship was *Rope Piece*, whose reception challenged the idealistic claims made on behalf of artistic collaboration, in which two or more artists intentionally work together to produce a work attributed to them. *Rope Piece* is credited both as the work of Hsieh and as a collaboration with Montano. The closest legal analogy to artistic collaboration is the concept of joint works. An idea Anglo-American law has recognized since at least the 1870s, the term *joint work* has been defined by the Court of Common Pleas in Great Britain as a "a joint laboring in furtherance of a common design."[106] In 1976, the U.S. Congress decisively established joint works as an authorship issue: "a work prepared by two or more authors with the intention that their contributions be merged into inseparable or interdependent parts of a unitary whole."[107] The idea of joint authorship in the art world was inflected by the highly publicized 1975 divorce of Robert and Ethel Scull that threw into relief the conspicuously large number of artistic collaborations occurring within the legally contested space of the family. Deciding who owned their substantial art collection was among the most heated points of debate, one the Appellate Division of the Supreme Court of New York tried to resolve by declaring that the joint acquisition of artworks suggests a legal joint venture "usually implicit in the nature of the marital relationship."[108] The court added, however, that there had to be "a pattern or a life-style" indicating that the parties were involved in a joint venture and that others perceived it as such.[109] The New York art world saw the couple as a team, and thus their art collection was a joint venture.

The Scull divorce raised doubts as to whether it is possible to have artistic collaboration in which all participating parties are genuinely equal, a question raised with increasing frequency by feminist critics and other commentators who openly wondered whether the idealistic aspirations connected to collaboration's subjugation of individual identity were mere alibis for unchecked dominion. As art historian Charles Green has discussed, such concerns were directed toward the perceived effacement of women and particularly of female partners, an injustice partly resolved by the tendency of artist teams since the 1970s to invoke the names of all members rather than that of a single male author.[110] Of *Rope Piece,* Jill Johnston has recalled that Montano allegedly felt "engulfed by Hsieh's dominance as author of the piece."[111]

Certainly, Montano struggled with the gender implications of this situation as well as with her own authorial instincts, writing that

> it was HIS PIECE . . . I was the woman joining the man, the mans [*sic*] piece, in the mans place, using the mans tracking record. that's never been easy for me, or for any woman (because we are expected to do that) . . . I realized I was primarily in it for the experience and training not for the glory of whose idea it was.[112]

The law may not have protected ideas from being copied or used, but art-world protocol credited certain works according to whose idea it originally was. Even when a work might legally qualify as a joint work, many artists scrupulously identified the source of its idea. For instance, Tom Marioni, to whom Montano handcuffed herself for three days as part of a 1973 work, stated that "she had the idea and I was a participant in the work, not a collaborator" (fig. 67).[113]

Artist and curator William Easton read Montano's frustration with Hsieh as evidence that the possibility of collaboration without one party playing the role of a "tyrannical author, an autocratic director, or a dictatorial conductor" was mere "wishful thinking."[114] Easton argued that it was not enough to fulfill the promises made in the name of collaboration; the psychological and emotional costs borne by those involved deserved acknowledgment. Other commentators have called attention to the role of friends like Cheng Wei Kuong, whose assistance they recognize as significant if not invaluable. Claire Fergusson credited Cheng as "the person who facilitated" *Cage Piece,* while performance studies scholar Adrian Heathfield observed that "the whole duration [in *Cage Piece*] is itself built on the shadow duration of Cheng's careful attendance."[115] In determining the authorial value of individual contributions, the question worth asking is whether the work would have happened without these contributions. Or, perhaps more importantly, would the work still have occurred if Hsieh had compelled his friends to sign a legal document relinquishing their claims to coauthorship?

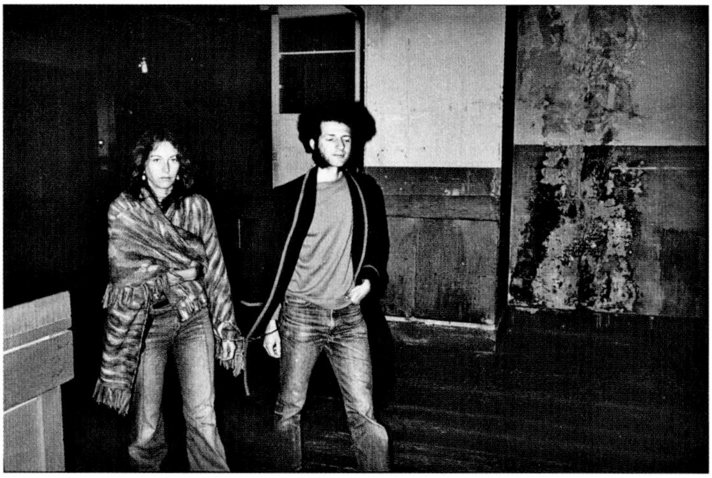

FIGURE 67
Linda Montano, *Handcuffed to Tom Marioni for Three Days,* November 2–5, 1973. Photographed for the University of California, Berkeley Art Museum, and Pacific Film Archive by Benjamin Blackwell. © Linda Montano.

The artist responded in the negative when he broke his year-long silence following the completion of *Cage Piece* by thanking "my friend, Cheng Wei Kuong."[116]

Not long after Hsieh and Montano finished *Rope Piece,* curator and critic Dan Cameron criticized collaboration as an artistic strategy based on an irreversible imbalance of power in his essay "Against Collaboration." Shaded by the fairness and equality rhetoric exceedingly popular in the U.S. political landscape of the late 1970s and early '80s, Cameron argued that collaborations were often based on established artists exploiting the work of lesser-known colleagues.[117] For instance, a "Keith Haring picture created entirely by LA2 [Angel Ortiz, a New York graffiti artist Haring collaborated with on many large works] is still a Keith Haring."[118] Cameron implied that collaborations produced states of forced consensus that reflected little of the participants' artistic characters. True, or legitimate, collaboration took place only when each participant contributed equally to a work's realization.

Cameron also suggested that collaboration was often a source of alienation rather than an instance of community formation, particularly when money was involved.[119] A case in point was the internal tensions within the Guerrilla Girls, the legendary group of women artists formed in 1985 to address the deep inequalities of the art world. "Anarchistic accounting practices" led some members to accuse another of embezzlement so that by the late 1990s, it became clear to many of the group's members that good faith was not enough to prevent conflict: "We really have no code beyond the Law of the Jungle."[120] Despite calls for greater accountability and structure, two older members would insist that they owned the copyright to posters created in the group's name, an assertion other members countered by turning to the spirit, if not the language, of joint authorship: "Most initial ideas were so transformed by group discussion that the final product could scarcely be tracked to its starting point."[121] The turn to legal concepts and counsel finalized the breakdown of what were once intensely close, and even familial, ties. The group's lawyer, Barbara Hoffmann, was sent a *New Yorker* cartoon of a hurricane inside a courtroom whose caption read, "I understand it's a Category 5 divorce."[122] For those outside the group, the Guerrilla Girls were read most legibly as a series of legal questions. As a literary agent asked Hoffmann,

> Are the Guerrilla Girls a legal entity? Would they be jointly liable or is their legal liability limited? What happens in the event of a suit . . . and what would happen if at some time in the future the group splits? Who would receive monies? Who would have control? And what happens in the future?[123]

Bonds of friendship and affection that may have guaranteed good-faith behavior in the past were replaced by legal language whose impersonal tone reinforced the absence of connection, save for a mutual interest in safeguarding the market value of previous production. In 1999, performance artists Ulay and Marina Abramović entered into a contract at the behest of Sean Kelly, Abramović's (and later Hsieh's) U.S. dealer.[124] The two longtime partners had commemorated the end of their personal and professional relationship in 1988 by walking toward each other from either end of the Great Wall of China. Despite the symbolism of this final collaboration, it was the contract specifying the economic rights of each party that marked the end of their relationship. Like a divorce ruling indicating the distribution of assets accrued during a marriage, the contract divided the joint output of the artists, with Abramović receiving the archives and Ulay a share of future sales.

Except for *Rope Piece,* Hsieh resists describing his works as collaborations, noting that the assistance he received from close friends during the enactments of *Cage Piece* and *Outdoor Piece* was entirely voluntary. The only reported exception was *Outdoor Piece,* for which an assistant was paid to forward him messages.[125] "I didn't think of ownership when conceiving my work," he stated.[126] Like many artists, Hsieh asserts that he and Montano did not discuss authorship, nor were there disputes over such. Montano has repeatedly stated that the idea for *Rope Piece* was Hsieh's, even though the two discussed the work for five months.[127] But asking whether *Rope Piece* legally constitutes a joint work illuminates some of the assumptions of current copyright law on one hand and those of artistic collaboration on the other. The standard for determining the existence of a joint work draws heavily from the ruling by Judge Pierre Leval in *Fisher v. Klein,* a dispute between two designers both claiming authorship of jewelry, decided in New York district court in 1990. Leval observed that "it is only where that dominant author intends to be sharing authorship that joint authorship will result," adding that the acceptance of suggestions by sculptors, painters, writers, architects, and other creators did not qualify.[128] The requirement of intent was further explicated a year later in *Childress v. Taylor,* where the Second Circuit proposed a two-part test other courts have widely adopted in deciding whether a collaborative project was jointly authored. In *Childress,* an actress (Taylor) claimed coauthorship of a play she had asked someone else (Childress) to write. The court held that despite Taylor's contributions, her research and suggestions did not make her a coauthor, as it was Childress who wrote the dialogue and narrative. "At the time the writing is done," there must be shared mutual intent for both writers to be joint authors and that each of the authors' contributions are "independently copyrightable."[129] Subsequent courts further qualified the nature of contributions, holding that "suggestions and refinements" to a script were insufficient proof of authorship.[130]

Would a project like *The Artist's Reserved Rights Transfer and Sale Agreement,* detailed in Chapter 1, be considered a joint work? Robert Projansky describes the process of writing it as if Seth Siegelaub was a client ("I drafted the contract"), and early legal discussions of the *Agreement* describe it as the "Projansky Contract." That the *Agreement* is sometimes referred to in art historical circles as the "Siegelaub Agreement" suggests its alignment with authorship models familiar to conceptual artists, where credit is commensurate with the source of the idea ("It was [Siegelaub's] idea," Projansky recalls).[131] Courts, in contrast, tended to assign authorship to the person or persons with final artistic control. Under this logic, Jeanne-Claude had a strong claim to joint-author status for *Running Fence.* Letters she signed on behalf of the Running Fence Corporation indicate her involvement in nearly every aspect of the work's production.[132] Additionally, letters regarding the acquisition of permits were often addressed to both Christo and Jeanne-Claude, thereby acknowledging them as equal decision makers. Yet Jeanne-Claude was routinely denied authorship credit, a point critic Robert Taylor observed in a 1977 article strikingly titled "In the Name of Integrity," in which he observed that Jeanne-Claude "doesn't get a line in the conventional reviews" even though the works then solely attributed to Christo depended on her "managerial prowess."[133] In 1994, Christo and Jeanne-Claude retroactively applied the joint name "Christo and Jeanne-Claude" to all outdoor works and large-scale temporary indoor installations.

For *Rope Piece,* the discussions Hsieh and Montano had before and during the work would be precluded from copyright protection. Photographs and recordings of conversations that Hsieh and Montano produced each day to document their work would be copyrightable. But other than verbal testimony, there is little to indicate who took which photograph when, or whether either Hsieh or Montano had sole authority over the other. Thomas McEvilley, who reviewed the work, observed that there was a "constant dependence on each other's approval to fulfill their moment-to-moment needs . . . each could veto any action suggested by the other."[134] In his mind, the extreme dependence nullified the pretense of collaboration: its very demands turned the work into a "renunciation of collaboration while it was going on."[135] *Rope Piece* modeled the impossibility of collaboration as a deliberate form of artistic production in which participants agree to create a work and share credit for their individual contributions. McEvilley provocatively suggested that performance works required such intensive commitment from the artists that the work eventually owned them rather than the other way around. *Rope Piece* "was no longer under the artists' control, and that was its great reality. From being its creators, they became its creatures."[136] Or as Hsieh said, "The work has its own life and will grow by itself."[137]

Jill Johnston described *Rope Piece* as "two people, equal before the law of the work."[138] She saw the performance as constituting its own kind of law, one based on upholding the division between art and life. For Montano, the "law of the work" meant flouting that separation, albeit through voluntary obedience to another's commands. Calling Hsieh a "master," she likened her participation in *Rope Piece* to a form of conscription into a military or religious order.[139] Performing surrender, acquiescence and subordination to hierarchy was not what the law of *Rope Piece* required. Upholding *Rope Piece* as law instead meant recognizing power as a resource held in common.[140] For genuinely radical collaboration to exist, participants had to be willing to surrender some, if not all, of their authorial claims. As Montano wrote in her notes: "Cooperate more, compromise and eventually learn to share power at times."[141] For his part, Hsieh pasted an article on IBM's corporate practice in one of his *Rope Piece* scrapbooks with the phrase "genuine respect for its employees as partners" underlined.[142]

Among the most underrated contributions of Hsieh's *One Year Performances* is how they effectively turned art into a means through which to speculate about the law's capacity to set standards for ethical behavior. About his works, Hsieh stated that "I don't blur art and life."[143] But the experience of hearing about, or seeing evidence of, his performances destabilizes the supposed boundary between art and life just enough to introduce the possibility of looking differently at some of the assumptions on which "life" activity is regulated.

Returning to the photograph of Hsieh standing outside the New York City Criminal Court, we note that the camera is too far removed to record his features in detail. Instead our gaze is directed to the words carved into the courthouse façade (an inadvertent echo of Hsieh's own laborious inscriptions in *Cage Piece*). The cropping of the image appears to literally cut the words to size, an act that leaves viewers to wonder about what it is we are actually seeing and reading. In this way, the photograph emphasizes how the perceived status of the law and its consequent authority depend on the ability to communicate intention through visual and physical forms. But it was not enough for artists to appropriate the language of the law or to disclose their repeated subjection to the authority of the legal system. In modeling the ideals of the law so consistently, Hsieh's first four *One Year Performances* and their accompanying documentation prompt us to ask whether and how the words about justice hovering over the artist's head might be something more than mere platitude.

5

ARTS OF DISENGAGEMENT

Sally Mann's "Immediate Family"

A VERY YOUNG CHILD LIES on an unmade bed, her eyes closed as if in sleep (fig. 68). Directly next to her is an amorphous stain, its contours just dark enough to stand out from the plain weave of the mattress. The spaces surrounding the bed are shrouded in darkness, making it difficult to precisely identify time or location. The distance between viewer and subject resonates with that found in some of the images documenting *Outdoor Piece*, which position us neither as Tehching Hsieh's companions nor as complete strangers. Here we look down upon the child, yet our viewpoint is not omniscient. Nor are we so close as to approximate the watchfulness of a parent gazing upon his or her child. The distance leaves open the question of what and who the child is to us.

Wet Bed was among the most recognizable examples of "Immediate Family," the series of photographs Sally Mann took of her children in and near her home in Virginia from 1985 to 1995. After some of the photographs were published as a book in 1992, "Immediate Family" became a popular target for politicians who

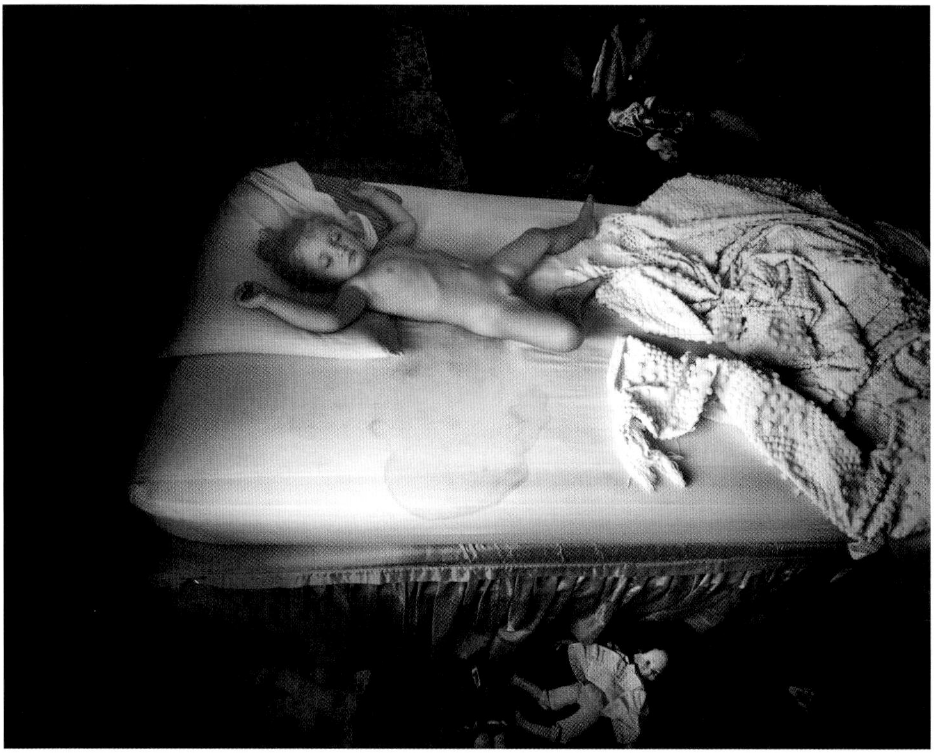

FIGURE 68
Sally Mann, *The Wet Bed*, 1987. Gelatin silver print. © Sally Mann. Courtesy of Gagosian.

used numerous antipornography laws, passed from the late 1970s to the '80s, to enhance their credibility in the eyes of their constituencies. Heightening the outrage was Mann's position as the subjects' mother, a category of identification shaped by numerous legal and ethical obligations. If Hsieh's *One Year Performances* emphasized how the personal and subjective are framed and mediated by the forms of the law, the reception of "Immediate Family" showed how personal choices made in the context of art were subject to both legal and extra-legal regulation.

Starting in the 1980s, the relationship between contemporary art and the law seemed deadlocked in a state of reciprocal vilification as new laws and legislative regimes brought intense pressure to bear on the supposed meaning of artworks. Controversy over photographs by Mann and other artists, including Jacqueline Livingston, Robert Mapplethorpe, and Andres Serrano, were prominent examples of a negative accountability that courts and lawmakers demanded from contemporary art and artists. Many works were self-censored or banned from public display, often at the advice of lawyers hired by institutions concerned with losing public and private funding.[1] Barbara Hoffmann, one of the first lawyers to write at length about contemporary art's relationship with the U.S. government, observed a "tension between art's subjectivity with its potential for controversy and government's need to promote the public good."[2] Yet even those who were self-funded were called to account for their works by lawmakers, police, and members of the general public. The political landscape compelled artists to defend themselves and their works in courts that ventriloquized the disapproval of small groups of people in the name of "community standards," even as the idea of community was tested by concurrent policy changes vis-à-vis multiculturalism and identity politics.

Negative accountability became even more visible in the late 1980s and early '90s, as legislators' calls to reduce or eliminate public funding for contemporary art became more vocal.[3] Government officials pressured artists seeking assistance to justify their professional, and even personal, behavior to courts and policy makers who rarely had to explain the reasoning behind their own decisions. The suspicion of potential wrongdoing became a pretext for a small group of mostly older white men to insist that their interpretations of artworks and artistic function be the standard for holding artworks accountable. In contrast to the voluntary disclosure embraced by artists in the late 1970s, this was a culture of interrogation, demanding artists to justify their behavior, including that taking place in their own homes.

Mann was never arrested, sued, or even formally charged with any crime. But the force of public criticism of Mann, her works, and her occupation was as punishing as any arrest or trial. Jeff Ferrell describes this situation as "cultural criminalization," whereby the media reconstructs as criminal the meaning of images produced by cultural workers, which can delegitimate "those targeted, though no formal legal charges are brought against them."[4] Yet even as Mann defended her works publicly, she also refrained from going to court or even filing a legal complaint, a move that read as a strategic disengagement from a legal framework that historically made few allowances for artistic photography. In one sense, such disengagement reflected how certain bodies of law, namely family and criminal law circa the early 1990s, were not the most productive venues to flesh out the complexity arising from the intersection of gender, age, and sexuality that "Immediate Family" threw into such sharp focus. It was also clear that lawsuits and protests did not always make things easier or better for contemporary artists. Elevating Mann's disengagement beyond simple indifference or pragmatic evasion was her willingness to accept moral disagreement without criticizing the moral character of her critics. In a time and place where reasonableness—the standard according to which the legality of actions was most frequently judged—depended on whose reasoning should prevail, Mann demonstrated another kind of integrity by suggesting how the act of looking, particularly at photographs, could function as a sustained questioning of viewing practices found in the law.

BETWEEN LAW AND ART

Mann's disengagement was especially compelling because of all artistic media, photography may be the most coded by its relationship to the law. Since the mid-nineteenth century, police in Western Europe and the United States have mobilized photography to record crime scenes, suspects, criminals, and prisoners as part of what many commentators have discussed as a dense network stitched together by shared interests in surveillance and power.[5] As a form of legal evidence, photography was initially greeted with skepticism by courts unfamiliar with its production techniques and because of what law scholar Jennifer Mnookin has pointed out as juridical anxiety over photography's potential discrepancies when compared with verbal and oral descriptions.[6] A century later, circumstances had become reversed, with one legal commentator, in 1946, going so far as to declare photography the "very highest type of evidence."[7]

While courts and lawyers placed astonishing trust in photographs as a reliable source of truth, the federal government under President Lyndon B. Johnson pointedly endorsed documentary photographs in the style of Walker Evans and New Deal–era social documentary. Such images were meant to burnish the image of the state by showing, as Johnson described it, how government took a "personal" interest in its citizens' welfare.[8] In contrast were the photographers whose self-identification as artists revolved around their deep skepticism about photography's capacity to bear unvarnished and dependable witness. Consider a selenium-toned Kodalith photograph by Les Krims (fig. 69). Taken in 1971 as an intentional copy of forensic photography, it depicts from above a naked young woman, her eyes closed and her limbs sprawled awkwardly on a linoleum floor.[9] Her legs are bent as if in mid-sprint, but her torso is contorted so as to recall fallen bodies, an interpretation reinforced by the congealed dark pool that appears to seep from beneath her back. Resembling wide-angle shots taken under standard forensic photographic procedure to establish the general crime scene, the image prominently features the shapeless pool, which to casual viewers might read as blood. Distance between the body and the imagined position of the viewer provides critical space within which to look back upon the genre of forensic photography as performing facticity rather than being factual.

Created when photography had yet to achieve full-fledged artistic recognition in the commercial market, this work, titled *Stack o' Wheats Murder #9, Celestial Chocolate Syrup Simulated Blood Puddle,* belonged to a series of three projects that rejected the uncritical ease with which photography was accorded evidentiary status. In an influential essay published in 1976, photography critic A.D. Coleman discussed how photographers like Krims deliberately created scenes resembling unstudied moments of daily life to produce what he called "falsified documents."[10] Yet there is nothing false about Krims's baroque tableaux, which elevated forensic photography beyond the register of satire and into the realm of camp. Near or next to each "victim" was a stack of pancakes, a reference to the tendency of some serial killers to establish a macabre claim of authorship over each crime. The series, titled "The Incredible Case of the Stack o' Wheats Murders," emphasizes photography as a medium inescapably subject to manipulation and forensic photography as a category whose capacity for unvarnished testimony was at best uncertain. Seen more broadly, the transparent staging of the images resists the instrumentalization of photography by the federal government in the name of the Great Society.

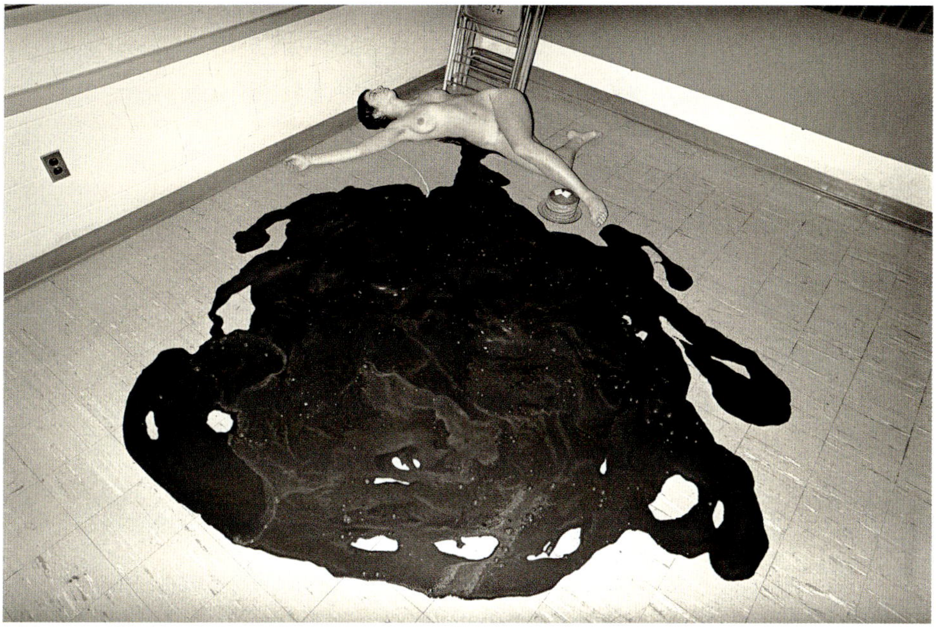

FIGURE 69
Les Krims, *Stack o' Wheats Murder #9, Celestial Chocolate Syrup Simulated Blood Puddle, Buffalo, New York*, 1970. From "The Incredible Case of the Stack o' Wheat Murders." Selenium-toned Kodalith paper print. © Les Krims.

Reluctantly signed into law in 1966 by President Johnson, who reportedly despised journalists "challenging the official view of reality," the Freedom of Information Act, which granted the public a legal right to access information from the federal government and its agencies, inadvertently paved the way for photographers like Mike Mandel and Larry Sultan.[11] Foreshadowing models of authorship based on the compilation and organization of found materials, their photobook *Evidence* consisted of fifty-nine photographs gathered from government agencies, private companies, and educational institutions in California between 1975 and 1977. While the images Mandel and Sultan gathered from corporations and other nongovernmental organizations were likely subject to copyright protection, those gathered from government agencies were exempt from such protection as "works of the U.S. government," or works prepared by a federal employee as part of his or her duties.[12] That the artists could gain access to more than two million images suggests a high degree of cooperation by the organizations and a culture of disclosure facilitated by the expansion of the Freedom of Information Act by Congress in the wake of public outrage over Watergate and demands for greater transparency. In its expanded version, the act reduced the burden on members of the public seeking information from government agencies, including narrowing the exemptions related to law enforcement.[13]

The *Evidence* photographs—collected in the photobook and displayed publicly in venues like the Los Angeles Institute of Contemporary Art—compelled viewers to

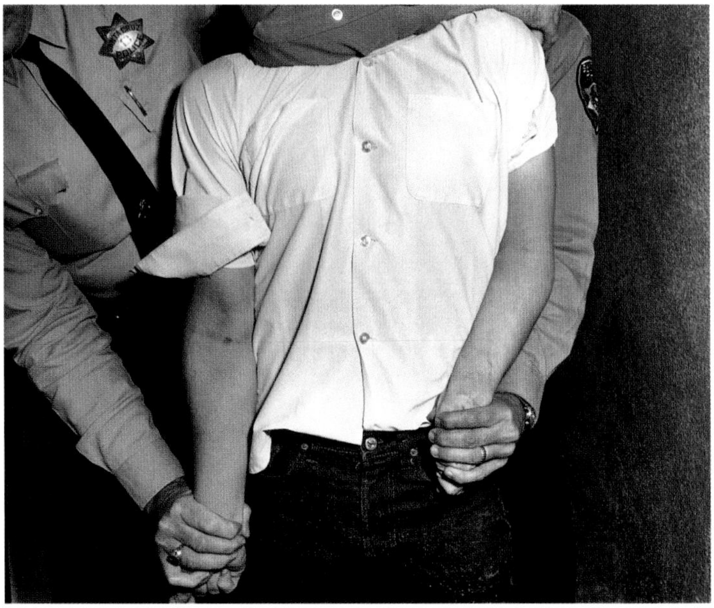

FIGURE 70
Mike Mandel and Larry Sultan, *Untitled*, from *Evidence*, 1977. © Mike Mandel and the Estate of Larry Sultan.

regard images originally intended to document industrial and technological processes as forms of cultural production. Just after the halfway point in the book is a photograph sourced from the police department in Santa Cruz, California (fig. 70). It thrusts us into the personal space of what looks like the scene of an arrest. A faceless police officer, his chin barely visible in the upper left-hand corner, restrains the arm of his quarry. His colleague holds down the other arm, while putting the alleged perpetrator in a chokehold. The faces of all three are cropped from view, likely a decision intended to exempt the picture from possible breach-of-privacy claims. The bodies of the two police appear strangely fused, their arms and hands adorned with similar rings looking as if they belonged to some octopus of enforcement. It is the opposite of the stills extracted from the video documenting New York City police forcibly hauling Tehching Hsieh into precinct quarters. Instead of confirming the occurrence of a past event, this photograph reclaimed by Mandel and Sultan raises doubts about the certitude of recorded events and of the susceptibility of allegedly objective documentation to human whim. First shown at the San Francisco Museum of Modern Art in 1977, *Evidence* resonated with the seminal group exhibition "Pictures" held at the nonprofit exhibition venue Artists Space in New York, also in 1977. According to that show's curator, Douglas Crimp, the intent was to "determine how a picture becomes a signifying structure of its own accord," where a photograph intentionally created as art could only be understood "in relation to other representations" rather than as a self-contained repository of decipherable meaning.[14] It was futile to mine images for stationary content, the very standard used by courts to determine a photograph's legality.

If *Evidence* aligned convincingly with law, it was because a preoccupation with the question of uncertainty compelled lawmakers and judges to cling more strongly to an evidentiary model of photography. The passing of numerous anti-child-pornography laws subjected creators, viewers, and distributors of photography to heightened consideration. For cases involving sex offenses against children, the bar for admitting photographic evidence was particularly low.[15] Laws such as the Sexual Exploitation of Children Act in 1977 framed photographs of human bodies, particularly of children and other protected classes, as potential evidence of the photographer's wrongdoing. Film developers were permitted to withhold photographs they regarded as morally suspect. Concurrent with this trend was a rise in cases involving obscenity, which vividly illustrated how visual images have affected the identity formation of law.[16] Obscenity represents the creation of a category that enables lawmakers and judges to exclude from public circulation images they deem unfit, "unspeakable," or without redeeming value.[17] But while it was relatively easy to condemn and punish obscenity, it was much more difficult to define what it was.[18] "My problem is not what to do about obscenity, but what to make of it," wrote legal scholar Abraham Kaplan decades earlier in a seminal 1955 article, "Obscenity as an Esthetic Category."[19]

Beginning in the late 1970s, law became a screen magnifying the scope of photography's communicative potential as photography's place in the law was grafted onto the question of law's place in photography. In 1979, Jacqueline Livingston, a professor of photography at Cornell University, publicly exhibited nine photographs of male nudes at the university, including a gridded montage featuring her son Sam. Livingston had photographed Sam nude in a friend's loft, then mailed the film to Kodak for processing, who informed her that she could either choose to have the film destroyed or let it be turned over to the district attorney.[20] Livingston's attorney recommended the former; the district attorney who was then up for reelection and known for actively prosecuting pornography cases would almost certainly have tried to have Livingston arraigned. Even after relinquishing her work, Livingston was nevertheless fired by Cornell, a decision she protested as part of the "Cornell Eleven," a group of eleven female faculty members who sued the university for tenure denial in one of the highest-profile gender discrimination lawsuits in academia in the 1970s.[21] While the suit against Cornell was progressing, Livingston published and distributed, in October 1979, a series of fourteen posters featuring photographs of her son, husband, and father-in-law. A gridded series of black-and-white images depicted Sam, from a state of undress to being overdressed (fig. 71). The representation is structured by the binaries of nude versus clothed and staged versus spontaneous; the first images show a playful Sam hamming it up for his mother's lens, only to conclude with him drowning in his father's suit, his expression correspondingly morose. It is hard not to read the work as a symbolic illustration of adult expectations regarding how children's bodies should appear.

Those defending Livingston's works raised the issue of viewer responsibility; critic Kathie Beals sounded only partly in jest when she advised viewers offended by tiny

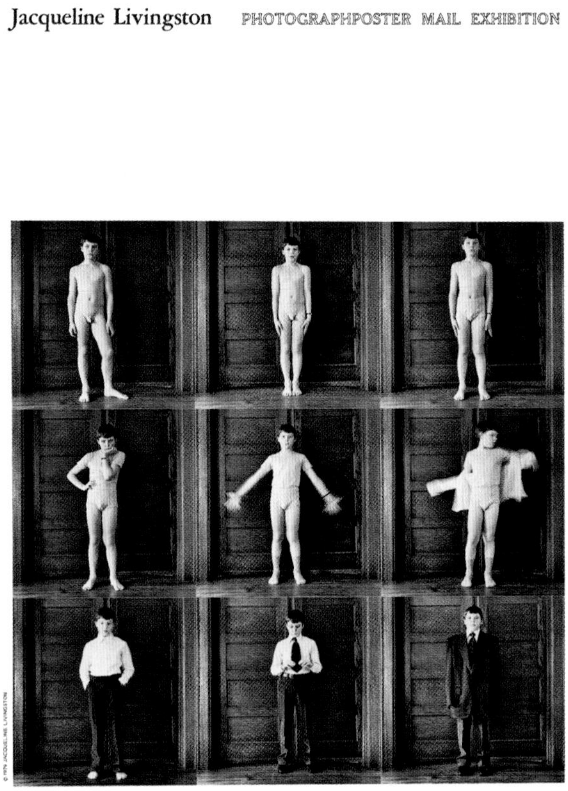

FIGURE 71
Jacqueline Livingston, *Photographerposter #4*, from the *Photographposter Male/Mail Exhibition*, 1979. Offset lithograph, $15\frac{3}{8} \times 14\frac{13}{16}$ inches. San Francisco Museum of Modern Art, Gift of Van Deren Coke. © Jacqueline Livingston. Photo: Don Ross.

images of Livingston's masturbating son to "step back about 10 feet."[22] More violent was the reaction of activist Nikki Craft against a different photographic work. Then an undergraduate at the University of California at Santa Cruz, she obtained and then mutilated a copy of "The Incredible Case of the Stack o' Wheat Murders" owned by the university library.[23] Concurrent with the highly publicized efforts of radical feminist Andrea Dworkin and legal scholar Catherine MacKinnon to outlaw pornography as a violation of women's civil rights, Craft poured chocolate syrup over torn pieces of the reproduced work, documentation of which she sold as her own work.[24]

So entrenched was the legal identity of photography as evidence that it was not until the early twenty-first century that the artistic status of photography became a consistent object of legal inquiry.[25] Despite the influence of photography on contemporary art in the late 1970s, for example, courts mostly excluded photography from the category of art. In his dissent from the majority decision in the 1976 case *Matter of Koner v. Procaccino,* Judge Jacob Fuchsberg criticized his judicial colleagues for letting the New York State Tax Commission decide that income derived from the sale of photographs not made at the behest of a client or for commercial promotional purposes failed to qualify as income derived from the practice of a profession. Fuchsberg argued that his colleagues had ignored "completely" that photography was a recognized art form.[26] That photographs could simultaneously be art and evidence subjected them to both aesthetic and legal judgment, a question Mann's "Immediate Family" raised more searchingly than almost any other set of photographic works.

A work like *Damaged Child* posed special questions because of its legibility as portraiture. In an essay so widely cited as to command something of the authority certain treatises have over particular areas of the law, the artist Allan Sekula noted how it was as portraiture that photography became "a system of representation capable of functioning both honorifically and repressively."[27] *Damaged Child,* a portrait of Mann's daughter Jessie, strongly recalls a cinematic close-up, an effect produced by the artist's use of an eight-by-ten large-format camera with short lenses with relatively little depth of field (fig. 72). Citing Gilles Deleuze, film scholar Mary Ann Doane argues that the close-up in film works to abstract the image "from all spatio-temporal co-ordinates."[28] Through this technique, "the image becomes, once more, an image rather than a threshold onto a world. Or rather, the world is reduced to this face, this object."[29] In *Damaged Child,* Jessie's head is curiously disembodied from the rest of her body. The right edges of her collar look whited out; the eyelet pattern is really visible only in the very center. The grid of her checkered gingham smock reads as blurry, not unlike a televised image transmitted through a poor signal. Her shoulders look as if they might dissolve into the background ether. Her face, in contrast, seems almost overarticulated. Even the smooth planes of her cheeks seem vaguely concave rather than flat. The small bulb at the end of her nose is clearly visible, as is a shallow dimple just below her lower lip. Perhaps most immediately evident is how individuated each of Jessie's hairs is. The image shows a plenitude of detail that actually starts to compromise the coherence of the picture, breaking it down to atomic particles best examined like laboratory specimens.

Among the most compelling defenses of "Immediate Family" was how the photographs themselves operated as self-contained worlds comprising separate, or rather separable, forms. Their capacity to perform as unmediated evidence of the actual lives of the Mann children was overshadowed by how efficiently the photographs worked as bounded domains. Not only is each scene framed to provide a distinct sense of enclosure, but the photographs turn on an interplay of spatial distance and proximity that provokes in viewers a sense of boundary between themselves, the actual physical object, and the scene. *Damaged Child* superficially resembles a school portrait but is oriented horizontally, not vertically. This lateral format indicates the stagedness of the image. In the book *Immediate Family,* each photograph is centered on a glossy white page with generous margins. Absent any other visual distractions, the reader must focus only on the image, eventually noticing how it is composed of various parts and relationships. Throughout "Immediate Family," Mann pays close attention to the edges of each photograph, frequently choosing to blur whatever it is that appears at the point where the world internal to the image gives way to

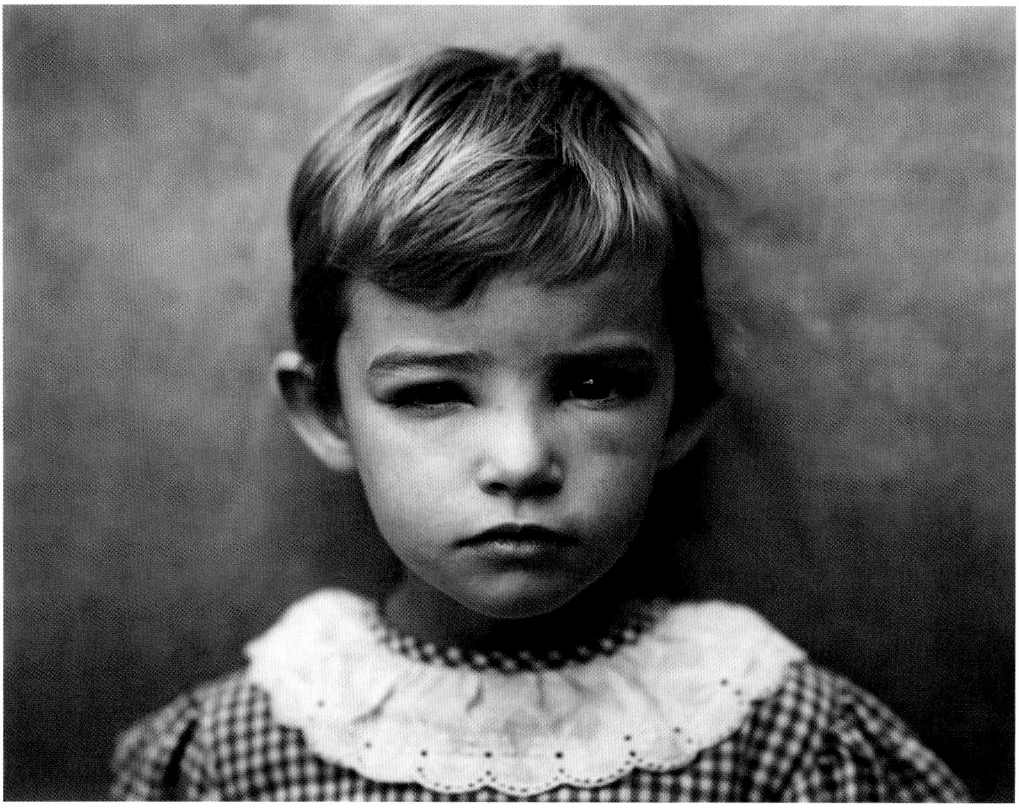

FIGURE 72
Sally Mann, *Damaged Child,* 1984. Gelatin silver print. © Sally Mann. Courtesy of Gagosian.

the stark white gutters. The blur diminishes the certainty with which we believe the photograph to be contiguous with our own world. Yet if the idea of the self-contained photograph failed to adequately shield Mann and her works from accusations ordinarily encountered in the juridical spaces of a legal complaint or a courtroom trial, it was because of photography's ontological fluidity. Photography as art still failed to outweigh the more entrenched notion of photography's ability to perform as evidence.

THE "ART DEFENSE"

As greater numbers of artworks were accused of obscenity, the "art defense," whereby the suspect image or object claims the status of artwork to escape punishment or liability, became increasingly visible. When the U.S. Supreme Court decided *Roth v. United States* in 1957, obscenity depended on whether the "average person, applying contemporary community standards," would consider that the material in question appeals to prurient interest "as a whole."[30] Another landmark Supreme Court decision, *Miller v. California* (1973), broadened the scope of obscenity to include both works "utterly" devoid of any "socially redeeming value" and those lacking "serious" literary, artistic, scientific, or political value.[31] *Miller* failed, however, to qualify what in *Roth* was an endorsement of arbitrariness under the guise of the "average person" having "community standards," and judges preferred to deflect actual consideration of images by focusing instead on their presumed target audience.[32] In the important First Amendment case *New York v. Ferber*, the U.S. Supreme Court declared that images regarded as child pornography may be banned without first being deemed obscene.[33] The 1982 decision helped open the scope of potentially liable images to include journalistic and other images encountered in the course of daily life.[34] Members of the *Ferber* court were divided; Justice William Brennan declared that it was "inconceivable how a depiction of a child that is itself a serious contribution to the world of art or literature or science can be deemed material outside the protection of the First Amendment."[35]

Owing to a striking variety of opinion within the judiciary as to what might sufficiently qualify as art, artistic value was an unreliable defense. As Christine Haight Farley has observed, "judges' views about art may be among their most closely held and least examined beliefs."[36] Given how judges in many nonfederal courts are elected, the closest approximation of these views may have been the responses sent to artist Jeffrey Vallance. In 1978, Vallance wrote each member of the U.S. Senate, asking them for a drawing and to express what they considered art. Titled *The U.S. Senate: A Survey on the Arts* (also called *Drawings and Statements by U.S. Senators*), Vallance's work is a startlingly illuminating look at lawmakers' attitudes toward visual art at a time when the legal status of artworks was in particular flux. A third of the Senate responded, usually with form letters filled with platitudes about the value of art as well as congressional publications on the history of the U.S. Capitol and the artworks it contained.[37] Yet Vallance also received small artworks from both advocates and opponents of arts legislation and funding. California senator and arts advocate Allan Cranston sent a semiabstract landscape of the Washington Monument, while arts funding opponent Strom Thurmond sent a drawing of a U.S. flag. Utah senator Orrin Hatch wrote in fervent defense of representational painting, which he claimed was being neglected in favor of "less talented" conceptual and abstract artists, while the Wisconsin senator William Proxmire submitted a green-and-blue abstraction that he challenged Vallance to decipher. Known for bestowing satirical "Golden Fleece" awards on government projects he deemed wasteful, Proxmire frequently targeted the General Services Administration's Art-in-Architecture Program for disbursing sizable grants to support public artworks, including conceptual and ephemeral works.[38] The most personal response may have been that of Arizona senator Barry Goldwater, who offered a drawing of a cactus with extended limbs, eloquent proof of how those empowered to make laws have their own predispositions that affect their judgment of images (fig. 73).

Following *Serra v. U.S. General Services Administration*, in which the Second Circuit in 1988 upheld the government's decision to remove Richard Serra's *Tilted Arc* from Federal Plaza, courts and legislatures became notably more engaged in the visual

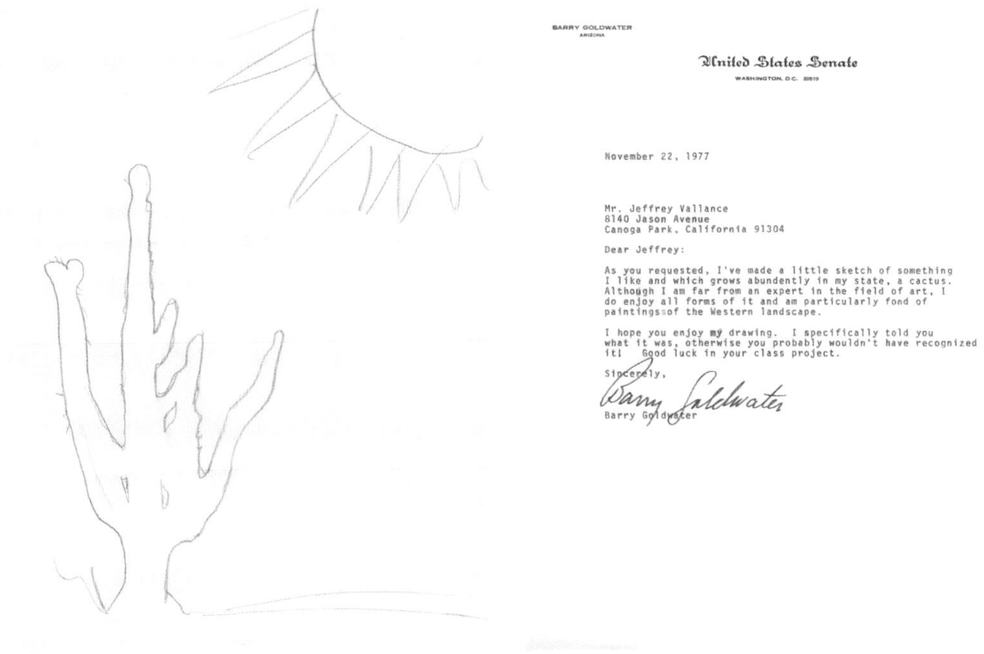

BARRY GOLDWATER
ARIZONA

United States Senate
WASHINGTON, D.C. 20510

November 22, 1977

Mr. Jeffrey Vallance
8140 Jason Avenue
Canoga Park, California 91304

Dear Jeffrey:

As you requested, I've made a little sketch of something I like and which grows abundently in my state, a cactus. Although I am far from an expert in the field of art, I do enjoy all forms of it and am particularly fond of paintings of the Western landscape.

I hope you enjoy my drawing. I specifically told you what it was, otherwise you probably wouldn't have recognized it! Good luck in your class project.

Sincerely,

Barry Goldwater

Barry Goldwater

FIGURE 73

Jeffrey Vallance, *Drawings and Statements by U.S. Senators,* 1978. Letter and cactus drawing by Senator Barry Goldwater. Typed letter with ink signature on paper, 8.5 × 11 inches, with pencil drawing on paper, 8.5 × 11 inches. From the series "Drawings and Statements by U.S. Senators," 1978. Pencil, ink, and marker on paper, with photocopies, photograph, and color lithography on cards. Courtesy of the artist and Tanya Bonakdar Gallery, New York. © Jeffrey Vallance.

analysis of works.[39] The Second Circuit even went so far as to declare that a "consideration of aesthetics is a legitimate government function."[40] Many incidents of what might be called judicial visual analysis occurred when determining the status of nude imagery. When controversy over Mann's photographs neared their peak, some judges considered the division between art and obscenity as a function of exposure (especially of body parts featured in pornography, including breasts, genitals, and buttocks) and behavior.[41] Decided in 1986, *United States v. Dost* was the first attempt to establish a standard of visual analysis for courts determining whether an image constituted child pornography. In deciding whether photographs of naked girls aged ten and fourteen were pornographic, the U.S. District Court for the Southern District of California indexed qualities like coyness to particular behaviors. A girl was "sexually coy" if she stared directly at a camera with her head tilted; "squinting and looking away from the camera" did not qualify.[42] Contrary to these almost formulaic equivalences was the extraordinary latitude granted to judges to determine for themselves what they considered age-appropriate behavior. A photograph depicting a girl whose genitals were exposed could escape condemnation so long as she was wearing "appropriate" clothing for her age and sitting "in an ordinary way for her age."[43]

Accumulated discourse concerning the dangers of child pornography, child abuse, and the general legal status of children eclipsed any possible discussion of subjectivity that might allow "Immediate Family" some independence from a legal history of photography. Recalling the responses to *Damaged Child,* Mann described how viewers wanted "to reach out and comfort the little girl with the battered face and then it gets into this whole interpretation thing. . . . People get so emotionally involved that they forget these are works of art."[44] The artist Connie Samaras argued that the issue is pushed even further in works like those of Jacqueline Livingston, which could not so easily use formalism as an alibi. They have "the look of photographs intended for mass consumption," particularly of snapshots that might be taken by anyone and that place the viewer "in the vantage point of producer."[45] Viewers were reluctant to accept the art defense, particularly in places like Britain, where antiobscenity laws were and are more strict.[46] Referring to Mann's work, journalist Julie Burchill fretted over whether such emphasis was a symptom of an endemic desensitization to wrongdoing: "As censorship has retreated, only the society of the spectacle has advanced; only the society in which the atrocity can be made into art, and therefore stops being an atrocity because it is no longer 'real.'"[47]

In his chronicle of art and illegality, critic Carl McCormick asserted that if "art is to truly mean anything outside its small private discourse, it cannot go before a judge and say 'but this is art.'"[48] But by describing her work as only images, Mann shifted the grounds of discussion to artistic and, thus, extra-legal territory, a move that also called attention to the fact that laws concerning obscenity must themselves appeal to ideas outside the law. Words common in obscenity cases—*appropriate, decent, lascivious*—are terminological orphans, undefined by existing legal doctrine and decided largely according to personal impression. While lobbying for the passage of a bill aimed at expanding the definition of child pornography, Colorado state senator Ken Arnold presented *Jessie and the Deer,* the photograph Mann took in 1985 of her smiling daughter in a ballerina costume, standing playfully next to a pickup truck and holding a dead deer (fig. 74). Arnold pointed to the photograph and allegedly exclaimed, "Look at that. It's like abuse is okay."[49] The legislator's imperative tone read as a gesture of deflection, made to draw attention away from the actual work of looking, which would likely yield multiple observations rather than a single, finite conclusion. Borrowing from Ariella Azoulay's contention that photography works by suturing makers, subjects, and viewers through acts of recognition, some of Mann's photographs suggest that the act of looking is itself an agreement to perform a certain role.[50] For example, *Wet Bed* casts viewers in the role of surrogate parents as they look down upon the image of the child. Yet some viewers may also feel that it unjustly casts them in the role of the pedophile looking on the naked girl as an object. The virulence with which some viewers protested Mann's photographs may have been motivated by how these images challenged the autonomy of viewers by casting them in certain positions without their consent.

Viewer disapprobation may also have reflected anxiety over the detachment Mann's images required from audiences. Seeing the children in the photograph *only* as images

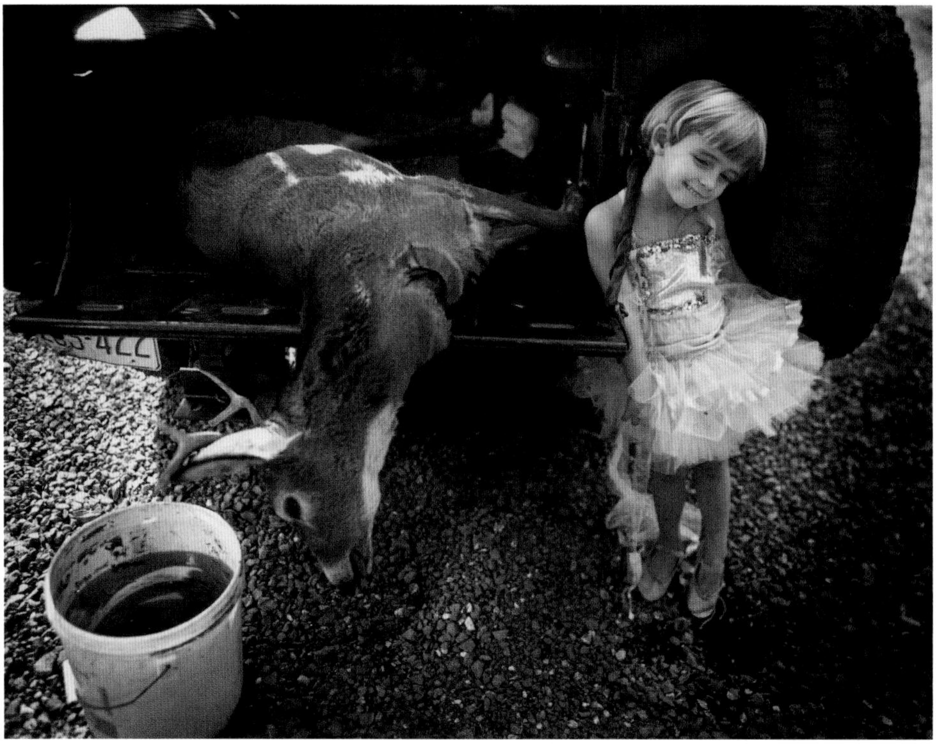

FIGURE 74
Sally Mann, *Jessie and the Deer,* 1985. Gelatin silver print. © Sally Mann. Courtesy of Gagosian.

is a tall order with a work like *Damaged Child,* in which the subject's face appears thrust into our line of vision from a nondescript background. Yet other images are most legible when we recognize as central the distance between the images and their referents. In *The Last Time Emmett Modeled Nude,* Mann's son Emmett stands naked in the water, his fingers rapidly skimming its surface (fig. 75). Situated near the center of pictorial space, the boy's body cuts through the water to form an inverted V-shape mimicking that produced by the reflection of the woods in the background. His head almost touches the point at which the two adjacent reflections of trees converge, emphasizing his body as the central axis around which the space of the photograph revolves. The depth of field has been altered so as to make even minute details visible. Emmett turns away from the camera; his right hand is drawn back as if to steady a shift of weight onto his right foot. His left arm appears to extend toward us, the hand spread in an ambiguous gesture that resembles, but does not completely register as, a greeting, offering, or self-defense. He lowers his head, projecting his gaze upward toward an unseen lens that appears to look down upon him. He does not smile, so the stare he delivers is as ambiguous in meaning as his open hand. Mann explained Emmett's scowl, remarking that it was "just his way of expressing that he was tired of posing."[51]

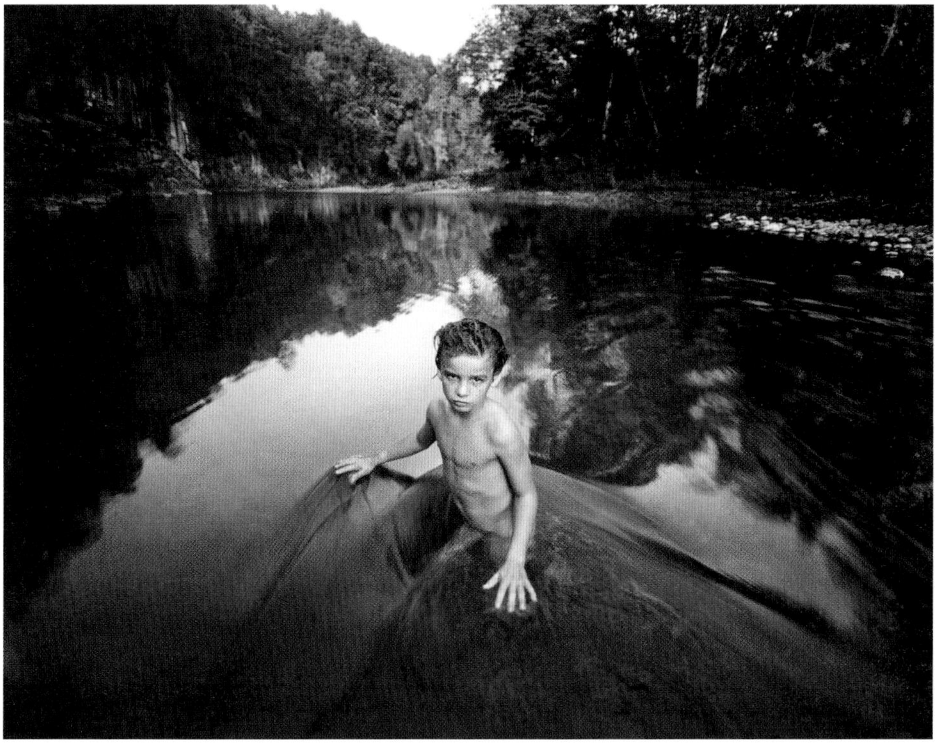

FIGURE 75
Sally Mann, *The Last Time Emmett Modeled Nude*, 1987. Gelatin silver print. © Sally Mann. Courtesy of Gagosian.

Although praised as "dazzlingly elegiac," *The Last Time Emmett Modeled Nude* is best remembered for the speed with which some viewers treated the image as if it were evidence of some immoral act or crime.[52] Unlike legally admissible evidence, Mann's photographs were not discussed according to accepted or proposed rules of judgment. They were considered proof that particular actions had happened—except for the action they actually demonstrated, that someone had photographed these children. Mann's photographs disturbed because their self-containment depended on reminding viewers how little they knew of the circumstances of their production.

In "The Importance of Permanence," a relatively little-known essay by Donald Judd, the artist lamented that "art has no legal autonomy."[53] While he urged the state and society to "revise some of its attitudes, laws and tax laws to make it easier" for artists to create and protect their works, he also warned, somewhat paradoxically, that "the government is too dangerous to get involved" in improving matters.[54] The danger extended beyond censorship, whether overt or indirect (through denial of grants and other financial support), lurking in the excessive force that law can exert over any form of authority recognized and inherent in the art world. It also lurked within the difficult potential bargain inherent in the art defense, which sometimes meant displacing affective force in favor of aesthetics; for instance, a critic remarked that the "formal beauty" of *Wet Bed* served to "counteract any sense of embarrassment."[55] Instead of acknowledging the productive discomfort so central to the experience of looking at Mann's photographs, such arguments reified the conception of the artist as a supplier of the inoffensively beautiful, which lined up with the attitudes of legislators and the government alike.[56] But while art was perhaps less sovereign than Judd and his colleagues may have hoped, Mann's emphasis on the images also tried to ensure that law would be reminded of its own inseparability from extra-legal concerns.

IN SEARCH OF THE REASONABLE VIEWER

By the early 1990s, artistic photography in the context of law figured most strongly in a debate about the idea of the viewer. The outcome of the Mapplethorpe case in Ohio depended crucially on the definition and selection of viewers, over which the defense team and the court had competing views. Acknowledging that New York City "has threatening connotations for many Cincinnatians," the defense intentionally brought in expert witnesses with midwestern connections.[57] Jurors were chosen with even greater care, given how Judge David Albanese refused to discount the ability of viewers inexperienced with art to determine a work's artistic value.[58] The defense team exercised its legal right of peremptory challenge to eliminate jurors who they sensed would favor the prosecution.

Enter the "reasonable viewer," a juridical fiction strongly resembling the imagined nameless lay viewer through which critics and art historians ventriloquize their experience of a particular artwork. The reasonable viewer assumed special importance after 1987, when the U.S. Supreme Court, in *Pope v. Illinois,* designated this viewer as the final arbiter of deciding whether allegedly obscene material had any socially redemptive value.[59] Prior to this decision, obscenity initially turned on the idea of community standards, or a form of social organization held together by a shared belief in the production of consensus. More liberal jurisdictions advocated an "exposure" standard. Consider Andrew J. Weisz, the Beverly Hills judge who in 1965 acquitted Chouinard Art Institute instructor Connor Everts of obscenity charges; the standard lay in determining whether "a person normally exposed to the various influences at work in our culture" would regard Everts's depictions of genitals "dirty."[60] In contrast, when Livingston displayed her work in 1979, the reasonableness standard turned on what would be reasonable for any viewer to assume of a photograph's content and the intention behind its creation. However incongruent, disproportionate, or unreasonable, a viewer's response was legitimate.

Courts, however, looked askance at responses based on visual analysis, even going so far as to suggest that it undermined the reasonableness standard. In *Allegheny v. ACLU,* the 1989 U.S. Supreme Court case involving the constitutionality of holiday displays situated on public land in downtown Pittsburgh, Justice Brennan stated his misgivings toward visual analysis: "I shudder to think that the only 'reasonable observer' is one who shares the particular views on perspective, spacing, and accent expressed in Justice Blackmun's opinion, thus making analysis under the Establishment Clause look more like an exam in Art 101 than an inquiry into constitutional law."[61] Judge Albanese offered a more temperate view, pointing out the lack of consistency regarding the interpretation of visual images. He cited Justice Antonin Scalia, who noted, in *Pope v. Illinois,* that "the fabled 'reasonable man' is of little help in the inquiry, and would have to be replaced with, perhaps, the 'man of tolerably good taste'—a description that betrays the lack of an ascertainable standard."[62]

Scalia and Albanese rightly invoked "taste" as the grounds tacitly underpinning many decisions concerning visual art—a history of taste ratified by the authority of law and politics. But taste is not synonymous with the act of viewing, a task judges continuously face when deciding whether a jury should consider the facts of a case or whether the case should be dismissed. In the same year of Albanese's decision, law scholar Katharine Bartlett called for judges to subject their analysis to "background principles and methods" that could act as "meaningful constraints" on what might otherwise be the clandestine freedom of judges to permit their subjective feelings to determine case verdicts.[63] "Meaningful constraints" do not require judges to be art historians or critics, but only to cultivate their capacity to discern certain features when looking at an artwork or object.

If courts clung to the flawed fiction of the reasonable viewer as they muddled their way through a world indelibly defined by visual imagery, it was because this fiction checked the interpretative excesses of legislatures, police, and the media. In the 1993 case *Boggs v. Bowron,* the U.S. District Court in Washington, D.C., ruled on whether the dollar bills that artist J.S.G. Boggs drew and exchanged to obtain various goods and services violated anticounterfeiting laws. In deciding against the artist, the District Court held that "a person of average intelligence and ordinary observation could not readily and immediately distinguish them from genuine currency."[64] The court noted that Boggs's artworks shared the "general pattern" of currency, noting similarities in size, color, and the placement of characteristic elements such as signature blocks and numeric features.[65] "General pattern" recalled the language of Otto Pächt, one of the leaders of the New Vienna School of art historians, celebrated for their efforts to make the interpretation of artworks more rigorous. Rather than identify differences in style or the alleged meanings of images, which he regarded as fatally subject to contextual circumstances, Pächt argued that artworks were governed by a system of relationships used to organize the work, including tensions between figure and ground, vertical and horizontal, and frontality and laterality.[66] His arguments foreshadowed the reasoning of the Second Circuit decades later when it found that broadcast networks HBO and Black Entertainment Television unlawfully used posters created by Faith Ringgold by placing them on the set of a television program. The court examined how and when Ringgold's work was visible on the offending portions of the program, observing that the poster was systematically parsed into "sections" and "quadrants," a determination that would not be out of place in the kind of formal analysis endorsed by Meyer Schapiro, the seminal art historian who pushed the New Vienna School's mandate for rigor further by insisting that art historical analysis depends on "relevant hypotheses, precise observation, logical analysis, and various devices of verification."[67]

Art historical approaches to formalism, and its emphasis on the accurate description of physical artworks, were not entirely incongruent with either the aims of the judiciary or its abilities. Rather than stress "artistic value" as a criterion, the challenge lies in articulating instructions that might guide judges when they have to engage in some form of visual analysis.[68] For although the "reasonable viewer" standard was theoretically intended to preclude outlier responses to a challenged work, in practice it granted permission to judges to express any opinion, no matter how egregious or damaging in its implications, so long as it was plausible. Evaluating image-analysis practices in copyright law, Rebecca Tushnet ascribes the inconsistency of judicial decisions founded on visual analysis as an example of "epistemic hubris."[69] Shades of similar hubris threaded through the glibness with which viewers of Mann's photographs made various extra-artistic claims regarding the subjectivity of Mann or her children. The sheer volume of comments either for or against particular images in "Immediate Family" reflected a sense of entitlement among viewers to freely express their unsolicited views, not only about what the images represent, but also what they might suggest about its maker, including Mann's fitness as a mother. Art historian Sarah Parsons describes Mann's images as being too close to reality, claiming they are too close to the inconsistency of the mother's gaze to be unproblematic.[70] Mann herself seemed to consider whether this was the case when she and her husband planned to renege on her publishing contract after seeing a group of preteen boys snickering over the images.[71]

The most reasonable viewers of all may have been Mann's children, who in fact had veto power over whether Mann could display certain photographs. They chose not to exclude nude images but only those that made them look like "dorks," "geeks," or "dweebs."[72] The use of such typical youthful pejoratives illustrates how the potential audience for "Immediate Family" also included other children as well as adults, a fact unaccounted for in most discussions. The children, too, could see; their agency in this regard is emphasized by how they look at Mann's camera almost in anticipation of when they would look back upon their photographic selves, reviewing with Mann the work their presence enabled.

If the priority is to find "a workable boundary between the real and imaginary in photographs," as art historian Anne Higonnet suggests in her book on the representation of children, a corollary issue is to ask what is reasonable to expect from jurists.[73] The certainty with which Mann's critics held fast to their beliefs about photographs functioning primarily as bearers of meaning registered as a kind of arrogance. One might say that "reasonable viewers" of Mann's works, then, were those who could acknowledge their own ignorance about what they were seeing. Law scholar Mary Jean Dolan has discussed the "exceedingly reasonable observer," or a viewer who considers the perspective of the other side when dealing with challenging images.[74] In Mann's case, such an observer might be expected to consider how sexual images can communicate nonsexual ideas and vice versa, as well as an opportunity for that viewer to prove her humility in the face of images whose power to unsettle demonstrated the fallibility of "epistemic hubris." Mann's disengagement from legal action doubled as an indirect plea to lawmakers and jurists to engage in close looking as part of their practice of reasonableness. It was also a disengagement from how artworks were commonly recognized within the law as forms of communication, namely speech.[75]

PHOTOGRAPHY BESIDES EVIDENCE

Disengagement had its limits. In 1991, the *Wall Street Journal* cropped, then redacted, Mann's photograph *Virginia at Four* (fig. 76). The image accompanied an article called "Critique: Censoring Virginia" and showed Mann's daughter with her eyes, chest, and crotch blacked out. The redaction showed how someone with no legal relation to Virginia Mann could impose their own ideas of privacy on her image. Thin rectangles of black transposed over various body parts—more commonly seen in a classified document than on a picture of a child—undermined any chance that readers might see the image as a coherent photograph. Rather, it was presented, in Mann's words, "as if it were Exhibit A in a child pornography prosecution."[76]

Often the most incisive observer of how her works circulated through different contexts, Mann emphasized how her photographs were being seen as legal evidence, a viewpoint also shared by advocates of her work. Her photographs were treated as proof of the likelihood of abuse, even when the depiction was staged.[77] Detractors read them as evidence that potentially established any number of crimes, from Mann's unfitness as a mother to the idea that child exploitation had taken place. Supporters treated these accusations as symptoms of perhaps a deeper insidiousness that threatened to regulate basic freedoms of speech, act, and thought. Intrinsic in both attitudes was a use of evidence with the intent to persuade without also considering how evidence might reinforce prejudices. Polemical interpretation of Mann's photographs was often counterproductive to the ideals embodied by the "reasonable viewer" standard or to the notion of viewer accountability.

Alert to the legal challenges faced by other photographers, Mann consulted at least one attorney in case "some crackpot" wanted to "make political hay" of her works.[78] Yet she declined an offer that law professor and free speech activist Edward de Grazia had made to file a lawsuit on her behalf.[79] The author of a history of the censorship of erotic materials, de Grazia was widely known in legal and publishing circles for his spirited defense of publishers of books that address overtly sexual matters, including Henry Miller's novel *Tropic of Cancer,* on the grounds that socially valuable material cannot be obscene.[80] For de Grazia, Mann's photographs represented a prime example he could use to extend his arguments concerning free speech. The hypothetical case would involve having certain laws declared unconstitutional when applied to her work, even though Mann had yet to be officially accused of breaking any law.

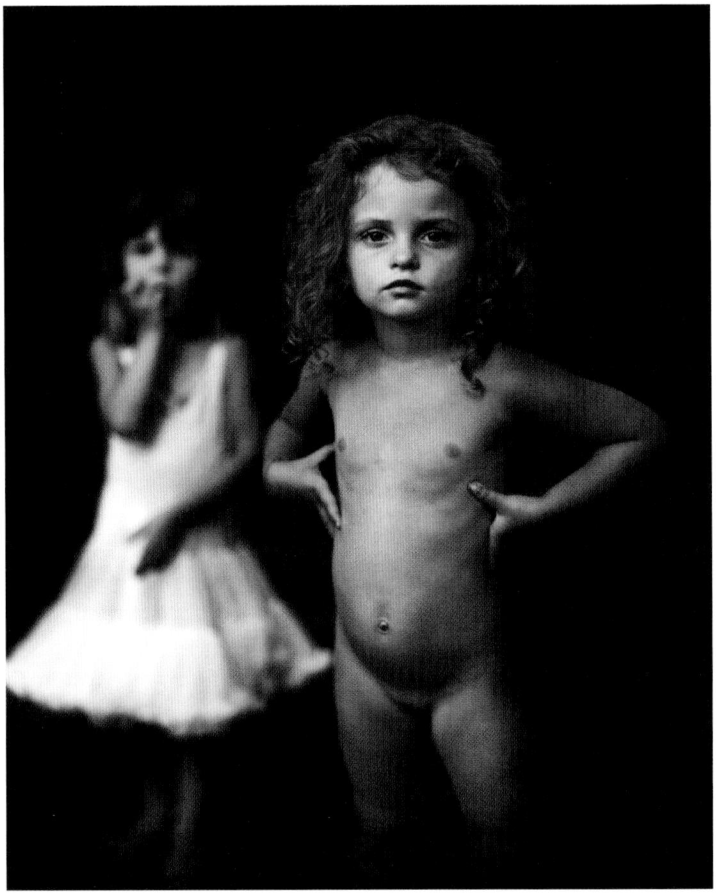

FIGURE 76
Sally Mann, *Virginia at Four,* 1989.
Gelatin silver print. © Sally Mann.
Courtesy of Gagosian.

As an artist of "recognized stature" whose work had been widely shown and discussed, Mann could have sued the *Wall Street Journal* under the recently enacted Visual Artists Rights Act (described in the Introduction) for violating her right of integrity. The redaction could very well convince a judge that it was an illegal distortion or mutilation of her work, with the form of mutilation seen as "prejudicial" to Mann's "honor or reputation." Another possible claim was copyright infringement, as it was unclear whether the newspaper secured permission from Mann to reproduce the photograph in this manner. Mann eventually decided against bringing suit, to avoid subjecting her child to an extremely hostile environment that would be considered unethical or abusive under most circumstances but was legally acceptable in a trial or deposition hearing.[81] Practically speaking, disengagement also avoided the uncertainty of the justice system; recall how, in the Mapplethorpe case, the Cincinnati Art Center gambled and lost when it attempted to preempt legal controversy by asking the Hamilton County Municipal Court for a declaratory judgment, a motion that decides on legal uncertainties. The motion was made on grounds that a legitimate museum could not be charged with obscenity. The court refused, and both the museum and its director were indicted a few days later.

In not seeking legal redress, Mann may have wanted to avoid an administrative system that showed little respect for the home as a space of personal autonomy. She observed that "like my children today, I wore no clothes until kindergarten interfered with my feral life, a life of freedom not only from clothes but from constraint of any kind, *limited only by the boundaries of our property*" (my emphasis). [82] But, contra the late 1950s, the home circa the 1980s was constantly subject to government intervention in the name of reducing child and domestic abuse.[83]

Mann's decision was also an attempt to keep the photographs out of the extra-artistic domains in which her detractors were so convinced they belonged. For Mann to begin legal proceedings would have permanently cast Virginia's participation as an issue of consent, and the photograph as a question of property. Her decision to abstain from litigation pushed back against the photographs' subsumption into pure context, as reflected in how viewers were primed to read Mann's works exclusively against the endless barrage of polemics concerning the family, child welfare, and free speech. She thus resisted mounting efforts to enable mere certitude of personal opinion to carry a set of politically motivated directives across the threshold of law. Uninterested in becoming yet another combatant in an arena defined by the tenacity with which participants clung to their own respective viewpoints while rejecting opposing ones wholesale, Mann instead channeled her energies toward getting viewers to allow themselves to see freely—that is, to let photographs generate questions rather than declarative statements.

On another level, Mann's photographs challenge viewers accustomed to thinking about representations of children as allegories of a larger social condition. Turn now to *Jessie at Five* (fig. 77). Bathed wholly in light, the flesh of Mann's daughter seems less real than almost any other child's. Nothing is hidden. Excessive light showcasing Jessie's face and upper body reads like overcompensation, as if we could not otherwise distinguish Jessie from her sister without this extra assistance. In an early, incisive review of "Immediate Pictures," critic Charles Hagen wrote that some of the works "seem so overblown, so blatantly symbolic, that they don't ring true."[84] Yet it is the artifice that reifies the picture's claims to documentation. The actions depicted "seem to have originated in the children themselves," Hagen adds.[85]

Jessie at Five reads as another kind of documentation, one intended to disrupt the certainty with which viewers see images of children. Mann literally makes light of the tendency to think that we know what a photograph means just because we have identified its most visually obvious element. "Here," Mann seems to say, "I will make it easy for you." We are placed just close enough that we might imagine ourselves calling the shots, even telling Jessie how to stand and turn. Particularly conspicuous is the color of the girl's skin against the dark foliage in the background. Bathed in light, her upper body is so blindingly white as to invoke the idea of racial whiteness. Certainly, this

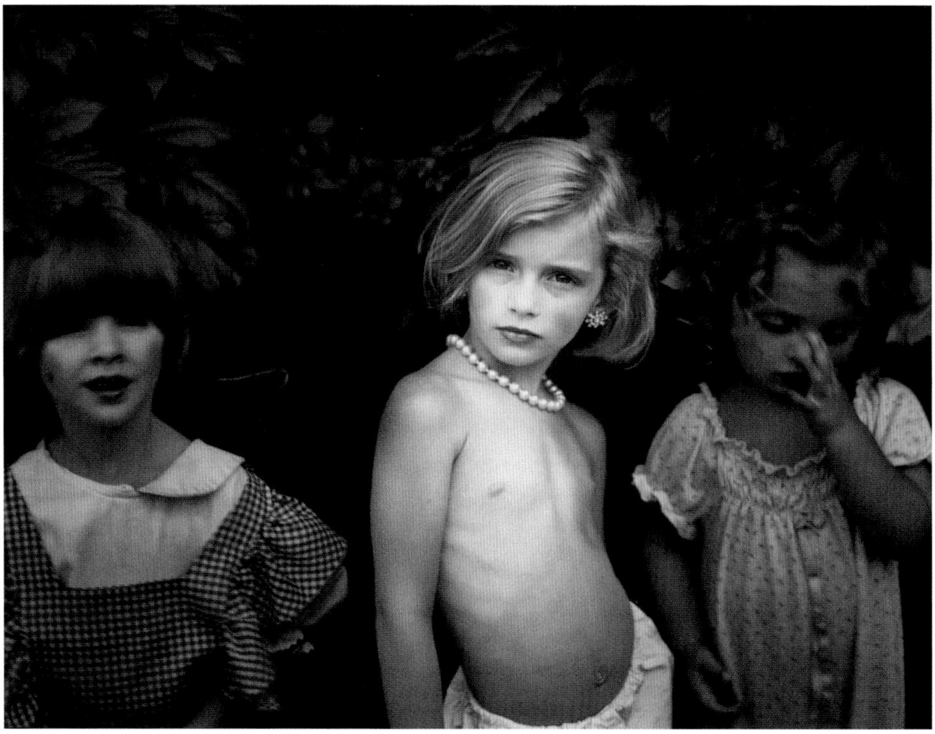

FIGURE 77
Sally Mann, *Jessie at Five,* 1987. Gelatin silver print. © Sally Mann. Courtesy of Gagosian.

coloring may explain the ferocity with which some viewers, particularly white male viewers, condemned these photographs as violations of an unspoken moral code. At the heart of the controversy surrounding Mann's photographs is a latent anxiety over who sees the white female body and how. But nearly all girls and women are subject to unwanted contact of a sexual nature at some point in their lives. The insistence that Mann's photographs of her daughters must necessarily be proof of some moral or criminal wrongdoing of a sexual nature emphasizes how even the images of girls are subject to endemic sexualization. As law scholar Amy Adler has contended, child pornography laws constitute yet another kind of sexualized representation of children.[86] Mann's images were condemned, their subjects compared to child prostitutes ("knowing, tarnished angels"), their eyes blacked out in the name of keeping the world safe from their supposed prurience.[87] Mann's conscious disengagement from the law was a step toward rejecting the sexualization of children's bodies while leaving intact the underexamined relationship between beauty and sensuality.

Referring to viewers who perform the role of surrogate parent in their reception of photographs like *Damaged Child,* Mann commented on how they "treat photography differently than painting."[88] Part of the suspicion against Mann's work recalls a longer history of legal ambivalence toward photography in relation to other artistic media. Legal scholars have sought to distinguish between nudity rendered "through some sort of mechanical apparatus" as opposed to nudity in "paintings, sculptures, or other reliefs"—that is, what the law generally considers art.[89] Obscenity law, in particular, required photography to prove itself more than painting had to, perhaps based on the reproducibility of photographs. Photography constantly provoked doubt about its worth, a point raised by an anonymous member of the Cornell University community in a letter criticizing the university's decision not to renew Jacqueline Livingston's contract: "If Livingston's contract was not renewed because her photographs [male nudes] affronted some uptight male faculty members, that is indeed an outrage. But if Livingston is leaving because the architecture department has mandated that photography goes when the budget gets tight, that is an even greater outrage."[90] As Livingston's travails demonstrated, it was one thing for a male sculptor to depict nude women; it was an entirely different matter for a female photographer to photograph nude men and boys.

The slowness and deliberation inherent in Mann's process, from her choice of camera to her method of film development, read as an intentional separation from how photography was generally regarded. The flesh Mann depicts is not the same as the flesh of a sculpture, or even of a depiction of sculpted flesh. There is something unreal about the body, which looks as if it was pressed into the physical surface of the photograph. Despite the flattening, the flesh shown here was regarded as being more indexical of an actual body than a freestanding sculpture. Accordingly, if looking at the work provokes such anxiety, is it because we are unsure what photography is or because we are unsure what it is not?

Emmett's Bloody Nose shows Mann's son lying on a floral upholstered floor one might expect in a living room or perhaps an unused spare room (fig. 78). Placidly lying next to him is another boy with similarly tousled hair, curling his left hand over Emmett's right in a gesture that is not easily read but could register as protective. Both boys gaze directly at the camera, their expressions largely neutral. Only here we see a profusion of blood streaming from Emmett's nose, flecking what in black and white reads as the alabaster porcelain of his skin, trickling down on his chin to pool in an amorphous blob on his white cotton turtleneck. High-contrast film makes the blood sharply visible. Unlike Mann's portraits of Jessie, the focus is not so much on Emmett as on the ambiguous point of contact between the two boys. Their cupped hands vaguely approximate the shape of a heart, which lessens any suspicions of apparent violence. Like most of the photographs in "Immediate Family," Emmett's face is finely articulated; we see, for example, his shiny bangs reflecting overhead illumination. The other boy's face is subtly dulled so that we look upon him as if through a slightly frosted plate. The tranquility of the scene is peculiar, contradicting what we might assume about the speed at which blood flows. Stranger still is how close to Emmett's world the photograph brings us. Unlike his sister in *Damaged Child,* his face is not so much thrust into ours as we are thrust into his personal space.

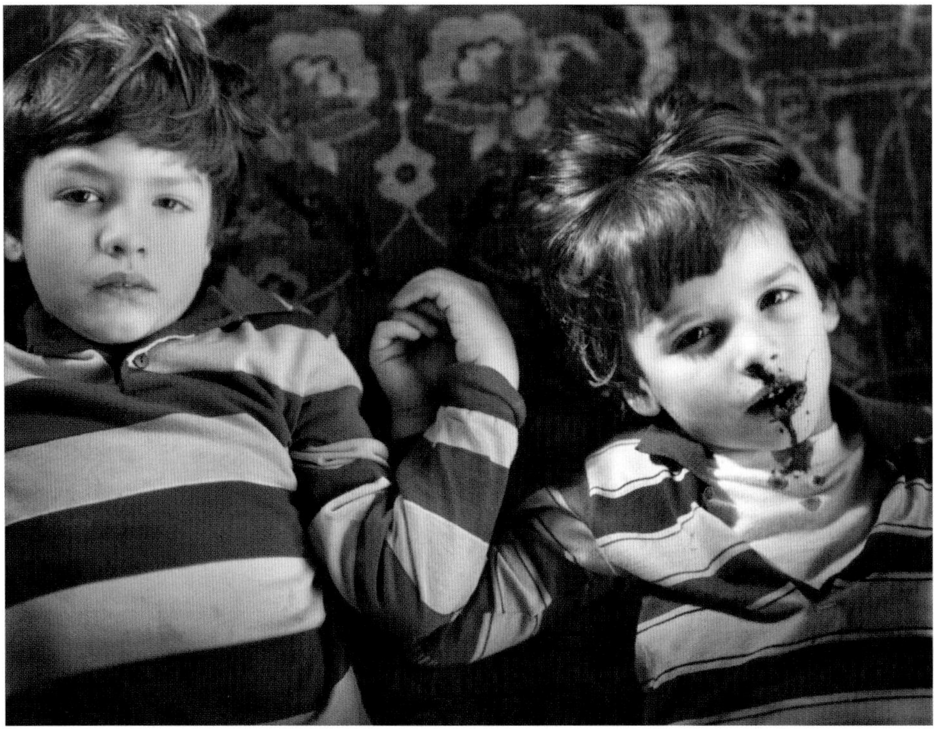

FIGURE 78
Sally Mann, *Emmett's Bloody Nose,* 1985. Gelatin silver print. © Sally Mann. Courtesy of Gagosian.

In defending photographer Jock Sturges, artist and critic Luc Sante highlighted the direct gazes of Sturges's subjects, which he read as evidence that they are "absolutely self-possessed in their acknowledgment of their bodies."[91] He added that Sturges's use of an eight-by-ten camera, not unlike that used by Mann, would have affected his subjects' interaction with the camera.[92] The heavy camera, the tripod, and the length of time needed to produce each shot would likely have affected sitter behavior. In Mann's *Candy Cigarette,* Jessie stands close enough to the bottom edge of the photograph to provoke a connection with the viewer (fig. 79). But she turns her body slightly away, just enough to have us note how the little girl on the right blocks us out of the picture. The angle at which Jessie folds her right arm across her body implicitly connects with the left elbow of the other girl. Arms akimbo, the latter's body acts as a screen, excluding us from further access to the world of the picture. Bodies are pictured in a way that imputes awareness to their owners. The girls stand as if they recognize how they are being photographed, even if it remains unclear whether they have full control over how they present themselves to the camera.

Virginia at Five shows far less bare flesh than *The Last Time Emmett Modeled Nude* (fig. 80). Her long, curly mane covers some of her face and drapes her shoulders like a

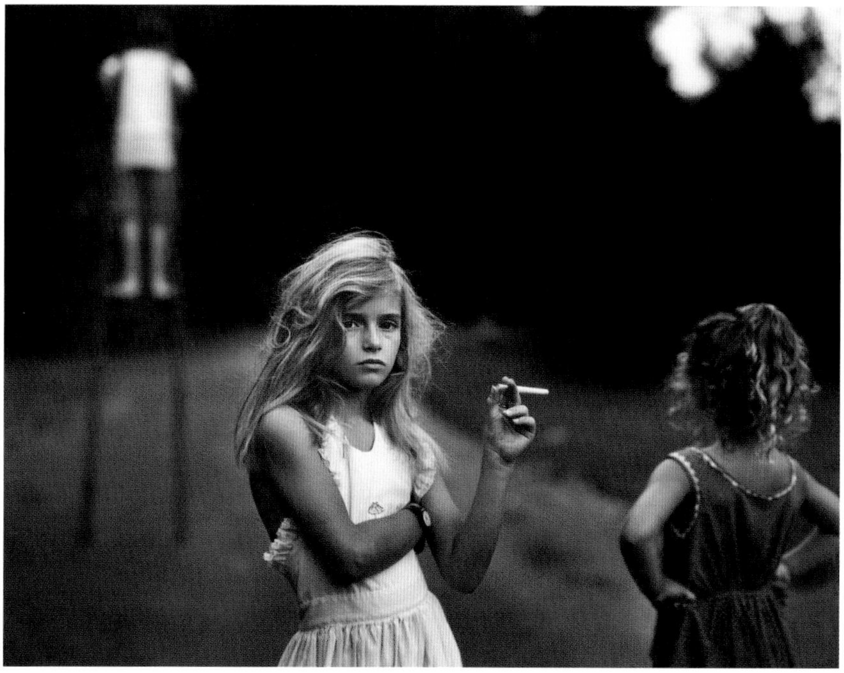

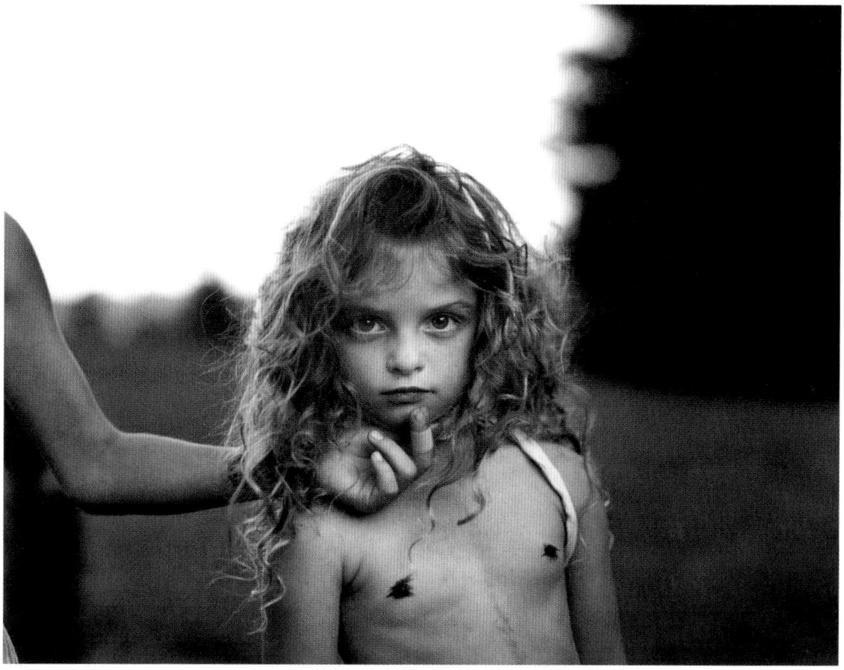

FIGURE 79

Sally Mann, *Candy Cigarette,* 1989. Gelatin silver print.

FIGURE 80

Sally Mann, *Virginia at Five,* 1990. Gelatin silver print.

mantle. Yet there is something untoward, and even intrusive, about the hand under her chin, caressing her as if she were a pet cat. Virginia seems oblivious to her sister's touch. She holds one shoulder higher than the other, as if to shift her weight and ground herself on one foot. More unnerving, however, is the suggestion that even a girl as young as Virginia understands that she will be looked at and, most importantly, *how*. As Mann observed of another photograph she took of a different girl in 1983, "There is just no way" adults "could protect the child from what she gives to the camera. I didn't tell her to cock her hip, or give that look . . . she knows her power and there was no way to prevent her from using it."[93] Even if Virginia Mann may not fully realize how she controls her own self-presentation, she may still convey a sense of control. Crucial here is how photography sets up its subjects to perform in ways that undermine efforts to gauge the intensity and magnitude of will. And that performance continues beyond the moment of creation.

BEYOND CONSENT

Photographs like *Virginia at Five* and *Candy Cigarette* rank among the most candid—and thus, for some viewers, unacceptable—depictions of children because of how frankly they dismiss preconceived limits on child agency and, by extension, legal ideas of consent. A mainstay of U.S. jurisprudence, particularly in criminal, contract, and family law, consent broadly defined entails informed and voluntary agreement to permit or perform a given act. Its position is murkier in parent-child relationships, for only when the vertical relationship between parent and child breaks down does law intervene.[94] Consent was integral to decisions involving the alleged exploitation of children, a group the law privileges because of its perceived fundamental vulnerability. The defense team for the Contemporary Art Center in Cincinnati was helped, for example, by the mothers having attended photo shoots involving their children. Their presence was regarded as implied consent to Mapplethorpe's image making.[95]

"I know what my mom likes sometimes, so I point it out to her," Jessie Mann stated in 1992.[96] Inherent in the younger Mann's statement is a distinct acknowledgment of her double role as daughter and assistant. Likewise, the photograph of Emmett's nosebleed was taken only after the boy brought it to the attention of his mother, when he "brought it (the nosebleed) home and said, 'Hey, look at this.'"[97] About Mann's initial decision not to publish the photographs, the children were outraged on the grounds that their authorship rights were being violated. "It destroyed them," she stated, adding that they "want the book published, [their attitude being that] they're our pictures as much as yours."[98] Likewise, the children were "quite adamant about wanting [the pictures] made. . . . They come home and they say, 'I thought of a good picture for you, Mom, or I found a good place.'"[99]

The cooperation of Mann's children was based on more than filial obligation; she paid them twenty-five cents a negative.[100] Although the sums were more supplemental allowance than market levels of compensation—think of the hourly fees paid to professional child models—they were nevertheless made in exchange for something Mann genuinely wanted, in this case visual access to bodies.[101] However casual, the transaction not only reframed the time of the children as valuable labor, but also pointed to a confluence of law, economics, and intimacy underwriting legal approaches to family relations in the 1990s. Law scholar Alan Hyde described, for example, how legal discourse "powerfully and relentlessly" corralled human relations into its preferred designations.[102] Love, for example, is filtered through conceptions of a marriage contract, while intrafamily relations are seen through the prism of competing rights. Margaret Brinig went even further, arguing that families actually work like businesses.[103] The idea of renting visual access recalls the grim scenario Carole Pateman laid out in *The Sexual Contract* concerning the asymmetries of power made visible when bodies are treated as property.[104]

Black's Law Dictionary defines *employee* as a "person in the service of another under any contract of hire, express or implied, oral or written, where the employer has the power or right to control and direct the employee in the material details of how the work is to be performed."[105] In respect to child employment, the State of Virginia is among the more protective of jurisdictions, generally forbidding children under fourteen to work, even with parental consent.[106] Among the few exceptions to the rule is when the employer is a parent and the employment is in an industry "other than manufacturing." The exception indicates how family law often assumes that a parent will naturally have the child's best interests at heart. Yet many photographs taken for "Immediate Family" depict relationships suggesting profound ambivalence toward the idea of collaboration. In *Candy Cigarette,* Jessie stands in the extreme foreground, her right arm crossing her body in a defensive posture. Her left arm is bent but extends cautiously forward. Held between her left index and middle fingers is a long, tubular white object that reads as a cigarette, mainly because of the way it is held. Her younger sister Virginia turns away from us, her sights perhaps set on her brother Emmett standing on stilts in the left-hand background. "Immediate Family" shifted the issue of consent from assumptions regarding the forms of agency available to children to the agency children exercise through form, particularly gesture and inflection. The spaces we as viewers enter upon seeing these images differ remarkably as a result, not just in terms of physical setting or distance but also in affective tone: in *Virginia at Five,* the tone is warm and inviting, while *Candy Cigarette* is shot through with equal parts suspicion and curiosity.

"I have no objections, none," recounted Jessie Mann about her participation in "Immediate Family," which she then contradicted, saying that "the few times I don't like [having my picture taken] is when I have a friend over and I'm just in my room and Mom says, 'Picture time,' and I don't really want to do it."[107] The scenario implies a rehearsal of the kind of parental authority used to command children; one imagines Mann saying "picture time" in the same tone used to announce "chore time" or even "meal time." She contends that the obedience of her children was grounded in a recognition of her own sense of obligation:

> The children look to me to make judgments for them. They have to trust my judgment that it's OK to hang a picture in a museum in which they're nude or hurt or somehow cast in an undesirable light. It puts huge responsibilities on me to weigh the art against my duties as a parent.[108]

Mann recognized the ambivalence of the situation her photographs created: "It's always interesting . . . to see just how far you can go. I break out into a sweat when I'm almost there and I've gone about as far as a reasonable human being can go in taking a portrait, and then I ask the next step."[109]

That Mann photographed her children at various ages, along with the titles of the photographs, questions the correlation between age and agency. The closest legal analogy would be regulation concerning the age of consent to sexual intercourse, which ranges from fourteen to twenty. But Virginia Mann made a persuasive case about meaningful consent arising in other situations. While her mother pointedly disengaged from politicians' and journalists' attempts to monopolize how and what photographs mean, Virginia wrote directly to the *Wall Street Journal,* informing the august chronicle that "I don't like the way you crossed me out."[110] Even if the law did not recognize Virginia Mann's deferred non-assent to her redacted image, the poignant admixture of dignity and hurt would be hard for adult readers to miss.

Mann staked her artistic integrity on insisting on the distinction between the worlds within and beyond the photographic frame. She emphasized her authorial claims to define when her art began and ended, a crucial gesture in a time and place where neither the public nor the courts placed much faith in the word of artists, even on the subject of their own works. Her integrity as a mother, however, stemmed from her ability to recognize children as capable of independent decision making within the context of artistic collaboration. That her recognition took place without recourse to legal advice allowed her to help preserve the integrity of the family, a unit of social organization acutely subject to legal intervention based on abstract conceptions of innocent children and their inability to choose for themselves. In Mann's hands, disengagement was part of a larger effort to preserve the distinction between art and life. For only with such a distinction could art function as a domain where the disquiet of everyday life could be explored frankly. Her attempts at disengagement were powerful declarations of independence for art, yet the constant stream of attacks against both Mann and her works demonstrated that any independence would be short lived. To borrow from legal scholar Elizabeth Porter's paraphrasing of Susan Sontag, photographs "exist to end in a legal document."[111] How to work within the enclosure of the law without capitulating to brittle legalism was the next task.

6

DOUBLE EMBODIMENTS

Felix Gonzalez-Torres's Certificates

TAKING A SHEET OF PAPER or a wrapped candy from a stack or pile by Felix Gonzalez-Torres ranks among the most iconic contemporary art experiences (fig. 81). Even when one is told that the artist wanted viewers to break the "no touch" rule defining museum and gallery spaces, participation feels transgressive. At least one viewer described feeling criminally complicit, nervously "scanning the exhibition space for surveillance cameras."[1] Others take candies by the handful (teenage boys are particularly eager). Audiences familiar with the story behind *"Untitled" (Portrait of Ross in L.A.)* take candy reverently, as if paying their respects to a grave in reverse. When the paper stacks are low, viewers sometimes take a sheet only to return it later, as if unwilling to deny someone else the opportunity of engagement. Massed into neat stacks or herded into a corner, the paper stacks and candy spills recall the rigorous geometry of Minimalist sculpture. The rigor promises us, as critic Jennifer Doyle writes of museum and gallery experiences, freedom from "the burdens of an emotional life."[2] But as the piles

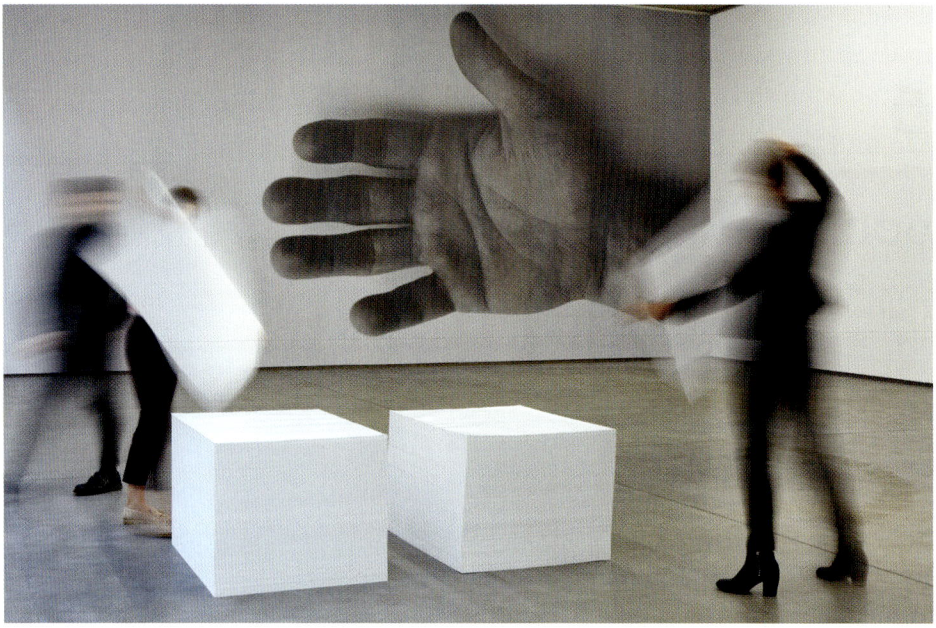

FIGURE 81
Foreground: Felix Gonzalez-Torres, *"Untitled,"* 1989/90. Print on paper, endless copies. 26 inches (at ideal height) × 29 × 23 inches (original paper size). Background: Felix Gonzalez-Torres, *"Untitled"* (*For Jeff*), 1992. Billboard, dimensions variable. Installation view: "Felix Gonzalez-Torres: This Place," Metropolitan Arts Centre, Belfast, 2015–2016. © Felix Gonzalez-Torres Foundation. Courtesy of Andrea Rosen Gallery, New York.

and stacks are depleted, feelings—particularly incomplete and inchoate ones—accrue in turn.

The production of feeling through direct physical and sensorial engagement with otherwise commonplace objects stems from the documentation that simultaneously accompanies and verifies the existence of many Gonzalez-Torres works, namely the certificates of authenticity and ownership transferred upon a work's sale. Commonly issued by artists and dealers to buyers anxious to both affirm the present value of their purchases and maximize potential resale value, certificates of authenticity belong to a category of financial documentation that includes receipts, invoices, and agreements generated upon, or in anticipation of, a work's sale. By the early 1990s, when Gonzalez-Torres's works attracted increasing commercial and critical attention, the certificate also overlapped with a nascent turn toward contracts. Unlike other certificates of authenticity that unilaterally impose the intentions of the artist on buyers, those of Gonzalez-Torres shared with owners some of his authority and duties. Here the idea of property exceeds what legal scholar Margaret Davies criticized as "the limited sphere of title to goods, land, or intellectual creations."[3] Titled "Certificates of Authenticity and Ownership" by the artist to indicate how they both verified a work's authenticity and explained its parameters, the certificates of Gonzalez-Torres proposed an alternative vision of possession as a fluid condition, with the owner having both unprecedented flexibility and responsibility from the moment of acquisition to when or if the work was sold. As both part of a well-established history of instruction-based artworks and a form of documentation increasingly recognized by the law, the certificates of Gonzalez-Torres read as an attempt to forge a sustainable working relationship between juridical privileging of ownership interests in visual-art cases and what might be called "art-world law," or the rules, customs, and other behavioral norms governing relationships between artists, institutions, dealers, and collectors.

Issued against a contested social, legal, and political landscape, the certificates resonated against a juridical system that reaffirmed its allegiance to private property while undermining the privacy claims of some of its most disenfranchised subjects. In a devastating reflection of how state interference usurped the role privacy had formerly played in defining the unique space of the home, the U.S. Supreme Court upheld the criminalization of sodomy in *Bowers v. Hardwick* (1986). Gonzalez-Torres condemned the decision, describing it as permission for the state to "actually go into" the bedrooms of gay men and lesbians and "penalize the way they express love to each other."[4] He added, "The body at this time in our history, at this time in culture, is defined not just by the flesh, but also by the law, by legislations, and by language first of all."[5] Yet courts just as adamantly defended property interests. Straight out of the "Culture Wars" playbook, *Wojnarowicz v. American Family Association* pitted a radical queer artist (David Wojnarowicz) against a religious arch-conservative (Donald Wildmon) who saw the artist's "depictions of sexuality" as "being nothing more than banal pornography."[6] But it was Wojnarowicz himself who initiated legal proceedings, on the grounds that Wildmon's organization, the American Family Association, had violated his moral and property rights.[7] Rather than grapple with the legal morass that obscenity had come to represent, Wojnarowicz emphasized how the American Family Association had violated his copyright and potentially damaged his reputation by selectively reproducing parts of his works. Despite agreeing with Wildmon that audiences "would be offended" by Wojnarowicz's works, presiding judge William Conner, a former patent lawyer who famously decided in 1981 that the First Amendment did not necessarily override the right of publicity, or an individual's right to control the use of her identity, ruled in the artist's favor.[8] For Wojnarowicz, who would die from AIDS in 1992 and for whom "the inevitability of death" was painfully concrete, property rights signified a pivotal opportunity to extend the life of his works beyond the time of his biological death by safeguarding their integrity in the most public and official manner possible.[9]

A year before Wojnarowicz filed suit, Gonzalez-Torres stated in 1989 that "you can't really oppose power in the same way you did ten years ago. Things have certainly changed a lot, the power structure is much more complex."[10] At this time, the artist began to issue certificates of authenticity for some of his works. Their flexible, and often ambiguous, language invited owners to create interactive, nondeterministic audience experiences directly challenging the underlying spirit of decisions like *Bowers.* In the words of Justice Harry Blackmun, the midwestern Republican author of *Roe v. Wade* who objected strenuously to *Bowers:* "The Court claims that its decision today merely refuses to recognize a fundamental right to engage in homosexual sodomy; what the Court really has refused to recognize is the fundamental interest all individuals have in controlling the nature of their intimate associations with others."[11]

"How can we talk about private events," Gonzalez-Torres asked, "when our bodies have been legislated by the state? We can perhaps talk about private property."[12] Among the most pervasive idioms for describing Americannness, private property held further implications for artists whose national and ethnic origin, racial background, and sexual orientation compromised their acceptance as Americans. As one of the few domains where cooperation occurred regardless of political preference or personal identity, the market held untapped potential as a political site. Deeply aware how precarious life was for an openly gay, nonwhite artist living with AIDS yet adamantly unwilling to capitalize upon his identity by wearing a metaphorical "grass skirt," Gonzalez-Torres stated it was "more threatening" that "people like me are operating as part of the market."[13] Through certificates that embodied rather than represented ownership by metabolizing elements of copyright and contract, he navigated market conditions and art-world protocol. Eventually shifting his works away from the metrics of supply, Gonzalez-Torres recast them as dynamic sources of doubt according to the legal frameworks to which he and they were unavoidably subject.

TITLE MATCHES: ARTISTS, DEALERS, COLLECTORS

Initially written by the artist, the certificates generally accompany six series of installations, although they have been issued to other works as well. One series involves stacks of paper from which viewers can take individual sheets. A second uses wrapped candies that can be variably installed (fig. 82). The third series pertains to billboards (fig. 83), while the fourth concerns strings of lightbulbs that may be configured according to the owner's preference (fig. 84). The fifth series consists of beaded curtains (fig. 85), and the sixth of text portraits composed of words and events painted directly on walls in a particular typeface (fig. 86). Authored by Gonzalez-Torres during his lifetime, the certificates were issued by his estate via the Andrea Rosen Gallery and then later by a foundation entrusted to provide information regarding the artist's works and motivations.[14]

When Gonzalez-Torres had his first solo exhibition in New York in 1988, artists, collectors, and dealers often differed on what having title to an artwork entailed. Case law throughout the 1970s and '80s steadily favored the swelling ranks of collectors, as judges considered it their duty to protect the latter against an industry they saw as woefully bereft of regulation. By the late 1980s, some courts even attempted to apply the concept of strict liability to sellers, making them automatically responsible for ensuring the authenticity and transferability of a work. Likewise debated was a

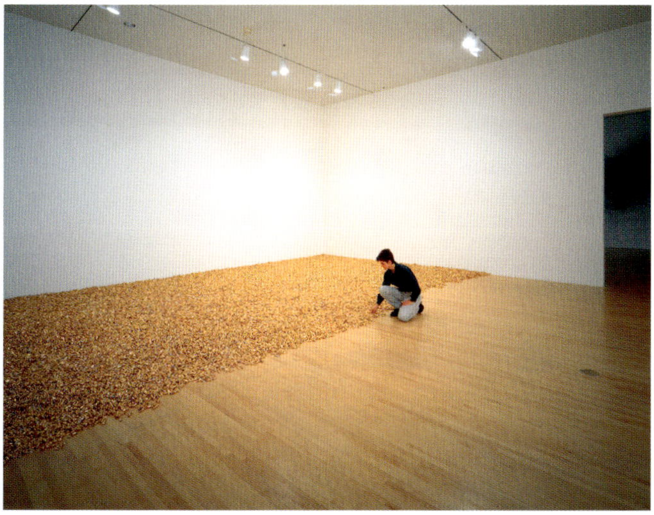

FIGURE 82
Felix Gonzalez-Torres, *"Untitled" (Placebo-Landscape-for Roni)*, 1993. Candies individually wrapped in gold cellophane, endless supply, dimensions variable. Ideal weight: 1,200 pounds. Installation view: "Felix Gonzalez-Torres: Traveling," Museum of Contemporary Art, Los Angeles, 1994. © Felix Gonzalez-Torres Foundation. Courtesy of Andrea Rosen Gallery, New York.

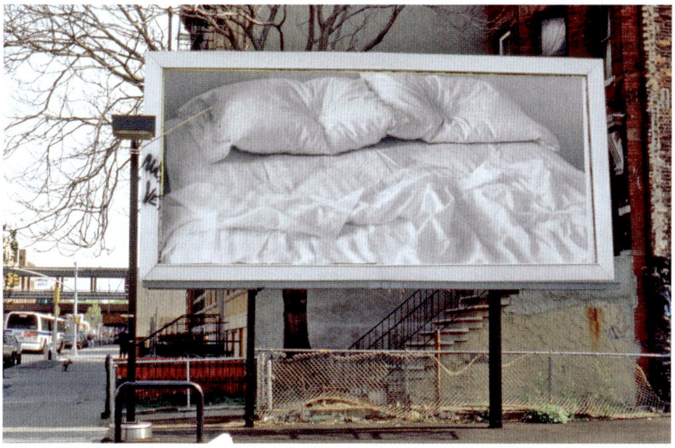

FIGURE 83
Felix Gonzalez-Torres, *"Untitled,"* 1991. Billboard, dimensions variable. Installation view: "Projects 34: Felix Gonzalez-Torres," Museum of Modern Art, New York, 1992. © Felix Gonzalez-Torres Foundation. Courtesy of Andrea Rosen Gallery, New York.

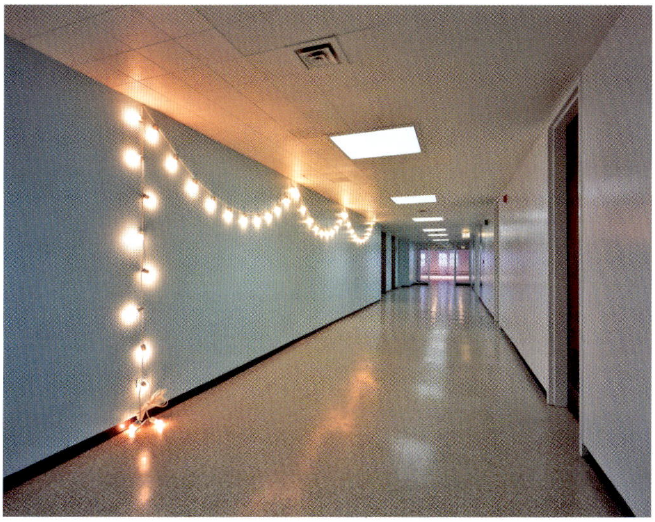

FIGURE 84
Felix Gonzalez-Torres, *"Untitled" (Summer)*, 1993. Lightbulbs, porcelain light sockets, and extension cord, dimensions variable. Installation view: "Felix Gonzalez-Torres: Traveling," Renaissance Society at the University of Chicago, 1994. © Felix Gonzalez-Torres Foundation. Courtesy of Andrea Rosen Gallery, New York.

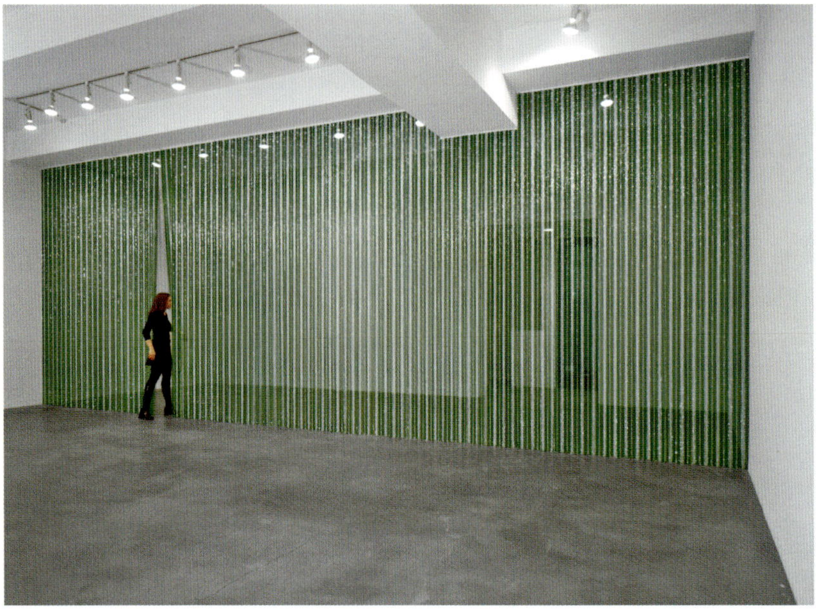

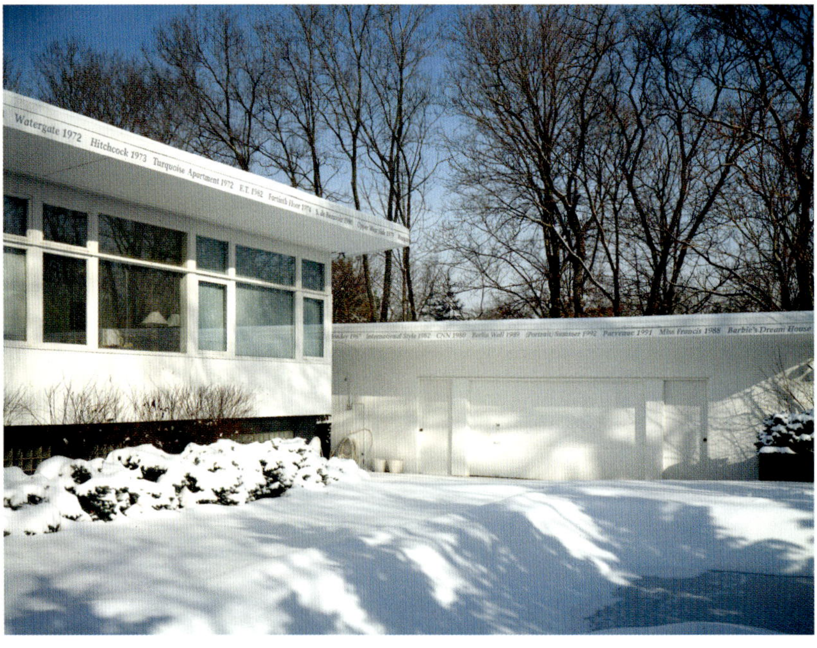

FIGURE 85

Felix Gonzalez-Torres, *"Untitled" (Beginning)*, 1994. Strands of beads and hanging device, dimensions variable. Installation view: "Untitled" (Beginning)," Andrea Rosen Gallery, 1997. © Felix Gonzalez-Torres Foundation. Courtesy of Andrea Rosen Gallery, New York.

FIGURE 86

Felix Gonzalez-Torres, *"Untitled" (Portrait of the Stillpasses)*, 1991. Paint on wall, dimensions variable. Photo: Cal Kowal. © Felix Gonzalez-Torres Foundation. Courtesy of Andrea Rosen Gallery, New York.

proposal to require sellers to act in the sole interests of the buyer.[15] Concurrently, dealers lobbied politicians to protect their interests, as they did when the Art Dealers Association of America lobbied Congress to reject the resale rights bill proposed by Senator Ted Kennedy in 1988.[16]

Artists retaliated against dealers they felt had wronged them by interfering directly with sales.[17] Disclaiming authorship, or what moral rights doctrine calls the "right of integrity," was a possibility, although it was not until the early 1980s that the law supported an artist's right to do that.[18] Another tactic was to threaten sellers and buyers with the possibility of a work's duplication. Frustrated with his Belgian gallerist, who he believed was less than forthcoming in transferring his share of the purchase price, artist Douglas Huebler felt compelled to reissue all the works that the gallerist had sold, but for which he had yet to be paid. While acknowledging that the collector "has acted in good faith and should not be punished," he was determined to teach the seller a lesson: "The dealer who takes the money and simply does not pass on the artists' [*sic*] share should not be allowed to operate in that way. So I said the only thing that could get Fernand's attention."[19] Other conceptual artists also issued multiples in an attempt to beat the market.[20]

Tension between artists and dealers came to an explosive head by 1977 in the infamous *Matter of Rothko* case decided by the New York Court of Appeals. Known as the "Watergate of the art world," the case involved the children of Rothko suing their father's executors over the management of his estate.[21] New York assistant attorney general Gustave Harrow, who represented the Rothko siblings, saw their extraordinary struggle as a resounding call for artists to secure their own interests; it was clear that dealers could not always be trusted to do so.[22] The following decade saw more artists suing their dealers for various acts of malfeasance, including the highly publicized dispute between the painter Peter Halley and the Sonnabend Gallery following his exhibition at a rival gallery in 1992.[23] Eventually settled out of court, Sonnabend claimed to have paid Halley substantial advances on works it argued Halley was obligated to sell through it. But securing of legal assistance was reserved for those with abundant economic resources, time, and knowledge. Connie Samaras pointed out how some artists, intimidated by the process of litigation and its attendant costs, chose to censor themselves rather than wage a legal battle that was practically guaranteed to be psychologically and financially exhausting.[24] Statutes like the California resale laws and legal initiatives such as *The Artist's Reserved Rights Transfer and Sale Agreement* failed to address the very real gaps of knowledge that reinforced a class hierarchy within the art world.

Even with the law on one's side, the chances of prevailing were slim against an abundance of resources. At the peak of his career in 1987, the painter David Salle appropriated the work of the lesser-known Mike Cockrill, who became aware of the use after seeing an exhibition of Salle's work at Leo Castelli Gallery. Cockrill protested, claiming that while appropriating a well-known image might be acceptable, to use “an obscure artist’s drawing . . . to activate his painting” was not.[25] He filed a lawsuit, one of the few ways an individual has of holding a more powerful party to account, but ended up settling, in part because of prohibitive litigation costs.[26] The real cost, however, was the damage to Cockrill’s reputation by those accusing the artist of trying to “cash in on my notoriety as a plaintiff. . . . Like I would never have been given a show if I hadn’t sued David Salle.”[27]

Long interested in the idea of the law as well as the process of its creation, Gonzalez-Torres may have known of the Visual Artists Rights Act (VARA) and other forms of legal recourse.[28] But VARA in some ways signaled the death of rights-based discourse, better known for what it failed to deliver than for what it did. The new law granted artists an unprecedented number of rights, regardless of whether they physically owned their works or the copyright to them, including the right to claim authorship of a work and to disclaim authorship for works they did not make or that had been changed in ways “prejudicial to the artist’s honor or reputation.” It thus represented a major benchmark in what had been an ongoing struggle for artists to control what became of their works, even after they were sold.[29] But as legal commentators quickly observed, VARA’s scope was far more limited than comparable legislation in Europe, which tended to grant broad protection even without being certain of the final outcome. Conversely, U.S. legislatures were less forthcoming, passing laws that covered only specific problems and a subset of artworks so narrow as to highlight the widening gulf between law and contemporary art.[30]

The circumscription of VARA also illustrated the limits of solidarity. Despite the turnout of art-world luminaries testifying on behalf of the law before Congress, the limitations of VARA showed plainly the inability of even a fairly consolidated art world to mobilize enough power to persuade lawmaker opinion. It was thus up to the individual artist to get what she wanted. Gonzalez-Torres had few illusions about what was needed to function adequately in an art world only partly regulated by a legal system whose first responsibility was to defend property rights. “Let’s not forget who wrote the Constitution that is ‘protecting’ our ‘rights’. . . . [It was] written by free white men with properties and titles—what I call the ‘Other,’” he stated.[31] In another discussion, he criticized the *Bowers* decision as an unjustified concentration of power in the hands of a limited number of people: “Nine people get together and decide who you can and can’t love.”[32] The critique might also extend to VARA, which continues to register as an attempt by Congress to define for all citizens the status of a “professional artist” under the conceit of “recognized stature.”

Seeking refuge outside the mainstream, however, was a non-option. “I’m not about to romanticize the margins. . . . There’s nothing out there,” he said to critic Nancy Princenthal.[33] In a conversation with Joseph Kosuth, he declared, “I do not want to be the opposition, the alternative. Alternative to what, to power? No, I want to have power. It’s effective in terms of change.”[34] But he implied that if artists wanted certain rights, they had to claim them by working within the system and, in particular, with the laws created to uphold it. After all, Gonzalez-Torres had belonged to Group Material, the New York collective founded in 1979 that braided artistic activity with citizen participation, including discussions concerning personal responsibility. In one such discussion, artist and curator Gino Rodriguez asserted that

> constantly referring to our 'powerlessness' and to 'them' and 'us' is a problem. One of the problem is that we keep saying 'you' . . . but we never point the finger at ourselves and say 'me'. . . . So long as we keep talking 'them' and 'us', we are saying we have no control or that we cannot assume control. . . . As long as there is somebody to blame you will never take responsibility for yourself.[35]

Gonzalez-Torres concurred in another discussion, stating that "we are all faced with a dilemma: do we do art or do we look at the society at large? Thinking about politics is one of the hardest things to put together. . . . Things are always interrelated. . . . Politics effects [*sic*] everyday life."[36] The interrelation was most vividly evoked in his certificates of authenticity, which framed his works as social situations that could exist outside the gallery rather than as finite objects contained in a designated physical space. For Gonzalez-Torres, having power included having "properties and titles" so as to lay down laws of one's own.

BILLS OF RIGHTS, OR CERTIFICATES OF AUTHENTICITY

Certificates, contracts, and other forms of documentation secure the legibility of so-called dematerialized artworks in a legal structure that recognizes visual art only as tangible, material forms. Kris Cohen describes *The Artist's Reserved Rights and Transfer Agreement* (detailed in Chapter 1) as a "legal prosthesis" intended to secure the value of the "dematerialized art objects [that Seth Siegelaub] worked so hard to promote."[37] Giuseppe Panza, the enthusiastic collector of Minimalist and instruction-based artworks, claimed that the works could not exist without the certificates.[38] In 1981, aware of how certificates of authenticity (sometimes called certificates of authenticity and ownership) helped guarantee the exchange value of artworks, the New York State Legislature passed the New York Art Multiples Disclosure Law requiring sellers to guarantee to buyers the authenticity of prints and photographs. Sellers who issued unreliable certificates could be liable for misrepresentation and product disparagement, and the usual claims could be brought against withdrawal of authorship. In addition to misrepresentation, sellers could be liable for not fully disclosing information that might affect perceptions of a work's authenticity. Case law and litigation did little, however, to alleviate the anxiety of artists, collectors, and dealers, as seen in the example of Bruce Nauman's dealers, who decided not to sell multiple versions of his work.

Attitudes regarding the use of certificates of authenticity and what they in fact entailed were thus unsettled. Art historian Martha Buskirk described them as being little more than "displaced signatures," while galleries treated bills of sale as virtual certificates of authenticity, with several containing various warranties.[39] Yet unlike most forms of commercial documentation from home deeds to checks, certificates of authenticity are sometimes irreplaceable, a fact that paradoxically reinforced the fetish for objects that conceptual art presumably challenged. Documenting authenticity and the role certificates played in this process received new attention in the early 1990s thanks to *Greenberg Gallery v. Bauman and Entwistle*. Among the most vivid instances of conflict between "the" law and the unwritten laws of the art world, this 1993 case involved a plaintiff accusing the defendant of selling it a forged work supposedly by Alexander Calder. Despite the testimony of the plaintiff's expert witness, whom the art world widely recognized as the leading authority on Calder, the U.S. District Court in Washington, D.C., ruled in favor of the defendant. Yet the reputation of the plaintiff's expert witness, who considered the work a fake, all but condemned the alleged Calder to a state of permanent market limbo.

Greenberg Gallery v. Bauman and Entwistle was remarkable for the variety of testimony offered regarding certificates. In his deposition taken by the defendant's attorney, the gallerist André Emmerich initially scoffed at the very idea of certificates, remarking that "I would consider it basically beneath my dignity. My letterhead should be enough. My good name rides with everything I sell."[40] According to Emmerich, the reputation of the dealer should be adequate grounds for determining a work's authenticity; in this case an invoice was "the best proof of authenticity [for a Calder that] I can think of."[41] "Good name," or reputation, was a category of value recognized throughout the art world. Presiding judge Louis Oberdorfer focused, conversely, on how close the signature on the work was to other Calder signatures, a decision consistent with commercial tendencies to value an artist's signature as a means of verifying a buyer's purchase.[42] The plaintiff's failure to challenge the signature's validity was "as important to a trier of fact as would be a prosecution's failure to offer fingerprint evidence about an article handled by a party or to explain by testimony its omission."[43]

For all their interest in verifying authorship and encouraging the disclosure of relevant information, courts and legislatures were curiously silent as to who, in fact, was entitled or qualified to issue certificates of authenticity. In 1995, the New York Supreme Court decided *Arnold Herstand v. Gertrude Stein, Inc.*, a case that involved the artist Balthus repudiating one of his own works.[44] The judge claimed that absent any sworn legal statement representing otherwise, the artist's opinion would determine the attribution of a work allegedly identified as his or hers. That the court in *Herstand* so quickly accepted Balthus's claims regarding the authorship of the contested work was due to the kind of documentation being offered, in this case a photograph of the work signed by the artist's former girlfriend. If the *Herstand* court was able to outsource its decision-making labor to the artist, it was because of the lack of any standards for either the form or content of a certificate of authenticity, California and New York laws notwithstanding.[45]

Still, artists continued drafting certificates for works that had yet to be made. Buyers purchased the right to fabricate the work, which in turn enabled artists to evade

U.S. tax law that otherwise prevented them from deducting the cost of production until the work was sold. Certificates for unrealized works put tremendous pressure on artists in two main ways. First, they required artists to convey their intentions accurately and in such a manner that a reasonable buyer would fully understand those intentions. Second, they recognized that an artwork was in fact separable into two parts: its invention (or conception) and its execution. Artists were thus required to trust buyers above and beyond what might ordinarily be expected from buyers of other goods. Conceptual artist Robert Barry wrote to his dealer about the potential risks of making works that could easily be reproduced, "We will just have to trust each other."[46] Barry's statement indicated a form of blind trust departing from theories of risk management that endorse trust only when it is justified.

Yet the lack of definition as to the scope and duration of said trust had unexpected, and sometimes disastrous, consequences. The outstanding case in point involved the certificates Donald Judd issued in 1974 to the Italian collector Giuseppe Panza for the plans of fourteen untitled and unrealized works. Panza consequently fabricated several works according to what he thought were Judd's instructions. The artist disowned the works, claiming that the fabrications did not satisfactorily meet his standards. In a 1990 letter, Judd angrily accused Panza of positivism: he "thinks my work has no existence beyond the paper in his files and that it can come and go as he pleases and as he designs it; now it can be multiplied as he pleases."[47] Upsetting Judd most of all was the very suggestion that he was not the ultimate arbiter of his own works, even though his certificates required any completed work to comply with his instructions and required Panza to notify the artist, his representative, or his estate that the work was being made.

The controversy was a function of two different approaches to contractual relationships. Assuming that both parties saw the certificates as virtual contracts, Panza—himself a lawyer—adhered to an orthodox legal approach, whereby the certificate only required him to act in good faith. In the event that he and Judd could not agree about the work, they should appoint "an independent expert in order to see if the work is correctly made or not."[48] Judd, on the other hand, seemed to regard the certificates as a guarantee that Panza would act in a fiduciary capacity. To him the certificates created a separate duty of reasonableness and fairness beyond what contract law generally holds as good-faith performance. The difference in viewpoint resonates with the move among courts to specify the limits of duties owed by parties to a contract, as in *Market Street Associates Ltd. Partnership v. Frey,* a heavily cited 1991 case in which Judge Richard Posner, ever the realist, famously commented that signing a contract does not obligate a signatory to become an "altruist" or "his brother's keeper."[49]

IN CONTRACTS WE TRUST?

The complexity of the agreements between Panza and artists like Judd and Asher vividly demonstrated how the process of acquiring an artwork became as much a part of the work as its display and circulation. The expansion of public art programs as well as occasional collaborations between artists and private industry, such as those between E.A.T. and Pepsi-Cola, made contracts an increasingly familiar part of the transactional everyday. Dealers became more receptive to using contracts in the early 1970s. Marilyn Fischbach, the founder of the eponymous New York gallery known for exhibiting Alex Katz and Eva Hesse, praised the contract as "something new" that could help her and other gallerists more efficiently manage their relationships with artists.[50] Even more enthusiastic was André Emmerich, who used the "Standard Form of Gallery-Artist Agreement" issued by the Art Dealers Association of America. He wanted to add a provision stipulating that the artist's consent must be secured before granting credit terms to a buyer for a period of more than a year.[51] Most artwork sales, however, continued to occur without written contracts. Lawyers were themselves undecided as to their efficacy. Remembering the failure of *The Artist's Reserved Rights Transfer and Sale Agreement,* Robert Projansky was particularly skeptical, while Jerald Ordover's apparent reluctance to assist his friend Seth Siegelaub in drafting the *Agreement* may have been motivated by his belief that it was the orality of agreements that best reflected the camaraderie that often developed between artists and dealers over a long period of interaction.[52] Of similar mind was Clifford Schaffer, an attorney for the artist Michael Asher who admitted to his client that "sometimes a lawyer's advice on how to handle business decisions wisely is misconstrued to appear as though one person does not trust the other."[53] More pragmatic was Louis Lefkowitz, who wryly observed that "the very hallmark of 'power'" for very successful artists is "their ability to resist being bound by any contract at all."[54]

In an unusually frank discussion about market practices at the New Museum in New York in 1975, several important New York gallerists, including Leo Castelli, Holly Solomon, Arne Glimcher, and Betty Parsons, stressed that buyers wanted a "a feeling of ownership, not of caretaking."[55] However, neither custom nor law could consistently guarantee all the rights an artist wanted. For every Walter Hopps willing to honor an agreement scrawled casually on a hot dog wrapper, there were at least a hundred Leo Castellis quick to dismiss contracts as not even "worth the paper they're written on."[56] And yet increasingly long and detailed contracts, such as the model co-drafted by Michael Asher and lawyer Arthur Alef, sought to reinforce the authority of the artist.[57]

The expanding scale and complexity of the U.S. artistic ecosystem made at least some knowledge of contracts desirable, if not necessary.[58] This was made dramatically evident in the *Tilted Arc* case, one of the most well-publicized conflicts between visual art and the law in postwar American history. The case, involving the U.S. government's removal and destruction of Richard Serra's sculpture *Tilted Arc,* has been extensively discussed as a matter of censorship and moral rights. Yet it also emphasizes just how much the law regarded contracts as the primary, and even sole, expression of artistic intention. Significant disagreement existed as to what the contract between Serra and the General Services Administration (GSA), the government agency that had initially commissioned Serra to create *Tilted Arc,* in fact meant. Serra's lawyers argued that the written contract—a standard form used by the GSA in commissioning artists to produce work—did not reflect the entirety of the agreement. For instance, the "work" mentioned in the standard contract did not refer to the actual sculpture, but only to the designs, sketches, and models prepared in anticipation of its execution, a specification not included in the contract but that GSA director Donald Thalacker stated was something "everybody seemed to understand and agree [to]." [59] In an undated memorandum assessing the case and possible legal remedies for Serra, attorney Anne Baker implied that the GSA contract was in practice recognized as a document that necessarily relied on agreements not explicitly included in the written text.[60] Likewise, Serra's counsel Gustave Harrow, himself a leading advocate of artists' rights, claimed that the government gave the artist "unequivocal" reassurances that his work would remain installed, and such reassurances "form a binding contract, which precludes removal without Serra's consent."[61]

The turn to contracts suggested what sociologist Frank Furedi has labeled a "blame culture," in which interpersonal disagreements are increasingly resolved through formal complaints and litigation. Trust becomes a resource in short supply as energy is directed toward allocating present and future blame to others.[62] But although the neutral objective voice might be accepted as good conceptual art practice, in a contract it could be alienating, a situation Gonzalez-Torres addressed by having his certificates become part of the ownership experience. Drafted at the height of the Judd-Panza conflict, the format and language of the certificates produce a reading experience closely analogous to that compelled by legally binding contracts, yet the certificates could also be changed to accommodate buyer needs to ensure the work could exist.[63]

That Gonzalez-Torres spent considerable time revising and reediting his certificates reflects an attempt to control the means by which his works were created and transferred.[64] Although he never consulted an attorney, his certificates contained terms and conditions that strongly recalled the legal definition of an *offer,* or a proposal made to another party in such a way that he or she could reasonably assume that any assent binds him or her to the terms of the proposal.[65] Performance studies scholar Joshua Chambers-Letson suggests that "the certificates signify an appropriation and reformation of the purchase contract."[66] Early versions issued before 1994 consist of several single-spaced paragraphs describing the parameters of the work and the intentions underlying its creation. The first two paragraphs include the title of the document and a physical description of the work, including title, media, dimensions, and control number. The third and fifth paragraphs describe the owner's rights and responsibilities concerning the work. The fourth paragraph describes the process of transferring title from one owner to another in the event that the work is sold.

Later certificates included a space for the buyer's signature and a legend informing buyers that "the signature below of [the buyer] indicates understanding, acknowledgment of, and agreement to these terms and completes the binding nature of this contract."[67] Not accepting the certificate's terms would mean compromising the status of the artwork as a bona fide Gonzalez-Torres. The certificates align with what legal scholar Margaret Radin calls "purported contracts," or paperwork "that contain[s] terms supposedly binding without your signature, and sometimes even without your knowing this is happening."[68] Issued in lockstep with the meteoric rise of Gonzalez-Torres's market after his death, particularly between 1998 and 2000, these certificates functioned as hybrid license-contracts that granted owners the right to manifest a work while also expecting them to honor certain terms regarding the work's production and circulation.[69] But reading a certificate is much like spotting issues in a law school exam; ambiguity is central to the production of knowledge through divergent interpretations.

Nevertheless, the early certificates are far more convincing as an extension of the work than as a species of legal documentation like a contract, license, or warranty. Were they binding contracts, the certificates would have entitled bearers to delegate the resolution of any interpretative conflict to the courts, whose capacity to administer justice amid the polarized ideological landscape of the late 1980s and early '90s was severely questioned by numerous artists, Gonzalez-Torres included. Outsourcing the regulation of interpersonal relationships to a third party whose own integrity meant taking sides in the form of a verdict was incongruent with his certificates, which transformed compliance into an ongoing conversation about possibilities rather than prohibitions.

THE FINE ART OF COMPLIANCE

Describing himself as "an extension" of Minimalism and conceptual art, Gonzalez-Torres belonged to a genealogy that delegated artistic intention to written instruction.[70] His artistic DNA thus also included getting others to comply with those instructions, a challenge Douglas Huebler faced with *Variable Piece #44/Global* (fig. 87). Printed directly on the work was a set of instructions directing each owner to send a photograph of him or herself to both the person who owned the work that preceded his or hers in the numerical sequence of the edition and the person who owned the following piece. Instructions were in fact conditions that had to be met in order for *Variable Piece #44/Global* to exist as an artwork; they declare that the work "will become original" after the owner has completed the instructions (fig. 88). In this way Huebler resembled Dan Flavin, who was among the first to explicitly reject the binary logic underscoring most forms of authentication by incentivizing his powers of authentication. Rather than immediately declare a work his or not, Flavin would partly certify it ("intermediate certification") when a buyer first purchased from him a set of instructions, and "completely" certify it upon their execution.[71] In a letter to Herman, Nicole, and Pierre Daled, who owned various editions of *Variable Piece #44/Global*, Huebler wrote that there was "no such thing as 'ART' in connection with this work *unless* each owner makes an exchange with two other owners at some point in time each year" (Huebler's emphasis).[72] Those not following Huebler's instructions would possess an "artwork," but not necessarily one the artist might claim as his own—to him such a

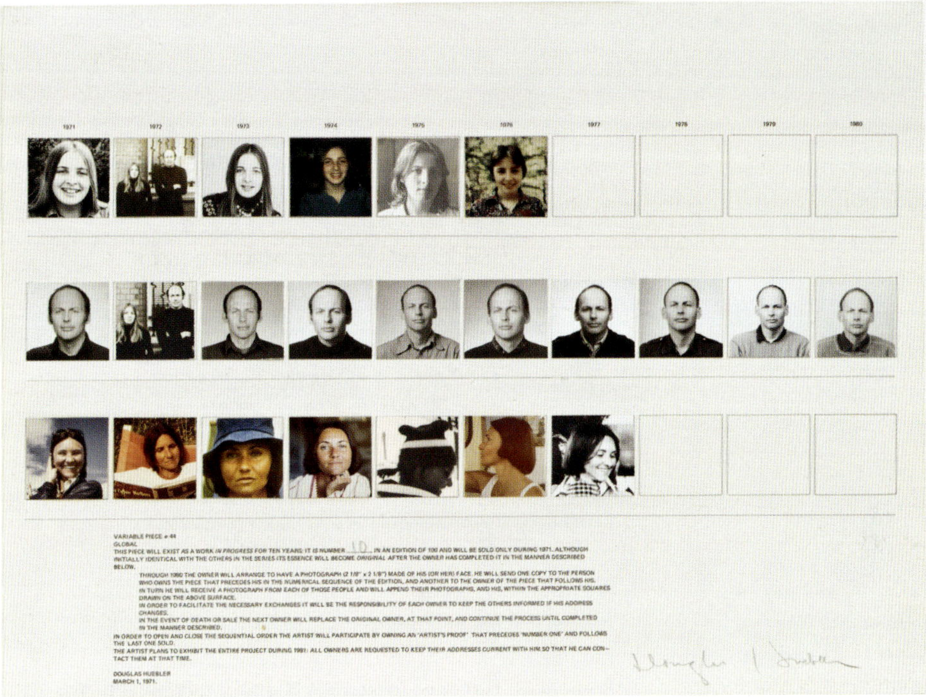

FIGURE 87

Douglas Huebler, *Variable Piece #44/Global,* 1971. Offset lithograph with collage additions, composition 9 15⁄16 × 22 1⁄16 inches; sheet 18 1⁄6 × 24 inches. Digital image © 2018 Douglas Huebler. Courtesy of Darcy Huebler/Artists Rights Society (ARS), New York, and Museum of Modern Art/Licensed by SCALA/Art Resource, New York.

work would merely be a "simple 'souvenir' of something or other."[73] To give his instructions additional rhetorical heft, Huebler reissued the instructions in the form of a typed statement resembling both a sworn legal document and a business letter. Although not specifically called certificates, these documents acted as certificates of ownership. New owners were requested to attach a photograph of themselves under the year that they bought the work "as soon as possible after receiving this information and the actual work."

Huebler noted that the work would not be his unless the instructions were followed, a prescription that effectively created a situation where the value of one owner's *Variable Piece #44/Global* depended on the actions of others. Some owners failed to heed the artist's conditions, thus potentially diminishing the value of their own investment. Huebler stated that those who "have not met the responsibility of 'ownership'" would be eliminated from a list of owners.[74] This was hardly satisfactory, as there was no way of making owners meet the artist's conditions. Huebler even went so far as to ask Daled—himself a supporter of artists' rights who helped fund the publication and distribution of *The Artist's Reserved Rights Transfer and Sale Agreement*—to intervene on

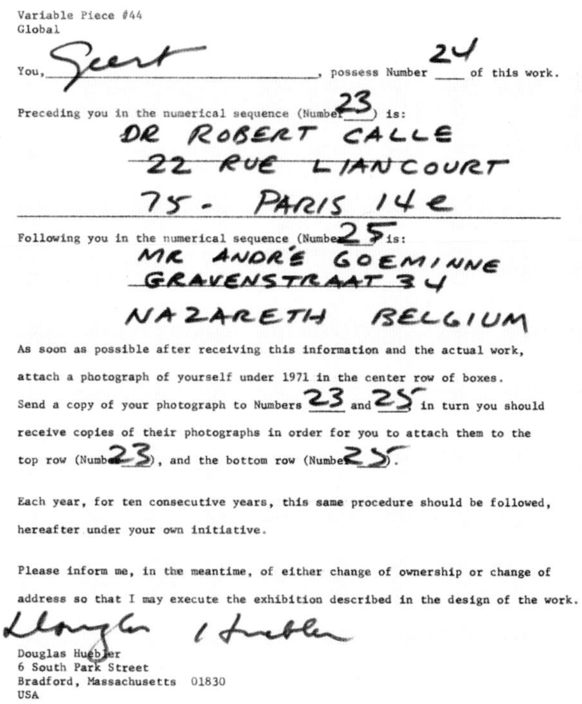

Variable Piece #44
Global

You, Geert, possess Number 24 of this work.

Preceding you in the numerical sequence (Number 23) is:
DR ROBERT CALLE
~~22 RUE LIANCOURT~~
75- PARIS 14e

Following you in the numerical sequence (Number 25) is:
MR ANDRÉ GOEMINNE
~~GRAVENSTRAAT 34~~
NAZARETH BELGIUM

As soon as possible after receiving this information and the actual work, attach a photograph of yourself under 1971 in the center row of boxes. Send a copy of your photograph to Numbers 23 and 25 in turn you should receive copies of their photographs in order for you to attach them to the top row (Number 23), and the bottom row (Number 25).

Each year, for ten consecutive years, this same procedure should be followed, hereafter under your own initiative.

Please inform me, in the meantime, of either change of ownership or change of address so that I may execute the exhibition described in the design of the work.

Douglas Huebler

Douglas Huebler
6 South Park Street
Bradford, Massachusetts 01830
USA

FIGURE 88

Douglas Huebler, *Variable Piece #44/Global*, 1971. Certificate: composition 8 3/8 × 7 1/16 inches; sheet 11 × 8 1/2 inches. Digital image © 2018 Douglas Huebler. Courtesy of Darcy Huebler/Artists Rights Society (ARS), New York, and Museum of Modern Art/Licensed by SCALA/Art Resource, New York.

his behalf with regard to a Belgian collector who failed to respond to Huebler for four years.[75] The most extreme case may have been Huebler's attempts to get Toselli, his Italian dealer, to pay for *Variable Piece* or to abide by its terms. The artist eventually threatened to place a giant advertisement in *Studio International* proclaiming that all of his works sold by Toselli three years earlier were "merely copies" and that anyone who owned such works would be illegitimate.[76]

Coercion, fear of punishment, and even moral responsibility were not enough, however, to ensure owner compliance. There was a sense of inherent failure in works requiring compliance, a failure accommodated, and perhaps even anticipated, by some artists whose certificates explicitly allowed for some noncompliance. The sculptor Fred Sandback, for instance, admitted in one certificate for a 1979 work that "new reconstruction will always be to some extent a further interpretation, and should be regarded as such without undue trepidation."[77] He provided photographs of previous installations as a guide but seems to have trusted at least some of his buyers to install his yarn-based work without a manual.

Art historian Miwon Kwon notes that a paradigm shift regarding artistic authorship took place in the 1960s and '70s. Rather than privilege the "artist's authorship as producer of objects," it was the artist's "authority to authorize in the capacity of director or supervisor of (re)production" that mattered, a shift dramatically illustrated by works like Christo and Jeanne-Claude's *Running Fence*.[78] The shift concurred with the 1976 Copyright Act, which gave copyright owners the right to authorize others to produce copies of their works. When Gonzalez-Torres first issued his certificates, considerable ambiguity existed over the scope and nature of authorization. For example, the executor or heir of an artist's estate was legally permitted to authorize the posthumous recreation or reproduction of works. Less clear was whether and how they could create new works where none previously existed. *Reality Properties: Fake Estates* was assembled in 1992 by Jane Crawford, Matta-Clark's widow, from documents the artist collected before his death, including deeds to residual land left over from surveying errors purchased by the artist at public auction in the early 1970s.[79] During his lifetime, Matta-Clark had expressed an intention to create from such land a standalone work using written and visual documentation of the property. Yet no record exists as to its final intended manifestation. While Crawford's decisions are hardly equivalent to those of critic Clement Greenberg, who posthumously stripped paint from a David Smith sculpture, her assembly of documents into collages initially deterred risk-averse institutions from buying the work.[80] Together with the growing number of questions from owners regarding the installation of works, the likelihood of comparable doubt may explain why Gonzalez-Torres's certificates grew longer and more detailed over time, particularly just before his death in 1996.

Yet the certificates moved beyond the questions of artwork commodification that so plagued some of his conceptualist predecessors, as well as the imperative of self-protection underwriting the contracts and certificates of Minimalism's stalwarts. Anticipating the flexibility of language in Gonzalez-Torres's certificates was the standard contract used by the Public Art Fund to commission artists for its "Messages to the Public" series. Founded by Doris Freedman, a former director of cultural affairs for New York City, the Public Art Fund enabled artists, including Gonzalez-Torres, to make and exhibit work hung in various publicly accessible venues in New York. Among its most significant projects was "Messages to the Public," which from 1982 to 1990 saw artists presenting a thirty-second animated work on a Spectacolor light board in Times Square. Drafted by an attorney, the agreement given to artists proposing a work strongly anticipated the tone of Gonzalez-Torres's certificates, particularly those involving lightbulb strings. "Bulbs are either on or off," they could not be dimmed, and "complex images must be illuminated in white."[81] The agreement also included recommendations ("The sign is most effectively used when bold images and broad gestures are employed") and even warnings ("Any fine lines must be in white as color will reduce the detail").[82]

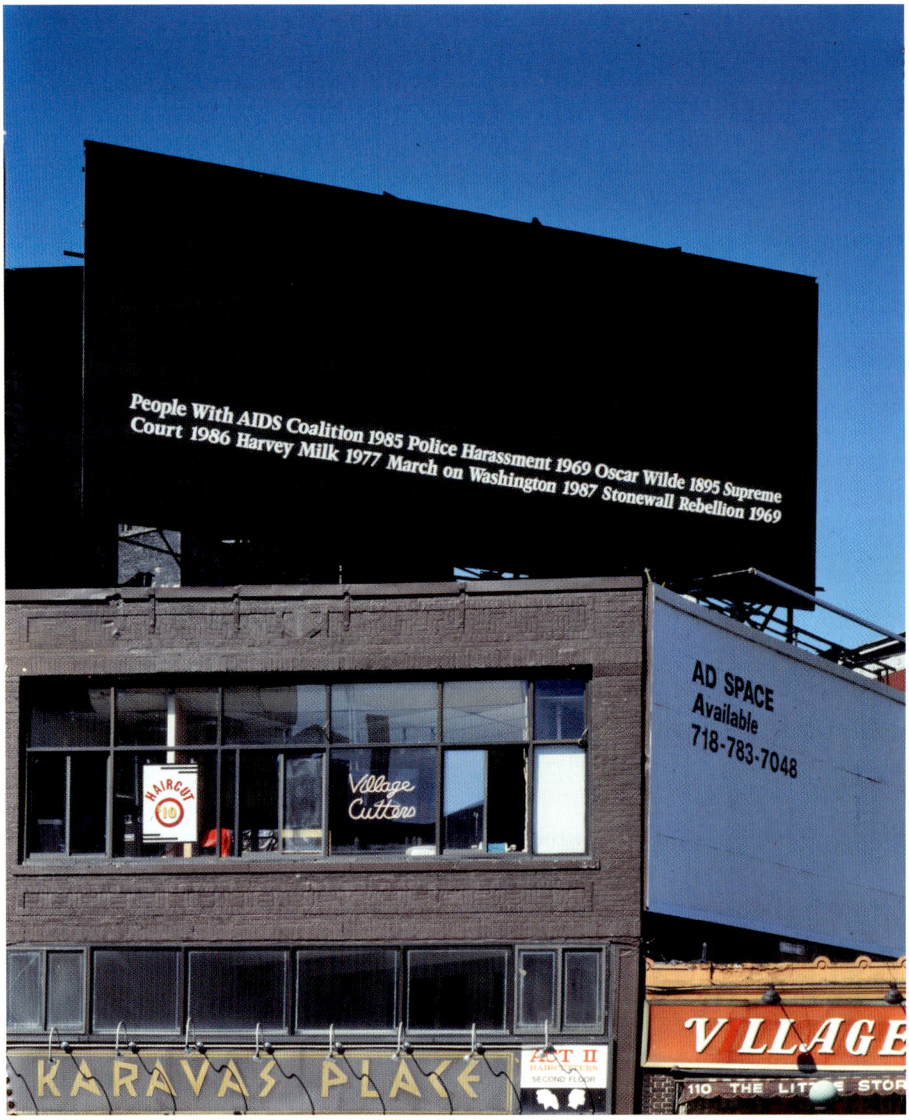

FIGURE 89
Felix Gonzalez-Torres, *"Untitled,"* 1989. Billboard, dimensions variable. Installation view: "Untitled" (Billboard), Sheridan Square, New York, 1989. Photo: Stanley Greenberg. © Felix Gonzalez-Torres Foundation. Courtesy of Andrea Rosen Gallery, New York.

For the Public Art Fund, Gonzalez-Torres proposed *"Untitled,"* a billboard that became his first public artwork. Scheduled for display in Sheridan Square in New York City from March to August 1989, the initial installation of the work commemorated the twentieth anniversary of the Stonewall Rebellion that occurred across the street from the billboard's location (fig. 89). It was a large rectangular billboard, a black expanse relieved only by two lines of white type reading, “People With Aids Coalition 1985 Police Harassment 1969 Oscar Wilde 1895 Supreme Court 1986 Harvey Milk 1977 March on Washington 1987 Stonewall Rebellion 1969.” The agreement he consequently signed with the Public Art Fund was not particularly unusual. It acknowledged the artist’s title to the work while granting to the Public Art Fund an irrevocable license to make a limited print edition of the billboard (up to 250 copies), stipulating that the artist will sign and date these editions. The contract also allowed the Public Art Fund to make photographs and other two-dimensional reproductions of “*Untitled*” without the artist’s prior consent; these were to be used for advertising and “for other purposes,” an open provision that meant, in theory, that they could sell these, although the Public Art Fund explicitly disclaimed any expectation of a direct financial benefit.[83] It did, however, reserve the right to remove work from display without first notifying the artist.

Not long after the maturation of Gonzalez-Torres’s certificates in the mid-1990s, the artist Renée Green stated in a roundtable discussion that “certain associations with the term ‘artist’ seem to, at times, limit people’s idea of what you’re capable of doing.” Her comment responded to questions asked of Judith Barry, another artist who used highly detailed contracts when producing artworks in an institutional setting.[84] In borrowing or nodding to contractual language in his certificates, Gonzalez-Torres may also have been trying to gain credibility in the legal and economic systems within which his works circulated.

THE WORD OF LAW

The resemblance between a Gonzalez-Torres certificate and a contract begs from readers a specific kind of attention in which the meanings of individual words are subject to more intense levels of scrutiny than may be applied to other documents. Like Tehching Hsieh, Gonzalez-Torres insisted on clarifying his meaning in the most direct terms possible, in order to minimize the risk of having the buyer mistake his intentions. Yet the certificates lack either the clarity or the precision generally expected of contracts, partly because they were initially drafted without outside legal assistance, but also deliberately.[85] It was therefore unclear just how closely owners were expected to abide by the terms of Gonzalez-Torres’s certificates. The level of detail is inconsistent. For example, one certificate for an early billboard work from 1991 grants its owner the “exclusive right to reproduce the billboard in public as often as they like, at what ever scale they like, at however many locations they choose.”[86] The wording of the certificate avoids a common mistake in contract drafting whereby *exclusive* and *sole* are used interchangeably. Several sentences, on the other hand, are so pointedly imprecise as to seem almost intentionally so. A standard phrase—“the physical manifestation of this work in more than one place at a time does not impugn this work’s uniqueness”—is unclear due to the improper use of *impugn*. A verb meaning “to doubt” or “attack,” it is most often used in legal contexts to assess witness credibility or in cases involving defamation. *Undermine* or *negate* would be more appropriate.

Yet these presumptive shortcomings of language—its looseness—may explain why owners have been so faithful to the certificate terms. "There are times when precision may kill a deal that should not be killed," cautioned legal scholar David Mellinkoff in his influential book *The Language of the Law.*[87] By using a word like *ideal* rather than the more standard *required* or *mandatory,* Gonzalez-Torres addressed what may be the most crucial aspect of any contract, the likelihood of its enforcement. He appeared to reject the punitive model of contracts, in which failing to fulfill a particular term could result in the punishment of the errant party. The model differs from that used to sell film and video works, a phenomenon that emerged in the 1990s, which specifically involved collectors signing purchase agreements that detailed very clearly how the works would be shown.[88] But while the obligations associated with the purchase of film and video works were largely to ensure the quality of the image, thereby casting film and video as themselves fixed objects, many Gonzalez-Torres works have elements that audiences can choose to physically take.

From a prospective buyer's standpoint, the least restrictive (or most permissive) of Gonzalez-Torres's certificates tend to be those accompanying his billboards and text portraits. Certificates for the former impose no restrictions on the size of the billboard or on how many can be shown at any given time. So great is this freedom that the artist seemed to retreat from the initial certificate by suggesting an "ideal" number of locations, which for most works is twenty-four.[89] The only condition is that the billboards be photographed, a term whose satisfactory fulfillment requires relatively minimal effort from the buyer. Gonzalez-Torres's text portraits are similarly expansive: buyers may extend or contract the length of the portrait, and the color in which the words are painted are equally left to buyers' discretion. Each accompanying certificate includes the text initially used for the portrait, which subsequent owners can decide to use in full, in part, or not at all; their choices too are recorded in the certificate. At the same time, he includes what he regards as "ideal" installation conditions—that, for example, the words be painted just below the point at which a wall meets the ceiling.

Next are certificates for the candies, paper stacks, and beaded curtains. In the first two groups, the owner is permitted to replenish the candies and paper stacks. For the beaded curtains, the owner must ensure that beads fill a given entrance completely from side to side as well as hang from the entrance top to the ground. That the works consisted of materials that were relatively inexpensive and easy to source may have reassured prospective buyers. The money and effort required to execute the certificate's terms were minimal in relation to the work's actual market value. Moreover, the potential cost of having to replenish the candies or paper is mitigated by the artist's granting permission that the owner may choose not to do so.[90]

Least permissive, at least on a superficial reading of their text, are certificates for Gonzalez-Torres's lightstrings. Accompanying each edition of *"Untitled" (March 5th) #2,* one of his first works to feature lightbulbs, is a certificate of authenticity that specifies the manner of installation (including the precise dimensions of the nail from

FIGURE 90
Felix Gonzalez-Torres, *"Untitled" (March 5th) #2*, 1991. Lightbulbs, porcelain light sockets, and extension cord, dimensions variable. Two parts, each approximately 113 inches in height. © Felix Gonzalez-Torres Foundation. Courtesy of Andrea Rosen Gallery, New York.

which the lightbulbs hang) in addition to listing the work's title, date, materials, and edition number (fig. 90). The owner decides only whether the lightbulbs should be on or off. On the same page as the description and instructions, a short legend reads, "This certificate is necessary to define ownership," followed by a space for the date and the artist's signature.[91] Yet unlike certificates of authenticity and ownership that

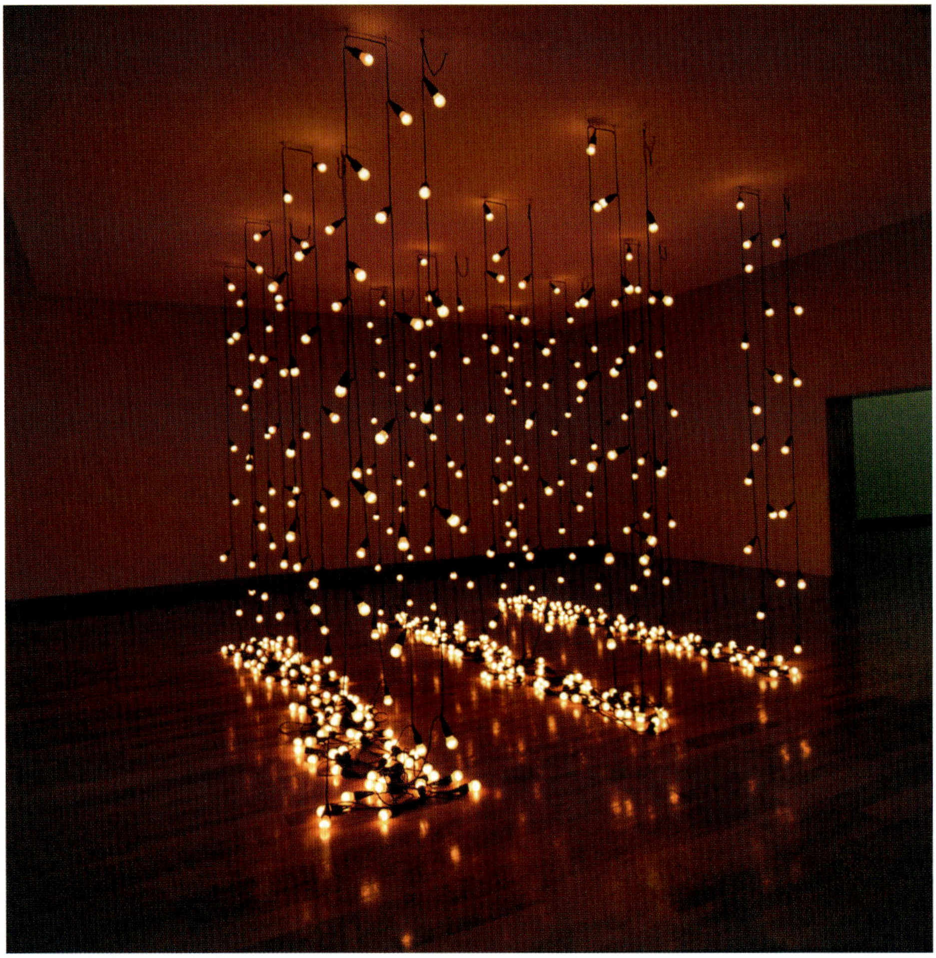

FIGURE 91
Felix Gonzalez-Torres, *"Untitled" (America)*, 1994. Lightbulbs, waterproof rubber light sockets, and waterproof extension cords, twelve parts, dimensions variable. Installation view: "Felix Gonzalez-Torres (A Possible Landscape)," Centro Galego de Arte Contemporánea, Santiago de Compostela, Spain, 1995–96. Photo: Archivo Fotográfico CGAC. © Felix Gonzalez-Torres Foundation. Courtesy of Andrea Rosen Gallery, New York.

are reissued upon the sale of a work, this certificate remains unchanged.[92] Other light-string certificates permit the owner to configure the work freely (figs. 91 and 92). Yet they mandate replacement of the bulbs when burnt out and that there had to be forty-two 22-watt lightbulbs.[93] The indication of quantity and energy output was to ensure sufficient brightness, but the specific quantity and type leave no room for alternative readings that would jeopardize the authority of the certificate as a source of information. Still, by giving owners the freedom to choose how best to install and reinstall the lightstring works, without further direction as to when or where, Gonzalez-Torres effectively delegated to owners the physical and mental labor of realizing the work.

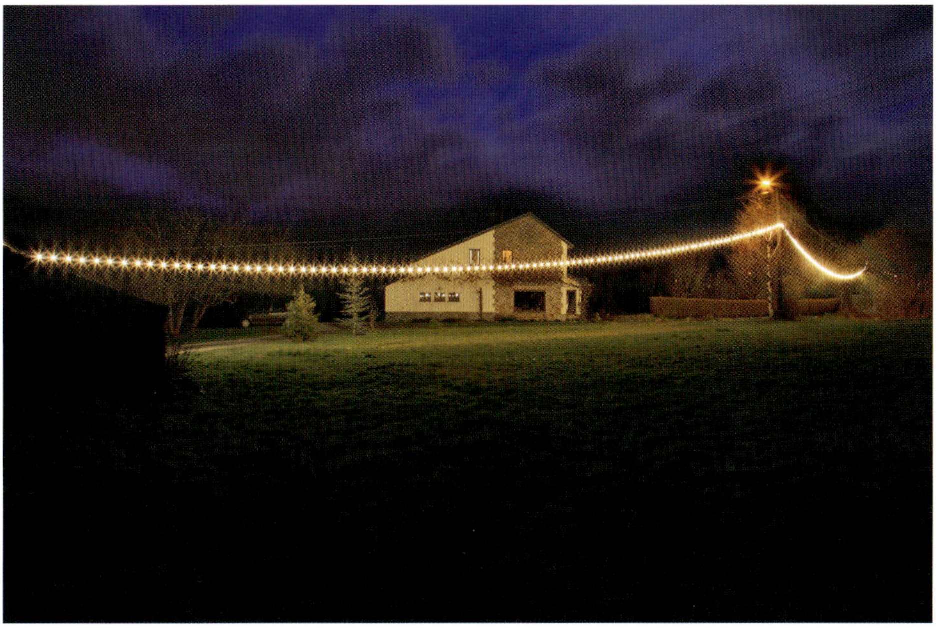

FIGURE 92
Felix Gonzalez-Torres, *"Untitled" (America)*, 1994. Lightbulbs, waterproof rubber light sockets, and waterproof extension cords, twelve parts, dimensions variable. Installation view: "Felix Gonzalez-Torres: Specific Objects without Specific Form," Wiels Contemporary Art Centre, Brussels, 2010. Photo: Sven Laurent. © Felix Gonzalez-Torres Foundation. Courtesy of Andrea Rosen Gallery, New York.

Unclear, however, was just how literally owners were expected to abide by the certificates' terms. The certificate of authenticity accompanying Andrea Zittel's 1993 work *Chamber Pot* bestowed upon owners "the right . . . to use the object in any way they choose" and "encouraged" them to do so. Yet the symmetry and elegance of the actual artwork practically dares the owner to exhibit it as anything other than an artwork, let alone put it to the use suggested by its title (fig. 93). It is as if Zittel is calling the buyer's bluff, betting (probably correctly) that his or her interest in preserving the value of the work would preclude him or her from fully exercising the privileges the certificate grants. Gonzalez-Torres deliberately refused to define the work's material parameters: "Is the piece the simple sheet of paper or is the piece the stack? Well it could be both, and I never define which one is which. I like that 'in-betweenness' that makes the work difficult to define."[94]

From a liability perspective, the looseness of Gonzalez-Torres's certificates' wording accommodated the concern some institutional owners were likely to have about their own responsibilities. Museums, for example, represent a type of owner characterized by sharp aversion to all forms of legal liability as well as correspondingly high levels of vigilance in safeguarding the tangible property it owns. Strategically vague

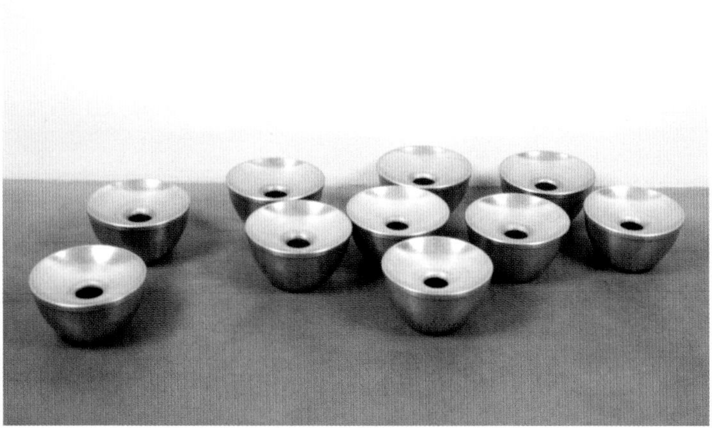

FIGURE 93
Andrea Zittel, *Chamber Pot*, 1993. Spun aluminum. Height: 5 ½ inches. Diameter: 9 ½ inches. © Andrea Zittel. Courtesy of Regen Projects, Los Angeles, and Andrea Rosen Gallery, New York.

language might reassure parties concerned about whether deviations from certificate terms would be regarded as actionable violations. Through the certificates, Gonzalez-Torres intuited how contracts are as much defined by imminent violation as they are by their potential to guarantee particular outcomes.

Comparing his own intentions with those of his conceptualist and Minimalist forebears, Gonzalez-Torres said, "I don't have that phobia of two inches . . . you know: 'if a work is two inches to the left, you have to destroy the work!'"[95] Miwon Kwon contends that Gonzalez-Torres's certificates permitted him "to work against the security of his own version of the stacks or piles, strings of light or beaded curtains as unchanging, original, and finite ideals for eternity."[96] Some deviation may also have been necessary to prevent the work from becoming what critic Robert Storr described as "just another fixed entity within a treasure house of things."[97] Additionally, by permitting owners of certain works to substitute one type of candy for another, Gonzalez-Torres improved the chances that these works would be realized in perpetuity. Theoretically, nothing prevents a collector from reproducing a different candy spill; depending on the certificate terms, buying one candy spill means acquiring the option to display any of the other spills.

But as Rollins insisted, Gonzalez-Torres's works were not "completely arbitrary or intuitive."[98] Unlike Lawrence Weiner, who claimed "there's no way to build a piece incorrectly," Gonzalez-Torres did set parameters for his instruction-based works.[99] Rosen notes, for instance, that the artist determined the size of his works on the basis of "standards."[100] There may have been no one "right size" of paper, for example, but certain factors, such as the proportions of the display venue, did affect how Gonzalez-Torres himself determined the formal appearance of the work. Storr observes that certificates concerning the candy spills direct the owner to routinely maintain the piles, a hint that the artist may have wanted buyers to adhere to a general standard of

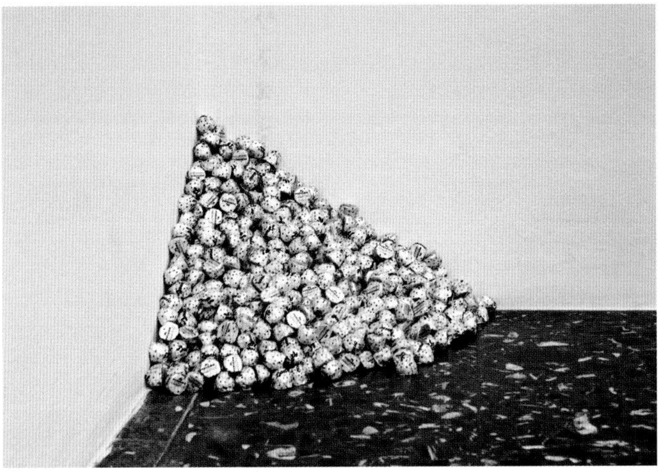

FIGURE 94
Felix Gonzalez-Torres, *"Untitled" (A Corner of Baci)*, 1990. Baci chocolates, endless supply, dimensions variable. Ideal weight: 42 pounds. Installation view: "Reversibility: A Theatre of De-Creation-Chapter III," Peep-Hole, Milan, 2012. © Felix Gonzalez-Torres Foundation. Courtesy of Andrea Rosen Gallery, New York.

execution. Gonzalez-Torres remarked, for example, that the height of his paper stacks should depend on how they appear in a given space.[101] In the case of the candy-based works that have *corner* in the title, such as *"Untitled" (A Corner of Baci)*, owners have often, but not always, installed the work in a corner (fig. 94). Site-specificity is crucial. Certificates accompanying the beaded curtains state that the curtain must fill the entirety of the space left open by a particular entranceway.

The adherence to "standards" is reflected in the prominence and consistency with which the word *ideal* appears throughout Gonzalez-Torres's certificates. Art historian John Paul Ricco suggests that the artist's use of the word *ideal* is malleable: it is a reference that "should be considered when installing and maintaining the work" but is not intended as an "unattainable end."[102] But *ideal* also resonates with the reasonableness standard often used to determine the lawfulness of a person's behavior. A particular height or configuration need not be followed to the letter, but there is an intimation that certificate bearers should be reasonable in deciding how high paper stacks should be or where candies are placed. An ideal height for the paper stacks is prescribed (the actual height of the original installation), but the buyer is free to choose any height, a freedom that could hypothetically lead him or her to erect a stack so tall as to make it impossible for some viewers to take individual sheets. In that case, would the paper stack still be considered a Gonzalez-Torres, given the certificate declaration that "a part of the intention of the work is that third parties may take individual sheets of paper from the stack"?

Unlike the contracts and certificates of his conceptualist and Minimalist predecessors, which prioritized firm options over individual preference, Gonzalez-Torres folded preferences into options in apparent recognition of the subjective, rather than rational, owner. A few certificates permit the owner to execute certain parts of the work according to his or her (or its) "liking."[103] Text portrait owners, for example,

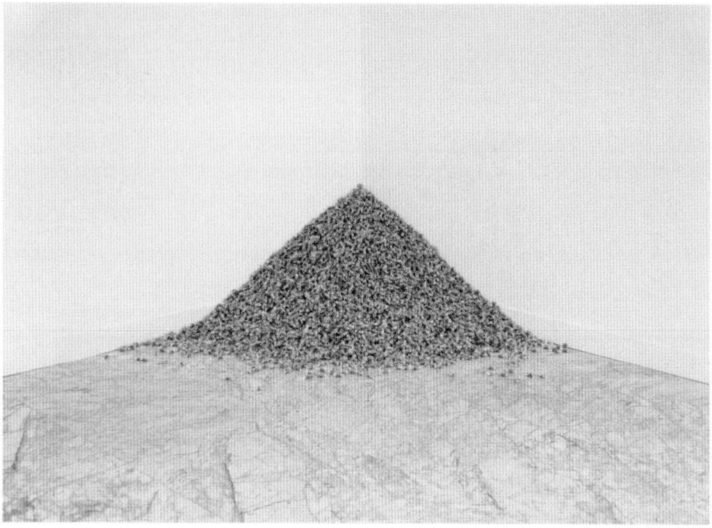

FIGURE 95
Felix Gonzalez-Torres, *"Untitled" (Revenge)*, 1991. Blue candies individually wrapped in cellophane, endless supply. Ideal weight: 325 pounds. Installation view: "The Savage Garden," La Fundación Caja de Pensiones, Madrid, 1991. © Felix Gonzalez-Torres Foundation. Courtesy of Andrea Rosen Gallery, New York.

have "the right to extend or contract the length of the portrait, by adding or subtracting events and their dates, and/or change the location of the portrait at any time."[104] Read against the repetition of *ideal* and *standards*, the promise of openness seems a challenge issued to collectors by Gonzalez-Torres. Consider the various manifestations of *"Untitled" (Revenge)* (fig. 95). In 1991, at the exhibition "The Savage Garden" at La Fundación Caja de Pensiones in Madrid, it consisted of a pile of small, cellophane-wrapped, greenish-blue, cube-shaped candies ("Blue Peppermint Ice Cubes") manufactured by the Chicago-based Peerless Confection Company, the artist's recommended supplier. After the company ceased operations in 2007, other institutions emphasized different aspects of the initial manifestation (fig. 96). Whether because of linguistic miscommunication, expense, or even a desire to test the flexibility of certificate terms, one institution seemed to have read "blue candies individually wrapped in cellophane" as candies individually wrapped in deep blue cellophane. It stands to reason that the certificates' openness invites owners to disagree with the artist and his representatives on the level of interpretation, so as to reverse the indexing of viewing experience to artistic intention, which sometimes felt more authoritarian than authoritative.

"NOBODY OWNS ME"

In 1994, Gonzalez-Torres collaborated with the upscale French clothing manufacturer Agnès B. to create a limited-edition t-shirt for a black-tie auction benefiting the New Museum of Contemporary Art, the formerly scrappy upstart that had hosted his first solo exhibition in 1988. Intended to attract "new blood" rather than "bejeweled ladies,"

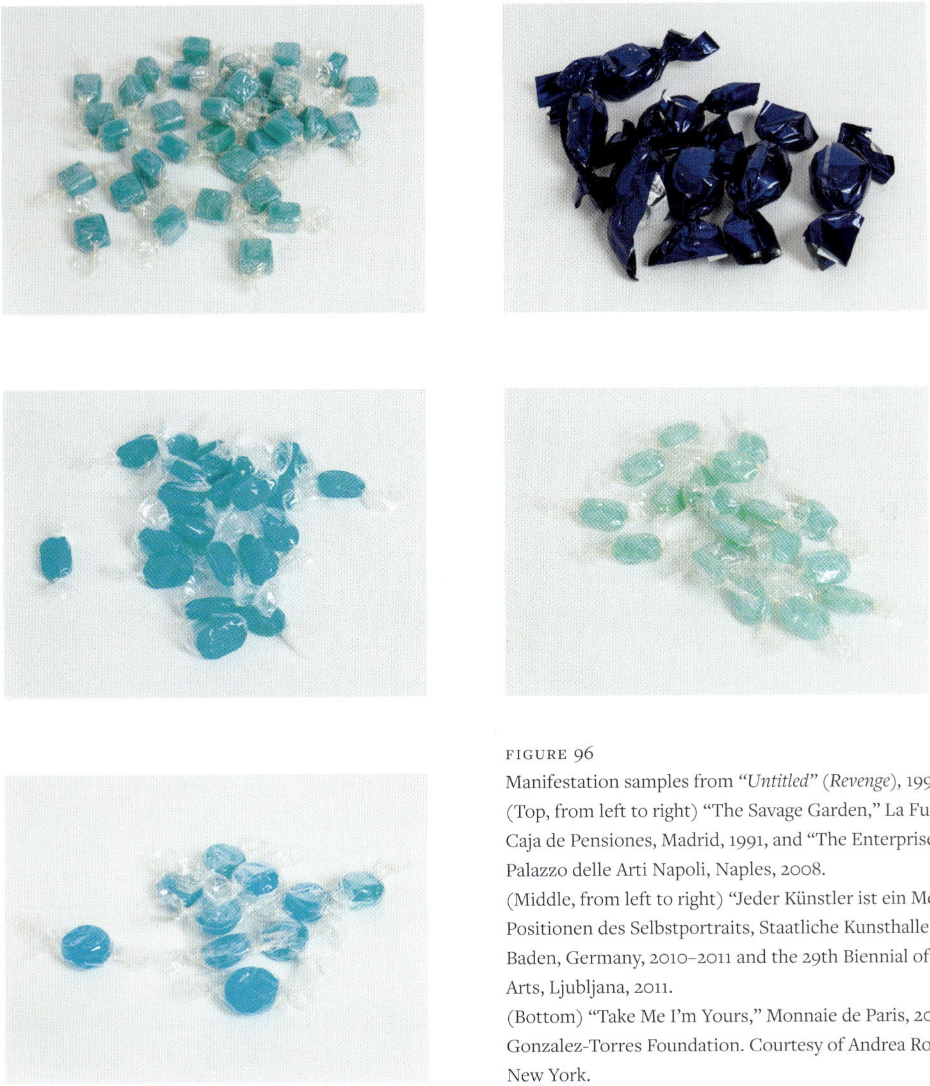

FIGURE 96
Manifestation samples from *"Untitled" (Revenge)*, 1991.
(Top, from left to right) "The Savage Garden," La Fundación Caja de Pensiones, Madrid, 1991, and "The Enterprise of Art," Palazzo delle Arti Napoli, Naples, 2008.
(Middle, from left to right) "Jeder Künstler ist ein Mensch!" Positionen des Selbstportraits, Staatliche Kunsthalle Baden-Baden, Germany, 2010–2011 and the 29th Biennial of Graphic Arts, Ljubljana, 2011.
(Bottom) "Take Me I'm Yours," Monnaie de Paris, 2015. © Felix Gonzalez-Torres Foundation. Courtesy of Andrea Rosen Gallery, New York.

each t-shirt read "Nobody Owns Me" on the back, a fitting rejoinder to legal and politically motivated circumscriptions of private life and, perhaps, of institutional eagerness to canonize the increasingly lionized artist.[105] The slogan might have doubled as the subtitle of his certificates, which the artist renamed "Certificates of Authenticity and Ownership" in 1993. Owning his work meant accepting the risk of not knowing exactly what was owned or what being an owner might eventually require. David Deitcher notes that a certificate from 1990 forbids the buyer from duplicating or showing a particular stack work in more than one place at a time.[106] The stipulation aligns with

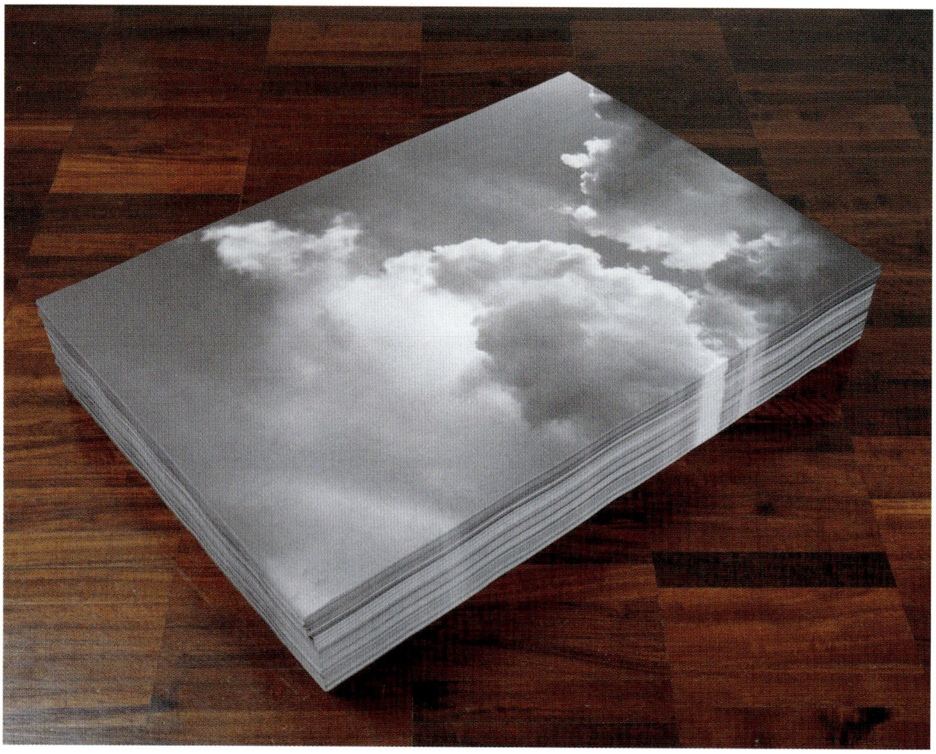

FIGURE 97
Felix Gonzalez-Torres, *"Untitled" (Aparición)*, 1991. Print on paper, endless copies. 8 inches (at ideal height) × 28 ½ × 43 inches (original paper size). Installation view: "Space of Time: Contemporary Art from the Americas," Americas Society, New York, 1993–94. © Felix Gonzalez-Torres Foundation. Courtesy of Andrea Rosen Gallery, New York.

common buyer expectations regarding the purchase of a unique work, namely, the principle of scarcity on which the legal construction of an artwork's economic value generally depends.[107] Gonzalez-Torres eased this restriction in other certificates, stating for example that the 1991 stack work *"Untitled" (Aparición)* may be reproduced—or, in the artist's words, "simulated"—for exhibition purposes (fig. 97). Deitcher argues that the artist may have included this revision to more readily accommodate growing museum interest and, by extension, his expanding schedule of exhibitions.[108]

Gonzalez-Torres's more flexible position recalls similar attitudes toward reconstructions. For a retrospective of Gordon Matta-Clark's work at the Institut Valencià d'Art Modern, the Holly Solomon Gallery indicated that *Dumpster Piece,* a work created from an industrial waste container, could be reconstructed if it was "identical in size and look" to the original made in 1972. It would up to the owner to decide whether this or the initial work (now better known as *Open House*) would be "the authentic piece . . . if it's the European dumpster, the California dumpster must be destroyed immediately to avoid any misuse with the material."[109] The logic mirrored how video artists like Bruce Nauman, Charles Ray, and Gary Hill permitted the use and circulation of exhibition copies in order to protect the master version. In like manner, Gonzalez-Torres provided that any "simulation" created for an exhibition would be destroyed after the show ended.[110] The flexibility he permitted may have also been a tactical maneuver to avoid the duplication of his works, even by museum professionals. The artist Andrea Fraser, for example, complained to her dealer that curators at the most reputable institutions seemed to think they could freely copy and distribute videos recording her performances.[111]

Owning a Gonzalez-Torres work meant thinking about ownership as a continuous process, subject to unexpected change. A precedent was Steve Kaltenbach's attempt to eliminate traditional views of artwork ownership in the contract he circulated for his work *Stone Maple* (1971–72). Directed toward museums, the contract stated that "at no time shall [the work] be owned by anyone," nor would money be exchanged for any reason. Absolved of maintenance responsibilities, museums could only have "custody" of the work, which ended with another museum's request to display the work.[112] The candy spills and paper stacks of Gonzalez-Torres might be compared to legal notions of alluvion (the extension of a landowner's property by deposits carried by wind and water) and its mirror opposite, diluvion (the diminishment of a landowner's property by erosion or other forms of attrition caused by natural forces). Land bounded by water tends to change in size and aspect, a recognition that grounds what common law holds as the nature of long-term ownership of property, its inherent subjection to gradual change.[113] Likewise, if the idea of change is inherently part of artworks, it follows that they can only be truly owned when held for long periods of time, or at least long enough so that they can be executed and shown in different ways.

The terms of the certificates make it potentially more difficult to sell a Gonzalez-Torres than to sell other works. But by continuing to offer what appears to be an endless supply of paper, regardless of how it is consequently used or even whether there is sufficient demand, Gonzalez-Torres thwarted the usual interactions on which economics depends. He openly declared his interest in the subversive potential of having more than one original at a time, noting how his replenishable stacks made at "the height of the 80s boom" undermined the idea of having an original work: "You could show this piece in three places at the same time and . . . it would still be the same piece. And it was almost like a threat—not only a threat but a reinterpretation of that art market."[114] Kwon describes this as "a struggle to establish new terms or systems of valuation that can respond adequately."[115] Similarly, Deitcher saw the artist as "trying to alter the system of distribution," which necessarily "depends upon the survival of the cultural economy that his gestures simultaneously undermine."[116] Letting audiences freely take the constituent components they would have seen as the work struck Gonzalez-Torres as perhaps the only response to a context where buyers were intensely, even pathologically, anxious to affirm their ownership status.

The certificates potentially ascribe to Gonzalez-Torres and his estate the right to control the product, a notion discussed in work-for-hire cases.[117] When Gonzalez-Torres was drafting his first certificates, the U.S. Supreme Court was considering *Community for Creative Non-Violence, et al., v. James Earl Reid.* At issue was whether the artist who produces a commissioned work retains copyright ownership or whether that ownership instead belongs to the organizer commissioning the work. The commissioning organization claimed ownership on the basis that it had "directed enough of [the artist's] effort to assure that, in the end, he had made what they, not he, wanted."[118] The court decided in favor of the artist, both because it determined the artist was not an employee of the commissioning organization and because of the amount of labor and time he spent in creating the work.[119] The decision supported an earlier model of authorship based on artists directly engaging in the production of work.

The language of Gonzalez-Torres's certificates resonates with the plaintiff's argument in *Community for Creative Non-Violence:* it "directs" enough of the owner's efforts to ensure that the work is what the artist wanted. It casts owners as subcontractors, and possibly even as virtual work-for-hire employees. Kwon states that "not only did Felix know that he would not be able to determine the work's future form," but he "was indebted to the owner's involvement."[120] Those buying Gonzalez-Torres's works were not his employees, nor were they paid by him or his representatives. Owners decide when to execute the terms of the certificate. But by delegating many of the functions ordinarily expected of artists, including sourcing materials and putting them together to create a tangible work, Gonzalez-Torres shifted the role, and perhaps the burden, of the artist as service provider onto owners in the form of a unique, and thus desirable, experience.[121]

Even more significant was how the certificates' openness augured the possibility of an authorship model more aligned with the free distribution of otherwise copyrightable work than with defensive and punitive models of copyright. In 2004, the artist Sturtevant made *Felix Gonzalez-Torres, Untitled (America)*, a near-facsimile of Gonzalez-Torres's *"Untitled" (America)* (fig. 98). Known since the mid-1960s for works closely resembling other works by well-known artists in a host of media, including land art and performance, Sturtevant heralded a recursive model of creation centered on assessing and choosing from existing data rather than producing works that looked conspicuously different from either their precedents or contemporaries. Jettisoning conventional notions of originality from artistic production, Sturtevant echoed inadvertently the iron-clad distinction the U.S. Copyright Office draws between originality and art.[122] Her process was hardly by rote, especially vis-à-vis Gonzalez-Torres, whose "intentions," Sturtevant remarked, one "really had to know."[123] Although she did not seem to have read the younger artist's certificates, the flexibility of Gonzalez-Torres's giveaway works had long been known in art-world circles; Susan Tallman in 1991 described how an artist, on asking whether she should preserve a sheet from a stack,

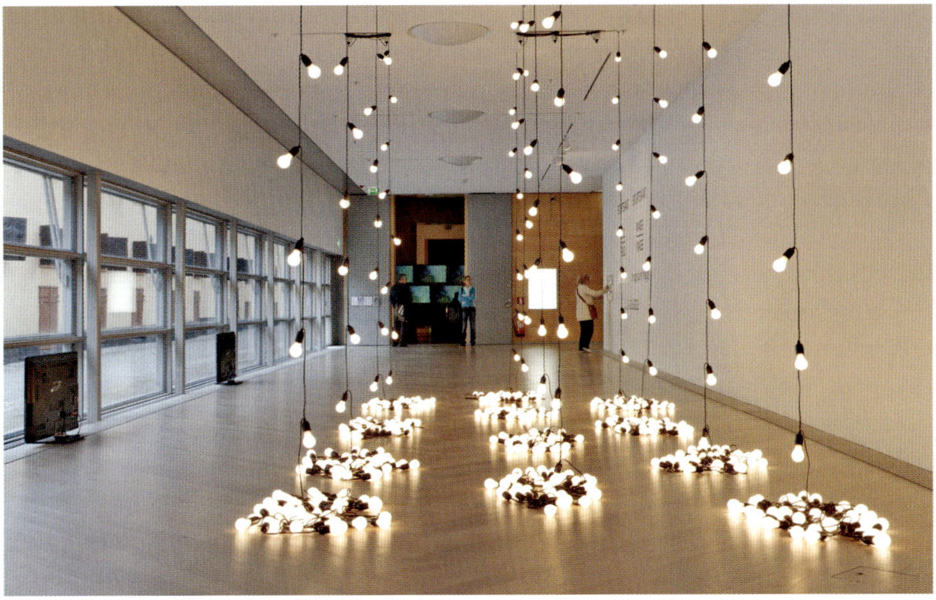

FIGURE 98
Installation view, Sturtevant, *Felix Gonzalez-Torres, Untitled (America)*, 2004. "Sturtevant: Image Over Image," Moderna Museet, Stockholm, 2012. © Sturtevant. Photo: Åsa Lundén/Moderna Museet.

was told "she should do with it whatever she liked."[124] The sheet no longer belonged to Gonzalez-Torres, yet the freedom granted may have obligated some takers to embark upon their own creative activity. The very existence of *Felix Gonzalez-Torres, Untitled (America)* delivers this possibility, consequently implicating Gonzalez-Torres's certificates to be retroactive grounds for a non-adversarial model of copyright based on producing and sharing knowledge for the many.

WHEN IS A GONZALEZ-TORRES WORK NOT A GONZALEZ-TORRES?

Sturtevant's choice of Gonzalez-Torres was especially judicious given how some of his work, namely the spills, curtains, and lightstrings, might not, in fact, be copyrightable under U.S. law. As the U.S. Copyright Office informed the artist Cady Noland, "a simple expression of rote designs and representation" does not meet its originality threshold; the law protects "expression" but not the idea from which it stems.[125] According to this logic of the text portrait certificates, adding and subtracting of events could potentially change the work until it is no longer recognizable as a work by Gonzalez-Torres, as Kwon discusses.[126] Candies in a Gonzalez-Torres heap may not themselves be the work, yet to exhibit one piece only might be seen as an unlawful attempt to show the work in an "altered, mutilated or modified form."[127] Not replenishing the spills or stacks might amount to destruction as a kind of death, given that viewer interaction, a key part of the work, can occur only when the idea takes physical form.

Contrary to U.S. copyright law, which discounts an artist's "conceptual choices" when determining originality, and in alignment with critical and commercial practices of the art world, the certificates of Gonzalez-Torres fixed his works as a function of their conception rather than their execution.[128] Early certificates specified that "the physical manifestation of this work in more than one place at a time does not threaten the work's uniqueness since its uniqueness is defined by ownership."[129] Perhaps mirroring the expanding global circulation of contemporary art, the phrase effectively permits owners to freely loan their works to multiple institutions concurrently. In the case of paper stack works, owners have the right to replenish the stack or simply allow the pile to disappear completely. The work need not be realized as a "fixed, tangible" object.

Yet institutional owners and lendees often defended the manifestation before the idea. Museum guards, whom Gonzalez-Torres deemed significant to the viewing experience, have been especially vigilant. In her review of the 1995 Gonzalez-Torres retrospective at the Guggenheim, Clara Hemphill wrote of how a guard scolded her for allowing her son to throw Gonzalez-Torres's candies in the air. The guard said the work was "supposed to invite interaction—but not too much!"[130] She later quipped that "perhaps Gonzalez-Torres' piles of candies become art when the museum guards yell at you not to touch them too much."[131] To the Guggenheim guards and many viewers, however, the candies constituted the work, a view applied to sheets of paper in the stack works. Although several certificates state that individual sheets "do not constitute a unique piece nor can be considered the piece," many have been offered for sale.[132] Rosen has noted that museums, apprehensive that their stack works might disappear even before a show began, asked Gonzalez-Torres's permission to prevent viewers from taking sheets during an opening.[133] That he eventually complied with such a request was a gesture of compromise, suggesting an awareness of the very real concern of institutional owners about the perceived damage of works acquired in the name of serving the public good.

The blurred distinction between idea and expression is further borne out by differences in insurance costs. Those borrowing the work bore the burden of insuring it for the cost of its production. For lenders, the candies indicated a right they purchased from the artist (in one owner's words, a loan meant giving someone else the temporary right to "reproduce a simulation").[134] In some cases, a relatively high value was assessed when identical replacements for a work's components could not be sourced, an indication of owners' attachment to objects.[135] For the candy spills and paper stacks, the cost amounted to less than a thousand dollars, a slim fraction of what the works they embodied might otherwise fetch on the market or at auction. Yet the Andrea Rosen Gallery has suggested that borrowers of *"Untitled" (Aparición)* should "make the printer aware that the material they are reproducing is actual artwork."[136] Gonzalez-Torres himself casually referred to the paper stacks as "sculptures," a description that his printer took up in referring to reams of paper generally: "His idea about his own work has been changed."[137]

Despite being a class of individuals with vested economic interests in preventing the mutilation or destruction of an artwork, owners of Gonzalez-Torres works differed considerably on what was a genuine risk. Some worried about the actual physical destruction of the constituent parts of a manifestation. Elaine Dannheisser, one of Gonzalez-Torres's first collectors, reportedly warned museums that the candy-spill works could be subject to a rat infestation, as hers was in 1994. Most institutions took no special measures to guard against such an incident, yet one used sugarless candy as a precaution, thereby suggesting an attachment to the idea of the work as inherently defined by tangible objects.[138] Many owners were fairly nonchalant about damage when it did happen, largely because of Gonzalez-Torres's insistence that the physical manifestation of his ideas was not the work itself, but an "exhibition copy," or, perhaps to diminish the stigma of describing a work as a copy, a "simulation of the work."[139] For museums, it lessened the burden of liability. "There's nothing that can happen to this work," wrote Amada Cruz, in reference to the billboard work *"Untitled"* (1991–93), while preparing for the artist's 1994 retrospective at the Hirshhorn Museum: "It's a refabrication—even if someone slashes the work—it's a simulation."[140]

Legal scholars Jack Balkin and Sanford Levinson have described authenticity in the law as a condition determined by a "community of consensus."[141] Yet during the years between Gonzalez-Torres's first solo show in 1987 and his death in 1996, community formation was still in process, as seen in the particular caution exercised by museums displaying works on loan, for whom having an authentic Gonzalez-Torres meant interpreting his intentions. Gonzalez-Torres may have found it "amusing" to receive endless faxes from museums asking "what they should do."[142] But for museums with the responsibility of showing genuine work, the lack of consensus surrounding how an authentic work of his might function and what it would look like was a pressing concern. When a candy-spill work, *"Untitled (Lover Boys),"* was shown at the 1991 Whitney Biennial, the museum interpreted Gonzalez-Torres's instructions to allow the public to know that they could "take one candy if they want" to mean that audiences should not be actively prevented from taking candies but that they should not be encouraged or directed to do so.[143] Conversely, the Museum of Modern Art in New York (MoMA), which owned *"Untitled" (Placebo)*, granted the Hirshhorn the option to display a sign allowing the public to take the candy.[144]

Most owners erred on the side of extreme caution, perhaps because in signing the certificates they also contracted with the art world at large. Many behaved as if they knew the VARA provision allowing changes to a work caused by its constituent materials or the passage of time so long as those changes were not the result of "gross negligence," or carelessness so serious as to exceed what a reasonable person might expect.[145] Yet institutional manifestation of work seemed governed by perceptions of civility and decorum, to the point that Gonzalez-Torres sometimes had to intervene. Struck by how viewers of his work at MoMA ate the candies, then threw their wrappings back into the pile, he asked that the museum leave the wrappers where they were despite the museum stipulating that the wrappers be discarded.[146]

The surest proof of owner intention may be the loan agreements that owners use to lend their Gonzalez-Torres works to other institutions for an exhibition.[147] By 1994, several loan agreements instructed lessees on how to install works and went so far as to indicate that the work must "not be transformed in any way" from its original dimensions.[148] In response to owner questions arising in the process of installing works, the Felix Gonzalez-Torres Foundation developed templates for more elaborate loan agreements, including recommendations for producing and installing the works. For owners using the foundation's template, the loan agreement becomes a de facto assertion of proprietary rights that reads as being more restrictive in the scope of rights granted than the actual certificate.

By granting owners considerable flexibility in determining how their purchases might appear, Gonzalez-Torres's certificates treat collectors almost like collaborators. Not surprisingly, many private collectors demonstrate unusual vigilance in following certificate recommendations. The certificates might also be read as invitations for owners to prove themselves as something other than consumers or property collectors interested primarily in maximizing their economic interests. Such owners might very well define what art historian John Tain calls the "rogue" or "activist collector," who, in lieu of collecting artworks as if they were any other asset type, dedicates herself primarily to prolonging the lives of the artworks she has.[149] Such collectors grew in number and prominence in the 1990s by establishing their own foundations, museums, and other institutions as a means of intervening in the ways artworks were discussed, produced, and circulated.

Gonzalez-Torres, or at least his estate, seemed to anticipate this breed of collector when the word *utmost* started to be paired with *discretion* in the certificates. A common filler in many legal agreements, *utmost* was added to replace an earlier term introduced in 1994 in which owners had to secure the express written permission of the artist if they wanted to lend his works elsewhere. "Utmost discretion" recalled similar phraseology in tort law, where *utmost* simply refers to a reasonable standard of care. Against a contractual context, *utmost* reads as mostly rhetorical window-dressing. More specific was *caretaker*, a term that appeared in a certificate for a text portrait sold jointly to the San Francisco Museum of Modern Art and the Art Institute of Chicago in 2002; the owner was "the caretaker [whom Gonzalez-Torres] entrusted with this work's evolution."[150] The "caretaker" designation suggests ownership as a temporary condition, one in keeping with the artist's apparent efforts to write into a world measured by assessments of economic value noneconomic qualities like respect and trust. The operative relationships were no longer determined by categories of "author," "buyer," "seller," and "owner." Instead the certificates demanded from owners proof of their integrity or, in this case, of their ability to fulfill another's will even if it meant having to act against their best economic interests.

Realizing a Gonzalez-Torres work remains a carefully regulated commitment, tempered by myriad contests between buyers and sellers, artists against both buyer and seller, and even the buyer against her own rights as an owner. The theoretical value of the certificate lies in the owner being able to freely show a particular collection of tangible objects as Gonzalez-Torres's work without the risk that he or she might be sued.[151] The risk was especially real for museums, whose aversion to liability and vigilance in safeguarding tangible property were noted above. For instance, the Hirshhorn had to make sure that the lightbulbs used in the Gonzalez-Torres retrospective were remade to adhere to national safety codes.[152] Ostensibly to assure owners of the artworks, the Hirshhorn promised to exercise "utmost care," a tort law concept mandating a higher degree of caution for others' safety where even the slightest negligence is grounds for liability.[153] Applied mostly to companies that provide accommodations or the transport of goods and people, "utmost care" signals residual attachment to ingrained views of artworks as objects, even when the certificate clearly permits the work's reconfiguration or reconstruction.[154] Consider, for instance, the priority the Art Institute of Chicago places on visual balance by replenishing candies of specific colors in *"Untitled" (Portrait of Ross in L.A.)* when visitors take those colors.[155]

During his lifetime, the artist instructed anxious museums to do "whatever you want," a response that not only knitted together obligation and choice as a function of desire and freedom but also suggested a refusal of the dualistic thinking that was categorizing queers as criminals via decisions like *Bowers v. Hardwick*.[156] The point was not simply about giving owners freedom of choice, but about claiming that there was no one right choice, just as Blackmun argued in *Bowers* that there was no one right form or approach to intimacy.

Doing "whatever you want" had other consequences, not least for Gonzalez-Torres himself. Although he disallowed giving individual candies and paper sheets the status of artwork, he thought it "weird" to see audience members "come into the gallery and walk away with a piece of paper that is 'yours.'"[157] Recounting how another artist took about twenty sheets from one of his paper stacks, he was initially pleased to think that they might become the basis of another's work, only to find that she had thrown them away.[158] His dismay, repeated over time, may have triggered his proprietary instincts, along with a generous helping of pique. In a later interview, the artist spoke of making conventional photographs he could "just" hang on "the fucking wall. . . . I don't want the public to touch them."[159]

In "Civil Rights Now," one of the more important group exhibitions featuring Gonzalez-Torres's work before his death, an implicit message was that the demand for rights was not simply a vague call to right injustices, but about cultivating an environment of sympathy toward "common issues of justice" underlying civil rights.[160] The challenge lay in grappling with difficult, and often illegible, feelings. True to form, the market has capitalized on feelings—since the mid-2010s, financial institutions have described art as "passion assets" in presumed reference to the emotional bonds between owners and their possessions. Yet even now, the elliptical language of Gonzalez-Torres's certificates continues to kindle a host of feelings, mirroring the unevenness of a world marked by failure and redemption. From this it becomes possible to imagine action beyond the official and unofficial laws now governing the relationships created by the sale of an artwork—relationships formed in the names of commerce and love alike.

EPILOGUE

THE TERMS OF ENGAGEMENT ARE REDRAWN by Carey Young in her 2005 work *Declared Void* (fig. 99). She sets the stage deftly and efficiently, using thick black vinyl lines to form a cube-like zone. A block of text just immediately to the right explains in the solemn timbre characteristic of legal writing how entering the zone means waiving one's constitutional rights. Developed by Young with intellectual property lawyer Robert Lands, the language has the tone of a disclaimer, an instrument for repudiating any potential legal claims that has become an ambient condition of everyday life.[1] The disclaimer epitomizes how responsibility, particularly for those who have the most economic and social resources, often means reassigning the burden of risk to those least able to bear its costs.

Spare as the work is, our attention latches onto any detail, including the thickness, color, and placement of lines. The austere presentation might come off as overly didactic, but I think Young was right to leave the installation as is. The withholding of further cues has us think about the strangeness of the lines and maybe their

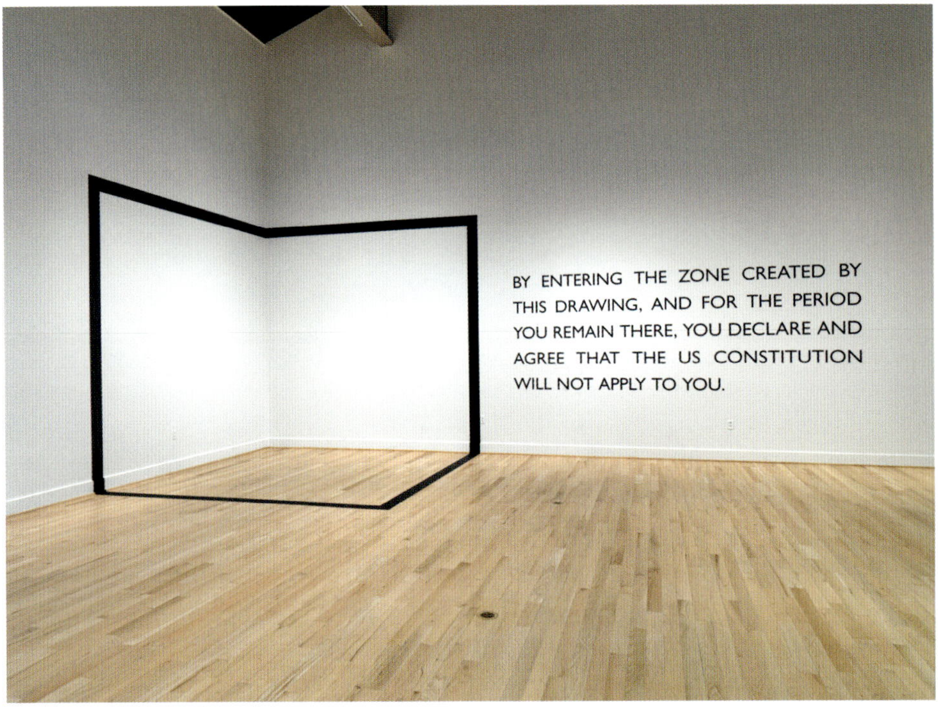

FIGURE 99
Carey Young, *Declared Void*, 2005. Vinyl drawing and text on wall, 133 × 133 × 133 inches. Courtesy of Paula Cooper Gallery, New York. © Carey Young.

arbitrariness, which the accompanying text situates next to the arbitrariness of law expressed through rules promulgated without explanation. The visually reductive presentation also enables Young to convey the pitch of law, in this case the contrived and even eerie neutrality channeled through the white-cube gallery setting and the bland inoffensiveness of Gill Sans font. Easily legible from a distance, the magnified words hyperbolize juridical demands that contractual terms be "reasonably conspicuous," language made familiar by case law upholding the validity of clickwrap agreements that require users to agree to a set of conditions before making an online purchase or using a website.[2] Whether users actually read or understand the largely nonnegotiable terms is irrelevant so long as the text is visible.

Young's text is exceedingly intelligible. It has to be, for the work depends on specific audience response. Said one viewer: "I made a beeline for the box, and stepped triumphantly inside. When I turned and reread the text, I felt, quite suddenly, alone and afraid. I sheepishly exited the box as quickly as I'd entered."[3] Like signing a Gonzalez-Torres certificate, apparent neutrality often gives way to a host of feelings that more concretely underscore one's place in the world than actual objects or locations do. The sudden shift from triumphant occupation to an uncanny sense of non-belonging catalyzed by *Declared Void* highlights feeling as law's substrate. Experiencing *Declared Void* offers other points of arbitration besides the law, a necessary task given how the law often tries to minimize or explain away feelings in order to preserve the illusion of its rationality and incorruptibility. Legal scholar Jennifer Nedelsky has called for the development of "a language of law whose metaphoric structure highlights rather than hides the patterns of relationship its constructs foster."[4] She asserts that the priority for jurists is to imagine how to be fugitives within the law, to escape from the usual ways of thinking about it in order to help law fulfill its goals more creatively and productively. For the legal imagination, contemporary art harbors the promise of representing an outside within which legal scholars might speculate on how best to deepen and improve the operation of law. Unlike law, where there is pressure to conform judgment to preexisting legal structures, artworks invite hypothetical thinking.

For many artists, modeling integrity means refusing wholesale the idea of emotional neutrality, including indifference to all conditions save those directly affecting private property interests. The artist and critic Simon Leung later stressed "the work of affect," or how "the psyche's interpellation with the look of law is not a supplement to, but the condition of political action."[5] His reference was to "The Look of Law," a 2006 exhibition at the University of California, Irvine, that explored, among other issues, how the force of law inheres unconsciously through its aesthetic manifestations in the wake of the 9/11 terrorist attacks. But as Leung notes, it is not enough to reveal the force of law or even to critique its shortcomings. There must also be some demonstration of how legal force resides in the emotional energy it can demand from those it governs.

Declared Void stages an encounter between art and law that results in generative friction that can "bring what we call law into being," a task legal scholar Pierre Schlag has argued is central to legal interpretation.[6] He contends that the law calls its subjects to think less about determining subjective intent by parsing the meanings of selected words or phrases and more about recognizing the phenomenological workings of law. The authority of the law and its subsequent enforcement frequently turn on regarding law as an aesthetic proposition, or what Schlag calls "legal aesthetics."[7] Is it a grid, where the main task is to divide and order inchoate behavior, as Young makes explicit in *Declared Void*? Is it a perspectival issue centered on acts of framing? Or is it a question of energy, where the task is to channel the flow and direction of the law by describing facts in particular ways? Who decides these forms?

The title of Young's work is a term often applied to agreements that no longer have any legal force. Here it belongs to a particular "geography of justice," the phrase legal scholar Kal Raustiala uses to describe the suturing of American law to territory where "simply by moving an individual around in space, the rights that individual enjoys wax and wane."[8] Personal misgivings aside, the ease with which gallery audiences can step in and out of the lines gestures more generally to extraterritoriality, one of the many legal fictions used to explain how one might physically be in a particular jurisdiction yet subject to the laws of another, or to no laws at all. An enclosure within a traditional gallery—itself a space bracketed from the unpredictability of the real world—*Declared Void* presciently alludes to the form of privatization, which, like the movement of bodies, exemplifies how the concept of place in the so-called age of globalism is defined more than ever by questions of jurisdiction. Indeed, Young's work was made during the rise of commodified privacy vis-à-vis spaces like "freeports," warehouses used by collectors and dealers for the temporary storage of artworks in transit, often located in countries with minimal tax laws and maximal privacy guarantees. Openly marketed since the early 1990s to appeal to collectors' desires for heightened security and privacy, the freeport has come to stand for a global art world defined by capital accumulation and transactional opacity.[9] It is art as private property writ largest.

If privacy is the heartbeat of privilege, its accelerated erosion increasingly defines everyday life for the vulnerable. An increasingly urgent point of intersection between art and the law, vulnerability has taken multiple forms. Artists grapple with the law as a function of the harm it causes those most subject to its punishment and least likely to challenge its assumptions. If a lasting priority for artists has been to ask how membership in a society is determined by the quality of one's participation in its formation, vulnerability has new currency given how so much of what passes for privilege is the untouchability and even unknowability of those who have control over the lives of others. Accountability exists only as calculations of economic profit and loss.

Since the early 1990s, the Spanish artist Santiago Sierra has staged ephemeral works by hiring disenfranchised or underprivileged individuals to perform menial acts (standing in a corner or moving concrete blocks) or subject themselves to physical alteration (being tattooed or having their hair dyed blond). Not surprisingly, works involving more extreme physical conditions often take place in jurisdictions where the rule of law is compromised, unstable, or nonexistent. Consider, for example, *8 People Paid to Remain Inside Cardboard Boxes,* a 1999 work where Sierra's temporary employees sat inside cardboard boxes in an unoccupied building in sweltering August heat. The work took place in Guatemala, where violations of labor law are rampant, and basic workplace protections often nonexistent.[10] Regardless of how unethical or unjust the performance may have seemed to viewers who mostly knew the work from documentation or hearsay, it was evidence of how the authority of the state to affect the lives of its constituents was now assumed by a select number of private individuals who enjoyed greater economic and political resources than the vast majority of citizens.[11]

Even in the United States, where national identity is so tightly associated with the rule of law as to carry over into pressuring foreign countries like Guatemala to enforce labor laws, Sierra was able to execute *12 workers paid to remain inside cardboard boxes* (2000) in New York City (fig. 100). A version of *8 People Paid to Remain Inside Cardboard Boxes,* the performance involved hiring from a government agency twelve individuals, mostly black and Mexican, to sit inside boxes scaled roughly to their proportions for four consecutive hours without a break.[12] That primarily minoritarian persons sit inside the boxes suggests that bodies so marked only exist unseen within

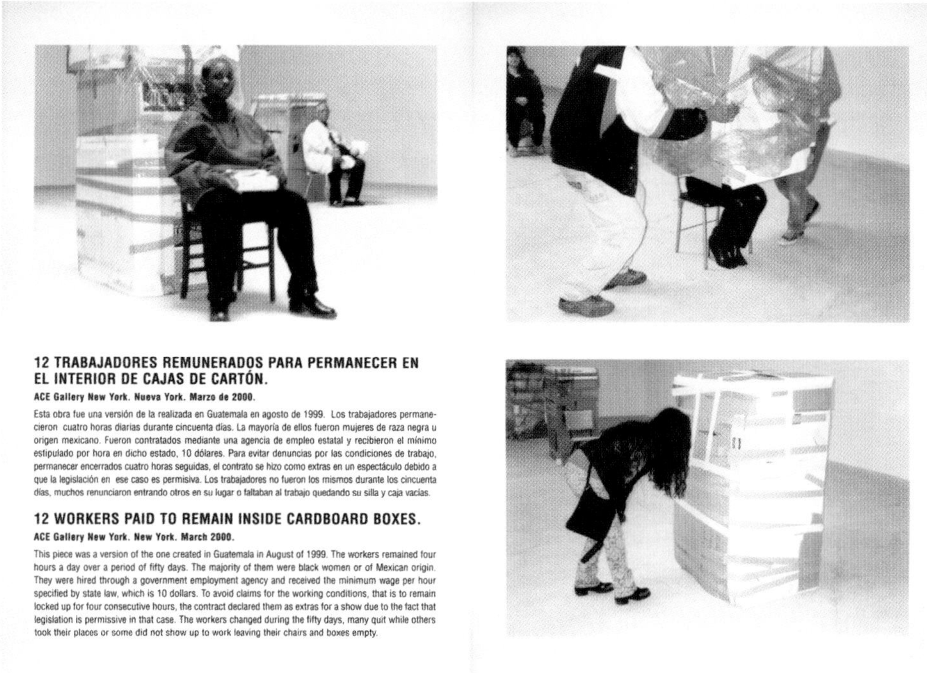

FIGURE 100

Santiago Sierra, *12 workers paid to remain inside cardboard boxes.* New York, March, 2000. Photographs (diptych), 17 3/8 × 23 3/8 × 1 1/8 inches. © Santiago Sierra.

the rarefied spaces of the gallery and museum (another Sierra work of 2000 involved a Mexican security guard paid to live behind a brick wall at the renowned New York contemporary art institution P.S.1 for fifteen days). Sierra claimed he was able to realize *12 workers paid to remain inside cardboard boxes* by describing the participants on their employment contracts as "extras" in a performance.[13] But the precautions he took to "avoid formal complaints being made about the working conditions" were unnecessary, given that neither federal nor New York state law requires employers to provide rest breaks to their employees. Sierra's medium inadvertently became what law in fact allows.

The work succinctly encapsulates Sierra's intention "to do things that are the most natural in the world."[14] Using bodies made doubly anonymous by their color and economic disenfranchisement in the service of a privileged, often white, individual or elite is so pervasive as to be among the defining characteristics of everyday life in the age of global privatization. What Sierra points out is how that which seems outrageous, immoral, or unethical is merely routine: commenting on a version of the New York performance held in Germany, one participant shrugged off presumptions of abuse, noting that "sitting around in narrow boxes—that's exactly what we do every day, anyway."[15] In such a context, acting ethically often means having the right contingency plan and enough money to outsource responsibility in the name of avoiding liability. One response is to reject this culture of risk aversion upheld by the policing of territories and the reinforcement of separation in the name of safety, security, and rationality. Such action requires a fugitive mindset that escapes what Fred Moten and Stefano Harney point out as frighteningly typical of real life, where "the only genuine and authentic mode of living in the world is to be recognizable within the terms of order."[16] The challenge is asking what kind of life is in fact possible, given how the crossing of boundaries does not result in their erasure.

12 workers paid to remain inside cardboard boxes would have been incomplete if the participants simply did as they were told; Sierra's projects underscore incertitude as a primary characteristic of agency. Several participant-employees chose to leave, out of boredom or exhaustion, thereby emphasizing how violability is as much a part of contract as performance. Most, however, fulfilled their contracts, perhaps out of fear that the employment agency Sierra used to staff his performance might retaliate by withholding future job opportunities. No one was coerced into staying or leaving, but for those who stayed, the matter of individual choice was heavily filtered through multiple structural considerations. As legal scholar Martha Fineman writes, contracts enable society to "reify individual choice in ways that mask society's role in perpetuating inequality."[17] Certainly, Sierra's works consistently illustrate the shortcomings of consent as a proxy for genuine freedom. Female drug addicts might agree to be tattooed in exchange for heroin or unemployed men to masturbate for minimal pay, but resulting audience outrage strongly insinuates an understanding of how consent can sometimes create situations as damaging as those resulting from open coercion.

In a 2008 article widely circulated in legal circles, Fineman makes a persuasive case for how and why the "autonomous and independent subject" of liberal political philosophy must give way to the "vulnerable subject" who is "far more representative of actual lived experience."[18] On this note, I close with Henry Taylor's 2017 painting *THE TIMES THAY AINT A CHANGING, FAST ENOUGH!* (fig. 101). Based on the video Diamond Reynolds streamed on Facebook just after her partner Philando Castile was shot by Mexican American police officer Jeronimo Yanez in July 2016 in Falcon Heights, Minnesota, the work approximates the dimensions of a history painting. Its size and scale bar viewers from committing the violence of looking away. Little about the painting resembles Reynolds's actual video, an indescribably surreal juxtaposition of the faceless cop yelling and crying, the balmy summer weather, and Reynolds's preternaturally calm description of events, which reads as survival instinct in its purest form. The painting has nothing of the urgency of the video or the risk Reynolds took to make it. Taylor has come too late to the scene and is thus forever barred from the event, save for images and texts mediated by other platforms. But it is this awareness of having come too late that binds Taylor's work to a much larger community of witnesses.

That Taylor is known for painting scenes of everyday life makes the work particularly striking. His aesthetic decisions signal relationships to other bodies of work in

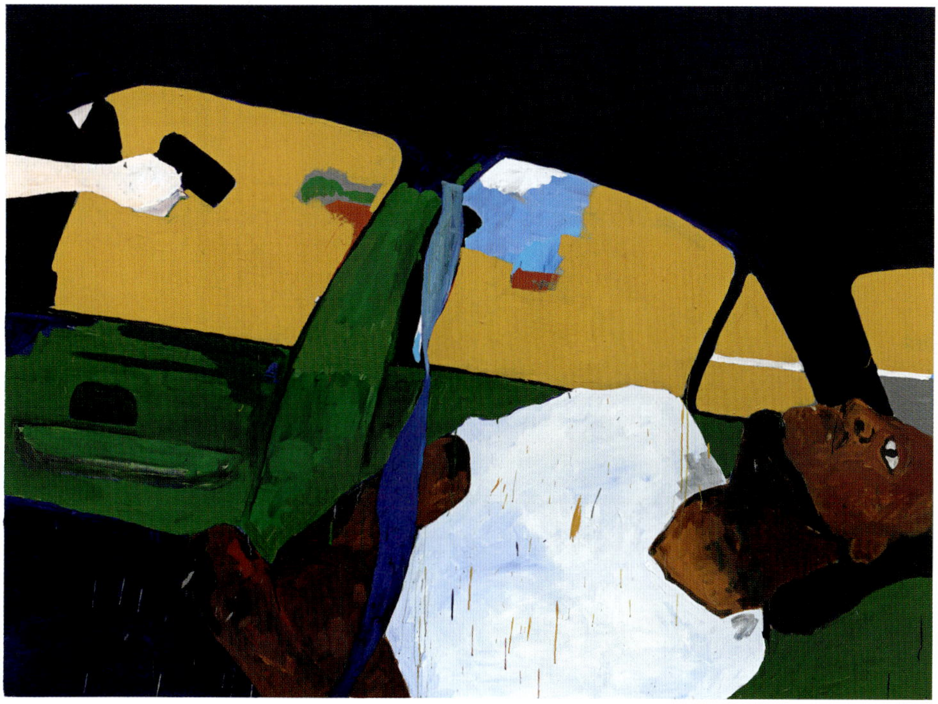

FIGURE 101
Henry Taylor, *THE TIMES THAY AINT A CHANGING, FAST ENOUGH!*, 2017. Acrylic on canvas, 72 × 96 inches.

ways that associate representation with historicity, almost as if he is painting to anticipate a history not yet salient. The profile of Castile recalls Ben Shahn's depiction of Nicola Sacco and Bartolomeo Vanzetti, the working-class men condemned to die in one of the most publicized miscarriages of justice in U.S. legal history (fig. 102). They lie with eyes closed, in telling contrast to the open ones of Massachusetts Superior Court judge Webster Thayer, whose political views compromised his ability to redeem justice's promise to be impartial and blind. Depicted in the painting's background, Thayer's ashen visage is as lifeless as the men his rulings doomed. Castile's left eye also remains open, but it is looking back at the killer, and even at us. This is less a scene to be looked at than one where we subject ourselves to scrutiny. Taylor understands how, in a split second, the compressed space of a car can feel as vast as an airplane hangar; here the space within is opened up to the viewer, swallowing her whole. It is a painting that concerns time but is not of it.

The painting registers, at the level of both facture and form, various ambitions and trepidations about representing crisis so recent as to make its historicization feel unjustly premature. Absent from the work is the taint of presentism that undermines so many well-intentioned gestures of representation. In choosing not to paint blood

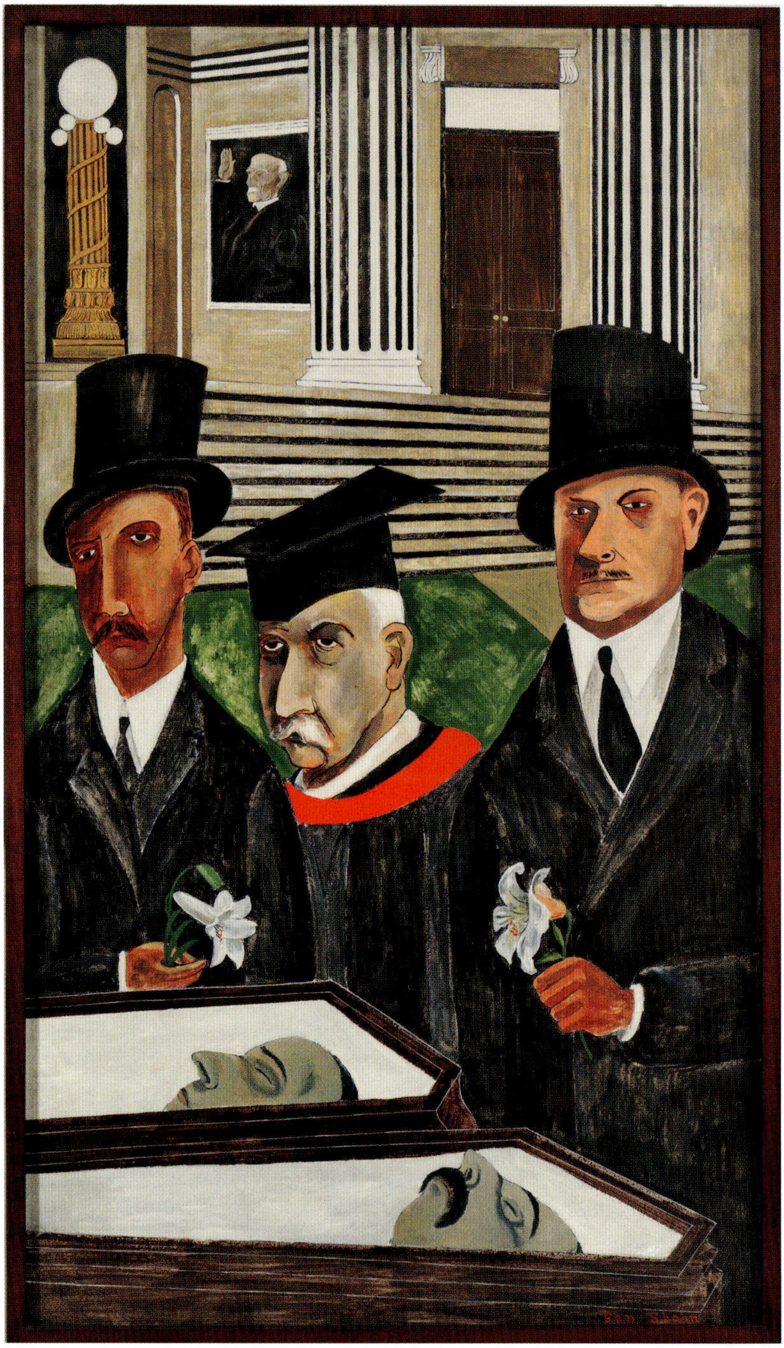

FIGURE 102

Ben Shahn, *The Passion of Sacco and Vanzetti*, 1931–32. Tempera and gouache on canvas mounted on composition board, 84 × 48 inches. Whitney Museum of American Art, New York; gift of Edith and Milton Lowenthal in memory of Juliana Force 49.22. Art © Estate of Ben Shahn/ Licensed by VAGA, New York.

on Castile's blindingly white shirt, Taylor reassures us that he recognizes the impossibility of capturing every nuance of the Castile murder. The drips of paint nevertheless embody the complex negotiation between the suggestive power of materials and the unpredictable capacity of painting to perform both remembering and forgetting. Drips and splatter disrupt the boundary between the internal world of the picture and the external world to which it refers.

Taylor's gifts as a colorist are in full view, and while they draw upon Bob Thompson's eye for generative incongruencies (the glimpses of dull red against the car's green upholstery are particularly suggestive), Taylor knows to keep the visual momentum from self-combusting into look-at-me showmanship. The lessons he learned from his lifelong mentor Jim Jervaise are in effect—sober phosphorescence is his tone. Phosphorescence is especially apt, in that it refers to how energy is absorbed by a substance released slowly in the form of light. Of the same chroma as the patch of ostensible sky, the twisting seat belt could be a lifeline, a rope thrown from the outside to liberate those still trapped within. The gun is abbreviated as a small black rectangle, a gesture that belies its frightening capacity for destruction. The arm is both anonymous and specific, its faint blush undertones a signal of law's presence. Here Taylor compromises how authority depends on its disembodiment in order to reemerge as plausibly neutral.

Yet, in contrast to the magnified head of Castile, the arm is strikingly inconspicuous. We know who is responsible for the killing, but the painting appears more concerned with undeserved death. The only sculptural image is Castile's face, his jawline and beard thickly rendered with a black line. Despite being supine, the head is lifted up, as if Taylor were attempting to salvage it from the wreckage produced by the effete arm of the unknown killer. Painterly buildup is extreme, as if the artist was trying to paint a head into existence that could double as a funeral pyre. It is all-seeing, eternal, but toppled from its pedestal. It is on the ground, and soon to be below it. But Taylor is far too ambitious a painter to be content with iconographical depiction, or even with coining a new visual language for discussing social injustice. He signals as much by the square patch of light blue paint that occupies a corner of one window. Almost directly above the very center of the painting, it consists of perpendicular brushstrokes, much as if Taylor was trying to clear the opaque dull maize covering both windows. Painted before Yanez was acquitted of Castile's murder, the work offers viewers the opportunity of judgment. Is Taylor suggesting that the death of Castile helps us see clearly, past the bleak banality of a world to which the unseen killer belongs? Or does the maize encroach upon the blue, a signal, perhaps, of the world where the U.S. Constitution does not in fact apply? What makes the painting work is its balance between emptiness and detail, between narrative and its construction. We see the brushstrokes from time to time, but never enough to make us think that Taylor's authorial touch is the subject.

Taylor is more than a creative producer of mnemonic devices. He understands just how easily images can be forced into playing prosthesis for viewers who would rather not remember such events or their own complacency in allowing them to pass unremembered. See how the folded arms look as if they are melting into each other, just as Castile draws his last breath. His fate as mute symbol is sealed by an overarching canopy of dark violet stretching across the full width of the canvas. Death frames the everyday, bears down on it, ready to flatten the living out of the picture. And it is death from which no one is exempt; its casualties include the identity of Castile's killer, who appears here beheaded and engulfed by the darkness that Taylor takes care to distinguish from blackness. We all are passengers in the funeral hearse.

The open eye of Castile frees Taylor's painting from the chokehold of earnest timeliness. Something we assume as fait accompli, left for dead, watches us with unrelenting force—perhaps the blank despair à la the open eyes of the trampled bodies in Picasso's *Guernica,* or even the imminent balefulness of a wronged soul. I think of the poster for the surprisingly underrated 1992 film *Candyman,* until recently one of the very few mainstream horror films to have a black main character. An enlarged, unblinking red eye stares at the viewer, its pupil a silhouette of the film's vengeful antihero, the Candyman—a reminder of the fatal folly of forgetting.

That Taylor's painting is overdetermined, able to feed into optimistic and pessimistic readings, is key. It is productively ambiguous, refusing to play along with the binary logics so prevalent now, which foreclose any possibility of thinking critically about viable alternatives. It is this ambiguity that allows the internally conflicted viewer to exist on multiple scales of operation rather than become a vanishing point on an ever-receding horizon of possibility. We wonder whether this emotional work, however necessary and acute, is simply not enough. Politically necessary as it may be, the sharing and disclosing of feelings has been so co-opted by populism that even genuine efforts at exchange threaten to devolve into an impasse of warring truth-claims. Integrity requires guarding against temptation to sequester works from critical or opposing viewpoints, yet new and more stringent demands on the viewer are in order, particularly in an era increasingly described as "post-truth." This requires not only critique and reflection, but also a higher bar for viewers. It calls for viewers to exercise vigilance, or a kind of focused, heightened attention analogous to what jurists call "strict scrutiny." Such vigilance demands that viewers assess everyday life as a question of legitimacy, to actively wonder not only about the correctness of a situation but about its rightness and justness, with an eye to the survival of the weakest and most vulnerable. It generates what might be called "liquid disruption": the heightened attention some artworks demand results in pauses, detours, and lapses that disrupt the flow of everyday life in formless, diffuse ways.

By initiating durational, locally specific encounters that enfold, rather than exclude, different kinds of viewers, artworks help create necessary psychological space within which to do the political and affective labor needed to bridge the sometimes gaping chasm between law and justice. If the unseen represents some of the greatest threats against freedom—the politicians masking their agendas with supposedly neutral language, the unacknowledged others boxing in contingent workers, the faceless police officer—artists are especially well placed to challenge this regime by making the unseen visible. Art poses hypothetical or disruptive situations that enable it to help forge a dialectic space wherein the law—the structure enabling politics to occur—can reflect upon the legal sensorium. If artists approach the law as a question of form, the experiences their works generate call upon the law to recognize multiple parties without relegating them to preexisting divisions. One must acknowledge others as subjects in order to create the possibility of a world where differences can be respected. It could even be claimed that mere acknowledgment is the point from which political power begins; it models a world where it is no longer necessary for one to suppress a part of oneself in order to belong to a particular side. On such grounds it will be possible to imagine the law as itself a leap of faith, made in hopes of reforming the boundaries that shape how we belong in, and to, the world.

NOTES

INTRODUCTION

1. "Rumbles," *Avalanche* 3 (fall 1971): 3–4.
2. Robert E. Keeton, "Assumption of Risk in Products Liability Cases," *Louisiana Law Review* 22(1) (1961): 166.
3. The counterexample would be Charlotte Moorman's efforts to deny culpability for her actions in her self-published text *Artist in the Courtroom (People vs. Moorman)*. For a discussion of this denial, see Kristine Stiles, "'Necessity's Other': Charlotte Moorman and the Plasticity of Denial and Consent," in *A Feast of Astonishments: Charlotte Moorman and the Avant-Garde, 1960s–1980s,* ed. Lisa G. Corrin and Corinne Granof (Evanston: Northwestern University Press, 2016), 174–175.
4. *Bates v. State Bar of Arizona,* 433 U.S. 350 (1977).
5. Margaret Jane Radin, "Property and Personhood," *Stanford Law Review* 34 (1982): 957–1015. Anthropologist Marilyn Strathern powerfully argued that it is in fact Euroamerican law that "requires that persons emerge as social agents when they are able to be in control (of themselves, property, others)." Marilyn Strathern, "Discovering 'Social Control,'" *Journal of Law and Society* 12(2) (summer 1985): 115.
6. Jonathan Simon, *Governing through Crime: How the War on Crime Transformed American Democracy and Created a Culture of Fear* (New York: Oxford University Press, 2007), 55.
7. For a history of the origins of "law and order," see Michael W. Flamm, *Law and Order: Street Crime, Civil Unrest, and the Crisis of Liberalism in the 1960s* (New York: Columbia University Press, 2007).

8. The metaphorical "city on a hill" exemplified Reagan's attitude toward American exceptionalism. Ronald Reagan, "Election Eve Address: Vision for America," 3 November 1980. www.presidency.ucsb.edu/ws/?pid = 85199, accessed 11 October 2017.
9. Examples include Corinna Weidner, ed., *Legal/Illegal: Art beyond Law* (Berlin: NGBK, 2004); Carlo McCormick, *Trespass: A History of Uncommissioned Urban Art* (Cologne: Taschen, 2010); and Leif Dahlberg, ed., *Visualizing Law and Authority: Essays on Legal Aesthetics* (Berlin: Walter De Gruyter, 2012).
10. Roberta Rosenthal Kwall, "Copyright and the Moral Right: Is an American Marriage Possible?" *Vanderbilt Law Review* 38(1) (1985): 8. Kwall discusses integrity as enmeshed with discussions about protecting human dignity. Also see Roberta Rosenthal Kwall, *The Soul of Creativity: Forging a Moral Rights Law for the United States* (Stanford, CA: Stanford University Press, 2010), 4.
11. Ronald Dworkin, *Law's Empire* (Cambridge, MA: Harvard University Press, 1986), 96.
12. Perhaps the best and most consistent example of lawyers grappling with the difficulty of translating visual material into words are U.S. Copyright Office review board letters explaining their decisions concerning copyright registration applications. www.copyright.gov/rulings-filings/review-board/index.html?loclr=blogcop, accessed 28 May 2018.
13. *Brancusi v. United States,* 54 Treas.Dec. 428 (Cust.Ct. 1928).
14. The full transcript of the case proceedings is published in Margit Rowell, André Paleologue, and Francesca Rose, eds., *Brancusi vs. United States, the Historic Trial, 1928* (Paris: Adam Biro, 2001).
15. Objects that were artistic and functional could be imported duty-free only after the Harmonized Tariff Schedule was enacted in 1989.
16. Sol LeWitt, "Paragraphs on Conceptual Art," *Artforum* 5(10) (summer 1967): 80.
17. Lucy Lippard and John Chandler, "The Dematerialization of Art," *Art International* 12 (February 1968): 31.
18. 17 U.S. Code §102.
19. Lowe's best-known contribution to the legal history of art was as a co-executor of the estate of celebrated sculptor David Smith. When Smith died, the Internal Revenue Service argued that the works' taxable value was close to $5.4 million, based on the retail asking prices for other Smith works set by the artist's dealer and estimates of the works' individual sale prices. Lowe counterargued that the taxable value was the sum obtained if all the works were sold at the moment of death. This meant that the retail value of each work would likely be lower given the sudden mass supply of Smith sculptures. The U.S. Tax Court partly acknowledged Lowe's claim by adjusting the value to $2.7 million, a rough mean between the amounts set by the IRS and the original value set by Lowe and his co-executors. *Estate of David Smith,* 57 T.C. 650 (1972).
20. Ed McGowin, quoted in J. Richard Gruber, "Ed McGowin and T.M. Dossett: 'True Stories' and the 'Southern Voice,'" *Ed McGowin: Name Change: One Artist, Twelve Personas, Thirty Five Years* (Mobile, AL: Mobile Museum of Art, 2006), 9.
21. Cliff Schaffer, telephone conversation with the author, 10 August 2017.
22. For a discussion of Morris's project and other earthworks made in the name of land reclamation, see Suzaan Boettger, *Earthworks: Art and the Landscape of the Sixties* (Berkeley: University of California Press, 2002), 239–240.
23. Robert Morris, "Art as/and Land Reclamation," *October* 12 (spring 1980): 98–99.
24. Lucia Saradoff and Sallie Batson, "Sculpture Marks Gateway to Soho," *SoHo Weekly News,* 15 November 1973. Another unprecedented issue concerned how the work occupied city-owned "taxable airspace" via projections from the wall into the sky above the Houston Street sidewalk.
25. *Board of Managers of Soho International Arts Condo v. City of New York, 2005 U.S. Dist. LEXIS 9139* (S.D.N.Y. May 19, 2005). Eventually a deal was struck to allow *The Wall* to be returned to its original location but raised to make way for advertising panels.

26. Lawrence Alloway, "Network: The Art World Described as a System," *Artforum* 11(1) (September 1972): 28.
27. Ibid., 29. Alloway's comparison is gleaned from *A Behavioral Theory of the Firm,* a classic work on organizational behavior by political scientist James March and economist Richard Cyert, published in 1963. The first major discussion of organizational management to address the significance of politics arising from competing individual and social preferences and its impact on a firm's operation, the book observed how each party in a given organization or "coalition" will lobby for its own preferences.
28. Rosalyn Deutsche, *Evictions: Art and Spatial Politics* (Cambridge, MA: MIT Press, 1996), 168; Hans Haacke, "Editorial-Artists vs. Museums, continued," *Art News* 70(5) (September 1971): 21.
29. Haacke observed to his gallerist, Paul Maenz, that his work prompted the *Village Voice* to investigate two of the properties featured. Haacke, letter to Paul Maenz, 27 November 1972. Galerie Paul Maenz Köln records, 1956–1991 (bulk 1970–1990), Getty Research Institute, Research Library, accession no. 910066, box 16, folder 1.
30. Vito Acconci, "Some Notes on Illegality in Art," in *Illegal America* (New York: Franklin Furnace, 1982), unpaginated.
31. Suzanne Lacy, quoted in Moira Roth, "Visions and Re-Visions: A Conversation with Suzanne Lacy," *Artforum* 19(3) (November 1980): 42.
32. Lacy observes that the police may have been less proprietary toward evidence at that time. Telephone communication with the author, 11 November 2017.
33. Despite an abrupt national surge in rapes in the late 1960s, rape laws changed very little. Camille E. LeGrand, "Rape and Rape Laws: Sexism in Society and Law," *California Law Review* 61(3) (May 1973): 920.
34. Lewis MacAdams, "The Law and the Power," *High Performance* 5(3) (fall 1982): 39.
35. Quoted in Hilary Robinson, "God! I Love Time: An Interview with Linda Montano," *n. paradoxa* 5 (2000): 65.
36. *National Endowment for the Arts v. Finley,* 524 U.S. 569 (1998).
37. Catherine Wood, quoted in Gabriella Giannachi and Jonah Westerman, eds., *Histories of Performance Documentation: Museum, Artistic, and Scholarly Practices* (New York: Routledge, 2018), 31. Photographs of performances have been sold as the performer's work since at least the 1990s. The *Chris Burden Deluxe Photo Book 71–73* began to appear at auction in 1995.
38. In 2010, the Regional Court of Düsseldorf ruled that photographs taken by an associate of Joseph Beuys of the late artist's performance infringed upon the copyright of the artist's estate and could not be publicly displayed. The German Federal Supreme Court overruled the decision, ironically because the photographs were the only documentation of the performance, thus making it impossible to decide whether "the overall impression of the photo series coincides with the overall impression of Beuys's performance." BGH, 16 May 2013—I ZR 28/12.
39. Roy Bongartz, "Question: How Do You Buy a Work of Art Like This? Buying Conceptual Art-Photos, Sets of Directions, Receipts," *New York Times,* 11 August 1974.
40. Acconci, "Some Notes on Illegality in Art."
41. 17 U.S.C. §106A.
42. 17 U.S.C. §101.
43. *Cohen v. G.M. Realty L.P.*, Case No. 15-CV-03230 (FB)(RLM) (E.D.N.Y., February 12, 2018).
44. Following his performance *Deadman,* in which he lay under a tarpaulin on La Cienega Boulevard in front of the Mizuno Gallery in Los Angeles, Chris Burden was arrested in 1972 for knowingly causing a false report of emergency. Rather than admit guilt, which would likely have resulted in a fine or probation per California Penal Code §148.3, Burden insisted on a trial, which resulted in the jury voting 9–3 in favor of conviction. The presiding judge, George Zucker of the Beverly

Hills Municipal Court, dismissed the case rather than order a retrial, a highly unusual outcome that suggested Zucker's acceptance of Burden's work as art and a desire for administrative efficiency. Barbara Smith, "Burden Case Tried, Dismissed," *Artweek* 4(8) (24 February 1973): 2.

45. Amy Adler, "Fair Use and the Future of Art," *New York University Law Review* 91(3) (June 2016): 610.
46. *Rogers v. Koons*, 960 F.2d 301 (2d Cir. 1992).
47. 4 Melville B. Nimmer & David Nimmer, *Nimmer on Copyright* §13.05 [D][3], at 13–229 (1997).
48. Pierre N. Leval, "Toward a Fair Use Standard," *Harvard Law Review* 103(5) (March 1990): 1111.
49. The Second Circuit did not completely discard the significance of artistic medium, noting with satisfaction how Koons did not try to argue for the validity of his copy by invoking the difference between a painting and a photograph. *Blanch v. Koons* 467 F.3d 244 (2d Cir. 2006).
50. Richard Prince, cited on Gagosian Gallery website, 2015. www.gagosian.com/exhibitions/richard-prince—june-12–2015, accessed 10 December 2016. On the correlation between large size and photography's artistic status, see Michael Fried, *Why Photography Matters as Art as Never Before* (New Haven, CT: Yale University Press, 2008).
51. Ada Louise Huxtable, "Sprucing Up the Bank of Tokyo," *New York Times,* 28 December 1975.
52. Ibid.
53. Grace Glueck, "Bank Cuts Up a Noguchi Sculpture and Stores It," *New York Times*, 19 April 1980.
54. Ibid.
55. Keeton, "Assumption of Risk," 166.
56. Anthony Giddens, "Risk and Responsibility," *The Modern Law Review* 62(1) (January 1999): 3.
57. A well-known example is the Common Rule, the U.S. federal regulation concerning research involving human subjects. "Minimal risk" exists when "the probability and magnitude of harm or discomfort anticipated" is not greater than those "ordinarily encountered in daily life." See also *Restatement (Second) of Torts* §496-A-E (1965), which defines the assumption of risk in civil cases partly as the risk of harm. What constituted an assumption of unacceptable risk in civil lawsuits was a flashpoint for tort law scholars throughout the 1960s. James Fleming, "Assumption of Risk: Unhappy Reincarnation," *Yale Law Journal* 78(2) (December 1968): 185–197.
58. George J. Church, "Sorry, Your Policy Is Canceled," *Time,* 24 March 1986, 20. The figure was quoted in connection to skyrocketing insurance premium costs threatening the service industry.
59. Billy Klüver, letter to Jerald Ordover, 18 January 1968. Experiments in Art and Technology records, 1966–1993, Getty Research Institute, Los Angeles, accession no. 940003, box 168, folder 3.
60. California Civil Code sections 1738, 1738.5 to 1738.9.
61. Allan Frumkin, quoted in Grace Glueck, "When Art Imitates Life, Controversy Arises in Art and Legal Circles," *New York Times,* 23 December 1980. *Silberman v. Georges,* 91 A.D.2d 520 (N.Y. App. Div., 1st Dept. 1982). The jury in the original case, tried in 1980, awarded each of the plaintiffs $30,000 in damages.
62. Barrie observed that U.S. museums were gripped by a fear of liability for at least a decade after the trial. Steven Litt, "Dennis Barrie Looks Back on His Cincinnati Obscenity Trial 20 Years after His Acquittal," *Plain Dealer,* 5 October 2010. www.cleveland.com/arts/index.ssf/2010/10/dennis_barrie_looks_back_on_hi.html, accessed 11 December 2016.
63. *Close v. Lederle,* 303 F.Supp.109 (D.Mass.1969).
64. Close tried to have the First Circuit decision reviewed by the U.S. Supreme Court. Although his petition was denied, the intention to pursue the matter to the fullest extent possible despite the modest financial and professional stakes conveys the seriousness of Close's commitment to defending his interests. *Close v. Lederle,* 400 U.S. 903 (1970).
65. *Close v. Lederle,* 424 F.2d 988 (1st Cir. 1970).

66. Ibid.

67. For a comprehensive collection of documents and analyses on the *Tilted Arc* hearing and its aftermath, see Martha Buskirk and Clara Weyergraf, eds., *The Destruction of Tilted Arc: Documents* (Cambridge, MA: MIT Press, 1991).

68. Seven works were in question; five were from Mapplethorpe's *X Portfolio,* depicting queer sexual acts, and two were of children, *Rosie* (a little girl on an ornate stone bench exposing her genitals) and *Jesse McBride* (a naked young boy perched on an upholstered chair).

69. Mark Jarzombeck, "Sights of Contention: The Mapplethorpe Trial and the Paradox of Its Formalist and Liberal Defense," *Appendx* 2 (1997), www.appendx.org/appendx/issue2/index.htm, accessed 1 February 2016.

70. For a succinct overview of the *Radich* cases, see Steven C. Dubin, *Arresting Images: Impolitic Art and Uncivil Actions* (New York: Routledge, 1992), 107.

71. *United States Ex. Rel. Radich v. Criminal Court of the City of New York,* 385 F. Supp. 165 (S.D.N.Y. 1974).

72. Joan Rothfuss, *Topless Cellist: The Improbable Life of Charlotte Moorman* (Cambridge, MA: MIT Press, 2014), 195–203.

73. Jack Newfield, "Ten Worst Judges," in *Verdicts on Lawyers,* ed. Ralph Nader and Mark Green (New York: Crowell, 1976), 269–284. Based on interviews with fellow judges and lawyers as well as reviews of court transcripts, the list featured those "most totally insensitive to civil liberties, the most biased against the poor, and/or as standing for cruelty, stupidity, or ill-temper." www.ncjrs.gov/App/Publications/abstract.aspx?ID = 47634, accessed 8 December 2017.

74. Until *Reed v. Reed* was decided in 1971, Utah state courts, for instance, favored men over women as estate administrators, while state legislatures claimed that men "as a rule" were more "conversant with business affairs" than women. *Reed v. Reed,* 404 U.S. 71 (1971).

75. Miranda Fricker, *Epistemic Injustice: Power and the Ethics of Knowing* (Oxford: Oxford University Press, 2009), 30.

76. Linda Nochlin, "Why Have There Been No Great Women Artists?" *Artnews* 69(9) (January 1971): 70.

77. Coined in 1958 to criticize the formation of an unequal society based on differing intelligence levels, *meritocracy* was defended as a social ideal by Daniel Bell, "Meritocracy and Equality," *Public Interest* 29 (January 1972): 29–68. Yet Bell unconsciously affirms Nochlin when he defines the meritocracy as "the men who are best in their field, as judged by their peers." Ibid., 66.

78. The most comprehensive account of the trial and its aftermath is investigative journalist Robert Katz's *Naked by the Window: The Fatal Marriage of Carl Andre and Ana Mendieta* (New York: Atlantic Monthly Press, 1990).

79. Ruby Rich, "Remembering Ana Mendieta—The Screaming Silence," *Village Voice,* 23 September 1986, 23. The Andre-Mendieta tragedy was widely publicized in the mainstream press, including a lengthy cover story written by Joyce Wadler for *New York Magazine* ("A Death in Art," *New York Magazine,* 16 December 1985: 38–46).

80. Rich, "Remembering Ana Mendieta," 24.

81. Judd Tully, "Andre Acquitted," *New Art Examiner* 15(8) (April 1988): 24.

82. Howardena Pindell, "Who Suffers Censors . . .," *New Art Examiner* 16(5) (January 1989): 1.

83. For a discussion of artistic criminality in Surrealism, see Jonathan Eburne, *Surrealism and the Art of Crime* (Ithaca, NY: Cornell University Press, 2008), particularly 173–214.

84. Jonas Mekas, "On the Misery of Community Standards," *Village Voice,* 18 June 1964, reprinted in *Movie Journal* 143. "Community standards" was the standard used by the New York City Criminal Court to determine the film's obscenity.

85. Gordon Matta-Clark may have been among these colleagues; in apparent response to an earlier letter, Jaroslav told Matta-Clark that "the secret to obtaining an alternate identity is to obtain

an unquestionably valid birth certificate in another name," adding that the certificate should belong to someone who died long before "he became entangled in this paper morass that many of us are now trying to escape." Jay Jaroslav, letter to Gordon Matta-Clark, 4 September 1972. Estate of Gordon Matta-Clark, on deposit at the Canadian Centre for Architecture (CCA), Montreal.

86. The first Congressional acknowledgment of identity theft was "The Identity Theft and Assumption Deterrence Act," Senate Report No. 105–274, 1998. www.congress.gov/congressional-report/105th-congress/senate-report/274/1, accessed 5 February 2018.
87. Jaroslav, telephone communication with the author, 21 January 2018.
88. Kenneth Baker, "Art: Jay Jaroslav's Identity Crisis," *Boston Phoenix*, 8 May 1973.
89. Unsigned, "Historical Background of the People's Flag Show," undated. The Judson Memorial Church Archive, MSS 094, box 4, folder 50; Fales Library and Special Collections, New York University Libraries.
90. *Hendricks v. Hogan*, 324 F.Supp 1277 (S.D.N.Y. 1971).
91. "Discussions with Barry Le Va," *Avalanche* 3 (fall 1971): 75.
92. On Barry Le Va and his interest in the language and viewing practices of detective novels, see Michael Maizels, *Barry Le Va: The Aesthetic Aftermath* (Minneapolis: University of Minnesota Press, 2015), 37–40.
93. Dennis Oppenheim, quoted in Gavin Morrison and Fraser Stables, *Lifting: Theft in Art* (Aberdeen, UK: Atopia Projects, 2009), 45.
94. Jeannette Ingberman, *Illegal America* (New York: Exit Art Press, 1982), unpaginated.
95. Ibid. 18 U.S.C. 17 holds that anyone cutting, defacing, perforating or cementing together any bank bill, draft, or note issued by the Federal Reserve System "with intent to render such bank bill, draft, note, or other evidence of debt unfit to be reissued, shall be fined under this title or imprisoned not more than six months, or both."
96. John Perreault, "Crimes of the Art," *SoHo Weekly News*, 2 March 1982, 45.
97. Ibid.
98. Ernesto Menendez-Conde, "Art, Social Criticism and Mass Media: An Interview with John Perreault," *Art Experience NYC* 1(2) (spring 2011): 30.
99. Perreault, "Crimes of the Art," 45.
100. Ann Messner, telephone communication with the author, 6 October 2017.
101. Ann Messner, "Stealing at the Summer End Sale," *Lifting: Theft in Art*, 34.
102. Acconci, quoted in *Illegal America*.
103. Bruce Mitchell, "Body Art: A Legal Policy Analysis," in *Law, Ethics and the Visual Arts*, vol. 1, ed. John Henry Merryman and Albert E. Elsen (New York: M. Bender, 1979), 162–175.
104. Burden and his partner Nancy Rubins resigned from the faculty of UCLA after one of his students used a gun in a simulated performance of Russian roulette. Regarding the act as domestic terrorism, he demanded that the student be suspended. No criminal charges were pressed against the student. http://articles.latimes.com/2005/jan/22/local/me-profs22, accessed 11 July 2016.
105. Mitchell, "Body Art."
106. Jacques Derrida, "'Force of Law': The Mystical Foundation of Authority," trans. Mary Quaintance, *Cardozo Law Review* 11 (1989–1990): 231.
107. Kristine Stiles, *Concerning Consequences: Studies in Art, Destruction, and Trauma* (Chicago: University of Chicago Press, 2016), 171.
108. Burden argued that the university's failure to act "created a hostile and violent work environment." Quoted in Jenny Hontz, "Gunplay as Art Sets Off a Debate," *New York Times*, 5 February 2005.
109. Robert Horvitz, "Chris Burden," *Artforum* 14(9) (May 1976): 31.

110. Frazer Ward, "Gray Zone: Watching 'Shoot,'" *October* 95 (winter 2001): 125.
111. Michael Leja, *Looking Askance: Skepticism and American Art from Eakins to Duchamp* (Berkeley: University of California Press, 2004), 246.
112. Roberta J.M. Olson, "A Fence in Name Only and an Interview with Christo," *SoHo Weekly News*, 14–20 October 1976, 20.
113. Bleistein v. Donaldson Lithographing Co., 188 U.S. 239 (1903).
114. On the development of a conceptual art market in Western Europe, see Sophie Richard, *Unconcealed, the International Network of Conceptual Artists 1967–77: Dealers, Exhibitions, and Public Collections* (London: Ridinghouse, 2009).
115. Judith Malina, cofounder of the Living Theatre, the oldest experimental theater in the United States, recalls Projansky and Ordover collaborating in 1968 on a memorandum outlining basic legal rights for actors of the Living Theater to consult when apprehended by the police. Malina, *The Enormous Despair* (New York: Random House, 1972), 21. About Ordover's significance in the New York art world, see Richard Kostelanetz, *Artists' Soho: 49 Episodes of Intimate History* (New York: Fordham University Press, 2014), 231–233.
116. Scott Hodes, *The Law of Art & Antiques: A Primer for Artists and Collectors* (Dobbs Ferry, NY: Oceana, 1966). According to Hodes, the 1966 edition sold around 7,500 copies. Telephone conversation with the author, 5 January 2017.
117. John Henry Merryman, "Art and the Law: Part I A Course in Art and the Law," *Art Journal* 34(4) (summer 1975): 332.
118. Examples include Franklin Feldman and Stephen E. Weil, *Art Works: Law, Policy, Practice* (New York: Practicing Law Institute, 1974); Leonard DuBoff, *Deskbook of Art Law* (Washington, DC: Federal Publications, 1977); and Stephen E. Weil, *Beauty and the Beasts: On Museums, Art, the Law, and the Market* (Washington, DC: Smithsonian Institution Press, 1983). Weil was an attorney who became the deputy director of the Hirshhorn Museum in 1974; that same year, DuBoff, then a professor at Lewis and Clark Law School, organized the first national conference on art law.
119. Peter Bürger, *Theory of the Avant-Garde,* trans. Michael Shaw (Minneapolis: University of Minnesota Press, 1984), 22. Originally published in German in 1974.
120. A particularly eloquent instance of art history putting law on metaphorical trial is Richard Meyer's discussion of the Mapplethorpe case. Richard Meyer, *Outlaw Representation: Censorship and Homosexuality in Twentieth-Century American Art* (New York: Oxford University Press, 2002), 159–224.
121. John J. Costonis, "Law and Aesthetics: A Critique and a Reformulation of the Dilemmas," *Michigan Law Review* 80 (January 1982): 373–377. U.S. courts in the early twentieth century rejected government efforts to police aesthetics, which they characterized as subjective preferences.
122. Ibid., 411.
123. Arthur C. Danto, *The Abuse of Beauty: Aesthetics and the Concept of Art* (Chicago: Open Court, 2003), 27.
124. Elaine Scarry, *On Beauty and Being Just* (Princeton, NJ: Princeton University Press, 2001), 39.
125. T.J. Clark, "On the Social History of Art," in *Image of the People: Gustave Courbet and the 1848 Revolution* (Berkeley: University of California Press, 1999), 15. First published in 1973.
126. Connie Samaras, "Feminism, Photography, Censorship and Sexually Transgressive Imagery: The Work of Robert Mapplethorpe, Joel-Peter Witkin, Jacqueline Livingston, Sally Mann, and Catherine Opie," *New York Law School Law Review* 38 (1993): 82. The quote on Mapplethorpe's work is taken from the reported court testimony of Janet Kardon, who organized "Robert Mapplethorpe: The Perfect Moment" in 1987.
127. Christine Haight Fairley, "Judging Art," *Tulane Law Review* 79(4) (March 2005): 805, 849.

128. *Miller v. United States* 431 F.2d 655 (9th Cir. 1970).
129. The jury acquitted the CAC and Barrie after less than two hours' deliberation.
130. For an accessible introduction to the history of the law and humanities movement, see Austin Sarat, Matthew Anderson, and Catherine O. Frank, "Introduction: On the Origins and Prospects of the Humanistic Study of Law," in *Law and Humanities: An Introduction,* ed. Austin Sarat, Matthew Anderson, and Catherine O. Frank (New York: Cambridge University Press, 2010), 1–46.
131. Important discussions include *Law and the Image: The Authority of Art and the Aesthetics of Law,* ed. Costas Douzinas and Lynda Nead (Chicago: University of Chicago Press, 1999), one of the first and most influential anthologies tracking the relationship between visual images and the law from antiquity to the present; Richard Sherwin, *Visualizing Law in the Age of the Digital Baroque: Arabesques and Entanglements* (New York: Routledge, 2011), notable for urging jurists to cultivate stronger visual literacy in light of how communication occurs through visual, as well as verbal, means; and Peter Goodrich, *Legal Emblems and the Art of Law* (Cambridge: Cambridge University Press, 2015), on the role and authority of emblems in legal judgment.
132. For a probing discussion of the use of visual images in case opinions, see Elizabeth Porter, "Taking Images Seriously," *Columbia Law Review* 114 (2014): 1687–1782.
133. Amy Adler, "Fair Use and the Future of Art," 610–618.
134. Rebecca Tushnet, "Worth a Thousand Words: The Images of Copyright Law," *Harvard Law Review* 125 (January 2012): 758.
135. See, for example, Nancy Troy, *The Afterlife of Piet Mondrian* (Chicago: University of Chicago Press, 2013); Marjorie Heins and Tricia Beckles, *Will Fair Use Survive? Free Expression in the Age of Copyright Control* (New York: Brennan Center for Justice, NYU, 2005), 23; Michael Corris, "Immortality Sucks! How the Estate of the Artist Writes History," *Art Journal* 76(1) (summer 2017), 158–169; and Steve Westbrook, "A Refrain of Costly Fires: Visual Rhetoric, Writing Pedagogy and Copyright Law," in *Composition and Copyright: Perspectives on Teaching, Text-Making, and Fair Use,* ed. Steve Westbrook (Albany: State University of New York Press, 2009), 98, 106. In Julian Stallabrass's *High Art Lite: British Art in the 1990s,* permission denial was indicated by blank squares with the legend "Permission to reproduce denied." A classic essay on the burden of proof in defamation suits is Marc A. Franklin and Daniel J. Bussel, "The Plaintiff's Burden in Defamation: Awareness and Falsity," *William and Mary Law Review* 25(5) (1984): 825–889.
136. The vast majority of image guardians I have encountered have been models of cooperation and, often, generosity. However, it is not uncommon to pay anywhere from $70 per image to upwards of $1,000, especially when the image and copyright sources differ. Given the need for high-quality illustrations in art historical scholarship and the nonprofit (indeed, profit hemorrhaging) nature of most academic publications, such fees are nothing short of usurious.
137. Art historian and dealer Bendor Grosvenor suggests that a class-action lawsuit against museums charging scholars costly fees to reproduce images of artworks in their collections might address the issue of "copyright overreach" affecting the production of scholarship. Bendor Grosvenor, "How to Identify a Wreck," *The Art Newspaper,* 18 December 2017. http://theartnewspaper.com/blog/diary-of-an-art-historian, accessed 18 December 2017.
138. James Boyd White, *The Edge of Meaning* (Chicago: University of Chicago Press, 2001), xii.
139. In 2008, Christo and Jeanne-Claude received the annual Great Negotiator Award from Harvard Law School's Program on Negotiation.
140. *Kelley v. Chicago Park District,* No. 1:04-cv-07715 (N.D.Ill. 2008).
141. Ibid. Coar's decision, however, was later overturned by the 7th Circuit, which took a more literal view of VARA, stating that the wildflower display did not qualify for VARA protection because it did not explicitly conform to any of the media named in the statute. *Kelley v. Chicago Park District,* nos. 08–3701 and 08–3712 (7th Cir., 2011).

142. David Coar, telephone communication with the author, 2 November 2016.
143. Examples of this expanding body of scholarship include Alison Young, *Judging the Image: Art, Value, Law* (New York and London: Routledge, 2005), which proposes that images, particularly photographs, are points where identifications shaped by legal beliefs are made; and Sonia Katyal's study on intellectual property, advertising, and contemporary art (forthcoming from Yale University Press).
144. Peter H. Karlen, "Art in the Law," *Leonardo* 14(1) (winter 1981): 51. Also see Karlen, "Legal Aesthetics," *British Journal of Aesthetics* 19 (1979): 195–212, for a similar discussion of the relationship between art and law in Great Britain.
145. Quoted in "Vito Acconci by Richard Prince," *Bomb Magazine* 36 (summer 1991), http://bombmagazine.org/article/1443/vito-acconci, accessed 28 September 2015. *Cariou v. Prince*, 714 F. 3d 694 (2d Cir. 2013) considered whether Prince's use of Patrick Cariou's photographs qualified as fair use or if they infringed the latter's copyright. Although the case eventually settled out of court in 2014, it provoked extensive debate as to the legal status of appropriation. For a legal analysis mindful of art historical concerns, see Adler, "Fair Use and the Future of Art," 559–625.

CHAPTER ONE. PARTNERS IN ADVOCACY

1. See, for example, Michelle O'Malley, *The Business of Art: Contracts and the Commissioning Process in Renaissance Italy* (New Haven, CT: Yale University Press, 2005), on how artistic activities in the Renaissance were shaped by legal frameworks, particularly through the language of contracts; Joseph Koerner, *The Moment of Self-Portraiture in German Renaissance Art* (Chicago: University of Chicago Press, 1993), 203–223, on how Albrecht Dürer sought to legally prevent the replication of his works in sixteenth-century Germany; and Frederic J. Schwartz, *The Werkbund: Design Theory and Mass Culture before the First World War* (New Haven, CT: Yale University Press, 2006), 147–212, discussing how the formation of authorial identity among industrial designers as authors in early twentieth-century Germany was profoundly mediated through developments in intellectual property law.
2. An example was the Artists Rights Association, an organization formed in New York that in 1974 held a sale of works accompanied by a resale contract. One of its founders, Judy Pendleton, was particularly active in the promotion and distribution of *The Artist's Reserved Rights Transfer and Sale Agreement.*
3. On the emergence of the Art Workers' Coalition and its political significance, see Julia Bryan-Wilson, *Art Workers: Radical Practice in the Vietnam War Era* (Berkeley: University of California Press, 2011).
4. Despite the AWC holding meetings at Paula Cooper's gallery, Cooper herself was not allowed to attend. Maria Eichhorn, "Interview with Paula Cooper," in *The Artist's Contract* (Köln: Buchhandlung Walther König, 2009), 231–251. Cooper sold Jackie Winsor's works using *The Artist's Reserved Rights Transfer and Sale Agreement.*
5. Milton Friedman, "The Social Responsibility of Business Is to Increase Its Profits," *New York Times Magazine,* 13 September 1970.
6. Siegelaub had initially approached Jerald Ordover to draft the contract. When the latter was unable to do so, Siegelaub asked Projansky. Eichhorn, "Interview with Robert Projansky," 231.
7. "The Upshot: What Is Your Opposite Job," *New York Times,* 8 August 2017. www.nytimes.com/interactive/2017/08/08/upshot/what-is-your-opposite-job.html?_r = 1, accessed 8 August 2017. According to the site, the opposite of a historian is a lumberjack.
8. "Summary Report for: 19–2012.00—Physicists," *O*Net Online,* www.onetonline.org/link/summary/19–2012.00, accessed 8 August 2017. For a detailed survey of the Occupational Information Network, see Nancy T. Tippins and Margaret L. Hilton, eds., *A Database for a Changing*

*Economy: Review of the Occupational Information Network (O*Net)* (Washington, DC: National Academies Press, 2010).

9. "Summary Report for: 27–1013.00—Fine Artists, Including Painters, Sculptors, and Illustrators," *O*Net Online*, www.onetonline.org/link/summary/27–1013.00, accessed 8 August 2017.
10. *Kuwabara v. U.S.*, 260 F. 104 (9th Cir., 1919) held that while aliens who were contracted laborers could be prevented from entering the United States, "professional actors, artists, lecturers, singers, nurses, ministers of any religious denomination, professors of colleges or seminaries, persons belonging to any recognized learned profession, or persons employed as domestic servants" could not.
11. *State v. Cohn*, 184 La. 53 (Supreme Court of Louisiana, 1936) held that skilled artisans whose jobs required more manual than intellectual labor should be exempt from an occupational license tax. In *Matter of Voorhees v. Bates* (308 N.Y. 184, 1954) the first case ever decided by the New York Court of Appeals involving "one of the arts," the bar for artists seeking to prove professional status was flexible. "Recognizing the realities of artistic development," the court took length of training into account but not "advanced formal education."
12. David M. Sokol, "The Founding of Artists Equity Association after World War II," *Archives of American Art* 39(1–2) (1999): 23–24.
13. On the history and impact of the amended law, see Aaron Shkuda, *The Lofts of SoHo: Gentrification, Art, and Industry in New York, 1950–1980* (Chicago: University of Chicago Press, 2016), 101–105.
14. For a selection of Maciunas's published thoughts on nonart from 1964 to 1965, see Jon Hendricks, ed., *Fluxus etc./Addenda II: The Gilbert and Lila Silverman Collection* (Pasadena: Baxter Art Gallery and California Institute of Technology, 1983), 165–167.
15. Shkuda, *Lofts of SoHo*, 141. The artist certification committee included artists and nonartists as well as dealers.
16. *Louis H. Porter*, 437 F.2d 39 (2d Cir. 1971).
17. *Porter v. Commissioner*, 28 T.C.M. 1489 (1969).
18. Attracting renewed interest in the early 1970s were earlier artist collectives such as the Artists' Union, active in New York City in the 1930s. Gerald M. Monroe, "The Artists Union of New York," *Art Journal* 32(1) (autumn 1972): 17–20. For an incisive discussion of the ideological landscape that gave rise to the Artists' Union, see Andrew Hemingway, *Artists on the Left: American Artists and the Communist Movement 1926–1956* (New Haven, CT: Yale University Press, 2008), 75–188.
19. Bryan-Wilson, *Art Workers*, 56.
20. "Interview with Jean Toche, Co-Founder, Guerilla [*sic*] Art Action Group," www.as-ap.org/content/oral-history-interview-jean-toche-3, accessed 10 July 2016.
21. William Proxmire, quoted by Michael Straight, "Reflections on a Golden Fleecing at the Arts Endowment," *Washington Post*, 16 October 1977. Straight was the NEA's acting director.
22. Sol LeWitt, "Paragraphs on Conceptual Art," *Artforum* 5(10) (summer 1967): 83; and Grace Glueck, "Bringing Back Beardsley," *New York Times*, 19 February 1967.
23. The text of the contract is reproduced in full in *Work from the 1960s by Edward Kienholz* (Washington, DC: Washington Gallery of Modern Art, 1967), 35–37.
24. In 1971, Rubin Gorewitz founded Artists' Rights Today, an organization that tried to introduce new legislation allowing artists to deduct the full market value of their work for donations to public institutions.
25. Not intended for sale, such reproductions would only be shown for a limited time. The contract specifies that they would be displayed only in "public, noncommercial galleries."
26. Lawrence Wechsler, ed., "Edward Kienholz," part of *Los Angeles Art Community: Group Portrait* (Los Angeles: University of California Art History Program, 1977), 452. Compare the prices of

the tableaux, which generally ranged from $10,000 to $37,500, with an asking price of $5,500 for one of his best-known works, *Backseat Dodge '38*. Pricelist, Virginia Dwan Gallery, 1964. The Dwan Gallery Archives, MSS.002; box 2, folder 48; Center for Curatorial Studies Library and Archives, Bard College.

27. In 1970, Hans Haacke had already looked to Kienholz's contract as a reference. Haacke, letter to Paul Maenz, 6 December 1970. Galerie Paul Maenz Köln records, 1956–1991 (bulk 1970–1990), Getty Research Institute, Research Library, accession no. 910066, box 16, folder 1.
28. Lawrence Scott Bauman, interview with John Henry Merryman, "Legal Control of the Fabrication and Marketing of Fake Paintings," *Stanford Law Review* 24(5) (May 1972): 935.
29. Robert Projansky, "The Perilous World of Art Law," *Juris Doctor* 4 (June 1974): 16.
30. The early history of the agreement's creation has been extensively discussed by Alexander Alberro, *Conceptual Art and the Politics of Publicity* (Cambridge, MA: MIT Press, 2003), 163–166.
31. For an overview of artworks as investments in the 1960s, see Sophie Cras, "Art as an Investment and Artistic Shareholding Experiments in the 1960s," *American Art* 27(1) (2013): 3–12.
32. See Roseanne Martorella, "Corporate Patronage of the Arts in the U.S.," in *Art and Business: An International Approach on Sponsorship*, ed. Roseanne Martorella (Westport, CT: Praeger, 1996), 17–28; and Marjory Jacobson, *Art for Work: The New Renaissance in Corporate Collecting* (Boston: Harvard Business School Press, 1993).
33. Some of Kosuth's early works, including *Grass, Vegetation, Green, Lawn* (1966), were unaccompanied by certificates of ownership because the artist confessed having "no understanding" of the problems that might arise by transfers of title. Kosuth, letter to Gerhard Sohst, 11 July 1978. Galerie Paul Maenz Köln records, 1956–1991 (bulk 1970–1990), Getty Research Institute, Research Library, accession no. 910066, box 12, folder 1.
34. Hans Haacke, letter to Paul Maenz, 14 April 1973. Galerie Paul Maenz Köln Records, Getty Research Institute, Research Library, box 16, folder 1.
35. See Maciunas, "Conditions for Performing Fluxus Compositions, Films and Tapes," c. 1965. Reproduced in "Aspects of Fluxus from the Gilbert and Lila Silverman Collection," *Art Libraries Journal* 8(3) (autumn 1983): 21.
36. Bob Watts, "Addendum to Pop-1964," 27 March–10 April 1971. Robert Watts Papers, 1883–1989, bulk 1940–1988, Research Library, Getty Research Institute, accession no. 2006.M.27, box 11, folder 16.
37. "Some hysterical outbursts have recently resulted from . . .," c. 1965, in "Aspects of Fluxus from the Gilbert and Lila Silverman Collection," 22.
38. In 1976, Matta-Clark priced a set of ten slides illustrating *Splitting* at $20. Two color prints called "Hole in Floor, N.J.—A & B," each 11 × 14 inches, were $600. Contract between Matta-Clark and Yvon Lambert for works on consignment, 25 October 1975. Estate of Gordon Matta-Clark, on deposit at the Canadian Centre for Architecture (CCA), Montreal.
39. Gordon Matta-Clark, letter to Joan Simon, 23 June 1976. Estate of Gordon Matta-Clark, on deposit at the CCA. Even after Matta-Clark's death, some dealers attempted to sell as Matta-Clark works contact sheets or photographs taken for documentation purposes. Lance Fung, facsimile to Klaus Lüpke, 10 June 1994, Holly Solomon Gallery records, c. 1948–2003. Archives of American Art, Smithsonian Institution, box 35.
40. "AWC Open Hearing," January 1969, quoted in Andrea Fraser, *Museum Highlights: The Writings of Andrea Fraser* (Cambridge, MA: MIT Press, 2007), 60.
41. Seth Siegelaub and Robert Projansky, "The Artist's Reserved Rights Contract: A Reply to Professor Benston." Siegelaub Papers, I.A.97, Museum of Modern Art Archives, New York. Gift of Seth Siegelaub and the Stichting Egress Foundation, Amsterdam.

42. Berne Convention for the Protection of Literary and Artistic Works, 9 September 1886, Treaty Doc. No. 27, 99th Cong., 2d Sess. 41 (1986). France and Germany had moral rights protection for artists even before signing the Berne Convention. On the early history of artists' moral rights in France, see Georges Michaélidès-Nouaros's classic study, *Le Droit Moral de l'Auteur* (Paris: Librarie Arthur Rousseau, 1935). The U.S. signed the convention in 1998.

43. Consider, for example, the contract issued by Multiples Inc., the company that published and distributed boxes of photographs for the group exhibition "Artists and Photographs," organized by the critic Lawrence Alloway in 1970. The company sent a contract to numerous artists, including Jan Dibbets, Douglas Huebler, Sol LeWitt, Joseph Kosuth, and Robert Smithson. One hundred dollars was offered in exchange for "all rights including copyright for the material you have sent to us." Siegelaub, who called the arrangement "pure bullshit," was especially upset by the rate of return for the organizers, who would net roughly $30,000 for the sale of editions produced for the exhibition, having invested only $2,000. Seth Siegelaub, letter to Jerry Ordover, 5 February 1970. Siegelaub Papers, I.D.27, Museum of Modern Art Archives, New York.

44. *Crimi v. Rutgers Presbyterian Church,* 89 N.Y.S. 2d 813 (N.Y. Sup. Ct. 1949).

45. Even as late as 1987, artists sometimes transferred copyright to buyers. An example is Bruce Nauman's certificate for his 1987 video installation, *Clown Torture*. He stated that "copyright becomes the possession of the purchaser."

46. Sokol, "Founding of Artists Equity Association," 17.

47. John F. Kennedy, "The Candidates and the Arts," *Saturday Review,* 29 October 1960, 44.

48. Bauman, interview with John Henry Merryman, "Legal Control of the Fabrication and Marketing of Fake Paintings," 935. Bauman proposed the creation of an art registry that would house certificates of authenticity as a means of deterring forgeries (ibid., 939).

49. Franklin Feldman, "New Protection for the Art Collector—Warranties, Opinions, and Disclaimers," *The Record* 23(9) (December 1968): 662. In 1970, the California Sale of Fine Prints Act (the "Farr Act") was passed to enable prospective purchasers to make informed decisions about the value of a modern print. The act imposed on print dealers "the burden of disclosure or disclaimer of certain details relevant to the print's value." See, for example, *Tunick v. Kornfeld,* 838 F. Supp. 848, 851 (S.D.N.Y. 1993) and *Grogan-Beall v. Ferdinand Roten Galleries, Inc.*, 133 Cal. App. 3d 969, 972 (1982) (upholding the Farr Act but decertifying a class in an action by a purchaser against a gallery for failure to comply with the act's disclosure-disclaimer provisions).

50. Louis Lefkowitz, *Supplemental Memorandum of Attorney General in Support of Legislation Amending Article 12-C of the General Business Law Relating to the Artist-Art Dealer Relationship.* Senate Intro. No. 4375A, 6.

51. Ibid., 15.

52. Ibid., 13.

53. Lefkowitz, Senate Intro No. 4375A, Box 9, unnumbered folder, "Art Legislation, 1959–1973," New York Artists Equity Association records, 1920–2012. Archives of American Art, Smithsonian Institution.

54. Peter Plagens and Daniel Schneider, "Cents and Sensibility: Collecting the '80s," *Artforum* 41(8) (2003): 212.

55. Scott Hodes, "'Fake' Art and the Law," *Federal Bar Journal* 27 (1967): 73. Even in the late 1950s, certificates of authenticity did not seem to be common; "the custom of trade" was to be satisfied with a bill of sale.

56. Alvin S. Lane, "How the Bar Can Assist the Art Community," *The Record* 20(9) (December 1965): 5.

57. Although the unnamed dealer refused to disclose who had undertaken the forgery or from where the work was acquired, he or she refunded to Lane the purchase price. Alvin Lane, "My Perspec-

tive on Collecting," *The Terese and Alvin S. Lane Collection: Twentieth-Century Sculpture and Sculptors' Works on Paper* (Madison, WI: Elvehjem Museum of Art, 1995), 12.

58. N.Y. Gen. Bus. Law art. 12-F, § 219-h(c). (McKinney Supp. 1977–1978).
59. For an overview of U.S. cases regarding misrepresentation in the sale of artwork, see Patty Gerstenblith, "Picture Imperfect: Attempted Regulation of the Art Market," *William and Mary Law Review* 29(3) (1988): 501–566.
60. Michel Claura, letter to Seth Siegelaub, 6 January 1971. Siegelaub Papers, I.A.92, Museum of Modern Art Archives, New York.
61. Anna C. Chave, "Sculpture, Gender, and the Value of Labor," *American Art* 24(1) (spring 2010): 26–27. Jackie Winsor also observed that the *Agreement* appeared at a time when it was assumed that "women's work would never sell." Eichhorn, "Interview with Jackie Winsor," in *The Artist's Contract*, 182. Dorothea Rockburne was among those who agreed to use the *Agreement*. Seth Siegelaub, letter to Michel Claura, 15 June 1971. Siegelaub Papers, I.A.92, Museum of Modern Art Archives, New York.
62. Eichhorn, "Interview with Jackie Winsor," 185.
63. For an annotated compilation of sources regarding coverture in the United States, see Claudia Zaher, "When a Woman's Marital Status Determined Her Legal Status: A Research Guide on the Common Law Doctrine of Coverture," *Law Library Journal* 94(3) (2002): 459–486.
64. Cady Noland successfully used an abbreviated version of the *Agreement* with the additional provision that 15 percent of any gross resale profit realized be donated to Partnership for the Homeless, a charity established in 1983 to support the homeless, and that the buyer will not exhibit the work publicly without Noland's written consent. "Transfer and Sale Agreement," 16 April 1992; Colin de Land, American Fine Arts Co., and Pat Hearn Gallery Archives, MSS.008; box 14, folder 826, Center for Curatorial Studies Library and Archives, Bard College.
65. Seth Siegelaub, "Artists' Reserved Rights Transfer and Sale Agreement," *Studio International* 181 (April 1971): 144.
66. For an extended discussion of the *Agreement*'s shortcomings from a legal perspective, see Franklin Feldman and Stephen E. Weil, *Art Works: Law, Policy, Practice (Materials and Commentary)* (New York: Practising Law Institute, 1974), 95–97.
67. Monroe Price, "Government Policy and Economic Security for Artists: The Case of the Droit de Suite," *Yale Law Journal* 77(7) (June 1968): 1366. Price was closely involved with the Los Angeles art world, having founded Advocates of the Arts in 1974, which provided artists and arts organizations with legal and management services, and later serving as a board member of the Los Angeles Institute of Contemporary Art. One of the earliest clients of Advocates of the Arts was Suzanne Lacy, who solicited legal assistance in drafting a binding contract allowing buyers to purchase her body organs as artworks. Ed Ruscha claimed that Price "has taken [the protection of work] as a cause." Alexandra Schwartz, ed., *Leave Any Information at the Signal: Writings, Interviews, Bits, Pages* (Cambridge, MA: MIT Press, 2002), 135.
68. European collectors were reluctant as well; in one case, a prospective buyer told Hans Haacke it would only use the *Agreement* if it was translated into German. Hans Haacke, letter to Paul Maenz, 15 May 1971. Galerie Paul Maenz Köln Records, Getty Research Institute, Research Library, box 16, folder 1. Another collector, Peter Ludwig, expressed "outrage" at having to use the *Agreement* when buying *Manet PROJEKT 74*. Maria Eichhorn, "Interview with Hans Haacke," in *The Artist's Contract*, 76. The effect of not signing this contract would adversely affect Ludwig's future efforts to buy Haacke's art.
69. Rubin Gorewitz was among the few who supported the *Agreement* as an inherent guarantee of provenance and title. He argued it would consequently reduce the risk of theft. Michael McGrinder, "Artists' Rights Association," *SoHo Weekly News*, 31 October 1974, 10. However, even

well-known artists like Carl Andre suffered some losses by insisting that buyers agree to pay royalties.

70. In 1990, the dealer Colin de Land sent the artist Cady Noland a letter outlining what he considered "standard" art-world practice regarding artist-dealer relationships, including crediting photographs to the gallery, splitting the proceeds of any sale by half, and promising that all sales and loans be processed through a gallery. Colin de Land, letter to Cady Noland, 5 May 1989; American Fine Arts, Co., and Pat Hearn Gallery Archives, MSS.008, box 15, folder 884, Center for Curatorial Studies Library and Archives, Bard College. In response, Noland may have sent de Land a copy of the *Agreement;* de Land did not respond.
71. Seth Siegelaub and Robert Projansky, "The Artist's Reserved Rights Contract: A Reply to Professor Benston." Siegelaub Papers, I.A.97, Museum of Modern Art Archives, New York. Projansky later speculated that the *Agreement* would work only if "powerful dealers" adopted it. Eichhorn, "Interview with Robert Projansky," *The Artist's Contract,* 235.
72. Diane B. Schulder, "Art Proceeds Act: A Study of the Droit de Suite and a Proposed Enactment for the United States," *Northwestern Law Review* 61(1) (1966): 19–45. Siegelaub had a copy of this article.
73. Wayne La Com, "The Artist as a Non-Joiner," *AFEA Newsletter* 1(2) (summer 1973), unpaginated.
74. Artists who initially agreed to use the *Agreement* included Carl Andre, Sol LeWitt, Mario Merz, Dorothea Rockburne, Hans Haacke, Robert Rauschenberg, Mel Bochner, Brice Marden, Douglas Huebler, Robert Ryman, and Joseph Beuys. Seth Siegelaub, letter to Michel Claura, 15 June 1971. Siegelaub Papers, I.A.92, Museum of Modern Art Archives, New York.
75. Joanna Rees, "Viewings," *SoHo Weekly News,* 6 December 1973, 9. A notable exception was artist Kristine Holm, who implied that a resale rights requirement doubled as insurance for collectors by giving artists an incentive to inform collectors of the existence of duplicate works. Kristine M. Holm, "Do unto Artists," *Los Angeles Times,* 17 December 1978.
76. See Lucy Lippard, *Six Years: The Dematerialization of the Art Object from 1966 to 1972; A Cross-Reference Book of Information on Some Esthetic Boundaries* (New York: Praeger, 1973).
77. Seth Siegelaub, letter to David Shirey, undated. Siegelaub Papers, I.D.27, Museum of Modern Art Archives, New York.
78. Ibid.
79. Lippard, ix.
80. 17 U.S.C. Section 102(a) (1988).
81. Cited in John Slyce, "The Contract," *Art Monthly* 328(11–13) (July–August 2009): 12.
82. Lawrence Weiner, postcard to Seth Siegelaub, c. 1970s (?), Museum of Modern Art Archives, New York.
83. Ibid.
84. Robert Barry, letter to Paul Maenz, c. January–March 1971; Galerie Paul Maenz Köln records, Getty Research Institute, Research Library, box 16, folder 1.
85. Clifford Schaffer, letter to Giuseppe Panza, 21 June 1974. Giuseppe Panza Papers, 1956–1990, Getty Research Institute, Research Library, accession no. 940004, box 174, folder 27.
86. For an overview of art investment funds, particularly their proliferation in the 1970s, see Noah Horowitz, *Art of the Deal: Contemporary Art in a Global Financial Market* (Princeton, NJ: Princeton University Press, 2011). Art investment became yet another source of fraud; among the more creative was the "Guaranteed Investment Collection" fund offered by the Daniel Grossman Gallery. Participants could buy artworks Grossman owned with the option of reselling the work to him after ten years should they not like the works. Ken Friedman remarked on the scheme's absurdity, which allowed Grossman to use participants' original investment as an interest-free loan. "Putting out $100,000 for a decade to get $100,000 back after they've been

ravaged by inflation? That, to quote Tom Wolfe, is a laugh and a half." Ken Friedman, "The Art Economist," *Art Information Service* 2(1) (13 January, 1982): 3.

87. *John R. Thompson Co. v. United States,* 477 F.2d 164 (7th Cir. 1973).

88. Perhaps the most dramatic protest of tax law by an artist was when Arizona artist Ettore (Ted) de Grazia burned an estimated $1.5 million worth of paintings in 1976 to ensure that his heirs would not have to pay estate taxes on the works' full market value. The incident was widely reported in the popular media, cited by legal scholars and even in the *Congressional Record,* the official publication documenting the proceedings of Congress. "Congressional Record-Senate," 6 March 1981, *Congressional Record: The Debates and Proceedings in the Congress of the United States* (Washington, DC: U.S. Government Printing Office, 1981), 3768.

89. Robert Rauschenberg, undated statement, c. 1979, "W+N: Writings: Political and Social: Artist Tax Equity, 1976, 1979," Robert Rauschenberg Foundation Archives, New York.

90. Jeffrey C. McCarthy, "Federal Income Taxation of Fine Art," *Cardozo Arts and Entertainment Law Journal* 2(1) (1983): 63.

91. Letter to Siegelaub from Eugene Schwartz, 4 February 1971. Siegelaub Papers, I.A.99, Museum of Modern Art Archives, New York.

92. Ibid. Schwartz was quoted in James Servin, "SoHo Stares at Hard Times," *New York Times,* 20 January 1991.

93. Lawrence Weiner discussed how obligations should be as much a part of ownership as rights. Quoted in *Avalanche* 4 (1972): 69.

94. The lawyer Robert Rie told Siegelaub that the *Agreement* could work only if its provisions were a federal matter, one that potentially involved registering artworks as if they were patents or trademarks. Robert Rie, letter to Siegelaub, 5 February 1971. Siegelaub Papers, I.A.99, Museum of Modern Art Archives, New York.

95. *The Artist's Reserved Rights Transfer and Sale Agreement* was also discussed in John Henry Merryman's inaugural art law case, "A Course in Art and the Law," *Journal of Legal Education* 26(4) (1973): 554; and Thomas Kennerly Carroll Jr., "Statutory Copyright: A Valuable Right for the Visual Artist Part I," *Georgia Law Review* 7(1) (fall 1972): 143–146. In his extended analysis of the *Agreement,* Carroll speculates that the policy arguments for upholding the resale provision (promoting the arts in general and the economic welfare of individual artists) would not convince judges likely to see the provision as an "unreasonable restraint of trade."

96. Examples included Tad Crawford, *Legal Guide for the Visual Artist* (New York: Hawthorn, 1977); Robert E. Duffy, *Art Law: Representing Artists, Dealers, and Collectors* (New York: Practicing Law Institute, 1977); and Leonard Duboff, *The Deskbook of Art Law* (Washington, DC: Federal Publications, 1978). Also see Richard Weiner, "The Artist and His Gallery: Legal Agreements That Work," *American Artist* 38(378) (January 1974): 22–27.

97. The subcommittee referred to the *Agreement* as a uniform contract drafted by the nonprofit group Volunteer Lawyers for the Arts, but its discussion indicated that the contract in question was actually *The Artist's Reserved Rights Transfer and Sale Agreement.* See *Committee Reports of the ABA Section of Patent, Trademark, and Copyright Law* (Chicago: American Bar Association, 1974): 223–224.

98. Robert Hughes, "A Modest Proposal: Royalties for Artists," *Time,* 11 March 1974, 65; and George Benston, "Can Artists Share the Profit Their Work Earns?" *Wall Street Journal,* 21 April 1971. Discussing his documentary of the 1973 Scull auction, E.J. Vaughn wrote that the "the central issue of artist royalties . . . propelled me into the project." Edward Jeffrey Vaughn, *America's Pop Collector: Robert C. Scull, Contemporary Art at Auction,* Ph.D diss., University of Michigan, 1990, 55.

99. When a record price was paid for a work by Jasper Johns, an AWC member reportedly confronted Ethel Scull, asking whether she "ever resold a taxi" the way she resold art. Laurel Delp, "Tears, Money, Glitter," *SoHo Weekly News*, 24 October 1973, 7.

100. "People," *Time*, 29 October 1973. Ordover expressed similar indignation on behalf of Frank Stella in *Factor v. Stella* when the buyer held the artist accountable for his work not fetching a high enough price at auction even though the buyer had purchased the work directly from Stella at a much lower price. Letter to Irwin Spiegel from Jerry (Jerald) Ordover, 9 April 1975. Frank Stella Papers, 1941–1993, bulk 1978–1989. Archives of American Art, Smithsonian Institution, series 1, box 2.

101. Baruch D. Kirschenbaum, "The Scull Auction and the Scull Film," *Art Journal* 39(1) (fall 1979): 53. The confrontation between Rauschenberg and Scull was in marked contrast to Scull's fury in another scene where a young man, possibly a reporter, accuses the collector of profiteering. Reportedly Scull yelled back, "Who the hell do you think you're talking to?"

102. Scull would later be cited for his willingness to sign the *Agreement* as a means of further securing the value of his artwork holdings.

103. Karl Marx, *Capital*, vol. 3 (New York: Penguin, 1981), 515.

104. *Tobey v. Commissioner of Internal Revenue*, 60 T.C. 277 (1973).

105. The U.S. Tax Court analogized Tobey's work to farming. Farmers sold tangible goods that were the result of personal effort; any sales qualified as "earned income." The most detailed analysis of the Tobey ruling is Renato Beghe, "The Artist, the Art Market and the Income Tax," *Tax Law Review* 29 (1973–1974): 491–524. In 1979, the Supreme Court of Kansas expressly regarded artists as service providers, especially if the artwork had yet to be realized. A contract with an artist for a painting was "the rendition of service with goods incidentally involved." *Care Display, Inc. v. Didde-Glaser, Inc.* 225 Kan. 232 (Supreme Court of Kansas, 1979).

106. In 1971, Rauschenberg established Change, a foundation that would provide emergency grants to artists in need and that tried to negotiate better health insurance premiums for artists.

107. "Statement of Senator Jacob K. Javits on [the] Introduction of the Artists Tax Equity Act of 1979," 3, Robert Rauschenberg Foundation Archives, New York.

108. Rubin Gorewitz, "For Artists' Rights," *Art-Rite* 6 (summer 1974), 12.

109. Gorewitz considered proposing a barter tax system in which artists could pay taxes in artworks rather than cash. Other proposals included limiting the resale provision to only works bought after a certain date and extending its duration to include not only the life of the artist, but that of his or her partner. Ron Blumberg, "Report on November 22nd Meeting on AB1391," *AFEA Newsletter* 3(5) (December 1976): 3.

110. Rubin Gorewitz, "Artists' Royalties: Should There Be a Law?" *Art in America* 61(6) (November/December 1973): 23. Another important example was the National Employment Recovery Act of 1975, sponsored by Senator Claiborne Pell of Rhode Island, a major supporter of federal aid to the arts who played a major role in establishing the National Endowment of the Arts and the National Endowment for the Humanities. Pell wanted to fund the arts in the way they were supported during the Great Depression; his bill was cosponsored by Representative Edward Beard, who was a housepainter before entering politics.

111. The full text of the law is contained in California Civil Code §986.

112. The resale fee would be 7 percent of the difference between the purchase price and the selling price. Royalty payments would only be applicable for sales in excess of $500 and when the work's value had appreciated by at least 120 percent. "Statements on Introduced Bills and Joint Resolutions," *Congressional Record* 132(116) (9 September 1986): 2.

113. A California legislator since 1966, Alan Sieroty had written a number of art-specific laws beginning with the California Sale of Fine Prints Act of 1971, the first law in the United States to

regulate the sale of limited-edition prints by requiring sellers to disclose information that would help buyers make informed decisions about a print's value. Leith Johnson, draft interview with Senator Alan Sieroty, "P+E Activism: Artists' Rights: Proposed Legislation," Robert Rauschenberg Foundation Archives, New York.

114. Artists' Authorship Rights Act, ch. 994, 1983 N.Y. Laws 1933 (codified at N.Y. Arts and Cultural Affairs Law N. § 314.51–59 (McKinney 1984).

115. Rubin Gorewitz, letter to Ron Blumberg, 15 October 1976. "P+E Activism: Artists' Rights: General, 1973–1976," Robert Rauschenberg Foundation Archives, New York. Gorewitz ideally wanted to create an organization that would administer the royalty proceeds, reserving some of the fees for a general artists' welfare fund. The standard certificate of authenticity he proposed would give royalty recipients the option of contributing the royalty to a nonprofit organization assisting artists as a tax-deductible donation. Ever the accountant, Gorewitz argued that in cases involving substantial royalties, a donation would actually give the artist more take-home income by reducing her overall tax burden, thus putting her in a lower tax bracket than if she kept the royalties. Gorewitz in conversation with Roberta Loach, "The Artist and the Law," *Visual Dialog* 1(4) (June/July/August 1976): 37.

116. Gorewitz, quoted in Owen Findsen, "The Fight for Artists' Rights," *The Cincinnati Enquirer*, 23 May 1976.

117. Gorewitz in conversation with Roberta Loach, "The Artist and the Law," 38.

118. Leith Johnson, draft interview with Senator Alan Sieroty, "P+E Activism: Artists' Rights: Proposed Legislation" (unpublished).

119. John Henry Merryman, "The Wrath of Rauschenberg," *The American Journal of Comparative Law* 41(1) (winter 1993): 106.

120. Ibid., 126.

121. California Civil Code §986. Sieroty was himself among the few collectors known to actually honor the resale provision as of 1980. Carole M. Vickers, "The Applicability of the Droit de Suite in the United States," *Boston College International and Comparative Law Review* 3(2) (1980): 446, note 89.

122. In 2012, the CRRA was ruled unconstitutional by the U.S. District Court for the Central District in California in *Estate of Graham, et al., v. Sotheby's Inc.*, 60 F. Supp. 2d 1117 (C.D. Cal. 2012). Holding that the law violated the Commerce Clause of the U.S. Constitution, which effectively limits the power of individual states to encumber interstate commerce, the court ruled that the act burdens transactions taking place outside California by requiring royalties to be paid for sales of art taking place entirely outside California between parties not based or physically present in California. The Ninth Circuit effectively struck down the CRRA in 2018. *Close v. Sotheby's Inc.*, No. 16-56234 (9th Cir. 2018).

123. Tom R. Camp, "Art Resale Rights and the Art Resale Market: An Empirical Study," *Bulletin of the Copyright Society of the U.S.A.* 28 (1980): 146–183. Cited in John Henry Merryman, "The Wrath of Rauschenberg," *The American Journal of Comparative Law*, 41(1) (winter 1993): 106.

124. Rubin Gorewitz, "Artist Residuum Transposal," unpublished manuscript, undated. Irving Sandler Papers, 1914–2001, bulk 1950–2000, Getty Research Institute, Los Angeles, accession no. 2000.M.43, box 38, folder 48. Gorewitz also argued that the royalties would be tax deductible for collectors buying art for investment purposes.

125. Scull, quoted in Kiki Levathes, "Artists Find Friends in Fight for Rights," *New York Daily News*, 2 February 1975.

126. Quoted in Roberta Smith, "When Artists Seek Royalties on Their Resales," *New York Times*, 31 May 1987.

127. "Visual Artists Rights Act of 1987," H.R. 3221, Serial No. 104, 9 June 1988, 57. Renewed attention to resale payments, however, caused deep-seated friction within the art world. When the resale

royalty provision was reintroduced to Congress in 1987 as part of a bill by Senator Ted Kennedy, Elaine de Kooning urged R. Frederick Woolworth, head of the Art Dealers Association, to testify against the provision before Congress. She petitioned him to instead support legislation that would effectively permit the equivalent of a home-sale exclusion for artwork, whereby collectors could be exempted from paying tax on the proceeds gained from selling a work if they were used to buy another work by a living artist. Elaine de Kooning letter to R. Frederick Woolworth (Art Dealers Association of America, Inc.), 23 January 1988. Published in *H.R. 3221 Visual Artists Rights Act of 1987, Serial No. 104* (Washington, DC: U.S. Government Printing Office, 1989), 76. The tax exemption idea was Stephen Weil's, then deputy director of the Hirshhorn Museum. Stephen Weil, "Resale Royalties: Nobody Benefits," *Beauty and the Beasts* (Washington, DC: Smithsonian Press, 1983), 210–225.

128. *Visual Artists Rights Act of 1987*, 57.
129. McCarthy, "Federal Income Taxation of Fine Art," 4.

CHAPTER TWO. CIRCLING THE LAW

1. Charles Garoian, Roy Quan, and Dan Collins, "Christo: On Art, Education and the Running Fence," *Art Education* 30(2) (February 1977): 18.
2. Ibid., 19.
3. Hodes's father was Barnet Hodes, a leading Chicago attorney whose clients included the artist and arts patron William Copley.
4. Burt Chernow, *Christo and Jeanne-Claude: A Biography* (New York: St. Martin's Press, 2002), 224.
5. Barbaralee Diamonstein, "The Reminiscences of Christo and Jeanne-Claude Christo," Oral History Research Office, Columbia University, 1979, 18.
6. Julia Brown, "Interview Julia Brown and Michael Heizer," in *Michael Heizer: Sculpture in Reverse* (Los Angeles: Museum of Contemporary Art, 1984), 10; quoted by Suzaan Boettger, *Earthworks: Art and the Landscape of the Sixties* (Berkeley: University of California Press, 2002), 110.
7. Calvin Tomkins, "Onward and Upward with the Arts," *The New Yorker*, 28 March 1977, 61.
8. Diamonstein, *Reminiscences of Christo and Jeanne-Claude*, 18–19.
9. "Christo testing 'running fence' in Denver area," *Rocky Mountain News*, 17 January 1974.
10. Lloyd Wilson, who owned one of the parcels of land, insisted on a lease payment of $5,000 for property development purposes. The other owner, Stanley Kansgen, was described as being "almost flustered with the prospect of so much compensation [$2,400]." Jan van der Marck, "Summary of Visit to Rifle," 13 January 1971. The summary is published in Christo, *Christo: Valley Curtain* (New York: Harry N. Abrams, 1973), 31.
11. Jan van der Marck, "Trip to Rifle to Meet with Representatives BLM," 19 May 1971. Ibid.
12. More recently, Christo and Jeanne-Claude have established a limited liability company (LLC), a hybrid entity that allows for liability protection but without many of the restrictions traditionally associated with corporations. Although LLCs were formed by the late 1970s, they only became common in the mid-1990s. By 1996, every U.S. state had an LLC statute.
13. Van der Marck's reputation was a key reason for his selection as the director of the Museum of Contemporary Art Chicago. Jack Lind, "The Flying Dutchman of Contemporary Art," *Chicago Magazine* (spring 1969): 94.
14. Jesse Kornbluth, "La Vie de Boheme," *Savvy* (December 1983): 79.
15. Mrs. Frank O'Brien, letter to Jan van der Marck, 15 January 1969. "Christo: Wrap In Wrap Out" Exhibition Archive; Museum of Contemporary Art Chicago Archives, Chicago, box 4, folder 10.
16. Untitled document, Peter Howard Selz Papers, 1929–2014, bulk 1950–2005, Archives of American Art, Smithsonian Institution, reel 2344.

17. "Ephraim Ilin and the Modarco Fund: A Portfolio of Art Investments," *Art News* 72 (December 1973): 63–65.
18. Contract between Modarco and Christo, 23 July 1975. Burt Chernow Papers, 1930–2002, Archives of American Art, Smithsonian Institution, box 3.
19. Wolfgang Mieder, "'Good Fences Make Good Neighbors': History and Significance of an Ambiguous Proverb," *Folklore* 114(2) (August 2003): 168–171.
20. As denoted in the Estray Act of 1915.
21. For an example of this, see Ellickson's 1981 study of ranchers and fences in Shasta County, located some 250 miles from Sonoma County. Robert C. Ellickson, *Order without Law: How Neighbors Settle Disputes* (Cambridge, MA: Harvard University Press, 1991), 65–81. It is important to note that by the mid-20th century, the laws were shaped by long-standing custom.
22. *Ingwersen v. Barry*, 118 Cal. 342 (1897).
23. This definition stems from the Trespass Act of 1852, later codified in the California Food and Agricultural Code, Section 17121.
24. See Merrill S. Timmins, "Farmer's Bulletin, No. 2247," in *Fences for the Farm and Rural Home* (Washington, DC: U.S. Department of Agriculture, 1971).
25. John B. Jackson, "Barbed Wire and American West," in *Between Fences*, ed. Gregory K. Dreicer (New York: Princeton Architectural Press, 1997), 67.
26. Burt Chernow, unpublished interview with Jeanne-Claude and Christo, 16 August 1995, 379. Burt Chernow Papers, 1930–2002, Archives of American Art, Smithsonian Institution, box 3.
27. "Conversation with Christo: On *Running Fence* Project," *Domus* 549 (August 1975): 54.
28. Diamonstein, *Reminiscences of Christo and Jeanne-Claude*, 40.
29. Ibid.
30. Kevin Wallace, "The Fence Starts to Come Down," *San Francisco Chronicle*, 22 September 1976.
31. Paul Cummings, oral history interview with Christo, 28–30 August 1973, Archives of American Art, Smithsonian Institution.
32. Tomkins, "Onward and Upward with the Arts," 30–31.
33. Chernow, *Christo and Jeanne-Claude: A Biography*, 232.
34. *Environmental Impact Report* (Foster City, CA: Environmental Science Associates, 1975), 51.
35. Unsigned, "Editorials: Running Fence," *The Press Democrat*, 23 March 1975.
36. Mary Fuller, "What's in the Package: Is Christo Javacheff All Wrapped Up?" *Currant* 1(1) (April/May 1975): 56.
37. Rod Brewster, "Christo Running Fence Wins Board Approval," *Petaluma Argus-Courier*, 19 March 1975.
38. Ellickson, *Order without Law*, 78.
39. Lester Bruhn, "We don't like other people telling us what we can do," in Christo, *Christo: Running Fence* (New York: Abrams, 1978), 84.
40. Sample Easement Agreement, 2. Republished in *Environmental Impact Report*, 243.
41. Ibid.
42. Ibid., 244.
43. Unpublished notes from a conversation with Christo, 21 October 1971. Calvin Tomkins Papers, II.A. 35, Museum of Modern Art Archives, New York.
44. Chernow, *Christo and Jeanne-Claude: A Biography*, 232.
45. Cited in "The New Christo Project: Leaning Over the Running Fence," *Paris Review* 62 (July 1975): 136. By 1975, the steel posts used for the work's construction would be worth double what the artist had paid for them. Tim Findley, "Christo and the Battle of *Running Fence*," *City of San Francisco*, 13 July 1975.

46. Cited in Beth Coffelt, "The Curse of the Gawking Factor," *San Francisco Chronicle*, 4 July 1976.
47. Quoted in Jan van der Marck, "Introduction," *Christo—Wool Works* (Melbourne: National Gallery of Victoria, 1969), unpaginated.
48. Elizabeth C. Baker, "Artworks on the Land," *Art in America* 64(1) (January–February 1976): 96.
49. Ibid. (emphasis in original).
50. "Conversation with Christo: On *Running Fence* Project," 55.
51. Ibid.
52. Ibid.
53. Robert Morris, "Notes on Art as/and Land Reclamation," *October* 12 (spring 1980): 97.
54. Diamonstein, "Reminiscences of Christo and Jeanne-Claude Christo," 38; "Conversation with Christo: On *Running Fence* Project," 52.
55. Diamonstein, "Reminiscences of Christo and Jeanne-Claude Christo," 38.
56. One of Christo's attorneys, Paul Kayfetz, later sold photographs he took of the *Fence* for $250 each at Sonoma State College. Mary McChesney, letter to Calvin Tomkins, 8 November 1976. Tomkins Papers, II.A.66, Museum of Modern Art Archives, New York.
57. Ibid. Also reported by Charles Petit, "The Air Is Busy over Christo's Famed Fence," *San Francisco Chronicle*, 14 September 1976.
58. Charles L. Hamman, letter to Ernest Harris, 21 January 1974. Peter Howard Selz Papers, 1929–2014, bulk 1950–2005, Archives of American Art, Smithsonian Institution, reel 2344. A leaflet for permit applicants published by the California Coastal Zone Conservation Committee defines *structure* to mean "any building, road, pipe, flume, conduit, siphon, aqueduct, telephone line." Art was not explicitly mentioned, but the definition of *structure* was sufficiently broad as to potentially include works like *Running Fence*.
59. Ibid.
60. Peter Selz, letter to Christo, 7 March 1974 (on his discussions with the San Francisco Museum of Modern Art) and letter to Bill Rubin, 24 September 1974 (about a proposed Christo show at the Museum of Modern in Art New York). Peter Howard Selz Papers, 1929–2014, bulk 1950–2005, Archives of American Art, Smithsonian Institution, reel 2344.
61. Cited in "The New Christo Project: Leaning over the Running Fence," 136.
62. Tomkins, "Onward and Upward with the Arts," 10, 61.
63. Michael L. Fischer implied that state commissioners whom Christo targeted denied the artist his permit partly because of the negotiation tactics used. Michael L. Fischer, oral history interview, conducted in 1992 and 1993 by Ann Lage, Regional Oral History Office, University of California at Berkeley, for the California State Archives State Government Oral History Program, 78.
64. Staff Recommendation, California Coastal Zone Conservation Commission, Appeal no. 103–75, 5 July 1975.
65. Ibid. Mike Zagoroff, who had previously worked with Christo and Jeanne-Claude on their project for Documenta, observed that the engineers contracted to undertake the work did not take the project seriously, as indicated by their bringing outdated equipment and an insufficient kind and quantity of materials. Zagoroff, letter to Christo, 25 October 1971. Tomkins Papers, II.A.35, Museum of Modern Art Archives, New York. Christo himself remarked that "if I were General Motors, they would have never treated me that way." Unpublished notes from a conversation with Christo, 21 October 1971. Tomkins Papers, II.A.35, Museum of Modern Art Archives, New York.
66. Larry Richey, letter to Lewis A. Moran, acting director, Department of Conservation, 28 March 1975. Environmental Impact Statements, F3849:1813, California State Archives, Office of the Secretary of State, Sacramento.

67. "Conversation with Christo: On *Running Fence* Project," 54.
68. Tomkins, "Onward and Upward with the Arts," 80.
69. An example was Compadres de San Antonio, a corporation that possessed the westernmost portion of land traversed by *Running Fence*. Although it was blocked from developing its land, it permitted Christo to erect his work on it.
70. On the circumstances surrounding the formation of COAAST, see Richard Walker, *The Country in the City: The Greening of the San Francisco Bay Area* (Seattle: University of Washington Press, 2007), 194–196.
71. J.J. Dukeminier, "Zoning for Aesthetic Objectives: A Reappraisal," *Law and Contemporary Problems* 20(2) (1955): 219–220.
72. "Beauty may not be queen, but she is not an outcast beyond the pale of protection or respect. She may at least shelter herself under the wing of safety, morality, or decency." *Perlmutter v. Greene*, 259 N.Y. 327 (1932).
73. Dukeminier, 221.
74. Ibid., 226.
75. Zoning efforts were frequently and successfully challenged in courts to the point where at least one jurist argued for stricter standards of aesthetic review. Everett P. Priestley, "Beauty and the Police Power," *Colonial Lawyer* (1973): 10–12, 19.
76. In *Hutcherson v. Alexander*, the California Court of Appeal for the Fifth District held that obstructing the view of a property owner's premises was unlawful if that obstruction was intentional and permanent. 264 Cal. App. 2d 126 (1968).
77. Douglas Davis, "The Size of Non-Size," *Artforum* 15(4) (December 1976): 49.
78. "I'm not being paid to be a bit player in this guy's performance art, nor is my commission meant to be demeaned in this way, meant to be used or exploited in this way." Michael L. Fischer, oral history interview, conducted in 1992 and 1993 by Ann Lage, Regional Oral History Office, University of California at Berkeley, for the California State Archives State Government Oral History Program, 73.
79. Ibid., 74.
80. Ibid.
81. Section 2(c), Public Law 88–544 (16 U.S.C. 1131–1136), 3 September 1964.
82. Jan van der Marck, "Trip to Denver and Boulder with Christo," 7–9 April 1971, in *Christo: Valley Curtain*.
83. Suzaan Boettger, "Earthworks' Contingencies," in *Ethics and the Visual Arts*, ed. Elaine King and Gail Levin (New York: Allworth, 2006), 219–220.
84. Public Resource Code Sections 21100 and 21151 (1986).
85. Public Resource Code Section 21100 (1986).
86. *County of Inyo v. Yorty*, 32 Cal.App.3d 795 (1973).
87. California Coastal Zone Conservation Act of 1972.
88. *Friends of Mammoth v. Board of Supervisors of Moro County*, 8 Cal.3d 247 (1972).
89. Ibid.
90. Code of Ordinances, Sonoma County Municipal Code, Sections 23A-38.
91. *No Oil, Inc. v. City of Los Angeles*, 13 Cal.3d 68 (1974).
92. Ibid. The dissent was written by William P. Clark, with Marshall F. McComb and Louis H. Burke concurring.
93. California State Lands Commission Minute Item no. 8, 31 March 1975, 210.
94. The Regional Commission hearing was especially charged as its items of discussion included whether to sue Paul Kayfetz, one of Christo's attorneys, for failing to obtain a permit to repair his cliffside home. Both Kayfetz and Fischer claimed that the case had no bearing on *Running*

Fence. Don Stanley, "Annals of Ecology: Kayfetz vs. Fischer," California State Archives, Office of the Secretary of State, Sacramento.

95. North Central Coast Regional Commission Supplemental Staff Report, Permit #534, 24 April 1975. F3849:1813, California State Archives, Office of the Secretary of State, Sacramento.
96. Margaret Azevedo, Memorandum to North Central Coast Commissioners, 14 April 1975. F3849:1813, California State Archives, Office of the Secretary of State, Sacramento.
97. John P. Crevelli, Secretary of COAAST, letter to the North Central Coast Regional Commission, 8 April 1975. F3849:1813, California State Archives, Office of the Secretary of State, Sacramento.
98. Ibid.
99. In her self-published memoir, Jean Hinkle, COAAST member and the wife of Bill Hinkle, the chair of the Sonoma County Board of Supervisors, recounts that COAAST did not initially take sides in the debate regarding *Running Fence*: "Our only concern was the need to protect the coastal zone part of the route." It was this incident that triggered COAAST's "only philosophical rift." Jean Hinkle, *All Political Power* (Las Vegas: Chuck and Jean Hinkle, 1995), 449.
100. Staff Recommendation, California Coastal Zone Conservation Commission, Appeal no. 103–75, 5 July 1975.
101. Ibid.
102. Ibid.
103. "Artist's Fence Is Trimmed," *San Francisco Chronicle*, 19 June 1975.
104. Cited in *Running Fence Corp. v. Superior Court*, 51 Cal.App.3d 400 (1975).
105. Ibid.
106. Ibid.
107. Ibid.
108. Ibid.
109. Ibid.
110. Ibid.
111. Ibid.
112. Ibid., footnote 14.
113. Cited in "Christo: Plain and Fency," *Time* (20 September 1976): 74.
114. Ronald Raymond, letter to Sonoma County Board of Zoning Adjustments, 23 November 1975. Republished in *Final Environmental Impact Report: Running Fence* (Foster City, CA: Environmental Science Associates, 1975).
115. Doug Korty, transcript, "In the Matter of Christo Running Fence," 3 December 1975, 77. Republished in *Final Environmental Impact Report: Running Fence*.
116. Ibid., 2.
117. Ronald Raymond, letter to Sonoma County Board of Zoning Adjustments, 23 November 1975.
118. Tomkins, "Onward and Upward with the Arts," 68–69. Even those formerly affiliated with the Coastal Commission began to speak against the plan; a prominent example was John Mayfield, the former chairman of the North Coast Regional California Coastal Zone Conservation Commission, who decried the plan's "ludicrous" infringements on ownership. Quoted in Mark Raymond, "Mayfield Blasts Coastal Plan; Will Continue to Criticize," *Ukiah Daily Journal*, 29 August 1975.
119. California State Lands Commission Minute Item no. 4, 26 February 1976, 133.
120. California State Lands Commission Minutes, 26 February 1976, 19.
121. Ibid., 21.
122. Details of the construction were painstakingly documented in *Christo: Running Fence*.
123. Thomas Albright, "This Fence Isn't for Straddling," *San Francisco Chronicle*, 2 September 1976.
124. Jerry Carroll, "Wrap It Up and Throw It Away," *San Francisco Examiner and Chronicle*, 27 April 1975.
125. *Running Fence Corp. v. Superior Court*, 51 Cal.App.3d 400 (1975).

126. Mary Crawford, "Route Advice for the Compleat Fence Viewer," *San Francisco Chronicle,* 12 September 1976.
127. Tomkins, "Onward and Upward with the Arts," 73.
128. Ibid., 45.
129. Frank Broadhead, acting executive director of the Coastal Commission, Letter to Roger Green, counsel, U.S. Army Corps of Engineers, 29 September 1976. Box 3, Folder 1, California State Archives, Office of the Secretary of State, Sacramento.
130. Ibid.
131. Ibid.
132. Before working with Christo, Kayfetz made his living primarily as an expert witness and as a consultant; most of his legal work involved "tilting at environment winmills [*sic*]." Burt Chernow, telephone interview with Paul Kayfetz, 13 January 1996. Burt Chernow Papers, 1930–2002, Archives of American Art, Smithsonian Institution. Kayfetz claimed that Christo assured him that the work would fully comply with the law.
133. Ibid.
134. Scott Hodes, interview with Richard Holland, 14 May 2013, *Bad At Sports.* http://badatsports.com/2013/episode-402-attorney-scott-hodes-the-india-art-fair-2013-with-tanya-gill/, accessed 12 August 2015.
135. Scott Hodes, telephone conversation with the author, 5 January 2017. Hodes remarked that after suggesting the two-week period, Menary then turned to the California attorney general's representatives, asking if the proposed period "was all right with you?" The attorney general did not appeal Menary's decision.
136. Keith Wallace, "The Running Fence's Illegal Leap," *San Francisco Chronicle,* 8 September 1976.
137. Burt Chernow, telephone interview with Paul Kayfetz, 13 January 1996. Burt Chernow Papers, 1930–2002, Archives of American Art, Smithsonian Institution, box 3. Christo's broken promise did not stop Kayfetz, however, from taking photographs of the offending part of the work. Kayfetz also stated, "I'd of done the same thing [if I were Christo]." Ibid.
138. Alfred Frankenstein, "An Art Critic's View of the Fence," *San Francisco Chronicle,* 9 September 1976.
139. Tomkins, "Onward and Upward with the Arts," 45.
140. Ibid., 80.
141. Lynn Hershman, letter to Calvin Tomkins, 10 September 1976. Tomkins Papers, II.A.66, Museum of Modern Art Archives, New York.
142. Douglas Davis, "Esthetic Terrorism," *Newsweek,* 9 August 1976, 78.
143. Ted Dougherty, contractor for *Running Fence* and *Valley Curtain,* quoted in Chernow, *Christo and Jeanne-Claude: A Biography,* 254.
144. Tomkins, "Onward and Upward with the Arts," 80.
145. Jean Hinkle, *All Political Power,* 453. The board's demands seemed to have little effect on the political fortunes of at least two members: Charles Hinkle and Bill Kortum were voted out of office in June 1976.
146. Gordon Ashby, quoted in Coffelt, "Curse of the Gawking Factor."

CHAPTER THREE. CLAIMS FOR DEFIANCE

1. Gordon Matta-Clark, letter to Wolfgang Becker, 2 February 1976. Estate of Gordon Matta-Clark (EGMC), on deposit at the Canadian Centre for Architecture (CCA), Montreal.
2. Matta-Clark assisted Christo in building a model of *Valley Curtain.* In 1971, Matta-Clark made two works based on this model, *Mock Christo Curtain: Wall between Legs* and *Mock Christo Curtain: Wall in Hand.*

3. Undated draft, "Interview between Wall and Matta-Clark," EGMC, CCA, Montreal.
4. Matta-Clark, "Proposal for Anarchitecture," EGMC, CCA, Montreal. Republished in Gloria Moure and Gordon Matta-Clark, *Gordon Matta-Clark: Works and Collected Writings* (Barcelona: Ediciones Poligrafa, 2006), 383.
5. In his exhaustive history of U.S. property law, Gregory Alexander notes how the influential Welsh legal reformer James Humphreys observed that intangible things had replaced land as the primary "form of property" as early as 1826, due to high rates of urbanization and industrialization. Gregory Alexander, *Commodity and Propriety: Competing Visions of Property in American Legal Thought, 1776–1970* (Chicago: University of Chicago Press, 1997), 113, 259.
6. Felicity Scott, *Outlaw Territories: Environments of Insecurity/Architectures of Counterinsurgency* (New York: Zone Books, 2016), 110.
7. Lou Gottlieb, an owner of one of the properties declared "open land," quoted in the *Press Democrat* (1967). Scott, *Outlaw Territories*, 79.
8. Gordon Matta-Clark, Small Cards. EGMC, CCA, Montreal.
9. Gordon Matta-Clark, letter to Harold Stern, 10 July 1971. EGMC, CCA, Montreal. Republished in Stephen Walker, *Gordon Matta-Clark, Art, Architecture and the Attack on Modernism* (London: I.B. Tauris, 2009), 48.
10. Cited in Judith Russi Kirshner, letter to Gordon Matta-Clark, 25 May 1978. EGMC, CCA, Montreal.
11. Pamela Lee, *Object to Be Destroyed* (Cambridge, MA: MIT Press, 1999), x–xv.
12. Ibid., 112.
13. Leonard D. DuBoff, *Deskbook of Art Law* (Washington, DC: Federal Publications, 1977), 20, 24.
14. Lee, *Object to Be Destroyed*, 81. Original quote from "Splitting the Humphrey Street Building," interview by Liza Béar, May 1974, first published in *Avalanche* (December 1974): 34–37.
15. The most famous of these other buyers was Jack Gasnick, an eccentric hardware-store owner. The long-time "apartment-living" Manhattanite routinely bought gutterspace, including a plot with a single apple tree, to "get a share of the good environment," a relative scarcity for apartment-dwelling Manhattan residents. Quoted in Alastair Bonnett, *Off the Map: Lost Spaces, Invisible Cities, Forgotten Islands, Feral Places and What They Tell Us about the World* (London: Aurum, 2014), 147. Another buyer even collected such parcels to give as Christmas gifts to friends "who have just about everything else." Dan Carlinsky, "'Sliver' Buyers Have a Field Day at City Sales," *New York Times*, 14 October 1973.
16. Ibid.
17. Carl Strock, "City Land Auction Draws Buyers to Sliver Properties," *Schenectady Gazette*, 25 October 1984.
18. "Interview with Gordon Matta-Clark," September 1977, published in Gordon Matta-Clark, *Gordon Matta-Clark* (Antwerp: Internationaal Cultureel Centrum, 1977), 11.
19. Nicholas Blomley, "Cuts, Flows and the Geography of Property," *Journal of Law, Culture and the Humanities* 7(2) (June 2011): 205.
20. Matta-Clark and Davidovich had photographed sites that had not yet been purchased prior to the October 1973 public auction. Jeffrey Kastner, Sina Najafi, and Frances Richard, *Odd Lots: Revisiting Gordon Matta-Clark's Fake Estates* (New York: Cabinet Books, 2005), 45.
21. On the circumstances regarding the posthumous creation of *Reality Properties*, see ibid., 54–59.
22. Matta-Clark, quoted in Donald Wall, "Gordon Matta-Clark's Building Dissections," *Arts Magazine* 50(9) (May 1976): 76.
23. Maud Lavin, "Gordon Matta-Clark and Individualism," *Arts Magazine* 58(5) (January 1984): 140.
24. "Interview with Gordon Matta-Clark," 10.
25. Gordon Matta-Clark, unpublished notes, undated. EGMC, CCA, Montreal.
26. The Noise Control Act of 1971, N.J.S.A. 13:1G-1.
27. Gordon Matta-Clark, letter to Jorard Piltzer, 18 August 1975. EGMC, CCA, Montreal.

28. Gordon Matta-Clark, letter to Pontus Hulten, 17 January 1975. EGMC, CCA, Montreal. In a letter to Lauren Ewing, Art Department, Williams College, 17 January 1975, Matta-Clark called his projects "re-structured works." EGMC, CCA, Montreal.
29. Gordon Matta-Clark, "A Proposal by Gordon Matta-Clark," undated. EGMC, CCA, Montreal. Republished in Moure and Matta-Clark, 132–133.
30. Donald Wall, "Gordon Matta-Clark's Building Dissections," cited in *Gordon Matta-Clark,* 44.
31. Gordon Matta-Clark, unpublished draft, undated. EGMC, CCA, Montreal. Republished in Moure and Matta-Clark, 141.
32. Quoted in "Rumbles," *Avalanche* 3 (fall 1971): 3.
33. Vito Acconci, untitled quotations, September 27, 1971. Ibid., 76.
34. Christo, quoted in Mary Jane Jacob, *Gordon Matta-Clark: A Retrospective* (Chicago: Museum of Contemporary Art, 1985), 41.
35. Joseph Kosuth, cited in Joan Simon, "Gordon Matta-Clark: Reconstructions," *Arts Magazine* 62(10) (June 1988): 85.
36. Robert Nozick, *Anarchy, State, and Utopia* (New York: Basic Books, 1974), 178–182.
37. Alfred Frankenstein, "Pier 18 Conceptual Projects of Artists," *San Francisco Sunday Examiner and Chronicle,* 4 July 1971.
38. "Interview with Gordon Matta-Clark," 9.
39. Ordover describes his earliest experiences working with artists in "What to Do Until the Lawyer Arrives," in Susan A. Grode, ed., *The Visual Artist's Manual: A Practical Guide to Your Career* (Garden City, NY: Doubleday, 1984), 73–74.
40. Ordover also handled more mundane matters, including artists' financial affairs. Rothfuss memorably recounts how he had "come to dread" Moorman's "frantic pleas for help that resulted from her habit of ignoring financial realities." Joan Rothfuss, *Topless Cellist: The Improbable Life of Charlotte Moorman* (Cambridge, MA: MIT Press, 2014), 257.
41. Jerald Ordover, letter to Gordon Matta-Clark, 11 February 1976. EGMC, CCA, Montreal.
42. Gordon Matta-Clark, letter to Mrs. Fredry Loizeaux, 27 January 1975. EGMC, CCA, Montreal.
43. J. Mark Loizeaux, letter to Gordon Matta-Clark, 5 February 1975. EGMC, CCA, Montreal.
44. "Gordon Matta-Clark: The Making of Pier 52, An Interview by Liza Béar, 11 March 1976," published in Moure and Matta-Clark, *Gordon Matta-Clark: Works and Collected Writings,* 218.
45. Ibid., 218.
46. Gordon Matta-Clark, in "Gordon Matta-Clark: Dilemmas—A Radio Interview by Liza Béar," WBAI-FM, March 1976, in ibid., 262.
47. Ibid., 11.
48. Gordon Matta-Clark, letter to Malitte Matta, 13 August 1975. EGMC, CCA, Montreal.
49. Gerard Hovagimyan, "Gordon Matta-Clark (A Remembrance)," *Gordon Matta-Clark: Experience Becomes the Object* (Barcelona: Ediciones Poligrafa, 2016), 47.
50. New York State Penal Law §145.10.
51. Gordon Matta-Clark, letter to Fredericka Hunter and Ian Glennie, 12 August 1975. EGMC, CCA, Montreal. Cited in Gordon Matta-Clark, *Gordon Matta-Clark* (New York: Phaidon, 2003), 12–15.
52. Mary Jane Jacob, *Gordon Matta-Clark: A Retrospective* (Chicago: Museum of Contemporary Art, 1985), 78.
53. Speaking of his attempts to gain information about subterranean land in New York City, Matta-Clark wondered openly to Béar why city bureaucracy seemed so "completely resistant" to providing any information. He found himself having to "literally wallow" in infrastructure. "Gordon Matta-Clark: Dilemmas—A Radio Interview by Liza Béar," 269.
54. Tony Rickaby, "Art Delinquency Notes 1974," *Tracks* 2(3) (fall 1976): 22.
55. Stanley Cohen, "Property Destruction: Motives and Meanings," in *Vandalism,* ed. Colin Ward (London: Architectural Press, 1973), 53.

56. Gordon Matta-Clark, letter to Marilyn Lubetkin, Contemporary Arts Museum Houston, 15 May 1975. EGMC, CCA, Montreal.
57. Eduardo Moisés Peñalver and Sonia K. Katyal, "Property Outlaws," *University of Pennsylvania Law Review* 155(5) (May 2007): 1098.
58. Jerald Ordover, interview with Thomas Crow, 19 October 2002, cited in Gordon Matta-Clark, *Gordon Matta-Clark* (New York: Phaidon, 2003), 8.
59. "Gordon Matta-Clark: The Making of Pier 52," 219.
60. Gordon Matta-Clark, letter to Wolfgang Becker, 8 September 1975. EGMC, CCA, Montreal. Cited in Gordon Matta-Clark, *Gordon Matta-Clark,* 8.
61. Ibid. Republished in Lee, 123.
62. David Bourdon, "The New Season: Pier Groups," *Village Voice,* 8 September 1975.
63. Ibid.
64. "Gordon Matta-Clark: The Making of Pier 52," 220.
65. Gordon Matta-Clark, letter to Jerald Ordover, 4 December 1974. EGMC, CCA, Montreal. Republished in Walker, 122.
66. Carol M. Rose, "Property as Storytelling: Perspectives from Game Theory, Narrative Theory, Feminist Theory," *Yale Journal of Law and the Humanities* 2 (1990): 56.
67. Gordon Matta-Clark, letter to Helga Retzer, 7 September 1975. EGMC, CCA, Montreal.
68. Jerald Ordover, letter to Gordon Matta-Clark, 19 September 1975. EGMC, CCA, Montreal.
69. Ibid.
70. Letter from Jerald Ordover to Gordon Matta-Clark, 21 October 1975. EGMC, CCA, Montreal.
71. Letter from Gordon Matta-Clark to Jerry [Jerald Ordover], 4 December 1975. EGMC, CCA, Montreal.
72. Statement by Gordon Matta-Clark for Jerald Ordover regarding work done at Pier 52, New York City, New York, 1975. EGMC, CCA, Montreal. Republished in Moure and Matta-Clark, *Gordon Matta-Clark: Works and Collected Writings,* 204.
73. Ibid.
74. In his tonic discussion of the legal right to destroy one's property, Strahilevitz discusses several cases involving building destruction that conspicuously occurred in the mid-1970s. Lior Jacob Strahilevitz, "The Right to Destroy," *Yale Law Journal* 114 (2005): 796–800.
75. "It must be clear that I give no one permission to copy slides of my work." Gordon Matta-Clark, letter to Joan [Simon?], 23 June 1976. EGMC, CCA, Montreal.
76. Statement by Gordon Matta-Clark for Jerald Ordover regarding work done at Pier 52, New York City, New York, 1975. EGMC, CCA, Montreal.
77. Gordon Matta-Clark, letter to Wolfgang Becker, 2 February 1976. EGMC, CCA, Montreal.
78. Jeff Ferrell, "Against the Law: Anarchist Criminology," *Social Anarchism* 25 (1998). http://library.nothingness.org/articles/all/en/display/127, accessed 11 July 2016.
79. An influential discussion on safety rhetoric, published not long after Matta-Clark executed his works, is Eugene Bardach and Robert A. Kagan, *Going by the Book: The Problem of Regulatory Unreasonableness* (Philadelphia: Temple University Press, 1982).
80. William Lowrance, *Of Acceptable Risk* (Los Altos, CA: William Kaufmann, 1976), 8.
81. Gordon Matta-Clark, "The earliest cutout works," typewritten statement, undated, in Moure and Matta-Clark, *Gordon Matta-Clark: Works and Collected Writings,* 137.
82. Judith Russi Kirshner, "Interview with Gordon-Matta-Clark," ibid., 334.
83. Messner observes that the bolt cutters in the photograph were not the ones actually used to break into the Delancey Street building. Telephone conversation with the author, 6 October 2017.
84. "Real Estate Show," *Cover* 1(3) (spring–summer 1980): 12.
85. Alan W. Moore, "Excavating Real Estate," *House Magic* 6 (2014): 16.
86. Ibid., 9.
87. Ibid.

88. Jimmy Carter, "Energy and National Goals: Address to the Nation, July 15, 1979," *Public Papers of the Presidents of the United States: Jimmy Carter, 1979, Book II* (Washington, DC: U.S. Government Printing Office, 1980), 1237.
89. Gary Indiana, "Slice of Art," *Village Voice,* 17 September 1985.
90. Real Estate Show folder, Political Art Documentation/Distribution (PAD/D) Archives, Museum of Modern Art Library, New York.
91. Cited in Natasha Kurchanova, "Lower East Side: The Real Estate Show Redux," *Studio International,* 5 December 2014. www.studiointernational.com/index.php/lower-east-side-the-real-estate-show-redux, accessed 2 October 2017.
92. Ann Messner, unpublished statement, September 1983. Cited in "Franklin Furnace Permanent Collection Information Sheet," 1983. Real Estate Show folder, PAD/D Archives, Museum of Modern Art Library, New York.

CHAPTER FOUR. RADICAL OBEDIENCE

1. Robert Jackall, *Wild Cowboys: Urban Marauders and the Forces of Order* (Cambridge, MA: Harvard University Press, 1997), 262.
2. Tehching Hsieh, "I Just Go in Life," in Adrian Heathfield and Tehching Hsieh, *Out of Now: The Lifeworks of Tehching Hsieh* (Cambridge, MA: MIT Press, 2009), 326.
3. Robert Braucher and E. Allan Farnsworth, *Restatement of the Law, Second—Contracts 2d* (St. Paul, MN: American Law Institute), §1.
4. Visitors recall how Hsieh refrained from interacting, and even acknowledging, those who came to see him in *Cage Piece.* Talking was not allowed. Kathleen A. Hughes, "Exile on Hudson Street," *SoHo Weekly News,* 13 December 1979.
5. Tehching Hsieh, e-mail communication with the author, 30 November 2014.
6. Tehching Hsieh, "Statement for One Year Performance 1985–1986," 1985, Franklin Furnace Artist Files, Museum of Modern Art.
7. Hsieh, "I Just Go in Life," 326.
8. Cited in Delia Bajo and Brainard Carey, "In Conversation with Tehching Hsieh," *Brooklyn Rail* (August–September 2003). www.brooklynrail.org/2003/08/art/tehching-hsieh, accessed April 12, 2013.
9. Shoshanna Amielle Magnet, *When Biometrics Fail: Gender, Race, and the Technology of Identity* (Durham, NC: Duke University Press, 2011), 53–54.
10. On the origins of the term *illegal alien* in a U.S. context, see Gerald L. Neuman, *Strangers to the Constitution: Immigrants, Borders, and Fundamental Law* (Princeton, NJ: Princeton University Press, 2010), 177. For a survey of cases in which the "undocumented alien" is cited in court cases during the 1970s, see "Developments in the Law—Immigration: Policy and the Rights of Aliens," *Harvard Law Review* 96 (April 1983): 1286–1465.
11. Hsieh, "I Just Go in Life," 324.
12. Tehching Hsieh, correspondence with Jeannette Ingberman, 28 January 1982. Exit Art Archive, MSS 343, series I, box 283, folder 18, Fales Library and Special Collections, New York University Libraries.
13. Ray Langenbach, "Statutory Obligations: The Performances of Tehching Hsieh," *Art Asia Pacific* 33 (January/February/March 2002): 47.
14. For a summary of the act and its history, see Lawrence A. Fuchs, "Symposium: Strangers to the Constitution: Immigrants in American Law," *University of Pittsburgh Law Review* 44 (winter 1983): 493.
15. Bill Ong Hing, "Racial Disparity: The Unaddressed Issues of the Simpson-Mazzoli Bill," *Berkeley La Raza Law Journal* 1(1) (1983): 26–27.

16. The anxieties of this period were particularly well evoked in literary movements of the 1970s. See Sung-Sheng Chang, *Literary Culture in Taiwan: Martial Law to Market Law* (New York: Columbia University Press, 2004), 122–167.
17. This was in response to Chinese artist Xu Bing asking Hsieh whether his coming to the U.S. from Taiwan entailed "intervening in an international avant-garde cultural 'system.'" "A Conversation with Hsieh Tehching, from the *Black Cover Book*," originally published 25 October 1993, trans. Jon Solomon. *Art Margins* 4(2) (June 2015): 109.
18. Chris Burden, quoted in Glenn Phillips, ed., *California Video: Artists and Histories* (Los Angeles: J. Paul Getty Museum, 2008), 65.
19. *Financial Disclosure Act: Hearings Before the Subcommittee on Administrative Law and Governmental Relations of the Committee on the Judiciary, House of Representatives, Ninety-fifth Congress, First Session* (Washington, DC: U.S. Government Printing Office, 1977).
20. Burden, quoted in *California Video: Artists and Histories,* 65.
21. Montano and Hsieh posted advertisements titled "Artists Want Work," undated. Linda Montano Papers, MSS 386, box 42, folder 9, Fales Library and Special Collections, New York University Libraries.
22. Taiwanese in New York's Chinatown were targeted for particular surveillance due to fears over gang-related crime. "Chinatown Youth Gang," *SoHo Weekly News,* 25 November–1 December 1976. Not surprisingly, Hsieh was either unaware of or indifferent to such surveillance; he rented living quarters to Ai Weiwei in the early 1980s. Wang Yijun, "Xunzhe shijian, zou meiyou huícheng de lu-zhuanfang xingwei yishujia xiedeqing" [Follow time, take the path of no return—an interview with performance artist Hsieh Tehching], *The Reporter,* 21 June 2017. www.twreporter.org/a/2017-venice-biennale-interview-hsieh-tehching, accessed 19 January 2018.
23. Bruce Conner, letter to Kathy Cohen, 10 December 1973. Reproduced in Bruce Conner, *Prints* (Palo Alto: Galerie Smith Andersen, 1974).
24. From 1996 on, California would require signers of deeds involving real property to record their right thumbprint in a notary's journal. California Government Code 8206 (a)(2)(G). The new state law was intended to curb fraud—reasoning, as did Conner, that thumbprints, unlike signatures, were "virtually impossible to forge." Conner, cited by Mary Fuller, "You're Looking for Bruce Conner, the Artist, or What Is This Crap You're Trying to Put Over Here?" *Currant* 2 (May–July 1976): 10.
25. *Davis v. Mississippi,* 394 U.S. 721 (1969).
26. Fuller, "You're Looking for Bruce Conner," 59.
27. Explanations as to why Warhol's murals were censored are varied; recent scholarship suggests that New York state governor (and later Warhol client) Nelson Rockefeller ordered the removal on the grounds that the murals would tar the city's image. Larissa Harris, "It Just Had Something to Do with New York," in *13 Most Wanted Men: Andy Warhol and the 1964 World's Fair* (Queens, NY: Queens Museum, 2014), 16.
28. A copy of Warhol's authorization is published in ibid., 58. For an in-depth look at censorship in the arts in 1960s New York, see *Censorship in the Sixties: Documents, Memos, Articles, Bulletins, Photos, Letters, Newspaper Clippings, Etc.* (New York: Anthology Film Archives, 2007).
29. Richard Meyer recounts that Warhol's source was a friend's policeman lover. Richard Meyer, *Outlaw Representation: Censorship and Homosexuality in Twentieth-Century American Art* (Boston: Beacon Press, 2002), 142–143. *Kolb v. O'Connor,* 142 N.E.2d 818 (Ill.App.Ct. 1957). *Dissemination of criminal justice information : hearings before the Subcommittee on Civil Rights and Constitutional Rights of the Committee on the Judiciary, House of Representatives, Ninety-third Congress, second session, on H.R. 188, H.R. 9783, H.R. 12574, and H.R. 12575* (Washington, DC: U.S. Government Printing Office, 1974).

30. See ibid.
31. William H. Rehnquist, "Is an Expanded Right of Privacy Consistent with Fair and Effective Law Enforcement?" *University of Kansas Law Review* 23 (1974): 3.
32. *Barnes v. United States,* 124 U.S.App.D.C. 318 (1966).
33. "A Conversation with Hsieh Tehching, from the *Black Cover Book,*" 115.
34. Rachel Hall, *Wanted! The Outlaw in American Visual Culture* (Charlottesville: University of Virginia Press, 2009), 10.
35. The notebooks are in the Linda Montano Papers, MSS 386, box 42, folder 11, Fales Library and Special Collections, New York University Libraries.
36. Hsieh, e-mail communication with the author, 11 October 2014.
37. Peter S. Munoz, "The Right of an Illegal Alien to Maintain a Civil Action," *California Law Review* 63(3) (May 1975): 776–781.
38. 42 U.S.C. 1981 (1970).
39. Reproductions of Hsieh's statements of intent can be seen at http://one-year-performance.com, accessed 16 May 2013.
40. Hsieh, e-mail communication with the author, 11 October 2014.
41. Benjamin Buchloh, "Conceptual Art 1962–1969: From the Aesthetic of Administration to the Critique of Institutions," *October* 55 (winter 1990): 118.
42. Vito Acconci, "Performance after the Fact," *New Observations* 95 (May–June 1993): 29.
43. See http://one-year-performance.com, accessed May 16, 2013.
44. Richard Posner, quoted in *Scribes: Legal Writing Today* 8 (2001–2002): 36.
45. *Weisz v. Parke-Bernet Galleries, Inc.*, 67 Misc. 2d 1077; 325 N.Y.S.2d 576 (1971).
46. Hsieh, e-mail communication with the author, 13 June 2013.
47. Unpublished manuscript, "Art/Life One Year Performance," Linda Montano Papers, series II, box 43, folder 1, Fales Library and Special Collections, New York University Libraries.
48. Montano stated that she met Hsieh, who was then looking for a partner to whom to be tied, in 1983. Exit Art Archive, MSS 343, series IV, box 177, folder 16, Fales Library and Special Collections, New York University Libraries.
49. Linda Montano, "Living Art: Time Spent Artfully Alone or Not Alone," unpublished statement, 26 December 1975. Linda Montano Papers, MSS 386, series II, box 43, folder 1, Fales Library and Special Collections, New York University Libraries.
50. Montano seems to have explored the possibility of applying this idea in a proposed work called "Two Person Piece." Ibid.
51. José Esteban Muñoz, *Disidentifications: Queers of Color and the Performance of Politics* (Minneapolis: University of Minnesota Press, 1999), 11.
52. Hsieh, e-mail communication with the author, 11 October 2014.
53. Ibid. For the statement accompanying *Cage Piece,* Hsieh was assisted by artist Ming Fay, who helped adjust the grammar. Tehching Hsieh, personal communication with the author, 18 April 2013.
54. See, for example, Lawrence Solan, Terri Rosenblatt, and Daniel Osherson, "False Consensus Bias in Contract Interpretation," *Columbia Law Review* 108 (June 2008); and Steven Shavell, "On the Writing and the Interpretation of Contracts," *Journal of Law, Economics, and Organization* 22 (2005): 289–290.
55. Calvin J. Karlin, "Readability Statutes—A Survey and a Proposed Model," *University of Kansas Law Review* 28 (1980): 531, 532–535.
56. In the late 1970s, the readability of insurance contracts was determined through the Flesch Reading Ease standard, which assigns readability levels based on the average number of syllables per word in texts and average sentence length measured in terms of the number of words per sentence. Ibid., 535.

57. *National Equipment Rental v. Hendrix*, 565 F.2d 255 (2nd Cir., 1977).
58. *National Equipment Rental v. Szhukhent et. al.*, 375 U.S. 311 (2nd Cir., 1964).
59. U.C.C. 1–201(b)(10).
60. Kay Larson, "A Year in the Life," *Village Voice*, 1 October 1979.
61. Kathy O'Dell, *Contract with the Skin: Masochism, Performance Art, and the 1970s* (Minneapolis: University of Minnesota Press, 1998), 14.
62. Heathfield and Hsieh, *Out of Now: The Lifeworks of Tehching Hsieh*, 68.
63. Claire Fergusson, "Doing Time: A One-Year Performance by Sam Hsieh," *High Performance* 82(4) (1979): 10.
64. Thad Ziolkowski, "The Implosive Quest of Teching Hsieh," *New Observations* 108 (September–October 1995): 11.
65. Kathleen A. Hughes, "Artist Explores Essence of the Daily Grind by Punching in Once an Hour for a Year," *Wall Street Journal*, 24 April 1981.
66. Barry Kahn, "One Year at a Time: Sam Hsieh's Annual Acts," *Live* 6/7 (1982): 42.
67. Kathleen A. Hughes, "Long and Very Close Relationship Looms for Two Artists in New York," *Wall Street Journal*, 6 July 1983.
68. Jill Johnston, "Hardship Art," *Art in America* 72(8) (September 1984): 178.
69. Peggy Phelan, *Unmarked: The Politics of Performance* (New York: Routledge, 1993), 146.
70. Ziolkowski, "Implosive Quest of Teching Hsieh," 11.
71. According to critic Lee Weng Choy, Hsieh deliberately chose to wash dishes because it allowed him to work late at night, when the risk of discovery by immigration officials would be less. Washing dishes also gave him greater flexibility to do with his time as he wished. Cited in Kon Gouriotis, "Tehching Hsieh: An 'Untimely' Contemporary," *Art Monthly Australia* 271 (July 2014): 20.
72. Hsieh, cited in Andreas Gedin, "Tehching Hsieh: Passing Time," *Nordic Art Review* 4(1) (January–February 2002): 67.
73. Kahn, "One Year at a Time," 41.
74. See American Law Institute, *Restatement (Second) of Contracts* 205 (St. Paul, MN: American Law Institute, 1981).
75. Kathleen A. Hughes reported that after Hsieh bought a second loudspeaker and alarm in January 1981, the total number of punch-ins missed decreased from twenty-one to three. Hughes, "Artist Explores Essence of the Daily Grind."
76. Montano recalls that it took about fifteen minutes to tie the rope. At the end of *Rope Piece*, witnesses signed a typewritten statement attesting to this: "I, Pauline Oliveros, in July 4, 1983, attached a lead seal to Tehching Hsieh's rope. I also engraved my signature on that seal. On July 4, 1984, I personally confirmed that the seal had not been removed and that said seal, inscribed by me, was still complete intact." Typewritten draft statement dated July 4, 1984, Linda Montano Papers, MSS 386, series II, box 42, folder 6, Fales Library and Special Collections, New York University Libraries.
77. Ibid., folder 13. In one of the many volumes of newspaper clippings Hsieh kept at this time, several concern tips on anger management. Ibid., folder 10.
78. Hsieh's scrapbooks are contained in ibid., folders 10–12.
79. Johnston, "Hardship Art," 179.
80. J.M. Balkin and Sanford Levinson, "Interpreting Law and Music: Performance Notes on the 'The Banjo Serenader' and 'The Lying Crowd of Jews,'" *Cardozo Law Review* 20 (1999): 1519.
81. Hughes, "Long and Very Close Relationship Looms for Two Artists."
82. Hsieh, e-mail communication to the author, 30 November 2014.

83. Max Liljefors, "Body and Authority in Contemporary Art: Tehching Hsieh's One Year Performances," in *Visualizing Law and Authority,* ed. Leif Dahlberg (Berlin: Walter de Gruyter, 2012), 228–229.
84. Hughes, "Artist Explores Essence of the Daily Grind."
85. Kathleen Ann Hughes, "The Arts," *OMNI* 4(3) (December 1981): 34.
86. Jerry Tallmer, "He's Got His Art to Keep Him Warm," *New York Post,* 22 February 1983.
87. Hughes, "Exile on Hudson Street."
88. Susan Silas and Chrysanne Stathacos, "A Conversation with Linda Montano," www.mommybysilasandstathacos.com/2012/07/19/a-conversation-with-linda-montano/, accessed 8 February 2015.
89. Hsieh, e-mail communication with the author, 11 June 2013.
90. Kathleen A. Hughes, "Mr. Hsieh's Latest Performance: Keeping Warm Was the Easy Part," *Wall Street Journal,* 11 June 1982.
91. Hsieh, "I Just Go in Life," 328.
92. Heathfield and Hsieh, *Out of Now: The Lifeworks of Tehching Hsieh,* 44.
93. One of the most celebrated criminal defense lawyers in New York before his appointment to the bench in 1978 and known for his realist views of the justice system, Erdmann once stated that it was much easier to defend the guilty because "you don't have the responsibility of saving him from unjust punishment." Quoted in James Mills, "I Have Nothing to Do with Justice," *Life* 70(9) (12 March 1971): 66.
94. Jonathan Siskin, "Still Doing Time," *High Performance* 5(3) (fall 1982): 76.
95. Cited in Hughes, "Mr. Hsieh's Latest Performance."
96. Fergusson, "Doing Time," 10. Also see Jeanette Ingberman and Papo Colo, "I Choose to Do This," *Artcom* 18 (1982): 17.
97. Mike Pearl and Larry Nathanson, "Gotta Have Art, Says Judge with a Heart," *New York Post,* 22 June 1982.
98. *Fenster v. Leary* turned on the rule for common-law vagrancy, which initially defined a vagrant as a person "(1) being without visible means of support, (2) being without employment, and (3) being able to work but refusing to do so." The court overturned the law, alleging that the anti-vagrancy statute interfered with a person's right to conduct herself in the manner of her choice so long as her actions do not interfere with those of others. *Fenster v. Leary,* 53 Misc. 2d 774 (1967). In *Papachristou,* the Supreme Court held that anti-vagrancy laws criminalized "activities . . . historically part of the amenities of life as we have known them." The court went on to hold that the scope of the law was too great, allowing police "unfettered discretion" to arrest anyone on suspicion of past or future criminality. *Papachristou v. City of Jacksonville,* 405 U.S. 156 (1972) at 164, 168.
99. 1981 N.Y. Laws ch. 991.
100. Ellen Baxter and Kim Hopper, *Private Lives/Public Spaces: Homeless Adults on the Streets of New York* (New York: Community Service Society, 1981), 6–7.
101. Hsieh, e-mail communication with the author, 18 April 2013 and 11 June 2013. The artist remarks that "I stayed alone through the piece, no one followed me for documenting the work."
102. As Joe Hannan recalled, "If I recognized Tehching Hsieh on the street, I don't remember it." Quoted in Frazer Ward, *No Innocent Bystanders: Performance Art and Audience* (Hanover, NH: Dartmouth College Press, 2012), 144.
103. John R. Coleman, "Diary of a Homeless Man," *New York,* 21 February 1983, 32.
104. Ingberman and Colo, "I Choose to Do This," 18.
105. Hughes, "The Arts," 34.

106. *Levy v. Rutley*, L.R., 6 C.P. 523, 529 (1871).
107. 17 U.S.C. §101.
108. *Scull v. Scull*, 94 A.2d 29, 462 N.Y.S.2d 890 (1st Dept. 1983).
109. Ibid.
110. Charles Green, *Third Hand: Collaboration in Art from Conceptualism to Postmodernism* (Minneapolis: University of Minnesota Press, 2001), 132.
111. Johnston, "Hardship Art," 178–179. Montano later expressed guilt over what she saw as Johnston's "rejection" of Hsieh, wondering whether Johnston failed to "see beyond" the negativity "when things were difficult [between herself and Hsieh]." Linda Montano, letter to Jill Johnston, 17 June [no year written]. Linda Montano Papers, MSS 386, series II, box 43, folder 1, Fales Library and Special Collections, New York University Libraries.
112. Linda Montano, unpublished manuscript, "Art/Life One Year Performance," undated. Ibid.
113. Tom Marioni, signed open letter, 28 July 1999. Ibid., folder 33. Marioni's letter reads as a deferred response to someone accusing Marioni, the "bad white male," of "handcuffing" Montano to him. Tom Marioni, letter to Montano, 17 January 1997. Ibid.
114. William Easton, "Collaboration and Other (Not So Scandalous) Plots," *Fiberarts* 21(2) (September/October 1994): 46.
115. Claire Fergusson, undated manuscript, 1. *High Performance* magazine records, 1953–2005, Getty Research Library, accession no. 2006.M.8, box 25, folder 29. Heathfield and Hsieh, *Out of Now: The Lifeworks of Tehching Hsieh*, 29.
116. Wang Yijun, "Xunzhe shijian, zou meiyou huícheng de lu."
117. Dan Cameron, "Against Collaboration," *Arts Magazine* 58 (March 1984): 83. Interestingly, installation and display workers for *Running Fence* were paid $2.40 per hour, about 20 percent more than the hourly minimum wage in California at the time.
118. Ibid., 83. Haring in fact regarded LA2 as a coauthor on at least one work, even when the younger artist was a minor. After selling a work circa 1981, Haring split the proceeds equally with LA2. John Gruen, *Keith Haring: The Authorized Biography* (New York: Simon and Schuster, 1991), 81. LA2's efforts for recognition as a collaborator and influence on Haring have largely been dismissed. For a critique of this dismissal, see Ricardo Montez, "'Trade' Marks: LA2, Keith Haring, and a Queer Economy of Collaboration," *GLQ: A Journal of Lesbian and Gay Studies* 12(3) (2006): 425–440.
119. In some cases, the conflict arose well after the initial moment of supposed collaboration. An example is the dispute over images of performance artworks taken by the photographer Rong Rong in Beijing in 1995. The furor exploded after Rong Rong and his subjects, including leading performance artists Ma Liuming and Zhang Huan, became recognized in the art capitals of Europe and the U.S. While Rong Rong claimed sole ownership of his photographs, some of his subjects argued that they were merely records of their work or, at best, joint works for which they and Rong Rong shared the credit. See Wu Hung, *Rong Rong's East Village, 1993–1998* (New York Chambers Fine Art, 2003), 9, 14; Carlos Rojas, *The Great Wall: A Cultural History* (Cambridge, MA: Harvard University Press, 2010), 161–162; and Keith Wallace, *Action-Camera: Beijing Performance Photography* (Vancouver: University of British Columbia Press, 2009), 74.
120. E-mail to Guerrilla Girls members, 2 March 2000. Guerrilla Girls Archive, MSS 274, box 3, folder 19, Fales Library and Special Collections, New York University Libraries.
121. Unidentified Guerrilla Girls, letter to Kristine Zaleskas, 15 December 2002. Ibid., folder 21.
122. Letter to Barbara Hoffman, October 13, 2003. Ibid., folder 19.
123. Charlotte Sheedy, letter to Barbara Hoffmann, cited in *Guerrilla Girls, Inc. v. Kaz*, 03 Civ. 4619 (S.D.N.Y. 2004). The letter was cited as evidence in a case where the incorporated group claimed copyright to the materials produced by offshoot groups formed by Guerrilla Girls members.

124. For a discussion of the contract and the circumstances of its formation, see Noah Charney and Edgar Tijhuis, "Ulay vs. Marina Abramović: How the Epic Legal Battle between Art-World Giants Went Down," *Salon,* 25 September 2016. www.salon.com/2016/09/25/ulay-vs-marina-abramovic-how-the-epic-legal-battle-between-art-world-giants-went-down/, accessed 5 October 2016.
125. Barry Kahn, "Sam Hsieh at Large in New York City," *Art in America* 70(6) (summer 1982): 146.
126. Hsieh, e-mail communication with the author, 17 April 2013 and 1 December 2014.
127. Among the options discussed over a period of five months prior to the start of *Rope Piece* was whether to have themselves monitored with a detector that would beep if either of them was outside an eight-foot space. Montano, unpublished manuscript, "Art/Life One Year Performance." Linda Montano Papers, MSS 386, series II, box 43, folder 1, Fales Library and Special Collections.
128. *Fisher v. Klein,* 16 U.S.P.Q.2d (BNA) 1798 (S.D.N.Y. 1990).
129. *Childress v. Taylor,* 945 F.2d 500, 505–06 (2d Cir. 1991).
130. *Erickson v. Trinity Theatre, Inc.*, 13 F.3d 1061 (7th Cir. 1994).
131. Maria Eichhorn, "Interview with Robert Projansky," in *The Artist's Contract* (Köln: Buchhandlung Walther König, 2009), 231.
132. An important example was Peter Selz's employment agreement with the Running Fence Corporation. Selz addressed both when giving updates about permits applied for and acquired.
133. Robert Taylor, "In the Name of Integrity," *Boston Globe,* 15 October 1977.
134. Thomas McEvilley, "Tehching Hsieh, Linda Montano," *Artforum* 23(3) (November 1984): 99.
135. Ibid.
136. Ibid.
137. Karlyn De Jongh, "Art/Life: A Conversation with Tehching Hsieh," *C Magazine* 105 (spring 2010): 9.
138. Johnston, "Hardship Art," 179.
139. Susan Silas and Chrysanne Stathacos, "A Conversation with Linda Montano," 19 July 2012. www.mommybysilasandstathacos.com/2012/07/19/a-conversation-with-linda-montano/, accessed 17 May 2015.
140. Patricia Maloney, "The New Endurance of Linda Mary Montano, Part 1," January 19, 2015. www.artpractical.com/column/women-in-performance-the-new-endurance-of-linda-mary-montano-part-1/, accessed 18 May 2015.
141. Undated note, Linda Montano Papers, MSS 386, box 42, folder 13, Fales Library and Special Collections.
142. Book 1, ibid., folder 10.
143. Hsieh cited in De Jongh, "Art/Life: A Conversation with Tehching Hsieh," 4. Fellow performance artist Ray Langenbach has similarly claimed that Hsieh insisted on separating *Time Clock Piece* from the life of the imprisoned. Langenbach, "Statutory Obligations," 49.

CHAPTER FIVE. ARTS OF DISENGAGEMENT

1. Several examples involving women artists are documented in Carol Jacobsen, "Redefining Censorship: A Feminist View," *Art Journal* 50(4) (winter 1991): 42–55.
2. Barbara Hoffmann, "Law for Art's Sake in the Public Realm," *Critical Inquiry* 17(3) (spring 1991): 540.
3. James Heilbrun and Charles M. Gray, *The Economics of Art and Culture* (Cambridge, MA: Cambridge University Press, 2001), 278–310.
4. Jeff Ferrell, "Cultural Criminology," *Annual Review of Sociology* 25 (1999): 405.
5. Classic texts on this point include Allan Sekula, "The Body and the Archive," *October* 39 (winter 1986): 3–64; and John Tagg, "Power and Photography: A Means of Surveillance: The Photograph as Evidence in Law," *Screen Education* 36 (winter 1980): 17–55.

6. Joel Snyder, "Res ipsa loquitur," in *Things That Talk: Object Lessons from Art and Science,* ed. Lorraine Daston (Cambridge, MA: MIT Press, 2004), 195–221; and Jennifer Mnookin, "The Image of Truth: Photographic Evidence and the Power of Analogy," *Yale Journal of Law and the Humanities* 10(1) (1998): 1–74.
7. Dillard S. Gardner, "The Camera Goes to Court," *North Carolina Law Review* 24(3) (1946): 236 (quoted in Mnookin, "The Image of Truth," note 10, 3). Gardner implies, however, that making full use of photography depends on judges and lawyers gaining a basic fluency with the techniques of photography in order to assess an image's accuracy (236).
8. Quoted in Erina Duganne, "The Failure of 'The President's Choice,'" in *Visual Research Methods: Images, Society and Representation,* ed. Gregory Stanczak (Thousand Oaks, CA: Sage, 2007), 121.
9. Les Krims, quoted in Abigail Foerstner, "In the Wicked World of Les Krims, More Spells Trouble," *Chicago Tribune,* 11 January 1985.
10. A.D. Coleman, "The Directorial Mode: Notes toward a Definition," *Artforum* 15(1) (September 1976): 56.
11. William Aspray and Barbara M. Hayes, *Everyday Information: The Evolution of Information Seeking in America* (Cambridge, MA: MIT Press, 2011), 255.
12. 17 U.S. Code §101. Each state may decide whether works made by its employees are entitled to copyright protection. California regards such works as in the public domain.
13. For a history of the Freedom of Information Act, see Michael Schudson, *The Rise of the Right to Know: Politics and the Culture of Transparency, 1945–1975* (Cambridge, MA: Harvard University Press, 2015), 57–62.
14. Douglas Crimp, "Pictures," *Pictures* (New York: Artists Space, 1977).
15. Benjamin V. Madison, "Seeing Can Be Deceiving," *William and Mary Law Review* 25(4) (1984): 713.
16. Adler describes how judges in the 1920s and '30s refused to describe sexually explicit materials on grounds that such materials were "like an infectious agent that had to be quarantined." Amy Adler, "The Perverse Law of Child Pornography," *Columbia Law Review* 101 (March 2001): 267.
17. Recall, for example, U.S. senator Jesse Helms's condemnation of Mapplethorpe's photographs in a congressional hearing: "There are unspeakable portrayals which I cannot describe on the floor of the Senate." Richard Meyer, "The Jesse Helms Theory of Art," *October* 104 (spring 2003): 137.
18. Adler claims an absent middle ground: "We as a society are left with a choice: either we protect art as a whole or we protect ourselves from obscenity. . . . It is impossible to do both." Amy Adler, "Post-Modern Art and the Death of Obscenity Law," *Yale Law Journal* 99(6) (April 1990): 1378.
19. Abraham Kaplan, "Obscenity as an Esthetic Category," *Law and Contemporary Problems* 20 (1955): 544.
20. Howard Smith, "Ruckus Aroused," *Village Voice,* 8 October 1979.
21. *Zahorik v. Cornell University,* 579 F.Supp.349 (N.D.N.Y. 1983). Predictably, the university settled out of court, thus avoiding any formal admission of wrongdoing. About 6 percent of Cornell's tenured faculty were women.
22. Kathie Beals, "Artifacts Meet at '70s Exhibit," *Herald Statesman,* 1 October 1982.
23. Joy Horowitz, "The Stack o' Wheat Photos Uproar," *Los Angeles Times,* 25 May 1980.
24. T.D., "Stack of o' Wheat Murder Pictures Destroyed," *Off Our Backs* 10(5) (May 1980): 10. Alluding to Krims's work as "violent pornography," Craft (legally known as Deborah Spray) claimed that "assertive, direct actions" were part of a larger refusal "to collaborate in our [i.e., women's] degradation." Although required to pay for replacing the destroyed copies, Craft was nominated for a university award for "outstanding contribution to campus understanding of ethical principles."

25. Most of these cases belong to copyright law. The earliest recognition of photography as art was by Justice Miller in the seminal U.S. Supreme Court case *Burrow-Giles Lithographic Co. v. Sarony,* 111 U.S. 53 (1884), which upheld Congress's decision to extend copyright protection to photographs. For a detailed analysis of the case and other examples where courts acknowledged photography as art, see Justin Hughes, "The Photographer's Copyright—Photograph as Art, Photograph as Database," *Harvard Journal of Law and Technology* 25(2) (spring 2012): 352–359.
26. *Matter of Koner v. Procaccino* (1976), 39 N.Y.2d at 301.
27. Allan Sekula, "The Body and the Archive," *October* 39 (winter 1986): 6.
28. Mary Ann Doane, "The Close-Up: Scale and Detail in Cinema," *differences* 14(3) (2003): 91.
29. Ibid.
30. *Roth v. United States* (1957), 354 U.S. at 489.
31. *Miller v. California* (1973), 413 U.S. at 23, 24.
32. Frederick Schauer, "The Return to Variable Obscenity?" *Hastings Law Journal* 28 (1977): 1275–1291.
33. *New York v. Ferber,* 458 U.S. 747 (1982).
34. Adler, "Perverse Law of Child Pornography," 263, note 295. Adler cited a case tried in Tennessee in 1998 in which a hidden recording of two girls taking a bath was deemed child pornography because the defendant ostensibly intended to use the recording for sexual purposes.
35. *New York v. Ferber,* 458 U.S. 747 (1982).
36. Christine Haight Farley, "Judging Art," *Tulane Law Review,* 854.
37. Suggestive of a general skepticism regarding lawmakers' willingness to engage with their constituents, William Wilson actually found the low rate of response "heartening." William Wilson "Some Politicians Get Right on It," *Los Angeles Times,* 21 April 1978.
38. Another Golden Fleece recipient in 1977 was the General Services Administration's Art-in-Architecture Program, for granting a $100,000 commission to Claes Oldenburg for *Batcolumn,* a hundred-foot baseball bat to be erected as a public artwork in Chicago. Quoted in Donald Thalacker and Joy Johannessen, *The Place of Art in the World of Architecture* (New York: Chelsea House, 1980), 150.
39. *Serra v. U.S. General Services Administration,* 847 F.2d 1045 (2d Cir. 1988).
40. Id. at 1051; also *Claudio v. United States,* 836 F.Supp. 1219 (E.D.N.C. 1993).
41. In New York, the 1967 judgment against Charlotte Moorman helped establish the public exposure of breasts as a dispositive factor for determining the presence of obscenity. As Judge Shalleck wrote, "There has been no reported interpretation in this state whether as a matter of law, publicly exposed female breasts are or are not an exposure of private parts" or whether such exposure is "lewd." "People v. Charlotte Moorman," *New York Law Journal,* 11 May 1967.
42. *United States v. Dost,* 636 F. Supp. at 833 (S.D.Cal. 1986).
43. Id. at 832.
44. Abigail Foerstner, "The Family of Sally Mann," *Chicago Tribune,* 19 September 1993.
45. Connie Samaras, "Feminism, Photography, Censorship and Sexually Transgressive Imagery: The Work of Robert Mapplethorpe, Joel-Peter Witkin, Jacqueline Livingston, Sally Mann, and Catherine Opie," *New York Law School Law Review* 38 (1993): 88.
46. Even as recently as 2010, the Photographers' Gallery in London, a respected venue for photography, was initially advised not to show Mann's photographs, including those published in *Immediate Family,* on grounds that it would violate various obscenity laws. Brett Rogers, "Foreword," in *Art & the Law—Child Protection—A Guide to the Legal Framework Impacting on Artistic Freedom of Expression* (London: Vivarta, 2015), 5.
47. Julie Burchill, "Death of Innocence," *Guardian,* 12 November 1997.

48. Carlo McCormick, "Trespass—Crossing the Boundaries Between Art and Criminality," in *Trespass: A History of Uncommissioned Urban Art* (Cologne: Taschen, 2010), 226.
49. Unsigned editorial, "This Dog Won't Hunt," *Denver Post,* 2 February 1998.
50. Ariella Azoulay, *The Civil Contract of Photography* (Cambridge, MA: MIT Press, 2012), 25.
51. Mary Ann Marger, "Pained Poses," *St. Petersburg Times,* 5 August 1994.
52. Margarett Loke, "Scenes to Make You Say 'Oh Boy!'" *New York Times,* 25 July 1997.
53. Donald Judd, "The Importance of Permanence," *Journal: Los Angeles Institute of Contemporary Art* 32 (1982): 5.
54. Ibid., 5.
55. Charles Hagen, "Childhood without Sweetness," *New York Times,* 5 June 1992.
56. In *Cernuda v. Heavey,* the U.S. Customs Service tried to justify its seizure of Cuban paintings under the Trading with the Enemy Act exempting from regulation any ideas or information protected by the First Amendment. The government unsuccessfully argued that the works of art did not qualify for the exemption, claiming that art was "only aesthetic." *Cernuda v. Heavey,* 720 F.Supp. at 1551 (S.D.Fla. 1989).
57. Marc Mezibov, "The Mapplethorpe Obscenity Trial," *Litigation* 18(4) (summer 1992): 13.
58. Ibid., 71.
59. *Pope v. Illinois,* 481 U.S. 497 (1987).
60. Cited in Robert Perine, *Chouinard, An Art Vision Betrayed* (Encinitas, CA: Artra, 1985), 189.
61. *County of Allegheny v. ACLU* (1989), 492 U.S. at 643–644.
62. *City of Cincinnati v. Contemporary Arts Center,* 57 Ohio Misc.2d 15 (Ohio Mun. 1990).
63. Katharine T. Bartlett, "Feminist Legal Methods," *Harvard Law Review* 103(4) (February 1990): 846.
64. *Boggs v. Bowron* 842 F.Supp. 542 at 561 (D.D.C 1993).
65. 842 F. Supp. at 561.
66. For a succinct discussion of Pächt and his thinking, see Christopher Wood's introduction to Otto Pächt, *The Practice of Art History: Reflections on Method* (London: Harvey Miller, 1999), 9–18. For an example of how Pächt's ideas could be employed in copyright cases requiring visual analysis, see Joan Kee, "Connoisseurship and Its Potential in Matters of Copyright," *Journal of Law, Culture, and the Humanities* 8(2) (June 2012): 333–349.
67. *Ringgold v. Black Entm't Television, Inc.* 126 F.3d at 76. Incidentally, the author of the *Ringgold* opinion, Jon O. Newman, was the presiding judge in the *Tilted Arc* case. Farley, "Judging Art," 818. Newman later proved himself a vigorous advocate of contemporary art when, in 2000, he rejected an attempt by New York City government to withhold municipal funds from the Brooklyn Museum after it hosted "Sensation," a traveling group exhibition that included several works accused of obscenity and blasphemy. Meyer Schapiro, "The New Viennese School," *Art Bulletin* 18(2) (1936): 258.
68. A recent attempt to suggest guidelines for courts considering photographic evidence while also taking into account the nature of photography is Jessica Silbey, "Evidence Verité and the Law of Film," *Cardozo Law Review* 31(4) (2009–2010): 1297–1299.
69. Rebecca Tushnet, "Worth a Thousand Words: The Images of Copyright," *Harvard Law Review* 125(3) (January 2012): 721.
70. Sarah Parsons, "Public/Private Tensions in the Photography of Sally Mann," *History of Photography* 32(2) (2008): 123–136.
71. Ann Gerhart, "Family of Mann," *Philadelphia Daily News,* 29 October 1992.
72. Woodward, "Disturbing Photographs of Sally Mann."
73. Anne Higonnet, *Pictures of Innocence: The History and Crisis of Ideal Childhood* (New York: Thames and Hudson, 1998), 162.

74. Dolan discusses the opinions of Justices Kennedy and Alito in *Salazar v. Buono* (559 U.S. 700), a 2010 U.S. Supreme Court case involving whether a war memorial in the shape of a cross violated the Establishment Clause prohibiting Congress from favoring one religion over another. Mary Jean Dolan, "Salazar v. Buono: The Cross Between Endorsement and History," *Northwestern University Law Review Colloquy* 105 (2010): 48.
75. *Roth v. United States*, 354 U.S. 476 (1957).
76. Sally Mann, *Hold Still: A Memoir with Photographs* (New York: Little, Brown, 2015), 146.
77. *Jessie's Cut* (1985), a photograph showing Mann's daughter Jessie with bloody stitches, reenacted a previous incident. Mann saved the bloody cloths from the actual event to stage this scene. Lizbeth A. Johnson, "Sally Mann—The Power of Everyday Life," *View Camera* 5(2) (March–April 1992): 31.
78. Sally Mann, quoted in Jonathan Valania, "Family Values: Sally Mann Uses Her 3 Children as Subjects," *The Morning Call*, 1 November 1992.
79. Foerstner, "Family of Sally Mann."
80. *Grove Press, Inc., v. Gerstein*, 378 U.S. 577 (1964).
81. Mann, *Hold Still*, 147. Both the newspaper and Sokolov sent letters of apology to Mann.
82. Sally Mann quoted in Jonathan Weinberg, *Ambition & Love in Modern American Art* (New Haven, CT: Yale University Press, 2001), 67.
83. John E. B. Meyers, "A Short History of Child Protection in America," *Family Law Quarterly* 42(3) (Fall 2008): 454–457. A damning example was the government removal of an estimated 25–35% of all Native American children from their homes prior to 1978.
84. Hagen, "Childhood without Sweetness."
85. Ibid.
86. Adler, "Perverse Law of Child Pornography," 272.
87. Margarett Loke, "Studying His Children's Faces: Portals into Lives Uncluttered and Vibrant," *New York Times*, 21 November 1997.
88. Foerstner, "Family of Sally Mann."
89. L. Steven Grasz and Patrick J. Pfatlzgraff, "Child Pornography and Child Nudity: Why and How States May Constitutionally Regulate the Production, Possession, and Distribution of Nude Visual Depictions of Children," *Temple Law Review* 71 (fall 1998): 609, note 10.
90. Unsigned, "Livingston v. Cornell," 9.
91. Luc Sante, "The Nude and the Naked," *The New Republic* (1 May 1995): 30.
92. Ibid., 30.
93. Mann, quoted in Johnson, "Sally Mann—The Power of Everyday Life," 30.
94. Katherine K. Baker, "Property Rules Meet Feminist Needs: Respecting Autonomy by Valuing Connection," *Ohio State Law Journal* 59 (1998): 1523–1597.
95. Samaras, "Feminism, Photography, Censorship and Sexually Transgressive Imagery," 82.
96. Richard Woodward, "The Disturbing Photographs of Sally Mann," *New York Times Magazine*, 27 September 1992.
97. Foerstner, "Family of Sally Mann."
98. Ibid.
99. Ibid.
100. Gerhart, "Family of Mann."
101. If Mann had paid any of her children more than $600 in 1993, the maximum allowable income for minors under IRS rules, they would have had to pay federal income tax. Internal Revenue Service, *Your Federal Income Tax*, Publication 17, No. 10311G, 1994, 8. Any tax liability, however, would likely be canceled by the credit Mann received by claiming the children as her dependents.
102. Alan Hyde, *Bodies of Law* (Princeton, NJ: Princeton University Press, 1997), 48.

103. Margaret F. Brinig, *From Contract to Covenant: Beyond the Law and Economics of the Family* (Cambridge, MA: Harvard University Press, 2000), 111.
104. Carole Pateman, *The Sexual Contract* (Cambridge, UK: Blackwell, 1988), 5–14.
105. Henry Campbell Black, *Black's Law Dictionary* (St. Paul, MN: West, 1991), 363.
106. Code of Virginia § 40.1–78.
107. Ibid.
108. Val Williams, "The Naked Truth," *Guardian*, 22 September 1992.
109. Mann, quoted in Johnson, "Sally Mann—The Power of Everyday Life," 30.
110. Vince Aletti, "Child World," *Village Voice*, 26 May 1992.
111. Elizabeth Porter, "Taking Images Seriously," *Columbia Law Review* 114 (2014): 1693.

CHAPTER SIX. DOUBLE EMBODIMENTS

1. Sandra Umathum, "Given the Felix Gonzalez-Torres's Case [*sic*]: The Art of Placing a Different Idea of Participation at Our Disposal," *Performance Research* 16(3) (2011): 94.
2. Jennifer Doyle, *Hold It against Me: Difficulty and Emotion in Contemporary Art* (Durham, NC: Duke University Press, 2013), 8.
3. Margaret Davies, "The Proper: Discourses of Purity," *Law and Critique* 9(2) (1998): 147.
4. Hans Ulrich Obrist, "Gonzalez-Torres, Felix," in *Hans Ulrich Obrist, Interviews 1* (Milan: Charta, 2003), 310.
5. Ibid., 309.
6. Testimony of David Wojnarowicz, court transcript of *Wojnarowicz v. American Family Association*, 90 Civ. 3457 (S.D.N.Y. 1990), 31–32.
7. The events leading up to the case are discussed in Steven C. Dubin, *Arresting Images: Impolitic Art and Uncivil Actions* (New York: Routledge, 1992), 214–218.
8. *Groucho Marx Productions, Inc. v. Day & Night Co.*, 523 F.Supp.485 (S.D.N.Y. 1981). Although the defendants who replicated the Marx Brothers in their play claimed their use was a parody and thus protected under the First Amendment, Conner observed that "the Marx Brothers themselves were a parody on life; the play does not present a parody on their parody" but duplicated the brothers' performance "as faithfully as possible." The decision was later reversed by the Second Circuit, which ruled that California law, not New York law, should have been applied.
9. Quoted in Matthew Rose, "David Wojnarowicz: An Interview," *Arts Magazine* 62 (May 1988): 60.
10. Quoted in Jim Drobnick, "Interview with Group Material," unpublished transcript, 21 June 1989, 18.
11. *Bowers v. Hardwick*, 478 U.S. 186 (1986).
12. "Joseph Kosuth and Felix Gonzalez-Torres: A Conversation," *Art & Design* 9(1–2) (1994): 76.
13. Tim Rollins, *Felix Gonzalez-Torres* (New York: A.R.T. Press, 1993), 20. Some homophobic senator is going to have a very hard time trying to explain to his constituency that my work is homoerotic or pornographic, but if I were to do a performance with HIV blood—that's what he wants, that's what the rags expect because they can sensationalize that, and that's what's disappointing." Felix Gonzalez-Torres, cited in "Felix Gonzalez-Torres by Ross Bleckner," *Bomb* 51 (spring 1995): 47.
14. Changes to certificate language must be approved by consensus of the Felix Gonzalez-Torres Foundation and its advisors. Lost certificates may be replaced if the owner can prove that the work was legitimately acquired by showing invoices and affidavits. Compare this with a 2012 lawsuit filed in the New York Supreme Court by an art collector and dealer named Roderic Steinkamp against Chicago art gallery owner Rhona Hoffman for having lost a certificate of authenticity and a diagram for Sol LeWitt's *Wall Drawing #448*, a work he owned. The plaintiff's complaint wavered between describing the certificates as "critical" to the work's value and

actually equating the work to the certificate. Nehemiah S. Glanc, *Complaint, Roderic Steinkamp against Rhona Hoffman and Rhona Hoffman Gallery, Ltd.*, 22 May 2012. The case was later settled out of court, but a corollary question arising from this case was whether the value of artworks depends mainly on their transferability.

15. Patty Gerstenblith, "Picture Imperfect: Attempted Regulation of the Art Market," *William and Mary Law Review* 29(3) (1988): 565.
16. Robert Rauschenberg, "Response to Meg Cox, *Wall Street Journal*," 14 November 1988. Box WN5, "W+N: Writings: Political and Social: Artists' Rights," Robert Rauschenberg Foundation Archives, New York.
17. Dealers sometimes manipulated salability as well. In 1969, a French gallerist intentionally destroyed an artist's market by selling the works cheaply. John Henry Merryman, "The Refrigerator of Bernard Buffet," *Hastings Law Journal* 27 (1975–1976): 1031.
18. The New York Artists' Authorship Rights Act gave artists exhibiting work within New York the legal right to disclaim authorship. New York Arts and Cultural Affairs Law § 14.53 (St. Paul, MN: West Publishing, 1984).
19. Letter to Herman Daled from Douglas Huebler, 19 May 1978. Herman and Nicole Daled Papers, partial gift of the Daled Collection, I.153, Museum of Modern Art Archives, New York.
20. But as gallerist and critic Anny De Decker noted, the art market of the 1970s easily absorbed these multiples, though not at the same pace as so-called original works. Sophie Richard, *Unconcealed, the International Network of Conceptual Artists 1967–77: Dealers, Exhibitions, and Public Collections* (London: Ridinghouse, 2009), 411.
21. The fullest account of the Rothko lawsuit is in Lee Seldes, *The Legacy of Mark Rothko* (New York: Holt, Rinehart and Winston, 1978).
22. Amei Wallach, "Court Rules in Art World's 'Watergate,'" *Newsday*, 23 November 1977.
23. *Sonnabend Gallery, Inc. v. Halley* (Sup. Ct. NY County 1992). For a discussion of the case in the context of artist-dealer relations generally, see Olav Velthuis, *Talking Prices: Symbolic Meanings of Prices on the Market for Contemporary Art* (Princeton, NJ: Princeton University Press, 2005), 66–71.
24. Connie Samaras, "Feminism, Photography, Censorship and Sexually Transgressive Imagery: The Work of Robert Mapplethorpe, Joel-Peter Witkin, Jacqueline Livingston, Sally Mann, and Catherine Opie," *New York Law School Law Review* 38 (1993): 77.
25. Cockrill, cited in "Follow Your Own Path: Mike Cockrill Interview by Joe Heaps Nelson," *Whitehot Magazine*, September 2012. http://whitehotmagazine.com/articles/interview-by-joe-heaps-nelson/2625, accessed 8 January 2017.
26. "We just took 2,000 bucks, because they were going to throw a lot of money at us, and we just could not afford to really take Leo Castelli to court. But we made our point!" Ibid.
27. Cockrill, cited in "Follow Your Own Path: Mike Cockrill Interview by Joe Heaps Nelson."
28. Julie Ault, e-mail communication with the author, 28 June 2015.
29. A poignant case in point was David Smith's futile attempt in 1960 to protest the unauthorized alteration of *17h's* (1950) following its sale. After failing to repurchase the work, he publicly declared in letters to *Art News* and *Arts* magazines his refusal to sell additional works to the parties in question. Rosalind Krauss, "Changing the Work of David Smith," *Art in America* 62(5) (September/October 1974): 32–33.
30. Justin Hughes, "Symposium II Art and the Law: Suppression and Liberty, the Line Between Work and Framework, Text and Context," *Cardozo Arts and Entertainment Journal* 19 (2001): 21.
31. Felix Gonzalez-Torres, "Practices: The Problem of Divisions of Cultural Labour," *Symptoms of Interference, Conditions of Possibility: Ad Reinhardt, Joseph Kosuth, Felix Gonzalez-Torres* (London: The Centre, 1994), 84. Originally published in *ACME* 1(2) (1992): 44–49.

32. "Politics and Election" Roundtable Discussion, 1. Group Material Archive, MSS 215, box 2, folder 11, Fales Library and Special Collections, New York University Libraries.
33. Nancy Princenthal, "Felix Gonzalez-Torres: Multiple Choice," *Art + Text* 48 (May 1994): 42.
34. "Joseph Kosuth and Felix Gonzalez-Torres: A Conversation," 76.
35. "Cultural Participation," 22 November 1988, 7. The other participants were David Avalos, Martha Gever, Lucy Lippard, Deborah Wye, Randall Morris, and Robert Farris Thompson. Group Material Archive, MSS 215, box 2, folder 11, Fales Library and Special Collections, New York University Libraries.
36. "Politics and Election" Roundtable Discussion, 3. The participants also included Bruce Wright, a New York State Supreme Court judge known as an outspoken critic of racism in the judiciary system.
37. Kris Cohen, "The Painter of Dematerialization," *Journal of Visual Culture* 15(2) (2016): 255.
38. Giuseppe Panza, letter to Avery Brundage, 23 July 1976. Giuseppe Panza Papers, 1956–1990, Getty Research Institute, Research Library, accession no. 940004, box 242, folder 2.
39. Martha Buskirk, "Certifiable," *In Deed: Certificates of Authenticity in Art* (Amsterdam: Roma, 2011), 99.
40. "Deposition of André Emmerich," 21 April 1992, U.S. District Court for D.C., 44. Barbara Mathes Gallery records pertaining to *Rio Nero* lawsuit, 1989–1995. Archives of American Art, Smithsonian Institution, series II, box 2, 43.
41. Ibid., 17.
42. Alexander Alberro, *Conceptual Art and the Politics of Publicity* (Cambridge, MA: MIT Press, 2003), 169.
43. *Greenberg Gallery v. Bauman and Entwistle,* Civil Action No. 91–0439-LFO, U.S. District Court for D.C., April 1, 1993, 19, footnote 10.
44. *Herstand v. Stein* (626 N.Y.S. 2d 74). While French moral rights law allows such repudiation, U.S. courts all but prohibit its practice.
45. In California, every certificate was required to contain the name of the artist, information regarding the artist's signature on the multiple, a description of the medium, a statement about any process used to create a multiple of an image produced in a different medium, for a purpose other than the creation of the multiple being described, and information about whether the artist was deceased at the time the master was made that produced the multiple.
46. Robert Barry, letter to Franco Toselli, 17 March 1972. Giuseppe Panza Papers, 1956–1990, Getty Research Institute, Research Library, accession no. 940004, box 8, folder 1.
47. Donald Judd, "Artist Disowns 'Copied' Sculpture," *Art in America* 78(4) (April 1990): 33.
48. Ibid.
49. *Mkt. St. Assocs.*, 941 F.2d 593, 594. (7th Cir. 1991).
50. Marilyn Fischbach, letter to Gene Davis, 1970. Gene Davis papers, 1920–2000, bulk 1942–1990. Archives of American Art, Smithsonian Institution, box 2, folder 15.
51. Herbert Hirsch, letter to André Emmerich, 3 April 1973, André Emmerich Gallery Records and André Emmerich Papers, c. 1929–2009, Archives of American Art, Smithsonian Institution, box 201.
52. Jerald Ordover, letter to Robert Douglas, 21 April 1967. René d'Harnoncourt Papers, IV.1, Museum of Modern Art Archives, New York.
53. Clifford Schaffer, letter to Giuseppe Panza, 19 December 1974. Giuseppe Panza Papers, 1956–1990, Getty Research Institute, Research Library, accession no. 940004, box 174, folder 27.
54. Louis Lefkowitz, "Supplemental Memorandum of Attorney General in Support of Legislation Amending Article 12-C of the General Business Law Relating to the Artist-Art Dealer Relationship Senate Intro. No. 4375A," 16.

55. Quoted in Nancy Ungar, "It's Artists versus Dealers," *Women Artists News* 5(4) (September–October 1975): 4.
56. Castelli, quoted in John Henry Merryman and Albert E. Elsen, *Law, Ethics and the Visual Arts* (New York: Matthew Bender, 1979), 37.
57. For a description concerning the background of the agreement's creation, see Kirsi Peltomäki, *Situation Aesthetics: The Work of Michael Asher* (Cambridge, MA: MIT Press, 2010), 69.
58. See Marc Selwyn, "Legal Eagles," *Art and Auction* 10(3) (October 1987): 188–193.
59. Deposition of Donald Thalacker, 4 February 1987. Legal records relating to *Richard Serra v. United States General Services Administration et al.*, 1985–1988, Archives of American Art, Smithsonian Institution, box 1.
60. The nature of public-art contracts with government agencies makes any modification to standard contracts "virtually impossible," as such changes result in long delays due to the necessity of acquiring approvals. Accordingly, GSA contracts lacked a common clause found in other contracts, one specifying that the written text fully encapsulates the "entire agreement and understanding between the parties . . . and there are no other agreements and understandings . . . with reference to the subject matter . . . that are not merged herein." Anne C. Baker, "The Legal Issues of Relocation." Legal records relating to *Richard Serra v. United States General Services Administration et al.*, 1985–1988, Archives of American Art, box 3. Barbara Hoffmann argued that Serra relied on both the oral statements of GSA administrators and what apparently was GSA practice. Hoffmann, "The Case of the 'Tilted Arc,'" *Public Art, Public Controversy: The Tilted Arc on Trial*, ed. Sherrill Jordan (New York: Americans for the Arts, 1987), 35–37.
61. Gustave Harrow, Memorandum, 22 April 1985, 4. Legal records relating to *Richard Serra v. United States General Services Administration et al.*, 1985–1988, Archives of American Art, box 2.
62. Frank Furedi, *Culture of Fear: Risk-Taking and the Morality of Low Expectation* (London: Cassell, 1997), 29.
63. Emilie Keldie, interview with the author, 11 December 2014.
64. Andrea Rosen, "'Untitled' (The Neverending Portrait)," in *Felix Gonzalez-Torres: Text*, ed. Dietmar Elger, exhibition catalog (Ostfildern-Ruit, Germany: Cantz, 1997), 48.
65. When new language is proposed or finalized for certificates, the Felix Gonzalez-Torres Foundation sometimes consults the foundation's attorney, John Sare, a specialist in trusts and estates. Emilie Keldie, telephone conversation with the author, 5 January 2018.
66. Joshua Chambers-Letson, "Contracting Justice: The Viral Strategy of Felix Gonzalez-Torres," *Criticism* 51(4) (fall 2010): 575.
67. Certificate of Authenticity, "Untitled" (L.A.), 1991, ARG no. 71.
68. Margaret Jane Radin, *Boilerplate: The Fine Print, Vanishing Rights and the Rule of Law* (Princeton, NJ: Princeton University Press, 2013), 8.
69. *"Untitled"* (*Last Light*), an editioned lightstring work of 1993, more than doubled in price from approximately $37,000 in 1998 (Christies New York) to over $100,000 in 2000 (Phillips New York). Candy-pile works rose even faster; compare *"Untitled"* (*Rossmore*), sold for approximately $177,000 at Christies London in 1998 to another work from 1991, *"Untitled"* (*Lover Boys*), which sold for $450,000 at Sothebys New York in 2000. The most resounding bellwether was *"Untitled"* (*Blood*), a non-editioned beaded-curtain work that sold for over $1.6 million at Christies New York in 2000. Prices for paper-stack works have generally risen more slowly, although the uneditioned *"Untitled"* (*Aparición*) sold for over $1.6 million in May 2011. The highest price paid for a Gonzalez-Torres work to date was for *"Untitled"* (*L.A.*), a candy-pile work sold at Christies New York in 2015 for roughly $7.7 million.

70. Felix Gonzalez-Torres, "Being a Spy: Interview with Robert Storr," *Art Press* 138 (January 1995): 20.
71. Heiner Friderich, letter to Giuseppe Panza, 20 January 1975. Giuseppe Panza Papers, 1956–1990, Getty Research Institute, Research Library, accession no. 940004, box 174, folder 27.
72. Douglas Huebler, letter to Herman, Nicole, and Pierre Daled. Undated, but most likely from 1975, given the postmark on the envelope. Daled, I.153, Museum of Modern Art Archives, New York.
73. Ibid.
74. Ibid.
75. Douglas Huebler letter to Herman Daled, 13 April 1975. Daled, I.A.97, Museum of Modern Art Archives, New York.
76. Douglas Huebler, letter to Franco Toselli, 30 June 1974. Minimal and Conceptual Art Documents, 1969–1989, Getty Research Institute, Research Library, accession no. 920025, box 1, folder 10.
77. Fred Sandback, Certificate of Authenticity for *Untitled,* 1979.
78. Miwon Kwon, *One Place after Another: Site-Specific Art and Locational Identity* (Cambridge, MA: MIT Press, 2004), 42.
79. Crawford referred to the work as "Realty Positions: Fake Estates" in a facsimile to Philip Dempsey, 26 June 1992. Holly Solomon Gallery records, c. 1948–2003. Archives of American Art, Smithsonian Institution, box 24. The photographs had previously been exhibited at 112 Greene Street in 1974. Jane Crawford, "Mythology: The Evolution of Fake Estates, Part II," in *Odd Lots: Revisiting Gordon Matta-Clark's Fake Estates,* 54.
80. Crawford responded to the Guggenheim's anxiety over the authenticity of the work, stating that the photographs could be reconfigured "however they preferred." Ibid., 54. The museum acquired the work.
81. Mark Saunders, "Agreement for Proposal to Produce a Work of Art for 'Messages to the Public,'" 14. Public Art Fund Archive, MSS 270, box 32, folder 6, Fales Library and Special Collections, New York University Libraries.
82. Ibid., 14–15.
83. Agreement between Public Art Fund, Inc. and Felix Gonzalez-Torres, 23 February 1989, Public Art Fund Archive, MSS 270, box 42, folder 8, Fales Library and Special Collections, New York University Libraries.
84. Judith Barry, Renée Green, Fred Wilson, Christian Philipp Müller, and Andrea Fraser, "Serving Institutions," *October* 80 (spring 1997): 124.
85. Recently, certificates have been amended with the advice of outside legal counsel.
86. Cited in Andrea Rosen, "'Untitled' (The Neverending Portrait)," 48.
87. David Mellinkoff, *The Language of the Law* (Boston: Little, Brown, 1963), 398.
88. Erika Balsom, "Original Copies: How Film and Video Became Art Objects," *Cinema Journal* 53(1) (fall 2013): 110. The sale of a limited-edition film or video includes both a certificate of authenticity and a contract specifying the owner's rights to exhibition and display. Ibid., 99.
89. If the work is borrowed, the exhibitor must install the work in a minimum of six locations. I thank Emilie Keldie for bringing this point to my attention.
90. U.S. tax law permits owners collecting for financial profit to deduct the cost of maintenance. Ironically, such deductions are less likely to be allowed for owners who collect for reasons other than profit. However, if an owner can prove that his or her collection constitutes an income-generating activity, she or he can deduct the same losses or expenses up to the amount of the gross income derived from the collection during the taxable year. On the different tax treatment for profit- and pleasure-seeking collectors, see Robert Anthoine, "The Collector of Taxes v. the Collector of Objects," *Taxes* 59 (1981): 917, 919–922.

91. Until the mid-1990s, certificates were signed by Gonzalez-Torres and Andrea Rosen, the executor of his will. After the artist died, the gallery, the artist's estate, and the work's owner signed the certificates.
92. For example, consider Certificate of Authenticity, *Untitled* (*L.A.*), 1991, ARG no. 71. Ownership "must be transferred through Andrea Rosen Gallery, with the new Bill of Sale accompanied by this original Certificate of Authenticity."
93. Rollins, *Felix Gonzalez-Torres,* 9.
94. Hans-Ulrich Obrist, "Gonzalez-Torres, Felix," 313.
95. Obrist, "Gonzalez-Torres, Felix," 311–312.
96. Miwon Kwon, "The Becoming of a Work of Art: FGT and a Possibility of Renewal, a Chance to Share, a Fragile Truce," *Felix Gonzalez-Torres,* ed. Julie Ault (Zurich: Steidl, 2006), 300.
97. Robert Storr, "When This You See Remember Me," ibid., 36.
98. Rollins, *Felix Gonzalez-Torres,* 8.
99. Willoughby Sharp, Liza Béar, and Lawrence Weiner, "Lawrence Weiner at Amsterdam," *Avalanche* 4 (1972): 70.
100. Rosen, "'Untitled' (The Neverending Portrait)," 49.
101. Rollins, *Felix Gonzalez-Torres,* 8.
102. John Paul Ricco, *The Decision Between Us: Art and Ethics in the Time of Scenes* (Chicago: University of Chicago Press, 2014), 186.
103. Kwon, "Becoming of a Work of Art," 299.
104. Ibid., 304.
105. Alexandra Peers, "Charities Draw Younger Donors with Hip Events and Door Prizes," *Wall Street Journal,* 25 April 1994.
106. Other certificates contain this prohibition against duplication, including those for *"Untitled"* (*Last Light*), 1993 and *"Untitled"* (*Silver Beach*), 1990.
107. An important example of this was print sale legislation. Introduced to the New York State Legislature in 1970, the prospective law required sellers to disclose the number of prints produced, the underlying assumption being that scarcity would automatically raise the price of prints via higher demand. For a critique of this reasoning, see "Legislation Introduced on Original Graphics," *Print Collectors' Newsletter* 1(1) (March–April 1978): 8.
108. David Deitcher, "Contradictions and Containment," *Felix Gonzalez-Torres: Catalogue Raisonné* (Ostfildern-Ruit, Germany: Cantz, 1997), 106.
109. Lance Fung, letter to Corinne Diserens, IVAM, 6 November 1992, Holly Solomon Gallery records, c. 1948–2003. Archives of American Art, Smithsonian Institution, box 35.
110. In a loan agreement with the Hirshhorn, Gonzalez-Torres required the museum to destroy any simulation following the end of his show and to prove that such destruction had occurred. "Loan Agreemeent with FGT, Untitled (1989/1994)." Smithsonian Institution Archives, accession 05-072: Hirshhorn Museum and Sculpture Garden, Dept. of Public Programs/Curatorial Division, Curatorial Correspondence, 1987–1994, box 1.
111. Under the pretext of "research," a MoMA curator apparently obtained videotapes of Fraser's performances, which were then copied and circulated without the artist's consent. Fraser subsequently priced her videos so that it would be cheaper for a museum or institution to purchase the work rather than screen it temporarily. Andrea Fraser, letter to Colin de Land, 14 November 1996; Colin de Land, American Fine Arts, Co., and Pat Hearn Gallery Archives, MSS.008, box 10, folder 597, Center for Curatorial Studies Library and Archives, Bard College.
112. Steve Kaltenbach, "Agreement," reproduced in *Contemporary Artists,* ed. Colin Naylor (London: St. James Press, 1989), 474.

113. Kevin Gray and Susan Francis Gray, *Elements of Land Law*, 5th ed. (Oxford: Oxford University Press, 2009), 12–13. I thank Emma Waring for this reference.
114. Obrist, "Gonzalez-Torres, Felix," 311.
115. Kwon, "Becoming of a Work of Art," 295.
116. David Deitcher, "The Everyday Art of Felix Gonzalez-Torres," *Felix Gonzalez-Torres* (Stockholm: Magasin 3, 1992), unpaginated.
117. *Aldon Accessories Ltd. v. Spiegel, Inc.*, 738 F.2d 548 (2nd Cir., 1984).
118. *Community for Creative Non-Violence v. Reid*, 652 F. Supp. 1457 (D.D.C, 1987).
119. *Community for Creative Non-Violence et al. v. Reid*, 490 U.S. 730 (1989).
120. Kwon, "Becoming of a Work of Art," 308.
121. The issue of the service provider and the presumptive psychological toll of fulfilling services contracted is poignantly illustrated in *Employment Contract (on Felix Gonzalez-Torres)*, a twenty-two-minute film by Pierre Bal-Blanc, who performed as a dancer in *"Untitled" (Go-Go Dancing Platform)* in 1991. For a discussion of the film, see Claire Bishop, *Artificial Hells: Participatory Art and the Politics of Spectatorship* (New York: Verso, 2012), 235. The final shot of the film shows the artist physically running away from the museum.
122. U.S. House of Representatives, Committee on the Judiciary, *House Report No. 94–1476: Copyright Law Revision* (Washington, DC: U.S. Government Printing Office, 1976), 51.
123. Oral history interview with Elaine Sturtevant, 25–26 July 2007. Archives of American Art, Smithsonian Institution. www.aaa.si.edu/collections/interviews/oral-history-interview-elaine-sturtevant-13622#how-to-use-this-collection, accessed 15 January 2018.
124. Susan Tallman, "The Ethos of the Edition," *Arts* 61(1) (September 1991): 14.
125. U.S. Copyright Office, letter to Andrew Epstein, 25 May 2018, 4. www.copyright.gov/rulings-filings/review-board/docs/log-cabin.pdf, accessed 2 June 2018.
126. Kwon, "Becoming of a Work of Art," 304. The wording is from the certificate accompanying *"Untitled" (Portrait of the Cincinnati Art Museum)*, 1994 (ARG no. GF 1994–9).304.
127. A comparable situation might be when a wrapped Christo work is unwrapped. The unwrapping might constitute an unlawful alteration, although such incidents have occurred only by accident.
128. U.S. Copyright Office, letter to Andrew Epstein, 25 May 2018, 5.
129. Quoted in Deitcher, "Contradictions and Containment," 106.
130. Clara Hemphill, "Is It Art, or Is It Candy?" *New York Newsday*, 18 April 1995. Taken aback ("How does one gauge the right amount of interaction, anyway?"), the reviewer wrote to Gonzalez-Torres, who responded via Guggenheim curator Nancy Spector that he was in fact "thrilled" that the reviewer's child had fun playing in the candy and that he was "sorry the guard interfered."
131. Ibid.
132. Two sheets from *"Untitled" (Somewhere better/Nowhere better)*, 1990, were sold on ebay in October 2015 for $44.25. www.ebay.com/itm/Felix-Gonzalez-Torres-Untitled-Somewhere-better-Nowhere-better-1990-/131617994531?hash = item1ea50b3723, accessed 28 October 2015.
133. Rosen, "'Untitled' (The Neverending Portrait)," 46–47.
134. Estelle Schwartz, letter to James Demetrion, 17 March 1994. The work referred to the paper stack *"Untitled"* 1989/90. Smithsonian Institution Archives, accession 05–072, Hirshhorn Museum and Sculpture Garden, Dept. of Public Programs/Curatorial Division, Curatorial Correspondence, 1987–1994, box 1.
135. Philippe Ségalot, letter to James Demetrion, 16 May 1994. "As the particular white beads this work is partly composed with are impossible to find anymore, the work ["Untitled" (Chemo)] couldn't be identically replaced should it be damaged during the show and this is why I have

indicated its market value." Smithsonian Institution Archives, accession 05–072, Hirshhorn Museum and Sculpture Garden, Dept. of Public Programs/Curatorial Division, Curatorial Correspondence, 1987–1994, box 1.

136. Andrea Rosen Gallery, *Felix Gonzalez-Torres Stacks,* undated. Smithsonian Institution Archives, accession 05–072, Hirshhorn Museum and Sculpture Garden, Dept. of Public Programs/Curatorial Division, Curatorial Correspondence, 1987–1994, box 1.

137. Felix Gonzalez-Torres, quoted by Bruce Ferguson, *Rhetorical Image* (New York: New Museum of Contemporary Art, 1990), 48.

138. Barbara MacAdam, "Sweet Horrors," *Art News* 94(5) (May 1995): 40.

139. "Exhibition copy" was used by institutions; they were also called "extra copies." Letter from Amada Cruz to Philippe Ségalot, 12 September 1994. Smithsonian Institution Archives, accession 05–072, Hirshhorn Museum and Sculpture Garden, Dept. of Public Programs/Curatorial Division, Curatorial Correspondence, 1987–1994, box 1.

140. Amada Cruz, untitled note to registrar Barbara Freund, 13 May 1994. Ibid. Hirshhorn staff expressed great concern over how to replace crushed beads, a problem that meant asking what constituted an acceptable substitute to the lender to whom the museum owed a legal responsibility via the loan agreement.

141. Jack Balkin and Sanford Levinson, "Interpreting Law and Music: Performance Notes on 'The Banjo Serenader' and 'The Lying Crowd of Jews.'" *Cardozo Law Review* 20 (1999): 1513–1572.

142. Hans Ulrich Obrist, "Künstler/innenporträts—Auszüge: Felix Gonzalez-Torres," *Der Standard,* 10 January 1996.

143. Richard Marshall, letter to Richard Gagliano, 12 April 1991; Registrar Memorandum to Public Education and Security, 21 April 1991. Whitney Museum of American Art, Frances Mulhall Achilles Library, Exhibitions 1931–2000 Archives, "1991 Biennial," box 155.

144. Letter from Cora Rosevear to James Demetrion, 28 April 1994. Smithsonian Institution Archives, accession 05–072, Hirshhorn Museum and Sculpture Garden, Dept. of Public Programs/Curatorial Division, Curatorial Correspondence, 1987–1994, box 1.

145. 17 U.S. Code §106A (c)(2).

146. Jo Ann Lewis, "Traveling Light Installation Artist Felix Gonzalez-Torres Shines at the Hirshhorn," *Washington Post,* 10 July 1994. Terms of the MoMA installation were set forth in a letter from Cora Rosevear to James Demetrion, 28 April 1994. Smithsonian Institution Archives, accession 05–072, Hirshhorn Museum and Sculpture Garden, Dept. of Public Programs/Curatorial Division, Curatorial Correspondence, 1987–1994, box 1.

147. The foundation takes a role by providing loan guidelines, or sample loan agreements upon request, although owners are not obligated to use them.

148. Jennifer Flay, letter to James Demetrion, 17 March 1994. Flay was conveying the wishes of Marcel Brient, the owner of *"Untitled" (Blood),* 1992, which the Hirshhorn borrowed. Smithsonian Institution Archives, accession 05–072, Hirshhorn Museum and Sculpture Garden, Dept. of Public Programs/Curatorial Division, Curatorial Correspondence, 1987–1994, box 1.

149. John Tain, "The Things You Own End Up Owning You: Art in the 1990s," unpublished symposium comments, University of Michigan, 24 October 2015.

150. As quoted in Kwon, "Becoming of a Work of Art," 308. From the certificate for *"Untitled,"* 1989 (ARG no. GF 1989–20), 4.

151. Emma Waring, e-mail communication with the author, 11 November 2014.

152. Kathy Watt, memorandum to Amada Cruz, 11 January 1993. Smithsonian Institution Archives, accession 05–072, Hirshhorn Museum and Sculpture Garden, Dept. of Public Programs/Curatorial Division, Curatorial Correspondence, 1987–1994, box 1. Similar was Cruz's decision to make

"Placebo 2" smaller in her proposal for the U.S. Pavilion at the 1995 Venice Biennale so that visitors could more easily access emergency exits per safety regulations. Cruz, letter to Felix Gonzalez-Torres, 22 February 1994.

153. Letter from Amada Cruz to Philippe Ségalot, 4 April 1994. Accession 05–072, Hirshhorn Museum and Sculpture Garden, Dept. of Public Programs/Curatorial Division, Curatorial Correspondence, 1987–1994, box 1.
154. Keith N. Hylton, *Tort Law: A Modern Perspective* (New York: Cambridge University Press, 2016), 262.
155. Lauren Weinberg, "Art Institute Candy Sculpture," *Time Out Chicago,* 19 March 2013. www.timeout.com/chicago/things-to-do/art-institute-candy-sculpture-whats-up-with-that, accessed 10 January 2018.
156. Obrist, "Künstler/innenporträts—Auszüge: Felix Gonzalez-Torres." An exception was the showing of *"Untitled" (Aparición),* a 1991 stack work in "Regarding Beauty," a group show at the Haus der Kunst Munich in 2000. According to Andrea Rosen and at least one Munich viewer, the work was shown with two signs, one prohibiting visitors from touching the stack of paper and another indicating that they may take a sheet of paper during the final week of the exhibition. The Andrea Rosen Gallery offered to contact the owner to have the work pulled from display unless the museum took down the signs.
157. Rollins, *Felix Gonzalez-Torres,* 13.
158. Ibid.
159. Jim Lewis, "Master of the Universe," *Harper's Bazaar* (January 1995): 133.
160. Maurice Berger, "The Crisis of Civil Rights," in *Civil Rights Now* (Winston-Salem, NC: Southeastern Center for Contemporary Art, 1995), 46.

EPILOGUE

1. Of her earlier work "Disclaimer," Young observed how disclaimers "increasingly surround us within our increasingly litigious society." Jon Wood and Carey Young, "Disclaimer" (Leeds, UK: Henry Moore Institute, 2004). www.careyyoung.com/disclaimer/, accessed 6 December 2017.
2. *Specht v. Netscape,* 306 F.3d 17 (2d Cir. 2002). No standard for conspicuity exists; however, size, color, and placement are central factors. In holding that Uber properly informed riders online that disputes would be arbitrated, the Second Circuit noted that despite the "small font," the "dark print contrasts with the bright white background, and the hyperlinks are in blue and underlined." *Meyer v. Uber Technologies, Inc.*, No. 16–2750 (2d Cir. 2017).
3. Cate McQuaid, "Making Their Points Simply and Effectively," *Boston Globe,* 28 January 2010.
4. Jennifer Nedelsky, "Law, Boundaries, and the Bounded Self," *Representations* 30 (Spring 1990): 163.
5. Simon Leung, "The Look of Law," *Art Journal* 66(3) (Fall 2007): 45.
6. Pierre Schlag, "The Aesthetics of American Law," *Harvard Law Review* 115(4) (2002): 1053.
7. Ibid., 1117.
8. Kal Raustiala, "The Geography of Justice," *Fordham Law Review* 73(5) (2005): 2504.
9. For an incisive view of art freeports, see Hito Steyerl, *Duty Free Art: Art in the Age of Planetary Civil War* (New York: Verso, 2017).
10. CALDH and the International Labor Rights Fund, *Labor Rights and Legal, Political, Economic and Cultural Obstacles in Guatemala,* 2004. CALDH (Center for Legal Action on Human Rights) was the first Guatemalan NGO to bring cases of human rights violations to the attention of the Inter-American Commission on Human Rights.

11. Shannon Jackson, for example, has criticized Sierra for instrumentalizing the anonymous participants in order to bolster his own authorial status. Shannon Jackson, *Social Works: Performing Art, Supporting Publics* (New York: Routledge, 2011): 68.
12. *Santiago Sierra: 300 Tons and Previous Works,* ed. Eckhard Schneider (Cologne: Walter König, 2004), 122.
13. www.santiago-sierra.com/20005_1024.php?key = 9, accessed 11 March 2017.
14. Teresa Margolles, "Santiago Sierra," *Bomb* 86 (winter 2003–2004): 64.
15. Stefan Heidenreich, "Santiago Sierra," *Frieze* 57 (March 2001): 108.
16. Fred Moten and Stefano Harney, *The Undercommons: Fugitive Planning and Black Study* (Brooklyn, NY: Minor Compositions, 2013), 125.
17. Martha Albertson Fineman, "The Vulnerable Subject: Anchoring Equality in the Human Condition," *Yale Journal of Law and Feminism* 20(1) (2008): 2.
18. Ibid.

INDEX

Note: Page numbers in *italics* refer to images or their captions.